THE MUCH TOO PROMISED LAND

America's Elusive Search
for Arab-Israeli Peace

THE MUCH TOO PROMISED LAND

America's Elusive Search for Arab-Israeli Peace

Aaron David Miller

BANTAM BOOKS

The opinions and characterizations in this book are those of the author, and do not necessarily represent official positions of the United States Government.

THE MUCH TOO PROMISED LAND
A Bantam Book / April 2008

Published by
Bantam Dell
A Division of Random House, Inc.
New York, New York

Book design by Melissa Sutherland Amado

Bantam Books is a registered trademark of Random House, Inc., and the colophon is a trademark of Random House, Inc.

Library of Congress Cataloging-in-Publication Data
Miller, Aaron David.
The much too promised land ; America's elusive search for Arab-Israeli peace /
Aaron David Miller.
p. cm.
Includes bibliographical references and index.
ISBN 978-0-553-80490-4 (hardcover)
1. Arab-Israeli conflict—1973–1993. 2. Arab-Israeli conflict—1993—Peace.
3. United States—Foreign relations—Middle East. 4. Middle East—Foreign
relations—United States. 5. Israel—Politics and government—1973–1993.
6. Israel—Politics and government—1993– 7. Palestinian Arabs—Politics
and government—1993– I. Title.
DS119.7.M4947 2008
965.05—dc22
2007038982

Printed in the United States of America
Published simultaneously in Canada

www.bantamdell.com

10 9 8 7 6 5 4 3 2 1
BVG

For my wife, Lindsay,
without whom there would be no love, joy,
and meaning in my life

Contents

Introduction:

"Where did you get those shoes?"

"The chairman will see you now. But the meeting will have to be short. He's not well." I had known Saeb Erekat, the PLO's lead negotiator, for twenty years and had never seen him so agitated.

As we walked down the corridor of Arafat's Ramallah headquarters, I thought about the chairman. I had seen him several months earlier, in August 2004. Then he was fiery and combative, reveling in his role as victim. He had described himself as an embattled but undefeated Arab general (the only one) besieged by the mighty Israeli army. Arafat's ominously black, compact machine pistol sitting on the conference table had set the tone for our meeting that day.

Now it was late October, and Arafat was reportedly very ill. Rumors hung as thick as the stale air in his headquarters. Did he have stomach cancer? Liver disease? Was he being poisoned by the Israelis? Did he have AIDS? I had no idea what to expect.

Saeb ushered me into the small windowless space that was serving as Arafat's bedroom, instead of the regular sitting room where Arafat usually greeted his guests. The room was unbearably hot. The heat, combined with the sight of his unmade bed, medications strewn about, and a strange-looking contraption that in better days probably dispensed oxygen, made me queasy. I started to sweat.

As Arafat entered the room, propped up by Abu Alaa, the Palestinian prime minister, on one side and quickly by Saeb on the other, I was shocked by what I saw. Arafat had lost a great deal of weight. His face, gaunt and white rather than pale, only accentuated his already large bug eyes and full lips. He was dressed in a stained light blue sweat suit. A knit cap had replaced his trademark kaffiyeh. And with his large black glasses, he could have easily passed for a badly dressed senior in a retirement community in Florida.

Arafat's footwear seemed to sum up the surreal character of the encounter. On his feet, the feet of the chairman of the PLO, symbol of national identity and pride to Palestinians, the embodiment of an arch-terrorist to many Israelis and Americans, were shower slippers from one of Israel's best hotels, imprinted with the words "Dan Tel Aviv."

I don't know what prompted me to say anything at all (maybe it was the heat), but I blurted out, "Mr. Chairman, where did you get those shoes?" Both Saeb and Abu Alaa looked down and, shaking their heads in disbelief, started to laugh. Arafat, on the other hand, looked confused and embarrassed, I suspect by his inability, in his weakened state, to understand the irony of donning footwear from a luxury Israeli hotel while the Israeli Defense Forces (IDF) kept him prisoner in his compound.

Saeb turned out to be right. The meeting lasted only twenty minutes. It was really more a monologue. Arafat focused on America, specifically on how the United States held the key—even now—to his fate and to the future of both the Palestinian and the Israeli peoples. He kept insisting that only we could "save the peace process" and that America must rise to its "historic responsibilities." There was no point in arguing. It had never worked when he was well, and it certainly wasn't going to have much of an impact now.

The monologue finished, Arafat embraced and kissed me, and I left. Within a week Arafat was flown to Paris for medical treatment. Within two weeks he was dead.

As I traveled back to Jerusalem from Ramallah that afternoon, I couldn't get Arafat's focus on America out of my mind. I had heard variations on this rap many times before. I never bought them, and more than likely Arafat, the consummate actor, didn't buy them either. America was certainly not the main cause of his problems, let alone the source of his salvation. And Arafat, and anyone else who followed this issue seriously, knew it.

Still, this eleventh-hour appeal directed at the United States by a dying Arafat started me thinking again about the American role in Arab-Israeli negotiations and peacemaking. I had resigned from the Department of State almost two years earlier, having spent more than two decades under both Republican and Democratic administrations trying to help Arabs and Israelis negotiate an end to their conflict. I left government not because I had lost faith in the power of American diplomacy but because the timeline for serious negotiations, let alone a settlement, seemed to have been pushed well into the future. By late 2004 everything we had hoped to achieve in Oslo and Camp David lay broken or bloodied somewhere. Now I wondered whether I'd been wrong all those years and what our legacy would be. In my blackest moments I thought about the words of the British governor of Aden who quipped that when Britannia fell beneath the waves, the British Empire would leave only two enduring monuments—the game of Association Football and the expression "fuck off."[1] Was this to be America's legacy in brokering Arab-Israeli peace? Was the conflict beyond resolution, the differences too great, and the hatreds too deep to be overcome even with American help?

For better than half a century American presidents, secretaries of state, and special envoys had wrestled with the same questions. And to what end? The promise of peace, harmony, and reconciliation in the promised land remains just that. The more I thought about it, the more it seemed that this land had been promised too many times to too many people. Those conflicting promises have haunted this troubled region for generations.

I figured historic Palestine was promised four times, at least, to its inhabitants: first by a Jewish, Christian, and Muslim God who offered an exclusive, even triumphal claim to the same land and its holy sites to those souls who were willing to follow; a second time by the British, who in an effort to protect an empire that stretched from Suez to India made conflicting commitments during the First World War to Zionists and to Arab nationalists; and third by the United Nations General Assembly, whose 1947 partition resolution proposed splitting Palestine into an Arab and a Jewish state.

But this book focuses on the fourth promise. That promise was made by America. I don't think we were cynical or duplicitous in making it, although perhaps we were naïve. We didn't strike secret covenants or political deals with the Arabs or Israelis. But in its policies and pronouncements America offered a more alluring prospect: a promise that over time, through negotiation, dialogue, and compromise, the needs of Arabs and Israelis could be somehow reconciled and that Americans could help deliver what God, the British, and the United Nations couldn't. The embodiment of the American promise was the passage in November 1967, largely through American diplomacy, of UN Security Council Resolution 242. It might have been a UN resolution, but for all practical purposes it became the prime directive of American diplomacy. Its language was ambiguous, but its main message was clear: land for peace was possible, but only through negotiations, in which the United States and others pledged to assist.

America's promise came with no guarantee; indeed, it was made with the clear understanding that Arabs and Israelis must bear the primary responsibility for negotiating their future. At the same time, America maintained that it would stand with the parties ready to help, and that American pragmatism, idealism, and power could assist them in ending their conflict and securing a comprehensive and lasting peace. With very few exceptions, every major statement or speech made by an American president or secretary of state on Arab-Israeli issues, from Richard Nixon through George W. Bush, contains a commitment to help the Arabs and Israelis negotiate their differences and reach peace.

On the rhetorical level, that promise was regularly made. But as the Israeli Prime Minister Levi Eshkol reportedly said: "I made a promise; I didn't say I'd keep it." In practice, whether and how the American commitment played out was driven by various administrations' perceptions of their interests, the crises and opportunities of the moment, the personalities and preferences of America's leaders, and of course, those of the Arabs and Israelis in the region. But one thing was clear. When success came, it resulted from America's leaders recognizing that the United States had a key national interest in advancing Arab-Israeli peace, and that they needed to make it a top priority.

Today many would argue that a comprehensive peace is more remote than ever and may not even be attainable. How come? What role have we played, for good or ill? And can we make a difference in helping to produce a solution? I wrestled with these questions when I left government, and they are the same ones that I grapple with today. This book, based on twenty years of participating in Arab-Israeli diplomacy and 160 new interviews with former presidents, secretaries of state, national security advisors, politicians, and diplomats, is my effort to answer them.

Two centuries ago the renowned British historian Edward Gibbon wrote that the word *I* was the vainest and most disgusting of pronouns. He's probably right. But this book—in the main, a story of why America succeeded and failed in Arab-Israeli peacemaking—is also, in a very real sense, my personal journey. It is a story of how a kid from Cleveland—with an ambition to become a history professor—got caught up in a rare piece of history himself, working for and advising (and not always wisely) six secretaries of state. I had the honor and privilege of working as a member of a talented negotiating team that spanned three administrations and of participating in most of the diplomacy around the Arab-Israeli issue for almost two decades.

This story is less about what I did than about what I heard and saw, and the impressions I gained from those experiences. Like Fitzgerald's Nick Carraway in *The Great Gatsby*, I was both in the story and outside it. I believed deeply in what we were doing at the time, maybe too deeply. Yet at the same time I had real doubts about some of our policies, particularly during the last two years of the Clinton administration and the two years I worked in the George W. Bush administration. I was often reluctant or unable to express those doubts. This book isn't intended as an "I told you so." I was as much a cheerleader for unworkable policies as anyone else. But in the past several years I have thought long and hard about what we did and, more important, about what we failed to do. We need to learn from both experiences. Honesty and clarity—minus any self-indulgent need to blame and recriminate—are important here. And I hope I can measure up to the task.

To maintain a broader perspective and gain some thematic altitude, I have covered not only the period in which I was involved but have looked briefly at the earlier years of the 1970s, specifically the diplomacy of Henry Kissinger and Jimmy Carter. These years were critical. They laid the foundation for much of the diplomacy that followed. And more important, both Kissinger and Carter, together with James Baker, for whom I did work, succeeded and in doing so became the three most consequential American figures in Arab-Israeli peacemaking. While these three squared off against issues and circumstances far less daunting than those their successors faced, we still have much to learn from their experiences. And we must learn, even with all the downsides of history's comparisons.

Finally, a word or two about Arabs, Israelis, and objectivity. The day after I landed in Israel in November 2001 on what was to be my last diplomatic mission, this time as an advisor to General Anthony Zinni, charged by the Bush administration with brokering a cease-fire between two guys (Ariel Sharon and Yasser Arafat) who didn't want one, we met with Shimon Peres, who was then foreign minister, in his Tel Aviv office.

Zinni, who knew the Middle East well, needed a refresher course on the Israeli-Palestinian conflict. And Peres, a master at distilled wisdom, was just the guy to give it to him. It was Peres, after all, who upon meeting the foreign minister of Iceland had once remarked what an honor it was for the representative of the chosen people to be meeting a representative of the frozen people.

Peres was in rare form that day, even against the backdrop of a bloody Israeli-Palestinian conflict. Like an old master preparing his charge for a dangerous journey, he told Zinni he would encounter three kinds of Arabs and Israelis on his mission: the righteous, the collectors of arguments, and the problem solvers. Zinni was instructed to ignore the first two and concentrate on the third.

I realized that Peres was right, but with one critical distinction. Most of the Arabs and Israelis I worked with had all three characteristics rolled into one. In varying proportions they all believed deeply in the rightness of their cause, and they all advocated that cause sometimes with an intensity that could drive you to distraction; and yet they could all come up with practical ways to solve problems. What made them so compelling wasn't that they had escaped the conflict that ground them down—they couldn't—but that, hardened by conflict and by their own natural prejudices and biases, they managed to struggle on, preserving a sense of humor, fairness, and, most important, hope for the future. In the end this struggle was about good people caught up in a nasty conflict who managed, however imperfectly, to preserve their humanity and faith in the future. As an American, I was glad I didn't live in their neighborhood, but I admired and respected their struggle.

Years ago it became painfully clear to me that when it comes to objectivity and the Arab-Israeli issue, there is no gold standard. Anyone who is seriously involved in these matters for any length of time is marked, typed, and cubbyholed by both sides—pro- or anti-Israeli, Jewish or non-Jewish, Arab or Israeli, and so forth. The amount of misinformation would have been comic had it not reflected such preconceived bias. A Palestinian asked me once if it was true that I was a rabbi; an Israeli wrongly assumed I was an observant Jew who sent my kids to an Orthodox school. And in perhaps one of the most laughable preconceptions of all, a high-ranking Egyptian official asked me if I was the heir to the Häagen-Dazs ice cream fortune, which he assumed—rightly, I later found out—had been started by Jews. My wife, Lindsay, used to maintain a file we jokingly called "fan mail"—essentially a collection of letters and news articles with the worst personal invective imaginable directed at those of us who worked on the negotiations. The fan mail was truly nonpartisan, coming from Jews, non-Jews, Israelis, Arabs, Americans, Christians, and Muslims. (One guy even sent a pack of matches with a note that read: "Go burn yourself.") Such responses are a sad but unavoidable fact of life in this business. For Arabs and Israelis caught up in the conflict, and I suspect for their partisans here at home, it is a deadly serious business. The desire to try to divine who is a friend and who is an adversary and to treat them accordingly is irrepressible.

Perhaps this sorting is inevitable. After all, we are nothing if not the sum of our experiences, biases, prejudices, and ethnic and religious backgrounds. As an American who happens to be Jewish, I had collected my own fair share of biases over a long period of time. Concern for Israel's well-being had become part of me, like some sort of ethnic DNA. Maybe the best we can do is to recognize those biases, make allowances for them, and set them aside in an effort to understand others' perspectives and do what we believe is right. In my case, this meant trying to further the best interests of the United States in the pursuit of Arab-Israeli peace. I have tried to do that throughout my career, and I have tried to bring the same honesty to this book as well. In those cases where I've failed, I've tried to point out my biases and prejudices. The story and what's at stake for America demand no less.

Part One

AMERICA'S PROMISE CHALLENGED

I was uneasy about the assignment, but there was no getting out of it. As part of our marathon negotiations over Israeli withdrawal from Hebron in 1996 and 1997, the United States had promised Arafat improvements in the Shuhada Road, a street that ran adjacent to neighborhoods and an important Palestinian market where hundreds of Israeli settlers bumped up against thousands of Palestinians.

My boss and the lead American negotiator, Dennis Ross, had with some relish volunteered me for the job. So one dark, threatening rainy day in January 1997 Jake Walles, our deputy consul general in Jerusalem, together with a civil engineer from USAID and a lot of security guys and I, traveled to Hebron. Our purpose was to survey the street and look for ways to create something of a buffer between Israelis and Palestinians, and to do it in such a way that it wouldn't feel like a wall between them—which, I might add, was probably exactly what they needed. I had barely broken 500 on my math SAT and knew nothing about roads. But that hardly mattered. There I was on my hands and knees with a tape measure calculating width differentials for a small street that had become a central sticking point in Israeli-Palestinian negotiations.

Hebron, to say the least, was never a friendly place. We worked quickly, under the suspicious and angry eyes of armed ultra-Orthodox Jewish settlers and dour and curious Palestinians. This was one of only two moments in two decades of diplomatic service when I felt threatened by being in a potential Israeli-Palestinian crossfire. But apart from heckling by the Israelis, we left without incident. The road was eventually finished, but today, in an ironic tribute to our efforts, the road is closed and has become a pedestrian mall for the Israelis. The shop fronts that USAID had restored for the Palestinians are now covered with anti-Arab graffiti.

Down on my knees that afternoon in Hebron measuring a road, I felt small and ridiculous, certainly as a representative of the world's only superpower. I should have realized a couple things. Once out in their neighborhood, powerful America wasn't so powerful. Regardless of what we wanted, the locals had timetables, agendas, and interests of their own. We could press them, cajole them, even threaten to walk away, but if we wanted to broker agreements, we had to get their cooperation. And sometimes to do so, we had to put up with indignities and the machinations of small powers that really were quite adept at manipulating big ones.

The other realization was more painful. When you're in a small world, you tend to become small, and when you're in the conflict-ridden world in which Israelis and Palestinians live, you tend to take on the concern for minutiae and the obsessiveness that can define that world. I'm sure it pleased Arafat to no end to have the world's biggest power groping around the streets of Hebron. In an odd sort of way our focus on his problems cut us down to size and brought us directly into his world. "They like you big," Fouad Ajami, one of the wisest and most honest observers of the contemporary Middle East, once said, "but they want to send you back small; they like you a virgin, but they want to send you back a whore."[1]

Looking back now, I understand more clearly what I didn't then. America's road to helping Arabs and Israelis move toward peace is strewn with two kinds of obstacles: those that come from Arab and Israeli politics and those that come from our own at home. For America, that journey brings both risk and possibility. Along the way, success of any kind—negotiating an agreement small, medium, or large—means being tough, smart, and sensitive to both challenges.

My early exposure to and experience in Middle East matters

made me skeptical about our chances of overcoming these challenges. But as I got caught up in the heady Arab-Israeli diplomacy of the 1990s, I put a great deal of faith, perhaps too much, in America's power to manage them. America, I thought, really could drive the diplomatic train and pull the locals along according to its own agenda. Unfortunately, as we'll soon see, far too much of the time it turned out to be the other way around.

Chapter One

A Negotiator's Tale

The room was packed. Secretary Baker's press secretary and close advisor, Margaret Tutwiler, had seen to that. Late Friday afternoon in Jerusalem—usually a time of quiet preparation for the Jewish Sabbath—had suddenly seen a frenzy of excitement. As scores of journalists had gathered in the banquet hall of the King David Hotel to await the arrival of the American secretary of state and the Russian foreign minister, anticipation was high.

The two men now entering the hall could not have represented a greater contrast in style or power. Boris Pankin, clad in a dark boxy Soviet-era suit out of the 1950s, embodied a once great empire in decline. Hungry for prestige and respectability, the Russians seemed not to care that they were being used as a decorative ornament in a ceremony orchestrated by the United States. And if they did care, they weren't complaining.

By contrast, Secretary of State James Addison Baker III was riding high. Tall and self-assured, he wore a dark suit, a crisp white shirt, and a trademark boldly colored tie. He had reason to be confident. Baker represented a country that was enjoying unprecedented influence in a region still shaken by America's lightning military victory over Iraq's Saddam Hussein.

On that late Friday afternoon, October 18, 1991, Baker and Pankin, on behalf of their presidents, Bush and Gorbachev, announced that formal invitations would be sent to Israel and to the Arabs to attend a historic peace conference in Madrid. That fall the United States was the only great power in an arc of small ones that stretched from Rabat to Karachi. If there was to be an American moment in the Middle East, this was surely it. And Baker knew that the moment might not last long. Later that day in Jerusalem he would quip with characteristic caution, "Boys, if you want to get off the train, now might be a good time because it could all be downhill from here."

I had no intention of getting off the train. For me the ride was only just beginning. The nine-month period of nonstop diplomacy in the run-up to the Madrid conference had been the most exciting time of my professional life. A dozen years had passed since Jimmy Carter's heroic success in bringing Anwar Sadat and Menachem Begin to a peace agreement. And while holding a peace conference of procedures like Madrid was certainly not the same as achieving a peace treaty of consequence between Egypt and Israel, it was still the most important breakthrough in Arab-Israeli peacemaking in more than a decade. To me, Madrid was reason enough to believe that with enough will and determination, American diplomacy could fashion something positive and hopeful from the raw material of a turbulent and changing region. And I could become part of it. I had become a believer.

Banking on No

As I look back now, it astonishes me that I ever got into the business of negotiations and diplomacy. Changing the world was definitely part of my family's history, but while I was growing up, it wasn't part of my personal temperament or interest. Born into an affluent Cleveland real estate family, I had parents and grandparents who were leaders in both the secular and Jewish worlds. During the 1950s my grandfather Leonard Ratner had been active in Zionist politics and philanthropy and would count Israel's first prime minister, David Ben-Gurion, and its fourth, Golda Meir, as personal friends. Leonard was an extraordinary man, an immigrant from Poland, one of nine brothers and sisters, who with piety, love of family, and an uncanny business acumen had sought his fortune in America, made one in the lumber and later the real estate business. My grandfather's love of Judaism and family was rivaled only by his passion for service to the community. He would talk to me endlessly about the importance of the Talmudic concept of *tikkun olam*, or "fixing the world." I'd listen respectfully, wondering most of the time what it had to do with me.

My father, Sam, a brilliant, driven man, was as tough, smart, and intimidating as anyone I'd ever known. Born to Russian immigrant parents, he'd served in the navy at Guadalcanal, then went to Harvard, married my mother, and entered the family real estate business, where his toughness and smarts made him an indispensable asset in dealing with the unions and zoning boards. Like so many second-generation American Jews, he was captivated by Israel's stunning military victory in 1967. Unlike most, he struck up close personal ties with Israeli prime ministers Begin and Rabin. A masterful fund-raiser for Cleveland's Jewish community and for Israel, he used persuasion, and, when needed, pressure. According to one story, he camped all night long outside the hotel room of a reluctant donor until the guy came up with an appropriate pledge for the United Jewish Appeal.

My father's view of the world was a grim one. And while he was tied deeply to America and its promise of success, his Jewish identity also ran deep. For him, the dark cloud of anti-Semitism and the Holocaust were ever present. He once challenged my brothers, sister, and me to name three of our non-Jewish friends who would hide us in the event the Nazis took over America. No matter how hard we tried, we could never win this game. To my father, Israel and the Jews were constantly in jeopardy, and in the end they could rely only on themselves. That in his later years he has emerged as a key philanthropist in both the Catholic and the black communities is a testament to a broader worldview not evident then. But growing up I remember him as a guy for whom the glass, at least when it came to what non-Jews would do for Jews, was half empty at best.

If my father's view of the world was based on what was probable, my mother Ruth's was based on its possibilities. She was a remarkable woman, way ahead of her time. Having never finished college, she went back for a Ph.D. in educational psychology. Active in Cleveland city politics as health director and community development director, she ran unsuccessfully for Congress in 1980 and was active at the national level in Republican Party politics, representing the United States abroad on women's issues and serving on the United States Holocaust Memorial Council. She later went on to represent the family's real estate interests in Washington and to lead its development of downtown Cleveland.

For my mother, nothing was impossible. She saw life as a glass neither half full nor half empty, but filling every day with new challenges, setbacks, and opportunities. What mattered in life, according to my mother, was how you handled these challenges. She taught me to look for the good in people, to accept their imperfections, and to believe in the capacity of human beings to change for the better.

Since I had powerful parents and grandparents who had a history of doing something about the world's problems rather than just talking about them, I of course shied away from anything to do with such aims. When I was thirteen, I made an obligatory bar mitzvah trip to Israel, and I made another with friends as part of a European excursion at twenty-one. My parents even created opportunities for me to meet important Israelis. During that second trip to Israel I attended a Druze wedding party in the hills near Haifa as the guest of my parents' friend Avraham Yoffe, one of Israel's storied military heroes in the 1956 Suez campaign. One of the other invitees was a slim and energetic Ariel Sharon, then commander of Israel's Southern Front, who arrived by jeep and within minutes was hugging and kissing the relatives as if he were a member of the family. At lunch I watched our Druze hosts crack the skull of a young lamb and offer its brains to the special guests. Sharon and Yoffe were eating and appeared to be enjoying themselves, so I had no choice. It was my first but not my last culinary adventure in the Holy Land.

Nonetheless I steered clear of anything that was either serious or political in nature, or that required a commitment. In fact,

my parents nicknamed me Hamlet because they saw me as inde-
cisive, contemplative, and rarely engaged. Growing up, I cared
about only two things: playing tennis and reading history—in
that order. Instead of doing something useful or educational during the summers, I played tournaments, taught tennis, or just
goofed off. When my hope to compete in tennis at the college
level went bust, I fell back on academics, specifically the pursuit
of a Ph.D. in American history.

To this day, the exact reason for my professional interest in
the Middle East is still not clear. I was Jewish and had been to
Israel a couple of times, but I was by no means active or interested in Jewish or Zionist politics. My entry point into the Middle
East was undoubtedly my Jewish upbringing and family connections. But I knew that mine was a narrow view of the region, seen
from a highly skewed perspective. When it came to Israel, I had
never been all that comfortable with the insular and exclusive
Jewish vantage points of much of the Jewish community and of
my parents. I saw myself as an American who happened to be
Jewish, not the other way around. Nor did I like the tendency to
divide the world into Jews and non-Jews and to assume the worst
about the latter. Intellectually and emotionally pulled by the secular non-Jewish world, I was open to a vantage point that was
broader and more complex. A fair amount of my discontent was
the natural rebellious soul-searching of a twenty-something acting out against parental controls and values. But it felt good, and
it was something I owned.

As an undergraduate at the University of Michigan, I had
taken a couple of Middle East history courses from Richard
Mitchell, a former Foreign Service officer who had written the authoritative study on the Egyptian Muslim Brotherhood. I'm sure
it's still true for college kids today: there are people whom you meet
along the way, outside friends and family, who can have a real impact on you and who, at the risk of sounding dramatic, can change
your life. Dick Mitchell was one of those people. He was a real
character—a goateed, chain-smoking, sandal-wearing, sheikhlike
figure who attracted both Arab students and controversy. His office

in Haven Hall was like a Middle East *hooka* or *shisha* bar. A soft-spoken, gentle man, Dick was open to new ideas and steeped in very old traditions. With his stooped posture and furrowed brow, he seemed at times literally burdened and bent by the weight of the Middle East history that he loved to pass on to his captivated students. To me, with my Jewish background, he became a kind of Pied Piper, telling stories that led me down the dim and narrow alleyways, through the bazaars and coffeehouses of Cairo, Damascus, and Baghdad, all the while never leaving Ann Arbor. Dick Mitchell pushed me out of my comfort zone into a virtual world of danger and possibility.

Well into work on a master's degree in American Civil War history, I began to have doubts about whether I wanted to teach American history, or even to teach at all. Frankly, I was bored. Studying Appomattox was fine but, as I thought about it, not nearly as alluring as the worlds of Arabia and Arafat. Moreover, the two professors at Michigan who influenced me most, Mitchell and Gerald Linderman, a historian of Americans at war, had both been foreign service officers before entering academia. Linderman, like Mitchell, was soft-spoken and thoughtful, possessed of the quiet confidence born only from years of practical and difficult experience. Gerry had been part of the American team that had opened the consulate in Kaduna, Nigeria. Both of these guys taught not merely from lecture notes and libraries but from recollections of their experiences and adventures abroad. The more I considered their pathway, the more sense it made to me. Why not offer students something more than book knowledge? I decided then that I needed to have some of those adventures.

In negotiations with the history department, represented by Mitchell and Bradford Perkins, a well-known historian of American diplomacy, we cut the following deal: if I could learn two Near Eastern languages (choosing from Arabic, Turkish, Farsi, or Hebrew) and pass preliminary exams in three fields of Middle Eastern study, the potentates would allow me to earn a Ph.D. in

Middle Eastern history. What initially seemed to me like a well-thought-out plan was really a leap into the unknown.

The truth is, I really had no idea what I was doing, or what I was getting myself into. How I thought I'd manage this transition—the new languages and fields of study—without any structure or guidance, I don't know. Staying in Ann Arbor, taking courses, and studying languages would have made more sense. But that would have been too rational. Risk-averse by nature, I pushed myself to become risk-ready. In 1973 there was only one place in the world where Arabic and Hebrew (my two choices) were spoken and studied seriously, and that was Jerusalem. I was married that May, and a week later my wife, Lindsay, and I, together with two footlockers containing two hundred books, moved to Jerusalem.

That year transformed us and pushed me in unanticipated directions. The Arab-Israeli conflict, I discovered, really did have two sides. It's hard to imagine now, but in 1973 you could still take a rickety blue bus from the central Arab bus station in East Jerusalem to Nablus, Ramallah, and Hebron in relative safety. And we rode that bus, meeting Palestinians from the West Bank. These encounters—one in particular with a young man from the village of Battier south of Bethlehem—weren't political but personal. We took long walks with Salih, whose tanned leathery skin made him appear much older than he was. Salih had soft brown eyes and a high-pitched voice, and when he laughed, which he did constantly, his entire wiry frame seemed to shake to its core. He made sure to keep our conversations far from politics, and we were only too happy to oblige him. We ventured to his village and got to know his large family, who greeted us with a warmth and hospitality we never forgot. Later that year we brought Lindsay's parents and grandfather to Battier—quite an adventure for the three of them.

Through these encounters I became familiar with at least part of the Palestinian story, which took its place alongside the Israeli narrative that was already fairly well ingrained in my consciousness. And I began to understand that whether by circumstance or design, Israel was an occupying power. That occupation was then only six years old, in its infancy really. In 1973 no more than several thousand Israelis lived in the West Bank and Gaza, and the Israelis had built few checkpoints, guard towers, bypass roads, or military installations. Even then Palestinians were hardening in response. As Salih's older brother, a teacher, made clear in a quiet but determined manner, "The Israelis will not be able to stay on our land."

But that year also taught me on a very personal level that Israel was a threatened nation. Five months after we arrived, the 1973 war broke out. As we sat in our Jerusalem apartment on the afternoon of Yom Kippur, Saturday, October 6, sirens shattered the stillness of the Jews' holiest day in their holiest of cities. Every apartment building was supposed to have a bomb shelter, and we were ordered to ours by a tough Israeli woman who headed up the apartment building's security committee. We sat on wooden benches, along with several older members of our apartment building, in a shelter that was in reality a garden shed. I felt ridiculous—this place wasn't going to provide much protection if we took a direct hit. We didn't know it then, but Egyptian forces had crossed the Suez Canal, overrunning Israeli positions on the canal's east bank, while Syrian troops attempted to push the Israelis off the Golan Heights.

We had never been in the middle of a society mobilized for war. Our parents pressed us to come home or at least go to Europe. But the thought of leaving made both of us uneasy. One reason was that we were committed to staying and helping in any way we could. We worked on a kibbutz through most of the war; afterward Lindsay would volunteer to help mothers whose husbands were still mobilized months later. But the other reason for not wanting to leave was that I was having the very experience and adventure I'd sought out; a piece of history might even be playing out before our eyes.

While Israelis in their late twenties had already endured wartime conditions in 1956 and 1967, for us the situation felt bizarre. We had experienced nothing like this in America. There had never been a national mobilization or moment of crisis to focus the national will or spirit. The closest thing I had lived through was the collective shock of President John F. Kennedy's assassination. I vaguely recall drills in elementary school in which we were asked to take cover under our desks in the event of a Soviet attack and a brief premonition of disaster during the October 1962 Cuban missile crisis. But until 9/11, most Americans my age felt no sense of impending or real threat.

Since the actual fighting was confined to the borders, Jerusalem displayed an eerie normalcy. But the nightly blackouts grimly maintained by the same woman who had ordered us to the shelter, the absence of many goods on supermarket shelves, and the disappearance of just about every male between the ages of eighteen and fifty-five were far from normal. After the cease-fire three weeks later, I went on a tour of the front lines in Sinai. What I encountered horrified me: a vast sandy moonscape, littered with the human and mechanical remains of one of the largest conventional land battles since the end of the Second World War. Everywhere I saw burnt-out tanks, half-tracks, gun emplacements, minefields, and bodies. Did this twilight zone represent the last great Arab-Israeli war, I wondered, or just the battle of the decade?

I thought the worst, returning to the United States older, wiser, and at the same time more confused. Arabs and Jews, I was convinced, had little chance for coexistence, let alone reconciliation. The prospects of reconciling the interests of an occupied nation with those of a threatened one seemed slim to none. To make matters worse, Dick Mitchell, with whom I had corresponded during the war, was having a meltdown. His views on the Middle East during the war had created such intense anger toward him from Jewish faculty and the Ann Arbor Jewish community, he informed me, that he would no longer accept Jewish graduate students. I left his office that day in tears, somewhere between shock, anger, and sadness that a man of such intellectual power and reason could get to such a point. His crisis was my first exposure to the domestic political realities of the Arab-Israeli issue and the absurd marking and typecasting that go along with a conflict that is being played out thousands of miles away. If Mitchell, a man whom I admired and respected, could not overcome these pressures, what hope did the rest of us have? Mitchell eventually agreed to cochair my doctoral committee. And Anwar Sadat's historic visit to Jerusalem in November 1977 (the year I received my Ph.D.) briefly raised my hopes. But I left Ann Arbor deeply pessimistic about the future and persuaded that while I could analyze this conflict up, down, and around, neither I nor anyone else could do much to resolve it.

Ironically, given all my doubts, my skepticism, and my "no can do" mentality, I ended up in Washington—the city, at least from the perspective of those who live there, of the "can do" or, to be more precise, of those who think they can do. My dissertation research on the origins of America's special relationship with Saudi Arabia had brought me into contact with the Historical Office, which was housed in the Department of State's Bureau of Public Affairs. This place seemed ideal for me. I could use my skills as a historian to edit recently declassified documents from the 1940s and 1950s. It was a pretty cushy first job, removed as it was from the pressures of what I imagined the real State Department to be. That was fine with me. What I knew about Middle Eastern history, combined with my midwestern skepticism and my experience of the year in Jerusalem, made me cynical about the use of diplomacy for pretty much anything of real value.

Unfortunately, within a year or so I was bored being a documentary editor but not at all sure I wanted to be part of the real State Department. So when Joe Montville, a brilliant but unorthodox Foreign Service officer, took a risk and offered me a position as the analyst for Lebanon and the Palestinians in the Bureau of Intelligence and Research (INR), I agonized for weeks about taking the job. Could I do it? Did I really want to? Hamlet would have been proud.

My experience at INR—I took the job—opened my eyes to the real-time world of diplomacy and policy but served only to deepen my skepticism about what America could accomplish.

No longer did my professional life involve studying the past, where everyone was dead and nothing changed. It was now tied to analyzing the present, and a phone call from the State Department operations center could ruin my weekend, keep me up all night, and challenge me to provide a short but accurate analysis of events I couldn't predict or control.

My job was to follow Lebanon and the Palestinians—two hopeless basket cases that produced an endless stream of bad news. More often than not my mandate was to bring that bad news to busy policymakers who, in my ever-negative view of the world, still needed to be reminded that nothing hopeful was ever going to occur in the Middle East. Still, I soon grew to love the job.

My time at INR occurred during the years of America's fateful involvement in Lebanon, when the Reagan administration, perhaps with the best of intentions, got caught up in the politics of small tribes—Israeli, Syrian, Lebanese, and Palestinian— with disastrous consequences. Beginning with Israel's June 1982 invasion of Lebanon, the situation went from bad to worse. That summer I worked ninety days straight monitoring the tortuous and deadly tangle of an Israeli-PLO war, the PLO's evacuation from Beirut, the assassination of the newly elected Maronite president Bashir Gemayel, and the Phalangist massacre of hundreds of Palestinians in the refugee camps of Sabra and Shatila. For America the stakes were increasingly perilous. In the early morning hours of October 23, 1983, an unforgettable call from State Ops informed me of a suicide attack on American Marines sleeping in barracks at Beirut's airport: that attack, which killed 241 Marine peacekeepers, presaged the extremist Shia confrontation with America decades later. To me an American policy that was designed to use Israel and the Christian militias to defeat Syria and its Muslim allies reflected bad analysis and provided few opportunities for peace. The glass of opportunity in Lebanon was neither half full nor half empty; it was empty, bone dry.

I laugh now when I recall my 1983 briefing of Donald Rumsfeld, then President Reagan's special envoy to Lebanon. Rumsfeld wanted me to show him on a map a specific "gap" or pass, through the mountains east of Beirut, through which Druze and Sunni forces might move to threaten U.S.-backed Christian militias. Already persuaded that the American policy of backing the Lebanese Christians invited certain failure, I could barely contain myself in the face of Rumsfeld's misunderstanding of the situation on the ground. Rumsfeld was one of the smartest people I'd ever met, but as he asked me to point out the gap, I thought to myself that the only "gap" I saw was the one between the envoy's ears.

Dan Kurtzer, my friend at State who would go on to have a brilliant career as ambassador to both Egypt and Israel, was the first to dub me "Dr. No." The title was richly deserved, and I was proud of it. I was always negative, ever cynical that American diplomacy could overcome the dead weight of generations of conflict. Diplomacy, particularly Middle East diplomacy, seemed to be for dreamers, for people who didn't understand the way the world really worked. A summer stint at our embassy in Amman, Jordan, only reinforced my conviction that the Jordanian option, or any other option to address the Arab-Israeli problem, was doomed to fail. Afterward I accepted a position on the secretary of state's policy planning staff, where I continued my dark forecasts and negative ways. I spent a good part of the mid-1980s attacking any proposal from State's Near Eastern Affairs (NEA) Bureau to involve the United States in the Arab-Israeli conflict, and I warned Secretary George Shultz that the Middle East was not a promised land of opportunity but a trap to be avoided, if possible—something he already knew from Lebanon and the failed September 1982 Reagan initiative.

But even George Shultz, a man of uncommon wisdom and judgment, believed with some justification that America at least had to try to manage the problem. In late 1987 the first Palestinian intifada broke out, and the next year the secretary traveled to the Middle East four times to try to produce an Israeli-Palestinian dialogue.

On the secretary's last foray to the Middle East, in June 1988, I had my most memorable undiplomatic moment but also perhaps my greatest impact on a secretary of state in a decade of service. Shultz was an avid tennis player, and while I was packing for the June trip, Lindsay persuaded me to take my racket. Sure enough, one night when we were in Cairo, I got a call from the secretary's staff summoning me to a doubles match early the next morning. It was a dramatic sight, date palms around the court, beautiful blue sky, and a real opportunity to demonstrate my tennis prowess. Whether I was nervous or just jet-lagged, I don't know. But one of my first serves caught my partner—the secretary of state—squarely in the back, just above the elastic brace he was wearing for support. My first trip with a secretary of state, I thought that morning, might also be my last. As the secretary grimaced in pain, yelling at me to hit my second serve, and the diplomatic security agents protecting him laughed themselves silly, I worried about my next assignment.

Getting to Yes

Being Dr. No is fine for a historian and may even be an added advantage for an intelligence analyst, but it was neither smart nor appropriate for someone charged with providing honest advice to the secretary of state. No matter how dubious the chances for success in Middle East diplomacy, the boss deserved a fair set of options, uncoated with either honey or vinegar.

There's no other way to say it: during the months of diplomacy that led to the Madrid peace conference, my views changed profoundly. On reflection, it was a good thing Jim Baker had given up tennis for golf. As I watched him announce invitations to Madrid that afternoon in Jerusalem, I couldn't believe the extent to which my fortunes and my own views had been transformed. Part of it was personal. An old government maxim has it that there's never a bad idea or meeting if you're somehow a part of it. Suddenly "being there" as part of a small, elite group had become extremely elating and important.

Two weeks later, at the end of October, I sat in Madrid's Palacio

Real, stunned by the historic conference unfolding around me. As I listened to the speeches, filled with bitterness and some hope, the gaps separating Arabs and Israelis made me shudder. Certainly life in the negotiations wouldn't be easy, but if America could put this conference together, why not aspire to do even more? In fact, with a tough negotiator like Baker, backed up by a president like George H. W. Bush, who understood the importance of Arab-Israeli peace to American national interests, why not reach for agreements or even peace treaties that would end the Arab-Israeli conflict once and for all?

Why not, indeed? For almost fifteen years thereafter, under Democratic and Republican administrations alike, I was part of a small group of diplomats and negotiators who tried to do precisely that, admittedly with very mixed results. Baker called us the peace processors or, when he was in an irreverent mood, the food processors. He'd order up some formulation or fix, and we'd mix it up in our diplomatic blender, usually with pretty good results. Mike McCurry, Secretary of State Madeleine Albright's and later President Clinton's spokesman, described our small team in a different way. Not since the Indiana Pacers basketball teams of the 1980s, he quipped, had a bunch of guys worked so well together. Even Colin Powell, who'd later roll his eyes at the thought of Bill Clinton playing host to Yasser Arafat for two weeks in the woods at Camp David, genuinely admired our dedication and creativity.

Looking back on those years now, I realize how special, even unique, they were. Rarely in the history of modern American diplomacy has such a small group of midlevel advisors worked on such an important issue over such a long period of time, with as much access to presidents and secretaries of state of both parties. That longevity had its downsides, but these years were certainly the most extraordinary and challenging of my professional life. Sometimes the Americans were able to rise to the occasion, at other times not. Negotiations demand a certain kind of personality. To be effective, you need to believe that things can change but have extraordinary patience if they don't. You need to be tough but empathetic, firm but practical. And above all, you need to be ready to endure the endless maneuvering and machinations of Arabs and Israelis for whom this conflict has sadly become a way of life, but still be able to threaten to walk away if circumstances require it. Robert Strauss, the former head of the Democratic National Committee who served as Jimmy Carter's special envoy to the autonomy talks in 1979 and 1980, laid out the frustrations best for me—even if you do everything right: "Working the peace process is like trying to wipe your ass with a wagon wheel. It goes round and round and nothing happens."

Settling for Maybe

I certainly felt that way many times. But in hindsight, I can see that for me working on the negotiations wasn't circular at all. Instead, the arc of my career as an analyst and a negotiator followed a clear progression. And my journey reflected the roller coaster–like ups and downs of the peace process itself. I began my career as Dr. No, a skeptic, an unbeliever really, in diplomacy and peacemaking; along the road to Madrid and in the Oslo years that followed, I underwent something of a conversion into Dr. Yes, a missionary spreading the word about the power of negotiations; and when, in the wake of the second intifada, everything we'd worked on collapsed, I fell back to something in between.

These transitions were not easy passages. They were very personal and complicated because a great deal was at stake for my country and for me. That I'm suspended now somewhere between despair and hope is not all that surprising given the turn of events; it's probably where I should have been all along. But as anyone who has ever been in the middle of a storm (and who's honest about it) will tell you, it's not always so easy to see things clearly.

In January 2003, after almost twenty-five years of working at the Department of State, I resigned from government. Since then I have come to question much about our policy and certainly the two principal articles of faith that kept me going all those years: first, that the Arab-Israeli conflict could be resolved as quickly as we imagined, or at all for that matter, and second, that America, working closely with Arabs and Israelis, could play a leading role in that effort.

In December 1998 I was sent to Israel to monitor the first phase of the recently concluded Wye River agreement. President Clinton had succeeded, against the odds, in getting Prime Minister Benjamin Netanyahu and PLO Chairman Yasser Arafat to take another step in the Oslo process. Having worked on achieving this unlikely success for over a year, I was on one hell of negotiator's high.

During that trip I gave a public talk in Jerusalem, in which I argued that the Arab-Israeli peace process had reached a point of no return. There would be setbacks, to be sure, but the process had achieved a kind of irreversibility that over time would allow us to move toward ending the conflict. It was as bold (and naïve) an argument as I had ever made. Four months later I received a highly unusual letter from Efraim Halevy, then the deputy director (and later director) of Israel's Mossad. Halevy questioned my assumptions and said he feared that the future held only confrontation. The current rivers of change flowing between Arabs and Israelis did appear positive, he admitted, but what would happen, he asked, "if the flow leaves more of the fish behind?"

The fact is that Halevy was right. No amount of "process," no feel-good signing ceremonies or interim agreements, can ever mask persistent, underlying grievances, traumas, and wounds. Nor can they transform a psychology of confrontation quickly or easily. Too complex and too nasty, the Arab-Israeli conflict has resisted any linear, speedy march toward peace. Having *evolved* in phases over time, it can only be *resolved* in phases over time. I knew this all along. But as caught up as I became in the diplomacy and desire to see conflict resolved, I focused too much on the possible and not enough on the probable.

As an American, however, the other core article of faith concerns and intrigues me more. Is America—as I came to believe—capable of helping Arabs and Israelis reach lasting solutions to the problem of the much too promised land? Can we really make good on our well-meaning pledge that, through negotiation, give-and-take, and compromise, we can help them achieve what God, the British, and the United Nations could not?

After more than thirty years of studying, analyzing, and negotiating the Arab-Israeli conflict, I believe the answer is still yes. We can't produce peace and reconciliation, but we can help to diminish conflict, defuse crises, and broker political agreements that might give Arabs and Israelis a chance to achieve these long-sought goals. Who are you going to believe, Groucho once said, me or your lying eyes? Just look at the historical record. With the exception of Oslo's Declaration of Principles (negotiated secretly between Israel and the PLO in 1993) and the Israeli-Jordanian peace treaty (negotiated directly between the two in 1994), the United States has been involved at some stage in every successful Arab-Israeli accord, and sadly it has participated in too many efforts that have failed.

But my *yes* is now a much more highly qualified one than it once was. The primary responsibility for peacemaking rests with the Arabs and Israelis, not with the Americans. The Middle East is their neighborhood, and its history and future is theirs. No matter how hard they or we may try, the conditions for Arab-Israeli breakthroughs will never grow in an American bell jar.

But a region in ferment needs American leadership. "To succeed in Arab-Israeli peacemaking," a senior American diplomat once told me, "you need balls this big." He put his hands into a circle roughly the size of a basketball. Even if the sun, moon, and stars are properly aligned, the chances for real and sustainable progress remain slight without a tough, forceful American role. And that's because the journey toward Arab-Israeli peace is littered with challenges and obstacles much greater than I imagined when I began. Commitment will get you started on that road. How far you get, however, is another matter. That depends on toughness and smarts, and on how well you can cope with Arab and Israeli politics, and on how well you manage your own.

Chapter Two

Gulliver's Troubles[*]:
A Great Power in a
World of Small Ones

The Secretary and the Tailor

On a diplomatic mission to Britain, Russia, and Israel, the American secretary of state decided to take a break and look for some new clothes. "For one hundred dollars, what can you make me?" the secretary asked the English tailor at a fine haberdashery near Piccadilly. "Not much, sir. Perhaps a vest." In Moscow the secretary put the same question to the Russian clothier. "Maybe a sweater" came the reply. Later in Tel Aviv, undaunted in his quest, the secretary asked the identical question of an old Jewish tailor in a small shop off Diezengoff Street. "For one hundred dollars, I can make you a vest, a sweater, a sport coat, and I'll throw in a pair of pants," he replied. Stunned, the secretary asked how the same money could buy so much more in Israel. "It's very simple," the old man explained. "Out here you're not so big."

The first time I heard this story it was attributed to James Baker. Later I asked him whether it was his yarn. Baker laughed

---

[*] The chapter title is adapted from Stanley Hoffman's *Gulliver's Troubles, or the Setting of American Foreign Policy* (New York: McGraw Hill, 1968).

and said no, but he wished it was. The story makes a powerful point that American diplomats and negotiators often forget or learn the hard way: for all their military and political muscle, great powers aren't always so great when they get mixed up in the affairs of small tribes.

I often thought about the secretary and the tailor—and the underlying paradox of who was big and who was small—as we flew out of Andrews Air Force Base, headed east into the Byzantine maze of Arab-Israeli diplomacy.

Here we were, on board the secretary of state's aircraft representing the most powerful nation on earth. We were traveling to tiny nations like Israel, no bigger than New Jersey. Then we would go to Syria, which Don Rumsfeld dismissed as "that peanut country," with an annual GDP smaller than that of Chicago. The exception was Egypt, with its population of nearly eighty million and an area more than twice that of California. But our ability to get Arabs and Israelis to agree on anything, let alone resolve the really tough issues such as Jerusalem, proved quite limited even when they asked for our help.

It wasn't that I expected quick or easy results. As a historian of the modern Middle East, I knew this was the Cadillac of conflicts—entrenched, bitter, and complicated. One conflict was bad enough, but this was really two rolled into one. An established state, Israel, and a Palestinian national movement that was seeking to become a state were fighting a historic and existential struggle over land, holy places, and identity. One side's gain was almost always seen as the other's loss. On a different level, states confronted one another. Essentially, it was Israel against its immediate neighbors (Egypt, Syria, Jordan, and Lebanon) and the broader Arab world, all acutely concerned by the Palestinian cause. And those kinds of struggles driven by memory, history, and national trauma are never resolved quickly or easily. They are generational.

As an analyst, I also knew that while Israel had signed peace treaties with Egypt and Jordan, and other interim and disengagement accords with the Palestinians and Syria, comprehensive or meaningful peace remained elusive. American diplomacy in the

Middle East appeared to resemble baseball (a game rooted in failure), a realization that was driven home to me as I sat through yet another losing Baltimore Orioles season at Camden Yards. After all, batting .400 in a major-league season, a feat achieved only once in the game's last seventy-five years, still means failing to hit safely six out of every ten times at bat. The odds really were not much better in America's Arab-Israeli diplomacy.

The gap between our power on paper and our lack of success on the ground always fascinated me. Our presence and our power at the plate were really impressive. In most cases we headed out on our diplomatic road trips at the urging of the Arabs and Israelis, with the support of the president and the backing of Congress, and with real leverage derived from the economic, security, and political support we provided to our friends in the region. At times we possessed an additional advantage: a crisis atmosphere that lent real urgency to making a deal.

But crises out there were a way of life. What often seemed urgent to us seemed more routine to them. And once we were out in what I dubbed "the neighborhood," our reach and influence could be quite deceptive.

In September 1996 Israel's opening of the Hasmonean tunnel in Jerusalem triggered a major crisis. That act resulted in the worst Israeli-Palestinian violence since Oslo, triggering confrontations that left eighty-five Palestinians and sixteen Israelis dead. It also triggered a negotiation. A summit hosted by President Clinton in Washington and attended by Jordan's King Hussein, Prime Minister Netanyahu, and Chairman Arafat launched our mission, which was to get Israeli-Palestinian negotiations back on track. With such a high-profile send-off and the worst crisis since Oslo, our mission, I figured, would be intense but short. What planet was I living on? Once in the neighborhood we were sucked into a three-month game of "gotcha" in which each side tried to demonstrate it could be more unreasonable than the other. I think Arafat won, but Netanyahu ran a very close second. Four months later Israelis and Palestinians signed the Hebron Protocol agreement that kept the Oslo process alive, but just barely.

The three-month negotiation made me feel at times like I was on the set of the Bill Murray movie *Groundhog Day;* every day was the same. We spent daylight hours negotiating with the Israelis in Tel Aviv or Jerusalem; our nights were devoted to meetings in Gaza with Arafat, including postmidnight suppers of fried food while the chairman ate nothing but skinless chicken, cooked vegetables, and yogurt. We were in bed by four A.M. and up by nine A.M. to start the whole routine over again. That New Year's Eve we celebrated at an Israeli truck stop near Gaza wondering whether we'd ever make it home again.

To continue the baseball metaphor, our hitting often proved no match for their pitching. Arabs and Israelis—even when they themselves seemed interested in reaching an agreement—threw curves, sliders, screwballs, spitballs, beanballs, knucklers, and a variety of junk pitches that you couldn't and didn't want to hit. The rare pitch that actually produced solid contact resulted from a combination of enormous patience, determination, and a good eye for what was possible.

Every trip reminded me of the long odds of reaching an agreement, let alone implementing one. We'd land, let's say, at Ben-Gurion Airport in Israel. The secretary would be met plane-side by the foreign minister (or some lesser light) and stroll down a carpet (it really was red), with loads of press and security monitoring their every move. It really was a sight. Since I was usually one of the last staff off the plane, I'd take a minute to soak up the scene (delay any longer, and I'd miss the motorcade, an unforgivable offense), which was particularly impressive at night. The floodlights illuminated the blue-and-white 737 embossed with the State Department seal, American flags on the tail, and the words "United States of America" running the length of the fuselage. Anytime, day or night, Cairo, Amman, or Damascus, an arriving secretary of state created real buzz and an impressive display of American presence.

The secretary and his "party" (a word I always found pretentious, particularly when invoked by a self-important staffer, as in the "party wants this or that") would be whisked away in a motorcade with sirens screaming, surrounded by every type of police vehicle imaginable. The ride to the Jerusalem hotel was always a wild one. Any veteran of these road trips will tell you that the most likely threat to American diplomats abroad is not a terrorist attack but an overanxious embassy driver behind the wheel of an armor-plated SUV doing seventy miles an hour, convinced he must remain within two feet of the vehicle in front of him. During one of these wild rides, in a motorcade in Alexandria, Egypt, my friend, the veteran Arabic interpreter and advisor Gamal Helal, badly fractured his ankle when he was thrown against the door of our van. Such motorcades, themselves symbols of American power, invariably annoyed thousands of Arabs and Israelis by tying up traffic anytime the secretary left the hotel.

At the hotel the controlled chaos continued as agents from our diplomatic security and from Shin Bet (Israel's FBI) ushered the secretary and a few lucky others through another throng of press and well-wishers in the lobby. Invariably an issue over some security procedure would arise between their guys and ours, the discussion leading, at least on one occasion I witnessed, to a pushing and shoving match. On another, a Shin Bet agent unholstered his weapon after one of the secretary's agents exiting his suite pushed him. Shin Bet was incredibly turf conscious and was one of only a handful of security agencies in the world that were allowed to position agents on the secretary's floor beyond the Marine guard. I always thought the Israelis should have been a bit more understanding since the same Shin Bet that was protecting the secretary was also bugging his and our hotel rooms. Out in the neighborhood we had no expectation of privacy, and none was given. Richard Shinnick, who ran trips for both Warren Christopher and Madeleine Albright, described life at these hotels in Israel and the Arab world as "living in a microphone." We learned to live with all kinds of indignities. On one trip our bomb dog who did luggage checks got sick, so we borrowed a small spaniel from the Israelis. That dog must have been really nervous because he proceeded to get on top of the luggage and piss his way up and down all over our bags.

Even with the bugs and dogs, though, we felt we were in control. These trips were akin to military invasions. The party would take over at least two complete floors of a five-star hotel, in addition to appropriating space for security, drivers, and admin, along with traveling press, medical personnel, and other assorted staff. Within hours our people would convert these areas into self-sustaining offices, complete with fax and copy machines, computers, and a secure phone system to support the mission. How the Washington advance teams and our embassies managed it all, sometimes on very short notice, while maintaining their composure and sense of humor in the face of "the party's" demands was never entirely clear to me. I do know that ambassadorial careers could be made or broken by performance during these secretarial visits.

Pushing a Foreign Service officer around was one thing; pushing paying guests out of a hotel room was something else. And it happened more than once, particularly when the secretary's trip had to be put together in a hurry and hotel rooms quickly secured. For me it once got personal. On one of Baker's early trips to Israel, I found a note in my hotel room from a Cleveland couple who knew my parents and who had been forced to relocate from the King David to another hotel. They wished me the best of luck even though I had been partly responsible for ruining their long-planned vacation. Frankly, they took this uprooting much better than I would have.

That we got just about everything we wanted on the housekeeping and amenities side only deepened our self-confidence. Israeli hoteliers aren't known for their great service, but hotel managers and staff had a stake in keeping us happy. They loved the PR, were really proud that a secretary of state was patronizing their hotel, and genuinely wished us success in our peacemaking mission. Every secretary of state I worked for preferred staying overnight in Israel. On the Arab side, whether we stayed in Damascus, Cairo, or Amman, everything was also arranged for us, but the food, medical treatment, and personal touch were just better on the Israeli side. Years ago I befriended a wonderful Israeli woman, Irit Gazit, who was guest relations manager at all three hotels that various secretaries used for more than a decade. Irit was irreverent and funny, with a keen sense of the absurd in life and in Israeli politics. She went to great lengths to keep four secretaries of state and their small teams happy. Once Irit baked Warren Christopher's favorite carrot muffins at her home when it was impossible for the hotel kitchen to do it on the Sabbath. And she ironed Madeleine Albright's outfits at three A.M. before the secretary's morning meeting. So I didn't bat an eye the day a treadmill and a cappuccino maker appeared mysteriously in Tony Zinni's hotel suite.

But once we were ensconced in the hotel—whether in Jerusalem, Tel Aviv, Cairo, or Damascus—the idea that we had real control or influence over much of anything quickly evaporated. Whenever we thought we had something fixed or agreed—especially then—we didn't. Once after the Saudis failed to deliver on an important press statement involving Arab representation at Madrid, Baker erupted, "These guys could fuck up a two-car funeral."

I was always acutely aware of how isolated we were and how limited our reach could be. Once in the neighborhood we were dealing with the locals' issues, fears, and internal politics on their timetables, not ours. If we wanted results—and there wasn't a secretary of state or envoy I worked for who didn't—you needed patience and the ability to tolerate and absorb indignities both large and small. In April 1996 Syrian president Hafez al-Assad embarrassed Warren Christopher by refusing to see him—a snub that the media latched on to as emblematic of our willingness to be jerked around by the Syrians. Of course, I was sympathetic to my boss and had no patience for the Syrians and the way they did business. But in the interests of the broader mission Christopher sucked it up. It was probably the right decision. What our friends in the press didn't know was that we were in Damascus to stage a surprise visit to Beirut by helicopter and had made a last-minute request for the Assad meeting. Still, the outcome of the incident didn't feel right, making it seem that Assad was taking us for granted, as if our frequent trips were making us part of the furniture.

When we traveled without the secretary, our ability to control our own destiny was even more limited. "Hurry up and wait" could have been the team's motto. "What about our dignity?" Martin Indyk, our ambassador to Israel, lamented as we whiled away the hours in Taba waiting for the arrival of an Israeli delegation hours overdue. What dignity? I thought, as Gamal Helal and I just looked at Martin and laughed.

This "out here you're not so big" problem is not simply a matter of perception; it's a reality, and it's the first mountain that has to be climbed if America is to manage this conflict, let alone succeed in brokering agreements between Arabs and Israelis. The past century was filled with attempts by outside powers to resolve national and ethnic conflicts in the Middle East, the Balkans, and Northern Ireland. An outside power can play a positive role, but it is at a distinct disadvantage. In conflicts where memory, identity, and history figure prominently, a great power—especially a great power from far away—has far less stake in a particular outcome than does a small power in the heart of the contested region.

Smaller nations will do just about anything to survive and are not inclined to listen to or even trust advice offered by a distant power whose political and physical survival is not at stake. The ghosts of the past, made real by history's fears and traumas, speak louder than the untested promise of a brighter future offered up by American diplomats. When our workday was done, we always had the luxury of returning to a normal life or simply moving on to a new assignment after a year or two. Arab and Israeli leaders—even the strong ones, such as Sadat, Begin, Rabin, and Arafat—had no such options. In fact, they were held accountable 24/7 by domestic politics, public opinion, and their own conception of how the terms of any agreement would shape their current political situation and place in history. At Camp David, when we pushed Arafat further than he wanted to go, I think his favorite line was "You won't get a chance to attend my funeral." And with the ghosts of Sadat and Rabin ever present, he was certainly determined to prevent that prediction from coming true.

Americans who understand these bitter regional realities and are able to find the right balance between being sensitive to these tribal and national traumas and not allowing American policy to be held completely hostage to them stand a much better chance of success than those who don't. And Americans who recognize the galactic gap between a secure and confident America and the traumatized and insecure world of Israelis and Arabs fare best of all.

American optimism is essential to sustain the effort, but too grandiose a conception always guarantees failure. Sadat's heroic bid to make peace with Israel really was an exception. This region hates big ideas, certainly those offered up from outside and usually those from inside as well. From the first Baghdad Pact, which tried to forge a Western-backed coalition of Arab states during the 1950s, to the current Iraq policies of George W. Bush, rejection has usually been the safer bet. Small tribes don't convert or transform easily. In fact, if there's any conversion, it's usually the other way around. The last three truly big ideas floating around out there—Judaism, Christianity, and Islam—came from them, and they converted us.

Fish for Neighbors

I grew up in a real estate family but never learned much about the business, except of course for the three L's—location, location, location. And the three L's of the real estate business apply just as much in the Middle East as they do in Cleveland, Ohio, maybe even more so.

Where you stand in life is almost always a result of where you sit and live. And Americans, Arabs, and Israelis have been sitting in very different places for years, in their case for quite a bit longer. The challenge involved in Arab-Israeli peacekeeping can't possibly be appreciated without a sense of how different those places really are.

The place where Americans live is quite extraordinary, exceptional really, and accounts for much of the way we see ourselves and the rest of the world. Jules Jusserand, France's astute ambassador to the United States from 1902 to 1925 (he clearly liked being in America), reflecting on America's good fortune, observed that the country was blessed among nations. "On the north, she had a weak neighbor; on the south, another weak neighbor; on the east, fish; on the west, fish."[1]

Jusserand knew that two oceans—our "liquid assets," so to speak—generate security, which breeds self-confidence. And together with our abundant natural resources and a unique political system, it has given America special advantages and a historical experience without parallel.

Since the American Civil War—an unbroken period of almost 150 years—we have been spared, on the security side, the crueler fate that has befallen much of the rest of the world. Without civil war, invasion, occupation, and the profound insecurity that is guaranteed by the presence of stronger and predatory neighbors, we have been shaped by a healthy dose of optimism, idealism, and pragmatism. As the first nation founded on the basis of an idea—the primacy of the individual—we also have come to believe deeply in the power and responsibility of individuals to improve themselves and the world around them.[2]

From time to time some of us have even believed that the rest of the world could learn a thing or two from us about life, liberty, and the pursuit of happiness. In fact, when we're at our best, without the excessive superiority and exceptionalism that make us talk more than we listen, we have a lot to contribute, and the rest of the world may even want to hear about it. At other times I'm not sure we care all that much about trying to transform the world in our image. We're not an empire in the classic sense, or even an empire in denial. Unlike the British, we lack a professional imperial class, let alone a generation of Americans committed to spreading our values abroad or building nations based on them. In some periods we've sought to export our exceptionalism, either out of a sense of opportunity—our late nineteenth-century manifest destiny—or, as today, in a time of crisis, in the wake of 9/11. But Afghanistan and particularly Iraq are exceptional, and the results thus far are, to say the least, ambiguous at best. Indeed, our wealth, physical security, and abundance have led many to believe that we have the option of limiting our involvement in the world and picking our fights.

Much of the rest of the world, certainly the Arabs and Israelis, does not have fish for neighbors, certainly not on the grand scale that our coasts afford. Sadly (both would say) they have each other. And as Mark Twain observed, perhaps from his own travels through the not-so-holy land as one of the innocents abroad, familiarity (in this case, proximity) breeds contempt and children. Experts have argued that the real problem in the Arab-Israeli conflict is that the sides really don't know each other. The more I thought about it, however, the more I came to understand that at least part of the problem is that they know each other too well. This fatal embrace locks both sides into a lethal struggle over the basic elements of life—land, water, security, and identity—and makes them different from each other and even more different from us.

I'd sometimes lose sight of this reality. Taken in by the Westernized, sophisticated manner and sheer likability of many of the Arabs and Israelis with whom we worked, I'd mistakenly assume that they were more or less like us.

This was particularly true of the Israelis, most of whom, after all, share many of our values, know America well, and understand how to talk to Americans. Benjamin (Bibi) Netanyahu, a Likud prime minister whom I'd known for many years, was about as Americanized as they came. Growing up in the United States with an American mother, Netanyahu had the best Americanized English of any Israeli I'd ever met. Madeleine Albright, who characterized Netanyahu as an Israeli Newt Gingrich, once quipped that Bibi was "so damn American" that it was sometimes tough to push back at him. I knew the feeling. During one particularly unpleasant meeting in Jerusalem, Bibi yelled at us for interfering in Israeli politics. I closed my eyes during his tirade and remembered my high school tennis coach yelling at me for throwing my racket.

But as American as Bibi seemed to be, his world and ours were quite different. We were about the same age. He was a veteran of one of Israel's most elite combat units and son of a prominent right-wing revisionist historian. His brother Yonatan was an internationally known Israeli war hero killed in the Entebbe hostage rescue operation in 1976. Despite our surface similarities, we came from different planets. Deeply suspicious of the State Department (Baker had temporarily banned him from the building after his over-the-top criticism of the United States), Netanyahu openly distrusted the American role in negotiations and viewed us as naïve and softheaded, particularly when it came to assessing the degree of Arab hostility toward Israel. There was more than a little condescension here on Bibi's part. But to be fair, our differences also flowed from where we lived. "You can afford to give the Arabs the benefit of the doubt from the safety and security of Washington," he once told me on a long plane ride we shared. "Out here in our neighborhood, we can't and won't." One of the peace process's great ironies is that Bibi Netanyahu, such a fierce defender of Israeli's independence when it came to negotiations, became the Israeli prime minister most dependent on American help during his three years in power (1996–1999). We would draft both of the key documents involved in agreements Netanyahu would conclude with Arafat, something Rabin and even Peres in later years would never permit.

Netanyahu was a tough and ideological Likud prime minister. But I also felt the difference in worldview with the Labor Party's Yitzhak Rabin. As much as Rabin respected, admired, and relied on America, he was still an Israeli caught up in a struggle that Americans might appreciate—even analyze correctly—but never fully understand. That sensibility was reserved only for those living on the knife's edge.

I met Yitzhak Rabin for the first time in April 1974. He was about to succeed Golda Meir as prime minister, and the traumas and wounds of the October 1973 war were still fresh. The occasion was a Passover seder at his home. Eager to impress him and talk (always a bad combination), I rambled on during dinner about Sadat's peace strategy toward Israel. Rabin sat impassively for several minutes, and then with a dismissive wave of his hand that I would come to know well over the years, he growled, "You don't live here, and you don't understand the Arabs." I didn't have much to say for the rest of the evening. This conviction that, however well intentioned, the Americans were naïve and didn't understand the Arabs, was shared by almost every Israeli with whom we worked. Frankly, I thought the Israelis, living on top of a volcano, had a point. But it created a distance even among close allies. When Rabin called the Declaration of Principles that Dan Kurtzer and I drafted in May 1993 "the worst American text" since Camp David, I wasn't happy about it, but it reflected a reality I came to appreciate.

I felt much the same sense of familiarity yet distance in dealing with my Palestinian and Arab colleagues. Saeb Erekat could have been the Palestinian Bibi. He had a green card, a degree from San Francisco State University, and an impressive command of English and the American vernacular. We were friends, as were our daughters and wives. I'd been to his home in Jericho, and he'd been to mine in suburban Washington. We'd shared many a water pipe, late into the night, talking about negotiations and life. At times, with his Ph.D. and his academic bent, he seemed like a graduate school colleague in Ann Arbor.

But then I'd watch him in negotiations, at meetings with Arafat, and on CNN defending Palestinian interests, and I'd realize how little we really had in common. Saeb often said that he wasn't pro-Israeli or pro-Palestinian, just pro-peace. It was a good line, and I think he meant it. But it really didn't reflect his reality. He was a Palestinian Muslim living under Israeli occupation whose every move—even with VIP permits, a driver, and a high-end European car—depended on Israel's sufferance. I lost count of the number of times Saeb would call us when we were in Israel to tell us he'd be late for a meeting because he was held up at a checkpoint, or ask for our help in getting the Israelis to help one of his colleagues. And his professional career—now that he had left the world of the university—was tied to Arafat's whims and to the rough-and-tumble vagaries of Palestinian politics. In Oslo in 1998 I once witnessed Saeb's colleagues hound and pound him so badly that they literally drove him out of the room. Palestinian politics, like Israeli politics, can be cruel and unforgiving. Without a street reputation, jail time, or participation in the armed struggle (Saeb had none of these credentials), you had to take more than your fair share of hits.

Saeb was also a father, and his world made him vulnerable in that role as well. Two of his four children went through the Seeds of Peace program, which brings young Arabs and Israelis together for coexistence and conflict resolution programs. We shared a commitment to Seeds. But then in 2002 he confided in me his fear that his youngest son, Muhammad, might be approached at school and pressured to become a *shahid* or martyr for the Palestinian cause. I was stunned. My son and daughter attended private schools in Washington, where my worst fear for them was that they might not get into the colleges they had their hearts set on.

The world of Arabs and Israelis was really not my world. That I had run into Jordan's King Hussein wearing blue jeans at a suburban Washington theater, watching Sean Connery in *The Rock*, or that his son Abdullah was a *Star Trek* fan (he actually appeared in a *Next Generation* episode), with videos lining the shelves of his office in Amman to prove it, didn't mean much. What did matter was that we lived in different neighborhoods, and that theirs could be a much rougher and nastier one than mine. As a young boy, Hussein had watched a young Palestinian murder his grandfather as he emerged from the al-Aqsa mosque in Jerusalem. And I'll never forget Muhammad Dahlan (former head of Palestinian security in Gaza), a man I admired and respected and who had opened up his home to my daughter, telling me about his execution of a Palestinian collaborator: "I shot him like a dog in the street."

As an affluent white American, I had a completely different frame of reference. I was passionate about my work and committed to advancing American interests by helping Arabs and Israelis sort out their problems. But for me, that work was never a life-or-death proposition. With my passport in my back pocket, I could go home, quit, or request another assignment. After all, I was lucky enough to have been born into a Western liberal democracy. No Qassam or Katyusha rockets fell on Chevy Chase, and no refugee camps blight its leafy prospects. When my kids went to school in the morning, I had no doubt they'd be back home safely when I returned that evening.

When you consider the simple fact that in recent years no Palestinian or Israeli parent could guarantee their own child twenty-four hours free from the threat of death or grievous injury, you begin to sense the difference in our worlds. "How protected and innocent were the Americans I met," Hanan Ashrawi, a shrill yet shrewd Palestinian negotiator and human rights activist, recalled of her first visit to America, and "how removed from the pain and complexity of life beyond their continent."[3] Hanan probably changed her mind about America-the-innocent after dealing with Jim Baker for a while. But her observation was still on target. Most Americans are sheltered and protected. And yet this detachment, I came to believe, could be an advantage. I called my friend Nahum Barnea, perhaps Israel's best political journalist, to offer my condolences when his son was killed in a terrorist bombing in Jerusalem in 1996. You know, Nahum said, "you don't live in this in neighborhood, which is precisely why you must continue your efforts toward peace." Freed from the existential worries of the Arabs and Israelis, America might be able to defuse and even resolve a nasty, bitter conflict, or so I thought.

It's a Small, Small World

Great powers, it has been said, meddle in the affairs of small tribes at their own risk. Just ask George W. Bush. But Iraq is only the latest cautionary tale of small creating trouble for big. The Middle East is littered with the broken illusions of great powers who believed they could impose their will on smaller ones: the French in Algeria; the Italians in Libya; the British and French in Suez; and the Russians, and after initial success the Americans, in

Afghanistan. The premier global example of small defeating great for the past millennium is Vietnam, a nation that has defeated the Chinese, French, and Americans. It's a fact of life: small guys who have a single-minded purpose and resolve can wear out and wear down big guys who may be focused for a time but are far from home with many other things to do. Small powers can't always best you, but they can always outwit and outwait you.

In Lebanon during the 1980s American Marines came to be viewed by many locals as just another militia in the ongoing struggle for military and political power. Our vulnerability to Shia terror attacks and to Syria, which managed to down several American carrier-based aircraft, made us look small and weak, as if we'd become part of their small world. Syrian president Assad prided himself on his ability to wreck the U.S. effort to broker an agreement between Israel and Lebanon. After all, he'd shown the superpower the power of the small and determined.

Israelis had no stake in diminishing America's influence in the region as long as they could advance their needs. At the same time, crises between Arabs and the Americans often served to cement American-Israeli ties. For Israelis, getting the big in bed with the small almost always helped, which was why American support for Israeli interests was deemed so important. The Israelis seemed to have a hard time appreciating that such coordination didn't always serve our interests, or theirs; perhaps they didn't care. In the run-up to Madrid Israeli foreign minister Arens proposed to Baker that the United States provide Israel with an assurance that we would vote with the Israelis in the UN against resolutions they didn't like. The United States was not ready "to turn its seat at the Security Council" over to Israel, Arens recalls Baker saying.[4] Having America in Israel's boat, even when it was leaking, may have made Israel more comfortable, but it could also make us look weak and ineffective.

The Arab-Israeli negotiations were filled with these heroic episodes of diplomatic downsizing—waiting for hours for meetings with Assad, putting tape measure to concrete on a Palestinian street, or changing yet another "happy" to "glad" to satisfy Israeli or Palestinian needs in a joint statement or letter of assurance, arguing for hours with Israelis over how many rifles Palestinian security forces could have and what caliber they could be, or debating endlessly whether a third redeployment of Israeli forces from the West Bank should take place "at the end of 1998," in the "last quarter of 1998," or at the "beginning of the last quarter." No third further redeployment ever took place.

But all the while, amid the minutiae of diplomacy, I was in good company. In May 1974 Kissinger, as he shuttled in search of a disengagement accord between Israel and Syria, complained about "retail rug-merchanting," particularly by Israel. At one point he reportedly exploded at the Israelis: "I'm wandering around here like a rug merchant in order to bargain over a hundred or two hundred meters. Like a peddler in the market! I'm trying to save you, and you think you are doing me a favor when you are kind enough to give me a few more meters."[5] Had he been involved in the U.S.-Syrian negotiations in 2000 over the four hundred meters Assad insisted on having off the shore of the Sea of Galilee, Kissinger would have felt right at home.

Size does matter. If I had to identity one defining characteristic that explains the behavior of Arabs and Israelis toward America and in negotiations with each other, it is their relatively small area and population, and the consequences that flowed from that reality—vulnerability, insularity, insecurity, and paradoxically even grandiosity. What distinguishes small nations from large ones, Milan Kundera, the Czech writer once observed, is not the number of their inhabitants; it is something deeper: "For the small nations, existence is not a self-evident certainty but always a question, a wager, a risk."[6] This sense of fragility was often masked by a toughness and boldness necessary to guard against predators in a hostile world. At the same time, Zionism, Palestinian nationalism, and Arab nationalism always seemed to me to be a kind of "fuck you" in the face of historical and contemporary forces that were poised at any moment to bury them.

This was not the case across the board. Among the key players in the Arab-Israeli arena, the Egyptians always seemed bigger, perhaps because of their 80 million population, their five-thousand-year history, or the self-confidence generated by their stability and pride of place as the Arab world's largest and most powerful state. By the time I joined the negotiating team, Egypt had already cut its deal with Israel, had survived the isolating disapproval of the Arab world, and had become the beneficiary of billions of dollars in American aid. After 1979 Egypt took on the role of a big brother, or beneficent great uncle, which sought—usually with our encouragement—to lend its support to peacemaking efforts. It was not by coincidence we'd often start our missions in Cairo, and we relied on Egypt to host negotiations and signing ceremonies. Tensions arose, to be sure, particularly as Palestinians, Jordanians, and Syrians competed for American attention and resources and as Egyptian and American strategies on what should be done in the Middle East diverged. Yet Egypt still loomed large in our perception and strategy. "No peace without us," Amr Moussa, Egypt's former foreign minister and now secretary general of the Arab League, once quipped to me, "and no war either."

An Egyptian diplomat and analyst, Tahseen Basheer, once provocatively observed that with the exception of Egypt, the Arab states were all "tribes with flags." I never accepted this judgment. The Arab states (and Israel) were modern polities with national identities, armies, and bureaucracies—all emerging, if at times dysfunctional, states.

But the more I thought about it, particularly in regard to Syrians, Palestinians, and even Israelis, whom I knew best, the more I came to accept the validity of Basheer's view. Beneath the external trappings of modernity, sometimes not very far beneath, lurked collective identities that could appear in times of crisis. Their bravado and toughness, particularly when they were under pressure, struck me as a way of masking their smallness and sense of vulnerability. In 1971 Amos Elon, an Israeli journalist, published his *The Israelis: Founders and Sons*, a brilliant interpretive study of what makes Israelis who they are. His last chapter is titled "In a Small Country." Elon argued that Israelis have an "elemental, almost tribal sense of sticking together" that flows from memories of the Holocaust and from the contemporary state of siege generated by the Arab-Israeli conflict.[7] Regardless of how that conflict is resolved, however, Israel will always be a small country, he says. Smallness can be a pleasant experience, but it can also lead to insularity, arrogance, and ethnocentricity.

I tracked Elon down (he lives part of the year in Italy) and asked him whether his conclusions had changed after the passage of thirty years. His answer intrigued me. Israel, as a nuclear power backed up by America, he said, was no longer a small country. But maybe with regard to Arab-Israeli peacemaking "you're the one who's shrunk in size and influence," he concluded. Elon was right, perhaps on both counts. The Israel of the 1970s was not the Israel of the early twentieth-first century. Its geopolitical position was bolstered by the region's finest military, by peace treaties with Egypt and Jordan, and by formal diplomatic relations with all five permanent members of the UN Security Council. Undergirding its military strength was a GNP on par with Ireland's and Portugal's and an economic output double that of Syria, Jordan, and Lebanon combined. Israeli cafés, restaurants, and hotels were full, and Warren Buffett had poured billions of dollars into an Israeli venture capital fund. Israelis probably feel more connected to the world now than at any other time in their short modern history.

But that sense of smallness and vulnerability remained. Seven years of Israeli-Palestinian confrontation had brought the Palestinian issue and suicide bombing directly into Israeli cities and towns. Having reoccupied much of the West Bank, Israelis once again were in the face of the Palestinians. The actual and metaphorical sense of fatal proximity to their neighbors remained, remedied neither by a separation nor by disengagement. Ariel Sharon had taken Israel out of Gaza before suffering his career-ending stroke, but Gaza refused to get out of Israel. Qassam rockets and kidnappings kept Israelis feeling vulnerable. Nor, it seemed, despite Israel's withdrawal from Lebanon in May 2000, would Lebanon get out of Israel. The summer 2006

Israeli-Hezbollah war demonstrated with a frightening clarity the paradox of big and small. That a small group like Hezbollah could hold off one of the world's most powerful militaries was shocking enough. Even more extraordinary was the Shia militia's success in using Syrian- and Iranian-supplied rockets to turn Israel for almost a month into two states—one from Haifa northward, where hundreds of thousands fled or lived in shelters, and the other to the south, where life functioned normally. If you needed a demonstration of what small and vulnerable meant— even as superior Israeli air power and artillery destroyed Lebanon's infrastructure—you found it that summer in Haifa.

"You know," Shlomo Avineri, one of Israel's foremost political philosophers, told me, using the Yiddish term for a small village, "in the end we're really just a shtetl with nukes." Richard Grossman, a British Labor politician, had similarly described Israelis as a traumatized people with an atom bomb; and Tom Friedman echoed it with his description of Israel as Yad Vashem with an air force. I know people hate these facile expressions because they seem to reduce Israel to a cardboard cliché. But I liked Avineri's characterization. It seemed to reflect Israelis' perception of themselves.

Here was a small country whose profound sense of historic vulnerability was validated on a daily basis by very real threats. And while it possessed tremendous military power, a significant portion of it could neither be utilized nor was terribly effective in the face of the threats the Israelis faced. The people possessed real strength and resolve but also felt a peculiar sense of fatalism and vulnerability. Small states bank on probability, not just possibility, and they worry a great deal. In the euphoric days after the signing in Washington of the Oslo agreement of September 1993, an Israeli official warned me to restrain my enthusiasm, as we were all in for serious trouble ahead. An Israeli poet had reflected the irony of his country's situation: "We build Jerusalem like men mounting the gallows."[8] This sentiment probably characterized the outlook of many Israelis with whom I negotiated over the years.

Israel may be perceived as a place of big ideas and larger-than-life personalities, but its sense of smallness and of the personal is unmistakable. Over the years I attended meetings between American secretaries of state and six different Israeli prime ministers in the cabinet room adjoining the prime minister's small office. The prime minister would sit at the center alongside a huge high-gloss wooden table, surrounded by various Israeli cabinet ministers and officials. The American secretary of state was seated in the center on the other side. Unusually large quantities of sandwiches, juices, soft drinks, nuts, and pastries (some of which weren't readily identifiable) would be arranged across the table. And then the fun would begin. No matter how hard various prime ministers tried, they could not eliminate the whispering, note passing, and moving around on the Israeli side. The amount of food and its copious and frequent ingestion added to the sense of disorder. The Israelis consumed heroically, although the government reduced the supply over the years, doubtless for budgetary reasons. Grandmotherly Israeli women pushed tea and coffee around the room to serve us individually. The large size of the table ensured that there would be too much reaching, passing, and scrambling for food during the meeting. The main event was the comic struggle for sandwiches. Every Israeli seemed to have a distinct approach. I once saw Sharon dismantle six sandwiches on a serving plate and reassemble them as a Dagwood, which he seemed to inhale in a single gulp. Eli Rubenstein (now a Supreme Court justice), who held various positions, including cabinet secretary and head of the Israeli negotiating team with the Jordanians and Palestinians, had a different strategy. He'd remove the meat and go for the bread and cheese, talking and eating all the while, rifling in his briefcase for a paper he never seemed to find.

It's hard to imagine a similar meeting involving a head of state, senior government officials, and a secretary of state taking place anywhere else in the world, with the possible exception of the Palestinian Authority. The informality, the lack of structure, and the personal character of these encounters could take place only in a small country that was bound closely together in crisis and war, in which senior officials with names like Bibi, Boogie (Moshe Ya'alon, chief of staff), Doobie (Dov Weissglas, Sharon's closest advisor), or Gilly (Gilead Sher, Barak's key negotiator with the Palestinians) related to one another with personal regard, playfulness, and affection, whatever their personal and political differences. At times I thought I was attending a relative's bar mitzvah party. That the Israelis played out such scenes before American officials reflected our close relationship with them and their general comfort level with us.

The concepts of size and intimacy are critical to understanding Israel's constant sense of vulnerability and traumatic memory. When visiting Israel, all secretaries of state made one mandatory stop, and most took advantage of an optional second. Such site visits, to use the term preferred by our protocol officers, reflected the historic and contemporary threats and fears with which Israelis wrestled. "I fight the Nazis at night and lose," the Israeli adage goes, "and I fight the Arabs during the day and win." For Israelis, the past was partly prologue, and they wanted every American official to understand why.

I must have visited Yad Vashem (Hebrew for "a memorial and a name"), Israel's memorial to the Holocaust, a dozen times in the company of secretaries of state and other envoys. The routine was always the same: it began with a tour of the museum; then the memorial flame was lit in the hall of remembrance, a dark, cold, and sunken chamber with the names of concentration camps inscribed on its floor; and then the visitors' book was signed. Press always covered the event, but there were rarely statements or speeches. The visit was designed to be a deeply personal reflective moment.

Yad Vashem sends an unmistakable message about the universal lessons of the Holocaust: that there is inhumanity and evil in the world; that silence in the face of that evil is now impermissible; and that the Nazis destroyed many minorities, including Gypsies, Catholics, Poles, homosexuals, and the disabled. But the point of the secretaries' visits was a very particular one: that the Nazi genocide was about the willful and obsessive destruction of Europe's

Jews as a people. (That the Nazis deported the entire Jewish community of Rhodes, over one thousand miles from Auschwitz, is still astounding.) The message of the Holocaust to the Jewish tribe was unmistakable: without a state of your own, you are the scum of the earth, the inevitable prey of beasts. And the Jews having secured that state, Yad Vashem's message to their key ally was to make sure that the state survives and prospers. I observed secretaries of state from James Baker to Warren Christopher, each with a differing emotional temperament, react to the Yad Vashem experience, and the tribal point was lost on none of them.

The helicopter tour of Israel, like the visit to Yad Vashem, left little to the imagination. We took several flights on our own, but the presence of an Israeli prime minister aboard always heightened the emotional impact. I flew once with Rabin and Christopher, then a second time with Sharon as he showed Zinni around during the spring of 2002. These trips were designed to make a single point: Israel lives on the edge of a precipice. Sharon flew Zinni north to the Lebanese border, east over the Golan Heights, and then south to Gaza and Sharon's farm, all within ninety minutes.

The prime minister couldn't have picked a better day. That afternoon Palestinians had carried out a suicide attack up north in Afula, and we circled that area for a time. Zinni had the headphones, but I'd heard the commentary before, and the drama that day could only have made it more compelling. Israel had little territorial depth, Sharon would be saying; the citizens and economic resources were concentrated in the narrowest area, Tel Aviv and its environs. Israel's waist was so slender that a hostile armored division driving from the West Bank could reach the Mediterranean in an hour, effectively cutting the country in half.

If smallness created vulnerability, it focused Israeli minds on efforts to compensate for it, overcome it, and survive and prosper as a modern state nonetheless. A message from a hypothetical Israeli prime minister to a hypothetical American president might go something like this: the Jewish people suffered the worst atrocities that could befall a people or nation; we Israelis now live in a dangerous neighborhood with no margin for error; we have neighbors near and far who at best tolerate us and at worst bide their time until they can get rid of us; we value your support and friendship, we really do, but don't fuck with us; after two millennia we are again masters of our future; and whatever that future may bring, we intend, as much as possible, to be its shapers.

I never heard an Israeli official articulate the message just this way, but that viewpoint was understood and reflected in many of Israel's policies toward the United States. And every American president and secretary of state understood and was sympathetic to the Israeli dilemma: statehood was a *necessary* but not a *sufficient* condition for Israel to be a normal, accepted, and secure state.

What constituted sufficiency was unclear, but as the historian Paul Johnson noted, the Jews were "learned and intelligent victims" and were thus interested in finding out.[9] Since 1948 the Israelis have searched with varying degrees of competency and success to find the answer. By using military power, they have defended themselves and have seized and settled additional territory. They have negotiated with Arabs and have taken unilateral steps, such as withdrawal, to return territory.

Throughout their climb up this dizzying military and diplomatic mountain, they have depended on the unwavering support of the United States, even while wondering whether one day American support might waver. The Israelis have not yet found the answer to their problem. But even if they do, I suspect that the imperatives of smallness, the risks of dependency, and the ghosts of the past will compel them to begin each new ascent for peace under the guiding philosophy of Prime Minister David Ben-Gurion's prime directive: it matters less what the goyim (non-Jews) say; what counts is what the Jews do.

If Israel, with all its military power, regional reach, and technological superiority, sees itself as a shtetl with nukes, then surely the Palestinians—divided, decentralized, and politically dysfunctional—represent a shtetl without them. Egypt had its pharaonic past and the grand visions of Nasser and Sadat. Syria had Hafez al-Assad, who had ruled longer than all his predecessors and whose tough Arab nationalism and ambitions gave Damascus diplomatic reach. Lebanon, for all its woes of civil war, still possessed in Beirut a dynamic capital and international marketplace. Jordan had King Hussein, the world's longest-ruling monarch before his death. His slight physical stature (we called him the PLK, "plucky little king") couldn't undermine his larger-than-life image and the broader regional role he sought to play. These were sovereign states with the trappings of modernity and, with the exception of Lebanon, control over their own resources, borders, and citizens.

Not so with the Palestinians. Here was a people either in diaspora, under occupation, or on the international dole, with no control over land, resources, or their own politics. Only after making many trips to the Middle East and having many conversations with Palestinians there and in America did I even begin to understand the impact of statelessness on Palestinians, how different their reality was, and to what degree history and memory shaped their approach to negotiations and to us personally.

Initially I was critical of and unsympathetic to the Palestinian position. While Jewish statelessness had driven some Zionists to violence and terror, others had exercised pragmatism and sought compromise. The term "Palestinian nationalist," however, seemed a synonym for "terrorist." In part, my lack of empathy grew out of American unease with national liberation movements in general, particularly with those that chose terror over politics, including attacks against Americans, as a political strategy. Where was the great Palestinian leader like Ben-Gurion or King Hussein, who could champion their cause in a manner that would favorably dispose Americans toward them? Unlike the Israelis, who had an American Jewish community that generally could be depended on as a champion, Palestinians had few allies in the United States to explain their plight, let alone to create a Hollywood mythology. No *Exodus* or *Cast a Giant Shadow* told the world of their suffering and heroism. No United Jewish Appeal raised money or mobilized a community, and few allies in Congress pleaded their cause.

During the first forty years of Israeli statehood, when Americans thought of Palestinians, they thought of refugees and terrorists, certainly not responsible statesmen or politicians.

Nor did the Palestinians get much help from their neighbors. On one level, the Arab world took up the Palestinian cause as its own, lobbying and campaigning emotionally through communiqués, UN resolutions, and summit statements. But on a more practical level, while the idea of justice for Palestinians resonated, the reality of their politics, especially the leading role of the Palestine Liberation Organization (PLO), did not. At best, the Arab regimes feared, used, and manipulated the PLO. With the exception of Egypt, every Arab state that shared common borders with Israel (Jordan, Lebanon, and Syria) had a bloody confrontation with the Palestinian national movement. Regional leaders both feared Arafat for the power of his cause on the Arab street and held him in contempt for his incompetence and clownish image. "That little shit," King Hussein snapped in an uncharacteristically impolitic moment, "he hasn't a clue what he's doing."

Opinion was even less charitable among the Israelis, who saw Palestinians both as a threat and as a painful reminder that their nation was founded, in part, on the displacement of another people. With some exceptions most Israelis I encountered in the 1980s had little respect for the Palestinians and little regard for their cause. Rabin, whose pragmatism restrained him from vilifying Arafat, simply didn't take them seriously. He believed that, with no military clout, no great-power support after the fall of the Soviet Union, and no political strategy worthy of the name, the Palestinians could be safely ignored; rather, the Arab states, particularly Jordan, should be engaged as interlocutors. Not until the outbreak of the first intifada in 1987–88 did Rabin realize that Israel had a Palestinian problem, one that could not be resolved by force. "They're now on the map," he told me shortly before Madrid, "and we may have no choice but to deal with them."

In the 1980s I wrote two books about the PLO and Palestinian politics, but I'm embarrassed to say I had almost no contact with actual Palestinians. My own ignorance about them—who they were and what they wanted—flowed from the simple fact that we didn't talk to them, at least not to the PLO. Throughout the 1970s the CIA had carried on extensive contacts with PLO figures on intelligence and security matters, and Kissinger had authorized limited contacts on political issues, as had Carter. But until the beginning of the first phase of the U.S.-PLO dialogue, from January 1989 to June 1990, our contact with Palestinians was confined to those on the West Bank and Gaza and to wealthy expatriates in Europe and the United States. To me they were cardboard characters more than anything else.

What the Palestinians lacked, it seemed to me, were the skills required to emerge as responsible political players. They appeared too eager to complain about their fate, too ready to blame others for it, and too unwilling—under most circumstances—to accept the extent to which their leaders had authored the misfortune of an entire people. Abba Eban, Israel's silver-tongued foreign minister, once immortally gibed that the Palestinians "never missed an opportunity to miss an opportunity." As late as 1988 I was arguing (wrongly) that no separate Israeli-Palestinian future was possible, and so the Palestinians should go for a confederation with Jordan.

When you get to know people by actually sitting down and listening to them, your views begin to change. During our efforts to put together the Madrid conference and in the ten rounds of unsuccessful negotiations in Washington that followed, I spent a great deal of time with West Bankers and Gazans. I got to know, like, and respect Palestinians such as Hanan Ashrawi, Faisal Husseini, Saeb Erekat, Haidar Abdul Shafi, Sari Nusseibeh, and Ghassan Khatib. Handpicked by the PLO, they were not, by their own admission, representative either of those in diaspora or of those in the refugee camps to whom they often referred. And they were under constant pressure, trapped as they were between the PLO on the outside and the "street" on the inside, not to mention their own internal disagreements. In Baker's first meeting with the Palestinians, their delegation had eleven members;

during his second, five; and in most of the meetings that followed, only three.

But they were great narrators of the Palestinian story, and that bleak story was characterized by exile, trauma, statelessness, military occupation, cruelty, and especially loss of identity. The *nakba*, Arabic for "catastrophe," the phrase they used to describe what for Jews were the stirring events of 1948, resulted in the permanent exile of almost 800,000 Palestinians. The *nakba* was not just a political and humanitarian disaster for the Palestinians: it destroyed an identity that had been rooted for centuries in the history and memory of land, village, and city, without the creation of another. The Palestinian tragedy was not simply about exile and refugees. It was an existential question about who Palestinians were and where they belonged.

Over the years another identity would emerge, a collective consciousness that had found the answer to the question: they were Palestinians, and they belonged, they had indeed a right, to a Palestinian state. And the PLO—the organizational embodiment of Palestinian nationalism and the idea that Palestinians have an identity and a legitimate claim to a place—deserves credit for promoting the answer. At the same time, the Palestinian existential crisis continued. Every time the Palestinian delegation was held up at a checkpoint, delayed at a border crossing, or had their computers confiscated by the Israelis, their identity was again called into question and their facelessness and powerlessness reaffirmed.

In the post-Madrid period we spent hours just trying to get the Palestinian delegation to Washington. I often wondered how it felt to them to face the Israelis as equals across the negotiating table or on CNN, only to return home and revert to the role of occupied persons, with the powerlessness and humiliation such status carried.

I'm not sure my newfound sensitivity mattered much. The Palestinians with whom we dealt felt cornered and abandoned. As Hanan Ashrawi recounted, Israelis got all the carrots and "we got the sticks and morbid forecasts about the consequences of saying no to American ideas." She was basically right. As Ashrawi and Husseini droned on about the detested occupation and the provocation of the settlements, we were prepared to do little about either. During his first meeting with them in Jerusalem in 1991, Baker made it clear that the Palestinians had to help him help them by getting to a peace conference. Any changes in the situation on the ground would result from a political negotiation. And we were prepared to subordinate everything, including legitimate Palestinian complaints about Israeli actions, to that goal. We would come to regret this pattern of overlooking Israeli (and Palestinian) behavior on the ground.

What impressed me most about the Palestinians' reality was how small their world actually was and how weak and dependent they had become. "All of Palestine," Ashrawi observed, "could be gift-wrapped and deposited in the corner of one American state."[10] And she was speaking as an optimist. By 1991 historic Palestine had pretty much disappeared into a division among Israel, Jordan, and the occupied West Bank and Gaza. The remnants were separated from one another with no guaranteed access for Palestinians anywhere on any given day. Jerusalem, east and west, had been annexed and enlarged (to include West Bank territory) and declared Israel's eternal capital. From the Palestinian perspective, 78 percent of historic Palestine was gone, leaving a truncated 22 percent available as the area for a Palestinian state. If you factored in all of the settlements, military installations, internal and external closures, checkpoints, and bypass roads, West Bankers and Gazans were living in a very small space indeed.

Politically, Palestinian space had become even tighter. Soviet support for the Palestinians, never all that reliable, vanished after 1991. Palestinians had no credible or serious channels either to the Americans or to the Israelis (the U.S.-PLO dialogue had been suspended in June 1990 over Arafat's refusal to expel a small Palestinian group on his executive committee for an attempted terror attack against Israel) and had developed no effective military or political strategy to attain statehood.

The PLO had been remarkably successful in gaining international recognition, keeping the Palestinian cause alive and giving Palestinians pride and identity. Yasser Arafat, one Gazan told me, "is a stone I throw at the Israelis every day." Defiance, however, was no substitute for a serious strategy. Arafat's support for Saddam in the Persian Gulf War had embittered the Gulf Arabs and denied him financial support. And the first intifada had demonstrated that the PLO leadership, in exile from the conflict area since 1982, had lost ground to Palestinians inside, who seemed willing to organize politically and take matters into their own hands. In short, the PLO was under enormous pressure, particularly on the issue of who would represent Palestinians at the peace conference the Americans seemed intent on organizing after the Gulf War.

No one described the plight of the PLO more eloquently than did Faisal Husseini with his story of the "Baker suit." Faisal, soft-spoken and usually very quiet, was perhaps the most credible Palestinian in the territories with whom we dealt. Descended from a prominent Jerusalem family, his father, Abdul Qader, was a storied Palestinian commander killed by the Israelis in battle during the 1948 war. Faisal, who would die of a heart attack in 2001, fought mightily to convince us that without PLO representation on the Palestinian delegation, including at a minimum persons from the diaspora and absolutely from East Jerusalem, Palestinian leaders would lose credibility or worse. Baker, however, was not prepared to oppose Israeli limitations on Palestinian representation, although he eventually worked out an arrangement by which a Palestinian from Jordan with ties to Jerusalem sat among the attendees.

To make his point, Faisal told the story of the man who had received a piece of fabric for a suit but couldn't afford a tailor. So he asked an unskilled friend to take on the task. The finished suit had one leg too long, a sleeve too short, and an ill-fitting collar. "How can I wear this suit?" he asked his friend. The answer came back readily: "Where the sleeve is too short, hold your arm in; where the pant is too long, push your leg out. To deal with the collar, just turn your neck to the right." The man complied with these directions and walked down the street in horrible contortions. One onlooker commented to another, "Look at that poor man, how misshapen he is." "It's sad," the other replied, "but you have to admit he's got the best tailor in the world." Faisal's point to Baker was clear. If Palestinians act strangely, it's only because the suit America is making for them doesn't fit. When Faisal was told that Jerusalemites, and he in particular, would not be included in the Palestinian delegation, he said to Baker, "Mr. Secretary, you're looking at a dead man."

The joint Israeli-Palestinian stitching and hemming known as the Oslo process was really an effort to make the suit fit. And to a degree, bringing the PLO into an open process of negotiation brought legitimacy to the enterprise, succeeded where ten rounds of Madrid-generated negotiations had failed to produce actual agreements, and opened up opportunities for Palestinians where none had existed before.

For the Palestinians, the paradox of Oslo was that, while it expanded potential political opportunities, it contracted the actual political horizon, something Arafat wasn't prepared for, although he had agreed to it. For Arafat, Oslo was a trade-off: in exchange for recognizing him as the only Palestinian partner for Israel and America, he agreed to an interim process that deferred big issues like Jerusalem and refugees, and focused on mundane matters, such as actually governing what would become the Palestinian Authority.

Oslo bestowed on Arafat the hoopla of a White House signing ceremony and the honor of a Nobel Peace Prize, but it made his world and that of the Palestinians much smaller. And combined with the confining interim arrangements that accorded Palestinians varying degrees of control but not much sovereignty, an already narrow world got a lot smaller.

The vast international stage on which Arafat had strutted now contracted to the West Bank and Gaza and, in truth, not really all of it. In seven years while working in the West Bank and Gaza, we met with Arafat almost always in Gaza and Ramallah, with a couple of meetings in Nablus, Bethlehem, and Hebron. His travel between the West Bank and Gaza, whether by Jordanian or by Egyptian helicopter, was constrained by security, politics, and his own refusal to be humiliated by this or that Israeli restriction. We never saw him in Jerusalem, which at least publicly was off-limits. During every encounter I felt as if we were meeting in a small, transparent box. Meeting space in his seaside Gaza compound, flattened by the Israelis in 2001, was cramped, and even the Mediterranean, which I could see from his office windows, seemed strangely small. That he died confined to his Ramallah compound (expanded but then partially destroyed by the Israelis in 2002) was consistent with the way he had lived during the last years of his life. His heady promotion of the Palestinian cause from China to Cuba was replaced by the more prosaic realities of governing a small authority with limited power. What had worked so well in the diaspora—during the 1960s, 1970s, and 1980s, a larger-than-life Arafat as a symbol—wore thin quickly, as many Palestinians groaned in the face of corruption, walk-around money, a proliferation of security services, and an authoritarian style of governance. Arafat lived fairly simply and carried tremendous power and authority. But he could not make a transition from symbol to statesman or even to CEO. And he would not delegate. Above all, in coming home to Palestine (or at least part of it), Yasser Arafat was reduced to scale, more human in a way, but also more imperfect. And Palestinians and certainly Israelis were not particularly impressed with what they saw.

Nor was I. I met Arafat for the first time in September 1993, when on the eve of the Oslo signing, I was assigned to be his control officer, a bizarre term when you consider the task at hand. I waited planeside along with Ed Djerejian, assistant secretary of state for Near Eastern Affairs, who kept needling me about what my mother would think about all this. And suddenly there he was descending the steps of his aircraft, looking confused and dazed. He seemed much smaller, less threatening than I imagined—and bore a striking resemblance to Beatle Ringo Starr with a kaffiyeh. He smiled, grasped my hand, and said how much he'd enjoyed my book on the PLO (the first of countless lies he told, but smart staff work on someone's part). I was flustered and disarmed. Reaching into my pocket, I fingered a container of Tic Tac breath mints and I asked him whether he wanted one. "Tic tock," he said, "what's a tic tock?" and moved on to shake the next person's hand.

So began my personal relationship with Yasser Arafat—a man who in a mere seven years would go from a pariah in American eyes to the most frequent visitor to the Oval Office in the year 2000. Through countless hours of meetings (and meals) with Arafat, I never got a sense of what drove him or what he really wanted. Once in a meeting at one of King Hussein's palaces in Amman where Arafat was staying, while searching for the men's room, I wandered into the guest room that Arafat was using as a bedroom. There, neatly folded on a turned-down bed, were pajamas, including what looked like a British-style nightcap. What a quaint scene, I thought, until my eye caught an automatic weapon on one of the bedside tables. It was a jarring reminder of who he was and the life he lived.

For reasons I still can't understand, the chairman took an interest in me, insisting that I sit by his side at meals. He also insisted on serving me, usually with his fingers. Arafat's meal was always the same: skinned chicken, vegetables cooked almost to extinction, yogurt, honey, and tea. The fish in Gaza was superb; the *kanafi*, with its phyllo dough, nuts, and honey, outstanding. But much of what we got would have made a cardiologist gag. The word of the day was *fried*. There was food that looked like pizza that I didn't even know you could fry. I didn't eat meat, but my good friend Gamal Helal in his never-ending game of gotchas would always tell Arafat in Arabic that I loved it, prompting the chairman to put huge pieces of lamb on my plate and then to scold me when I wouldn't touch it.

Arafat had many moods. He could be unctuous and deferential; indignant and angry; playful with his colleagues; and at times stone cold and almost catatonic, when he'd stare straight ahead, shaking his foot for long periods. This was a sure sign he was truly enraged.

But what really seemed to animate him was any real or perceived affront to his dignity and his pride, which, not surprisingly, he felt was under attack constantly by Israel and frequently by us. Much of his behavior was designed to protect that dignity. His famous Paris walkout on Madeleine Albright in October 2000 was prompted by Barak's keeping Arafat waiting too long. During these episodes he could become volatile and emotionally out of control. One stormy night in February 2002, together with Ron Schlicher, our consul general in Jerusalem, I went up to Ramallah to deliver a list of the names of thirty-three Palestinians responsible for terror attacks that the Israelis (using us as cover) wanted arrested. We gave Arafat the list. He exploded, alternately yelling at us and weeping uncontrollably. He was imprisoned in his own compound, he lamented, while his sister lay gravely ill in Amman. It got so bad that his aides had to escort him into another room. Within fifteen minutes he returned, kissing both our hands and begging forgiveness.

Above all, with every successive encounter, what struck me was his smallness and ordinariness against the backdrop of the very weighty cause he embodied. But whether he was ladling lentil soup into my bowl in Tunis like some solicitous Jewish grandmother, or calling me in Cleveland to extend his condolences after my mother's death, Arafat became all too human to me. In the end, a small man leading a big cause, he failed the expectations of Americans, Israelis, and his own people. Arafat had done much better on the larger but less consequential world stage. As a pragmatic leader, he proved incapable of functioning on the smaller but more important one in Palestine.

Gulliver and the Lilliputians

Small, as Gulliver and so many great powers have learned, doesn't necessarily mean weak. In the Arab-Israeli arena over the past half-century, in matters of war and peace alike, the locals have acted in ways that were beyond anyone's prediction or control. And how could America control what it had failed to predict?

From Suez to the Six-Day War to Israel's invasion of Lebanon and through two intifadas, the story line has been clear: small powers act; big powers react.

I often wondered why big simply couldn't make small comply. Why was it that $3 billion didn't seem to buy much in Jerusalem or Cairo? Why couldn't we make the Palestinians (the weakest party in the neighborhood) be reasonable? Why not just impose a solution?

The short answer is that when you need the cooperation of the locals, small isn't so small anymore. And the locals' dependence on America doesn't necessarily guarantee American influence. Despite Israeli actions we didn't like, U.S. administrations demonstrated real reluctance to withhold vital assistance. In the context of cold war politics and peacemaking, Kissinger and Nixon were worried about pressuring Israel too much lest they weaken an ally and embolden the Arabs and Russians. And using aid as a weapon invariably meant upsetting Israel's superbly organized supporters at home—a challenge that most administrations didn't want or need but that some were prepared to take on if the American national interest demanded it.

Even more problematic was the question of using leverage on locals who were not dependent on America but who may have wanted American benefits. The old saying that America's allies always have something to be worried about, and its foes always have something to hope for in terms of an improved relationship, didn't quite work here. Syria's support for terrorist groups made an improvement in bilateral ties unlikely. During the entire period of the on-again-off-again U.S.-sponsored negotiations between Israel and Syria, Assad, the "Lion of Damascus," remained on the list of state sponsors of terror for his support of Palestinian groups such as Hamas and Islamic Jihad and Lebanese groups like Hezbollah. There was never a domestic constituency in the United States willing to go to bat for Assad. And with good reason: unlike Sadat, Arafat, or Hussein, he rejected public diplomacy with Israel. His view of peace was a cold, even Arctic one. Indeed Assad's view of confidence building was to wage a proxy war via Hamas and

Hezbollah, as a way to remind the Israelis that they could never have *confidence* in him until the Golan Heights was Syria's again.

If carrots were unavailable, so were sticks. Not that we ever really tried sticks. The last real effort to press Syria when I was in government occurred when the Reagan administration tried to use Israel's invasion of Lebanon and the Christian Phalange to weaken and ultimately undermine the Syrian position in Lebanon. It was a boneheaded policy that lacked both the will and an understanding of local Lebanese politics, and it was countered by Syria's use of Hezbollah as a proxy and by the weakness of America's relying on Israel and the Christians to remake Lebanon. How many "how do we leverage Syria" memos I must have written during the 1980s. I never believed we were smart or tough enough to create real pressure on Syria using the Turks, internal opposition groups, Arab states, and Israelis. None of them wanted to play this game anyway for very long. In any event, by 1990 Assad, in the face of his own narrowing options, was open to closer ties to America and the coalition against Saddam. As the current administration flails in the face of confirmed Syrian obstructionism in Lebanon and Iraq, I can only imagine how many "let's leverage Syria" memos have recently been written without much effect.

Dealing with Arafat was another story. Using incentives or disincentives was like punching a bowl of Jell-O. As long as Israel needed him, so did we, and he knew it. The power of the Palestinian cause is a striking demonstration of the power of the weak. It is a terrifying but fascinating force to behold, and Arafat was its master. Salah Khalaf, one of the founders of Fatah, and head of Black September, said it best thirty years ago: the United States "has no grip on us, for we have nothing to lose... we are comparable to a breeze... and are feared because we have the ability to blow hot or cold over the entire Middle East."[11] Even years after that "breeze" blew back into the West Bank and Gaza to govern as the Palestinian Authority, neither American pressure nor persuasion seems to have changed Palestinian calculations. Arafat is gone; Abu Mazen has replaced him; yet Hamas has now emerged with a majority in the Palestinian Legislative Council and enough military and political power to defeat Fatah in Gaza and check its influence in the West Bank.

So we Americans, in part by circumstance and in part by design, are caught up in the conflicts of a world beyond our shores where we have interests, friends, and enemies, and where we deal with events we can't master. Like the optimistic Gulliver, we are faced by small powers with long memories, but the conflicts in which we have entangled ourselves in Iraq, Palestine, and Lebanon are far more complex and weighty than the war of the Lilliputians, which turned on the issue of whether the pointed end or the rounded end presented a more effective entry into the boiled egg. Sometimes we succeed. But more often than not we are distracted, hoodwinked, sidetracked, or just plain screwed by small powers who want to befriend and use us at the same time.

We don't play this particular game of nations very well. Avi Gil, one of Shimon Peres's closest advisors, reflected that "unlike you Americans, we stay in our positions for a long time, and we often return. We divine who's serious and who's not on our side, and we learn the tricks of the weak, how to ambush and how to test."

Gil's comments were honest and clear—qualities you don't often find in conversations with Arabs and Israelis, particularly during official diplomacy. Most important of all, he used the word "we," which not surprisingly means that Arabs *and* Israelis play the superpower when their interests demand it. Looking back, I counted at least four different kinds of responses and maneuvers that Arabs and Israelis used interchangeably when they weren't interested in accepting our ideas and initiatives.

Just Say No: Diplomacy is a get-along business, which bothers some people. It often lacks clarity and honesty. Diplomacy places a high priority on avoiding confrontation, since it relies mainly on persuasion, not on pressure. Even the smartest secretaries of state—Kissinger and Baker—will tell you to try to avoid slamming doors, to always leave yourself an option, a way out.

A superpower can say no with little fear of consequences, but so can small powers, even though they are weaker and dependent. Arabs and Israelis usually did not want to present the United States with a categorical no, and they searched for ways to avoid that unpleasant situation. After all, rejecting an American proposal could have negative consequences. But at times an American idea was, from the Arab or Israeli perspective, so ill-timed, so deficient in detail, or so threatening in its potential results that a quick and clear negative response became imperative. Israel took no more than a day to reject Secretary William Rogers's peace initiative of December 1969; three days after the U.S.-Soviet joint communiqué was announced in October 1977, Israeli foreign minister Moshe Dayan, reflecting an even harsher Israeli government reaction, met President Carter in New York to tell him the U.S.-Soviet approach was totally unacceptable. At Geneva in March 2000 President Bill Clinton presented Prime Minister Ehud Barak's final offer on the Golan to President Hafez al-Assad, who made it unmistakably clear within minutes that he wasn't interested.

Sometimes rejection came somewhat more slowly. After two weeks of summitry at Camp David, Clinton and Barak pushed Arafat to give a clear answer to American ideas on borders and the status of Jerusalem. And they got it. Early in the morning on the summit's last day, Saeb Erekat delivered the chairman's no. The ideas were unacceptable, even though Arafat wanted to continue negotiating.

But the "no of all nos" was Menachem Begin's rejection of President Reagan's peace initiative of September 1982. That initiative, developed in July and August, was an effort to improve American credibility in the wake of Israel's invasion of Lebanon and to forestall negative reaction at an Arab summit planned for September. As remarkable as it seems, the Reagan administration presented the initiative to Begin with every expectation that he would reject it. In this sense, Begin's no had little consequence. As it turned out, Begin's response foreshadowed the Arab answer: neither the Jordanians, nor the PLO, nor any other Arab party embraced the proposal either.

The presentation was left to Sam Lewis, the American ambassador to Israel, who personally presented the initiative to Begin. Lewis later recounted the episode to me. The prime minister,

68 | AARON DAVID MILLER

who had not taken a vacation in four years, was relaxing with his wife, Aliza, in Nahariyya, near the Lebanese border. He appeared stressed and worn down as a result of Israel's Lebanon invasion, a trauma from which he'd never really recover. Lewis, who was under instructions from Secretary of State George Shultz to deliver an "eyes only" message from the president, insisted on driving north to see Begin, who very much wanted to postpone the meeting for a few days.

When Lewis entered the house, he found Begin—whom he'd never seen without coat and tie—dressed informally in a sport shirt and slacks. Although tired, Begin seemed in a relaxed mood. They chatted briefly about Lebanon; then the ambassador dropped the bombshell, handing Begin the president's letter outlining the new U.S. initiative. Among other items, the letter laid out American opposition both to Israeli annexation of the West Bank and to a Palestinian state. The president proposed negotiations with Jordan over the West Bank's future, accompanied by a settlement freeze during the talks.

As Begin read the letter, from a president whom he liked and saw as a friend of Israel, he grew visibly upset. "Oh Sam," he finally said plaintively, "this is one of the saddest days of my life. Couldn't you let us enjoy our victory for one or two days?" His mood then changed to anger, and as he grew angrier, he accused the United States of violating not only the Camp David accords but the U.S. commitment to consult with Israel before undertaking such an initiative. As Begin fluctuated between anger, weary resignation, and an aggrieved bitterness, it became clear that what set him off most was the American decision to coordinate the initiative in advance with both the Jordanians and the Saudis.

Begin felt betrayed. Later that night, unknown to the Americans, he took his anger out on Bashir Gemayel, Israel's Christian ally in Lebanon and presumed partner in a projected Israeli-Lebanese peace treaty. As Gemayel politely resisted Begin's hard sell for a treaty, the prime minister became angry and abusive, treating the young Lebanese in a way that altered his view of the Israelis. The exchange would scarcely matter, for within weeks Gemayel was assassinated by pro-Syrian elements, and the Reagan initiative was dead. Just to make sure the Americans didn't miss the obituary, the formal Israeli cabinet reply to the president's initiative called for an expansion of Israeli settlements, a reminder that Israel sometimes will act as it chooses in the face of American pressure.

She Didn't Say No: A guy who has been married for years tells his friends again and again that should his wife pass away, he'll never remarry. Sadly, she dies, and within several months he's engaged to be married. His friends ask for an explanation. "I went to the cemetery to ask Dorothy what she thought." "Well, what did she say?" his friends asked. "She didn't say no," he replied.

Not saying no, in an effort to avoid stating a clear yes, can be an effective technique for a small power. It provides room to maneuver in their own politics or to buy time; it can be used to bargain for better terms or to send a message to your negotiating partner that you won't and can't be taken for granted, particularly if the stakes are high.

We faced such a problem with Arafat in the run-up to the Camp David summit. Arafat did not want to come to the summit. He genuinely feared that Ehud Barak would set a trap that would force him to make a decision. Worse, he did not wish to be put in a position in which he would have to say no to the president on a substantive issue such as Jerusalem or refugees. At the same time, he didn't want to say no to Clinton on process by actually refusing to show up at the summit meeting.

So, eager to get the best possible terms he could, Arafat did what Arafat did best—he prevaricated, warning us of the costs of a failed summit but never issuing an outright refusal to attend. He told Madeleine Albright in late June that he feared a failed summit would cause the Middle East to burn and asked how, if Barak couldn't return three villages in the Jerusalem area to the Palestinians, he could negotiate seriously on the final status of Jerusalem itself. At the same time he pushed for several more weeks of preparation without actually empowering his negotiating team to prepare seriously with us and the Israelis.

Ultimately he relented, surprisingly arguing not about whether the summit should be held but about when he could arrive. His yes, for all practical purposes, might as well have been a no. Arafat came to Camp David in body but hardly in spirit. His goal was to get even with Barak for chasing Assad first, by opening negotiations on Golan, while ignoring Israel's commitments to Palestinian needs. But above all he sought to survive the summit without creating a crisis with Clinton, his own public, or the Arab world.

The night Arafat arrived at Camp David, I went with Secretary Albright and others to meet him at the helipad. It was late, and as he stepped off the president's helicopter into the floodlights illuminating the dark woods surrounding him, he seemed exhausted but clearly exhilarated. I couldn't stop thinking that Arafat felt as if he'd finally made it. He was now being hosted by the president of the United States at a summit meeting with Israel that only one other Arab head of state had ever attended. "How are you, Mr. Chairman?" I said. "I'm here at Camp David," he replied, smiling broadly, confirming my suspicion, as he was driven off in a golf cart with his black and white kaffiyeh flapping in the cool night breeze.

Drag It Out Until the Initiative Dies or You Do: There's a wonderful story about a rabbi summoned to the czar to be told that his entire village must relocate to Siberia. Determined to avoid this fate, the rabbi tells the czar that if he cancels the decree, the rabbi will teach the czar's favorite horse to sing within a year. Returning to his village, the rabbi happily reports his success. "You can't deliver on that promise," the villagers reply. "I know," said the rabbi, "but in a year the czar, the horse, or I might die, or the horse might talk."

Playing for time in the hope of getting out of a tight spot has always been an effective Arab and Israeli response to ideas they don't like. Frankly, time was usually on their side. Nothing ever happens quickly in Arab-Israeli negotiations. In the spring of 1989 we confronted a situation that was rife with possibilities for delay. Israel was governed by a hard-line Israeli prime minister who was reluctant to move but who was saddled with a unity government whose Labor Party ministers wanted progress. The

PLO, with no chance at that point of being at the table, was suspicious and oppositional.

Yitzhak Shamir never moved quickly on anything. With great reluctance and largely under pressure from his Labor partners, he had proposed a four-point Israeli initiative whose centerpiece was Palestinian elections in the West Bank and Gaza. Even that proposal was a stretch for the prime minister. Intensely suspicious of the Arabs, secretive and tight-lipped from his days in the Zionist underground, he had a remarkable capacity, in the words of Eytan Bentsur, a senior Israeli Foreign Ministry official, to "wait with endless patience as his adversaries eventually wilted."[12]

Although Shamir and Baker would indeed find a way to work together on the road to Madrid, Shamir's suspicion of the United States and the new Bush administration ran deep. A few days before his first visit to Washington, the prime minister told Moshe Arens, his tough foreign minister, that Baker "was against us; a new hangman for the Jewish people." Arens, with whom Baker would also find an eventual modus vivendi, had already reached the same conclusion. Baker and Bush "will try to cut our balls off without mercy," he had told the prime minister.[13]

When it came to promoting the Israeli plan and responding to our modifications, Shamir had two speeds—slow and slower. He quickly realized where the train was going and didn't want to reach that particular destination. Barely a week after the Israeli initiative was announced, Baker had delivered his now famous "give up the dream" speech at the American Israel Public Affairs Committee's (AIPAC) annual meeting, which made clear that America believed Israel couldn't have peace and the West Bank at the same time. That speech, combined with our efforts to work with the Egyptians (who were fronting for the PLO) in an effort to turn Shamir's election dialogue into a Israeli-Palestinian negotiation on broader issues, doubtless persuaded him that this was no longer his initiative. He came to believe that the Americans, together with the Egyptians, the PLO, and the Israeli Labor Party, had hijacked it.

Shamir was right. By the end of 1989 Shamir's original four

points had been joined by Egypt's ten points, then by Baker's five points (which Israel accepted with elaborate conditions). Nineteen points in all, but a total progress score of zero. The game was on, but who was winning or how long it might take to conclude was hard to tell.

At the same time Israeli domestic politics were heating up. Labor, under Peres's leadership, was intensifying pressure to bring down the government if it wouldn't endorse the American plan. This was not what Shamir wanted; indeed, he would have preferred continued cooperation in a national unity format, but in a partnership with Rabin, Peres's key rival. We didn't help matters: President Bush, Israeli expansion of settlements always on his mind, introduced Jerusalem into the mix through public comments opposing settlement activity there. Like George Washington Plunkitt of Tammany Hall, Shamir "seen his opportunity and took 'em." Using Bush's comments to rally the Likud troops, Shamir voted against his own plan in the cabinet, fired Peres, who failed to convince Shas, the key religious party, to join him, and then survived a no-confidence vote in the Knesset. Three months later Shamir formed one of the most right-wing governments in Israel's history, including bringing in Ariel Sharon. Baker recalls feeling "battered, beaten, and betrayed." And maybe he should have. After all, in the end, the czar and the horse died. The rabbi had lived to fight another day.

Yes, But: Perhaps the most common form of parrying, delaying, countering, and even revising American plans or initiatives is the conditional acceptance. The normal ebb and flow of life produces many results through give-and-take negotiation. In the Middle East, where bargaining is like breathing, haggling precedes almost every transaction. No American proposal of consequence has ever been accepted unconditionally without serious modifications. In good-faith negotiations, this process is how agreements are actually reached. It's another matter entirely when Arabs and Israelis don't really want a proposal implemented and use the "yes, but" technique, either to avoid an outright rejection or to maneuver the other side into the first refusal.

The "yes, but" dynamic was the subtext of President George W. Bush's April 2003 road map for Israeli-Palestinian peace. With Iraq engaging almost the entirety of their attention, the Bush team either didn't see or care that Prime Minister Ariel Sharon and Chairman Yasser Arafat were engaged in a power struggle that left neither man interested in taking the steps required to begin implementing the road map. While the Palestinians disingenuously accepted the document "as is," the Israelis also agreed but advanced formal reservations in double-digits. Neither side believed the other was credible or serious about implementation; nor were they prepared to give the other any benefit of the doubt. Since the Bush administration exhibited no willingness to work intensively with either side, the road map has never been implemented.

A year earlier, in March 2002, Tony Zinni and I found ourselves in a similar situation, which indeed became a dress rehearsal for the road map's demise. Israelis and Palestinians were in the middle of perhaps their bloodiest confrontation, and we had been charged with the impossible task of ending it with a cease-fire.

Neither Sharon nor Arafat wanted an end to the fighting, but we labored on, working with the security chiefs on both sides to create a work plan acceptable to all that would end the violence. We had actually narrowed the differences and were approaching a critical moment in our efforts, or so we thought.

Tony had made clear from the beginning that he didn't want any agreement to be known as the Zinni plan. He knew that it was likely to join the ranks of the yet-to-be-implemented and nearly forgotten Tenet and Mitchell plans. Against my better judgment, I pressed him hard to consider putting out a proposal; otherwise there would be no going forward and perhaps a collapse of our efforts. After all, I joked to him, you're not the president; you signed up for mission impossible, and no one will blame you if you can't pull it off.

So were born the Zinni proposals. They had a shelf life of about three days. The Israelis had a dozen reservations but said yes, convinced that Arafat would never accept Zinni's proposals, and even if he did, they were not worried, because Israel's performance depended on that of the Palestinians. When Eval Giladi in the IDF's planning branch called me at my Jerusalem hotel with the Israeli yes, I was stunned. Israel had never accepted any U.S. proposal without some change. I called Tony and said that Sharon seemed determined, to use a James Baker phrase, to leave the "dead cat" at Arafat's door.

The Israelis had guessed right. The Palestinians' acceptance was light on "yes" and heavy on "but." Moreover, Arafat was now focused on getting out of his besieged headquarters in Ramallah to attend the Arab summit in Beirut. His goal, which he eminently achieved, was to avoid saying either yes or no to Tony Zinni. When Saeb Erekat called me with the Palestinian "yes, but," I remember frantically trying to push him the other way. I used language like "last chance" and "headed for the abyss." But who was I kidding? I knew Saeb too well. Holed up in his compound surrounded by the Israelis, Arafat was worried about more than the dead American cat at his door. As Israeli forces reoccupied the West Bank in reprisal for the Palestinian suicide attack on the Park Hotel in Netanya, the time for yes— and for diplomacy—was over.

As I headed out to the airport to return home from what would be my final diplomatic trip to Israel and the West Bank, I knew two things for sure: this wasn't the first time big America had been frustrated by smaller powers, and it wouldn't be the last. I also knew something else. Doing effective American diplomacy out in the neighborhood was intimately tied to managing our own politics at home. And that could be every bit as taxing as dealing with the Arabs and the Israelis, sometimes even more.

Chapter Three

Israel's Lawyers*: How Domestic Politics Shapes America's Arab-Israeli Diplomacy

In May 2005 I wrote an op-ed in the *Washington Post* that got me into a lot of trouble.[1] The article, entitled "Israel's Lawyer," made what I thought was an irrefutable point: if you wanted to succeed in Arab-Israeli peacemaking, you must be an advocate for both sides. Far too often the small group with whom I had worked in the Clinton administration, myself included, had acted as a lawyer for only one side, Israel.

The piece provoked an intense reaction, gauged by a couple hundred emails and a lot of phone calls. In the Jewish community some applauded my courage; others thought I was either wrong or irresponsible to give Israel's enemies more grist for their propaganda mills. I hardly felt courageous, since the point, to me at least, was so obvious. The week after the article appeared I happened to be in Cairo, where Arab journalists flooded me with requests for in-

---

* I first encountered the term "Israel's lawyer" in Henry Kissinger's Memoirs, *Years of Upheaval* (Boston: Little, Brown, 1982) 620. Dan Kurtzer and I used the term with Secretary Baker who, not surprisingly, loved it.

terviews. My use of the term "Israel's lawyer" had made me into a kind of minicelebrity in the Arab world, who had finally exposed the truth about Jewish political power. To make matters worse, I was later told that President Clinton or someone close to him was angry about what I had written. I've interviewed three of our four ex-presidents (Ford, Carter, and George H. W. Bush). My requests to see President Clinton have been repeatedly turned down. I have also now become part of the stump speech of the two professors, Stephen Walt and John Mearsheimer, who seem to have made a career out of warning people about the power of the pro-Israeli lobby. If there ever was an example of no good deed going unpunished, this was surely it.

The reaction to my op-ed shouldn't have surprised me. Like almost everything else associated with Israel, Jews, and domestic politics, it had been misunderstood, politicized, and hijacked in the service of what UCLA professor Steven Spiegel calls the "other Arab-Israeli conflict." That conflict is the struggle in Washington to influence American policy, politics, and public opinion on the Arab-Israeli issue.

It hardly mattered that the only point I was making was that mediators must respect the interests of both sides to reach agreements and that we were often too influenced by Israel. People heard what they wanted to hear depending on where they stood on the U.S.-Israeli relationship, the legitimacy of lobbying, and America's role in negotiations. And they used what they heard— accurate or not—to do battle in the service of their particular side and cause.

While conducting the interviews for this book, I encountered much the same problem. To the question "What drives the U.S.-Israeli relationship, and what role do domestic politics play in shaping it and America's role in negotiations?" the answer seemed to depend on how much value the interviewee attached to Israel and to America's support for the Jewish state. Wary people concerned that I would manipulate their words subjected me to plenty of spinning. But I felt that most seemed genuinely to believe what they were saying.

Those on the pro-Israeli side argued strongly that America's Israel advocacy derived primarily from common values. Malcolm Hoenlein, executive vice-chairman of the Conference of Presidents of Major American Jewish Organizations, dismissed domestic politics as a "factor on the fringes" in accounting for American support. Others, especially on the Arab-American side, gave greater weight to campaign contributions and political influence. With regard to the special relationship, James Zogby, president of the Arab-American Institute, argued that Congress and the administration are "pummeled into saying that [value drives the relationship] and fear has brought them to say it." Most said that our position was hopelessly intertwined, a mix of shared values and politics. "You'll never get it right," Morrie Amitay, AIPAC's executive director in the 1970s, told me with more than a trace of satisfaction in his voice.

Getting it right, however, is vital not only because of the sheer amount of distortion out there on the subject these days but because of the importance of the U.S.-Israeli relationship to our peacemaking efforts and to our interests in a critically important region. Domestic politics, as Anthony Lake, Bill Clinton's first national security advisor, told me, is like sex to the Victorians: "Nobody talks about it but it's on everybody's mind." Abraham Foxman, national director of the Anti-Defamation League, made the same point: the Jewish community "wants to exercise power and influence, but we don't like it when people talk about it." I think that it is time we start talking about it, but we need to do so in a way that is honest and clear and that doesn't engender conspiracies where there are none, or pretend that domestic politics doesn't influence our thinking about the Arab-Israeli issue when it does.

After twenty-five years of observing the political system, participating in Arab-Israeli diplomacy, and examining the policy process up close (like making sausage and writing legislation, not a pretty picture), I've come to some basic conclusions: in our system domestic politics has a strong voice in but not a veto over policymaking; AIPAC is the guardian of an already entrenched pro-Israeli tilt and is effective at making the case for a close U.S.-Israeli relationship but much less so when it comes to affecting American diplomacy toward the Arab-Israeli issue; an administration strongly committed to pursuing Arab-Israeli peace almost always trumps the opposition of domestic interest groups, but not without some messy fights; and a danger exists, particularly in the absence of strong U.S. leadership, that our *special* relationship with Israel, so important to our peacemaking efforts, can become *exclusive* with costs to our broader interests in the Middle East.

Finally, no conspiracy exists—no small bunch of Jews and conservative Christians compels an entire domestic and foreign policy establishment to support Israel against its collective will. The case for Israel is much deeper and bigger than that. It is rooted in the broadest conception of the American national interest: support for like-minded societies, that, correctly or not, are perceived by Americans to be more or less "like us."

That case is argued powerfully every day not by one metaphorical lawyer, as I originally thought, but by at least five discrete ones. First, a well-organized, affluent, and disproportionately politically active and influential Jewish community is focused on Israel as a survival issue. Second, a sophisticated congressional lobby builds on a minority of members who are passionately pro-Israel and a majority who don't care all that much, are open to persuasion on Israel, or fear retribution should they oppose the lobby's goals. Third, millions of conservative Christians are increasingly finding their political voice and are stunningly pro-Israel for reasons of theology and shared values. Fourth, in the wake of 9/11 the new threat from radical Islam has strengthened the U.S.-Israeli bond, as both governments foster the vision of democracy under threat from radicalism and terror, thus making the Arabs one of Israel's most effective advocates. Indeed, the threat of godless Communism that made America and Israel strategic partners during the cold war has now been replaced by the challenge of "too much God" from a strain of violent extremist Islam. And finally, the case for Israel is made by a "Jewish lobby of one"—an Israeli prime minister whose arguments can be compelling but are not always in America's best interest. This last lawyer, particularly in the person of Ehud Barak, played a particularly significant role during the Clinton years.

I can already hear the moans and groans from many in the pro-Israeli community who believe that the word *lawyer* is loaded and pejorative. Why does Israel need lawyers when the case for American support is so compelling? But I suspect these folks are not being honest with themselves. Jews worry for a living. The more advocates, friends, and lawyers push Israel in America, the better. I cannot tell you how many times I have heard many American Jews thank God for AIPAC, Congress, and now, increasingly, American evangelicals even though they may have doubts about their social policies.

Together Israel's lawyers present a case that no administration, Republican or Democratic, can ignore. The "other Arab-Israeli conflict" is over. Today the issue is no longer whether an American political leader is for or against Israel and a close U.S.-Israeli relationship but the degree to which they are. In a bizarre twist, American politics has morphed into Israeli politics. The nuances in support for Israel don't mirror disagreements between Republicans and Democrats so much as they reflect differences between Labor and Likud. The U.S. Congress has not had one long-serving member with an anti-Israeli or pro-Arab agenda since Paul Findley, who served in congress from 1961 to 1982. Public opinion polls continue to show strong majorities in support of Israel, regardless of Israeli actions. You can argue about this or that peace plan, or about how active America should be in Arab-Israeli peacemaking, but in political life in America today everyone of consequence says they're a friend of Israel. Bill Clinton was the most pro-Israeli Democratic president since Harry Truman, and George W. Bush is the most pro-Israeli Republican president ever.

Whether that level of consensus is always good for the national interest is another matter. Without its special relationship with Israel, America would have little influence in Arab-Israeli peacemaking. That simple fact is one of the best-kept secrets of American diplomacy. The Arabs know we have the confidence and trust of the Israelis and that under the right circumstances we can turn it into real influence, even pressure. Our phone rang for all those years, and is still ringing now, because we have that capacity. Sadat was the first Arab leader to understand that even though America was a biased mediator, it could be used to get him what he wanted. Arafat and Assad wanted America to do the same for them, but neither they nor the Israelis would yield enough to produce results.

At the same time, when the special tie leans too far in a pro-Israeli direction, we lose our capacity to be an effective broker, let alone an honest one. Kissinger, Carter, and Baker understood this fact and accepted that pushing Arabs or Israelis hard in negotiations was bound to produce domestic political repercussions. All of them understood that success depended on the special relationship but also that excessive pro-Israel or pro-Arab advocacy could cause their diplomacy to run aground or worse. In fact, I first discovered the term "Israel's lawyer" in Kissinger's memoirs. They knew they risked a fight with Israel's supporters but were willing to accept one as an occupational hazard of doing serious diplomacy. Not surprisingly, in Kissinger's, Carter's, and Baker's diplomacy, the pursuit of the national interest trumped the political interest. And this is as it should be. When presidents lead on foreign policy, domestic constituencies and lobbies usually follow, albeit sometimes uneasily. The case for Israel is a compelling one. We simply need to ensure always that, when we make it, the case for America is advanced as well.

The U.S.-Israeli Relationship: Common Values, Common Enemies

Writing in 1951, David Ben-Gurion, Israel's first prime minister, warned his countrymen against having illusions about great powers: "Let us not fool ourselves in thinking that America ever identified or will ever identify in the future with the state of Israel...there is no identity of interests between a world power...and a small and poor nation in the faraway corner of the Middle East."[2]

Ben-Gurion, despite his gloomy rhetoric, sought close ties with America and did not live to see how wrong he was. By the time of his death in 1973, the U.S.-Israeli relationship had matured but still looked nothing like the quasi-alliance that binds the two nations today. No Israeli prime minister would pay an official visit to the United States until 1964, the same year the Israelis received a few F-4 fighters, their first real military hardware from America.

The October 1973 Arab-Israeli war led to a decisive change in the relationship. Before the war Israel ranked twenty-fourth among the recipients of U.S. foreign assistance. By 1976 the Jewish state had become the single largest beneficiary of American aid. In the wake of the 1979 Camp David accords, American aid to Egypt and Israel rose sharply. Today these two countries comprise the largest two recipients of our foreign assistance outside of Iraq. Although economic aid to Israel zeros out in 2008, foreign military financing increased from $1.8 to $2.4 billion in 1998, and to $3 billion in 2008, not to mention the supplemental assistance that Israel has received over the years for counterterrorism activities, resettlement of immigrants, and security needs flowing from the implementation of peace agreements.

In 1985 Israel and the United States concluded a free-trade agreement. The United States is Israel's main trading partner, while Israel ranks twenty-second on our list. Today more than one hundred Israeli companies are represented on the big board in New York. In 1988 Israel was designated a "major non-NATO ally," one of only twelve such countries, affording it preferential treatment in bidding for U.S. defense contracts and access to expanded weapons systems at lower prices. And as a result of a strategic dialogue begun in the 1980s, Israel and the United States pre-position equipment and conduct joint military exercises. The United States and Israel never concluded a formal alliance, but there was really no need. The ties that bind the two are as close, resilient, and powerful as those created by any treaty that either nation could ever sign. In July 2006 President George W. Bush made clear that the United States would defend Israel militarily if it were attacked.

Ben-Gurion can be forgiven for not foreseeing these developments. But who could have predicted them? Abba Eban once remarked that in the history of international relations there was "nothing quite like the U.S.-Israeli bond." The political laws of gravity—disparity in size, mission, strength, and interest—would seem to make impossible the close, intimate, and protracted involvement of a great power with a small one.

What then drives this strange relationship? Why has America supported Israel since its birth in 1948? Why, despite divergent interests and crises both large and small, has the relationship not only rebounded but grown deeper, seemingly working itself into the fabric of American domestic and foreign policy?

Shimon Peres used to say that it was "common values, not common enemies," that defined the special relationship. As usual, Peres was right, but only partially so. Over time the mix of shared values and shared enemies created a unique closeness nurtured in America by Jews and non-Jews alike, deepened by common challenges and threats abroad. The U.S.-Israeli relationship is not primarily a strategic one. Despite all the intelligence sharing, pre-positioning, and joint exercising, Lawrence Eagleburger, former secretary of state, reminded me that during the moment of America's greatest strategic challenge in the Middle East—Saddam Hussein's 1990 invasion of Kuwait—he spent considerable energy in persuading the Israelis that they must not act unilaterally and must stay out of the conflict even if attacked. Those who measured the U.S.-Israeli relationship in strategic terms could not have dreamed of a better scenario—a radical Arab state attacking a Gulf oil producer—by which to judge the value of Israel as an ally. Whatever military help Israel could provide was decisively outweighed by the political need to prevent the transformation of the Persian Gulf War from a battle between Saddam Hussein and the world to an Iraqi-Israeli confrontation, which would have played into Saddam's strategy of mobilizing the Arab street and governments against the United States.

Still, common adversaries—the Russians and radical Arabs during the cold war and al-Qaeda, Iran, Hamas, and Hezbollah post-9/11—today reinforce and highlight those common values in a way that few other factors could. Tom Lantos, Democrat from California and the only Holocaust survivor in Congress, makes a point I often heard in many of my interviews: the American people "may not know the difference between Slovakia and Slovenia, but they have a fairly good idea that they would like to live in a free and open society of equal opportunity. You don't have to be a Middle East expert to realize that these societies [in the Arab world] are the antithesis... I mean you open the newspaper every morning and turn on television and 35 children going to school in Baquba or Ramadi or Baghdad have been blown to bits. This is not an appealing picture for the average American."

During the course of six decades of the U.S.-Israeli relationship, common values and common enemies mixed seamlessly and became mutually reinforcing. President Truman's decision in May 1948 to recognize Israel, eleven minutes after Ben-Gurion declared the establishment of the state, derived mainly from his commitment to Jews in the wake of the Nazi genocide. But as his close advisor Clark Clifford reminded him, the act was also smart geopolitics. After the Soviet Union had unexpectedly supported the partition of Palestine in late 1947 and was now poised to support statehood as well, Truman wanted to prevent Moscow from gaining a step on both the British and the Americans in the region.

The 1960s and 1970s tightened the linkage between values and enemies and thereby the linkage between America and Israel. Americans perceived Israel's stunning victory over the Arabs in 1967 as a triumph of a struggling young democracy, fighting for survival in a dangerous neighborhood. As *Washington Post* columnist E. J. Dionne Jr. puts it, there was "a gut sense then of Israel as the underdog on the block." As a Catholic growing up in a Jewish neighborhood in Massachusetts, he recalls that people rooted for the Israelis "the way they rooted for the Red Sox." And no one seemed to root for the other side. Until Anwar Sadat's historic visit to Jerusalem in 1977, the images people saw—as Norman Ornstein, resident scholar at the American Enterprise Institute and veteran political commentator and analyst, notes—

were Arab countries hostile to Israel "in bed with the Russians." So it was much easier to identify with the Israelis, as people who were just like us, than with the Arabs, who were not.

During the 1980s the association of common values and common enemies continued to strengthen the U.S.-Israeli relationship, though the bond frayed considerably. Israel's invasion of Lebanon and its rejection of President Reagan's peace initiative created friction. During the same period, however, far more consequential events were bringing America and Israel even closer. Richard Straus, a Capitol Hill veteran who is the editor of the much acclaimed *Middle East Policy Survey*, describes this period as a "revolution" in the U.S.-Israel relationship. Hijackings and bombings introduced Americans to terror. After two "oil shocks" in the 1970s the importance of Arab petroleum production began to decline. Above all, the rise of Ronald Reagan and conservative Republican support for Israel laid the foundation for the current strategic relationship and created the beginnings of wall-to-wall political support.

No longer was the case for Israel to be argued primarily by liberal Democrats. Disillusioned with Democratic policies on a range of domestic and foreign issues, bright young men and women deserted the party in large numbers to join the GOP, sometimes referring to themselves as neoconservatives, a phrase that morphed into today's readily recognizable neocons. Richard Perle, a leading neocon, had been mentored by centrist Democrats like Henry "Scoop" Jackson. Perle and other academics like Jeane Kirkpatrick provided intellectual arguments that would be married to the reflexively pro-Israeli sentiments of Reagan himself. In the president's value-laden view of the world, Israel figured centrally as part of the good team and an American ally against the evil empire and its minions. As former congressman and senator Robert Kasten, Republican from Wisconsin, one of Israel's strongest conservative supporters on the Hill (a self-described "thousand percenter"), told me, "Israel in its own way kind of fit into this basic theme that some of us were so proud to be a part of. With Margaret Thatcher and the pope and Ronald Reagan it was consistent...Israel during every step of the way, found itself on our side if you will."

Emblematic of the new pro-Israeli climate was George Shultz, Reagan's second secretary of state. Shultz, initially mistrusted by both the Israelis and the American Jewish community because of his association with Bechtel Corporation and the Arabs, created one of the most positive relationships any secretary of state had with Israel and its American supporters. Shultz told me that the "Jewish lobby represents a group that cares about the problem more than most people do so you want to pay a lot of attention to them." And he did. The secretary's pro-Israel sentiments were on full display in May 1987 at AIPAC's annual policy conference, where he actually led the audience in a kind of "hell no to the PLO" chant. The same George Shultz, however, within a year or so engineered the opening of a U.S.-PLO dialogue, after Arafat met long-standing U.S. terms. The dialogue was a bitter pill for many in the pro-Israeli camp to swallow, but it seemed much more digestible coming from Dr. Shultz.

During the scores of interviews that I conducted, value affinity emerged strikingly as the most important element in American support for Israel. With rare exceptions presidents and secretaries of state, Jews and non-Jews alike, all made clear that while domestic politics is an important factor, at the end of the day common values count most. This value affinity, the sense that "they're more like us than the other guys," included at least three basic historical or philosophical connections. First was the commitment of the West, particularly the United States, to the survival of the Jewish people in the wake of the Holocaust. The presence of the U.S. Holocaust Memorial Museum on the National Mall (one of the most frequently visited museums in Washington) has made that commitment manifest in striking form. American politicians routinely speak of Israel as the only democracy in the Middle East, and despite some limitations that are also familiar to Americans (social and economic discrimination against more than a million Israeli Arabs), the old bromide is true. Israel not only shares an open, pluralistic tradition similar to our own but has as well an immigration and pioneering experience to which Americans can relate. Finally, the contrast between Israel and its neighbors, particularly those Arab states and groups committed to terror, violence, and Israel's destruction, elicits sympathy from Americans, who after 9/11 have felt a greater identification with Israel's own battle against suicide terror. The people I interviewed did not speak of these matters as history but seemed to have validated them through personal experience.

Take Mark Kirk, for example. Kirk, a former Hill staffer and now a Republican congressman from the northern suburbs of Chicago, compared his own personal experience in dealing with nondemocratic leaders and with the Israelis. He found the former to be "utterly long-winded because they're surrounded by toadies." By comparison, a "walk into an Israeli prime minister's office is constantly a discussion about coalitions and balance and votes and blocs, which is our language."

Or listen to Andrew Kohut, president of the Pew Research Center, who has been polling and trolling for trends in American politics for years: "The public thinks of the Israelis as having values which are closer to the values of America." Kohut went on to explain: "If you didn't have a broad base of public support or acquiescence...you couldn't create the level of support for Israel that exists on the basis of lobbying." And that base of support remains deep, despite occasional ups and downs. In 1978 Kohut himself raised the possibility that Sadat's positive image in America combined with Begin's negative one might diminish support for Israel. But like so many dire predictions over the years forecasting the erosion of American support for Israel, this one never materialized. Tom Pickering, former undersecretary of state for political affairs and a career ambassador to just about everywhere, including Jordan and Israel, explains why: as the "state child" of the Holocaust and a democratic state in a nondemocratic region, Israel creates a very strong affinity for Americans.

Politics of Intensity: The Organized Jewish Community and Israel

"You're nothing but a self-hating Jew, and your boss is an anti-Semite," a man from Atlanta shouted at me. "You ought to be ashamed of yourself." It was the spring of 1990. I was briefing a group of American Jews at a Washington hotel on the administration's Middle East policy. I knew a tsunami of anger was building against James Baker for his statements on the Arab-Israeli issue. But there is nothing like a hostile audience to focus the mind. A year earlier Baker had told the annual AIPAC conference that Israel should give up the dream of holding on to the West Bank. A month before, frustrated with Shamir's stone-walling, he'd told a congressional committee that Israel should call when it was serious about peace. Baker actually gave out the White House phone number. When I interviewed former national security advisor Brent Scowcroft, he jokingly wondered why Baker hadn't given out the State Department number. Baker told me he'd never learned it.

But this guy from Atlanta was over the top, and it was getting personal. I had been working as part of Baker's Middle East team for over a year. And I was proud of what we were trying to do. Whose side was this guy really on anyway? Both as an American and as a Jew, I was offended. I knew there was more anti-Semitism at the local supermarket than at the Department of State. And while Baker could be tough, he was no anti-Semite. So I pushed back. "Let's get out of the gutter," I told Mr. Atlanta. "If you have problems with U.S. policy, let's talk about them. But don't drag the secretary of state or his staff through the mud while you're doing it."

For American Jews to be upset with presidents and secretaries of state is nothing new. The Jewish community had vented its anger previously at Kissinger and Carter too. The overriding reality is that American Jews see the survival of Israel as a key surety of their own survival. Other ethnic groups, of course, have played a role in foreign affairs. For decades Irish-Americans donated money and sometimes arms to the Irish Republican Army to aid its struggle in the Protestant North. Greek-Americans lobbied heavily about Cyprus. Cuban-Americans, concentrated in Florida and New Jersey, have exercised a near-veto power over national policy toward Castro since the mid-1960s. Citizens and residents of Hispanic origin have become central actors in the struggle over immigration reform.

No ethnic group, however, has the power and focus of the American-Jewish community. And although campaigns for Soviet (now Russian) Jewry and against anti-Semitism have mobilized Jews from time to time, it is the survival of Israel for which the Jewish community has consistently and tirelessly fought, organized, and rewarded or punished politicians. It is not always easy for outsiders to understand the extent to which Jews worry about Israel, or how easily its perceived jeopardy can create a crisis atmosphere. After all, every American president from Harry Truman to George W. Bush has made Israel's welfare a priority and worked hard to ensure it. The occasional friction between Washington and Jerusalem was inevitable in any relationship, particularly between two countries whose size, reach, and responsibilities are so different. Yet for the majority of the organized Jewish community these tensions have never been seen as natural or logical. In fact, even as they live in extraordinary peace and security, by comparison with the Israelis, many American Jews can be supersensitive to any bumps in U.S.-Israeli relations—a reaction that can be difficult for non-Jews to fathom.

Before we go any further, it is important to point out a couple of things. Significant percentages of American Jews do not identify with Israel in a primary way or are not affiliated with any Jewish organization, even synagogues. Somewhere between 25 and 40 percent of American Jews have ever visited Israel.

Moreover, when it comes to the U.S.-Israeli relationship or American efforts to broker Arab-Israeli peace, even the organized community is not monolithic. Organizations such as Americans for

Peace Now and the Israel Policy Forum have long pushed for a robust American diplomacy and are willing to acquiesce on firm U.S. policies toward Israel—let's say on settlements—to achieve Arab-Israeli peace. But these organizations do not set the tone or the agenda or drive the politics on these issues. More powerful groups such as AIPAC, the Anti-Defamation League, and the Conference of Presidents, whose orientation is more conservative, tough-minded, and at times defensive, play that role. Those advocates—and other well-connected, affluent Jewish community leaders who are willing to play the political power and influence game—are the ones who attract the attention of Congress and the administration, particularly when they feel that the American government is not being sensitive to Israeli needs.

American Jews committed to Israel worry for a living—I call this the "cosmic oy vey" syndrome, the tendency to worry about everything, combined with an inability to distinguish what is really worth worrying about from what isn't. Ira Forman, executive director of the National Jewish Democratic Coalition, observed that Jews have enemies and must be constantly vigilant but are "paranoid" when it comes to Israel. Doug Bloomfield, a former AIPAC lobbyist and Hill staffer, made the point a different way. The American Jewish community, he believes, is more defensive about Israel and more hard-line than any element in Israel. "It's [the community] six thousand miles away. It's an overworn paternalism. We have to defend them, we have to protect them. Many [Jews] still can't conceive that it's not a charity case." The level of insecurity is huge, he continues, and the need for reassurance great. "If you blow in their ear and you tell them you love them, and put your arm around them, you have a chance. Shultz learned that. Baker never did."

Try as we did during the Baker years, we could never persuade enough of the Jewish community that while pro-Israel rhetoric was lacking, pro-Israel actions were not. Frustrated by a hard-line Israeli prime minister who announced a new settlement almost every time he arrived in Israel and who was never really an empathetic guy to begin with, Baker did very little blowing in anyone's ear. Baker's phone number comment and his speech to AIPAC about giving up the West Bank, created suspicion, anger, and anxiety among American Jews and in Israel. In one presentation before a large Jewish audience, I cataloged all the pro-Israel things the administration had done: keeping Saddam in his box; the Madrid peace conference; and pushing hard for emigration of Russian and Ethiopian Jews. During the Q-and-A session, a man from Detroit stood up and simply said, "If things are so good, why do I feel so bad?" That summed it up.

Jews do more than complain. They have learned the lessons of history—how to worry, act, and take nothing for granted. And on Israel and other survival issues, like anti-Semitism, they organize. A thousand stories could illustrate the depth and strength of Jewish organization and drive on the issues of greatest import to the community. Monte Friedkin, a longtime Democratic activist, AIPAC board member, and fund-raiser, tells one of them about American Jews' efforts to support Edwin Edwards's campaign for reelection as governor of Louisiana against white supremacist David Duke. In one week Friedkin claims to have collected 250 one-thousand-dollar checks from Jewish donors all over the country. And in a scene reminiscent of *All the King's Men*, Friedkin walked into Edwards's office in Baton Rouge to deliver them. Edwards, who had been tried three times on racketeering charges (one of his campaign slogans in the race against Duke was "Vote for the Crook—This Is Important"), thanked Friedkin and told him not to worry about the election because he had all the "drivers" taken care of. "What drivers?" Friedkin asked. "All the taxicab drivers to take people to the polls so they can vote right," Edwards replied. "Do you think it was easy to get those checks?" Friedkin asked me. "First you have to know two hundred fifty people, and they've got to deliver. We're organized. They're all AIPAC members."

Part of the Jewish community's success is its ability to articulate a cause and make its voice heard. Jews are the most highly politicized ethnic group in the country. They constitute less than

3 percent of the population (roughly 5.3 million people), but they vote, organize, and campaign in higher percentages than most other groups. Graeme Bannerman, former staff director of the Senate Foreign Relations Committee, consultant, and lobbyist, put it this way. Jews are active "in the charities, they're in the PTA, city government; they're disproportionately active to any other ethnic group in the country. They did a congressional survey, and there wasn't a single congressman that didn't double the number of people they estimated were Jewish in their district."

Being small is not the issue, but being small and organizing with purpose and intensity is. David Saperstein, director of the Religious Action Center of Reform Judaism, points to the gun control scenario to explain this intensity. Polls regularly show that two-thirds of Americans want stronger gun control, but few of them base their vote for a specific candidate on the position of that candidate on gun control. Gun control activists, however, organize their lives around it. The issue is not what people say in polls but what percentage will organize, give money, write letters, and vote. Democratic congressman from California Henry Waxman makes much the same point. "In politics people who care intensely about any issue have a claim on getting attention on that one issue," he says, "whether it's abortion, gun control, help for corn growers to have an ethanol program, or for Jews who care a great deal about Israel."

That's certainly the case in Congress, and not only as a consequence of Jewish organizations like AIPAC and the Conference of Presidents. Nita Lowy, a Democratic representative from New York, told me a story about her attempt to influence a colleague to vote in favor of aid to Israel. He resisted, saying that his district had other priorities. Later, after getting three calls from influential community leaders who were not only pro-Israel but were involved in charities he cared about, he relented, saying he'd changed his mind.

Former senator Robert Kasten offers the best description of how individual American Jews can have an impact in Congress. Ideas or proposals originate with AIPAC only about a third of the time, Kasten estimates; in many instances knowledgeable and well-connected people in the community can get through to their senator or representative without the help of AIPAC or any other organization. Such a person, for example, might urge a senator to write a letter to the president or secretary of state on some Israel-related matter on which the administration has chosen to take an inadequately tough position. Kasten recalls "that a group of like-minded senators would sit down; staff would produce a letter written in good neoconservative, some would say pro-Israel [language] whatever, and we'll say good job, sign it, and give it to our staff. Where [is] this giant lobby in this? We could do it with or without [the lobby]."

Senator Carl Levin reinforces Kasten's point about the importance of support for Israel coming from individuals rather than from organized lobbies. Levin is a smart, direct, no-nonsense Democrat from Michigan who chairs the Senate Armed Services Committee. During almost three decades in the Senate he has earned the respect of both American Arabs and American Jews—no easy feat in the volatile politics of suburban Detroit, where most Jews in the state live, and in Dearborn, home of the nation's largest community of Arab-Americans.

Levin cited three factors that drive the U.S.-Israeli relationship: common values, strategic location, and an active pro-Israel community. But he urged me to keep in mind that these vary in importance according to different senators and representatives. Peering over his bifocals, he seemed somewhat impatient with my efforts to press him on what drove America's relationship with Israel: "I don't know if there's one kind of formula." Sometimes, he mused, personal experiences and relationships can shape a senator's or a politician's views. He urged me to go talk to Senator Daniel Inouye and Representative John Lewis about their experiences. He got me thinking that maybe in some cases lobbies and politics may not be decisive factors.

So I did. Senator Daniel K. Inouye, a Democrat from Hawaii and one of the few World War II veterans now in Congress, is a thousand-percenter in his support for Israel. I asked him for the reason for his strong support. "It doesn't come from political activity, I can assure you," he replied. "But that doesn't mean there's no politics," he continued. "When it comes to an Israeli issue or a Jewish issue, most people just go along. As you say, why make a fuss?

"Do you want to know when I became a supporter of Israel?" Inouye continued. Badly wounded during the Second World War, Inouye describes meeting a fellow amputee in the next bed who told him about "a stinking place, bodies were stacked up like wood." Horrified by these stories of Nazi atrocities against Jews simply because they were Jews, Inouye began to learn and study more. "I got to the point," he concluded, "where I nearly converted."

John Lewis, the charismatic African-American congressman from Georgia's fifth district, is another case in which personal experience, rather than purely political considerations, created an affinity with Israel. "I grew up," he told me, "hearing songs" about Moses, Pharaoh, and Egypt. Hence, "we have an obligation— almost a mission—that we have to look out for the children of Israel."

That early bond, born of the Bible, was reinforced during the civil rights movement, when Lewis, secretary of the Student Nonviolent Coordinating Committee, braved police dogs and billy clubs. "Many members of the Jewish community fell and died with us in the struggle for civil rights," he told me, his voice rising. The congressman then went on to talk about Israeli democracy, the Holocaust, and something else. Israel, he concluded, "is a state of impossible possibilities. We have to identify with that. We have to be part of that."

All politics, Tip O'Neill famously said, is local. In a real sense, much of politics is also personal. When the seminal experience of your own life—World War II or the civil rights movement— somehow becomes positively identified with Jews or Israel, meaner considerations tend to fall away. These guys don't need an education or a tour of Israel to rationalize their support; they have lived the reason why.

AIPAC: Guardians of the Tilt

With a compelling case to make, a predisposition among Americans to advance it, and an American public predisposed to hear it favorably, you wouldn't think that a sophisticated organization with a hundred thousand members and with a $40 million annual budget would be needed to sell the U.S.-Israeli relationship in Congress. But you'd be wrong. At least that's the feeling I got from my interviews. AIPAC is very necessary indeed.

AIPAC is actually small by megalobbying standards. The National Rifle Association, by comparison, has four million members and an annual budget of about $200 million. Ben Rosenthal, a staunch pro-Israel congressman from New York, used to say that AIPAC didn't matter all that much. Without the lobby, the United States and Israel would still be friends and the Middle East would still be a mess. Rosenthal was right. But to my question about AIPAC's influence, most of those who spoke to me had little doubt that the intensity of the bond would not be nearly as great. Without AIPAC, Tom Dine, who ran the organization in the 1980s and early 1990s, said, "you wouldn't have those extraordinary numbers" in assistance. Doug Bloomfield, the former AIPAC staffer, agreed: "The level of foreign aid to Israel is directly attributable to organized lobbying." Former New York congressman Steve Solarz said: "There would probably have been less aid" and "less reluctance to be publicly critical of Israel."

What does AIPAC do? How powerful is it really? And is it, as the *New York Times* suggests, "the most important organization affecting America's relationship with Israel"?

The answer is that AIPAC is a powerhouse but not all-powerful. Its influence on Congress is clear in maintaining and even increasing yearly assistance levels to Israel, but it does not win every battle there. When an administration proposes an action that is critical to its larger aims but that Israel and its supporters view as potentially harmful, such as arms sales to Saudi

Arabia in 1978 and 1981, or opposition to loan guarantees to Israel in 1991, the administration prevails, but sometimes not without a costly fight. Such a fight can enhance the lobby's power and reduce the willingness of the executive to fight again. But the idea that AIPAC gets everything it wants is just flat-out wrong. The fact is that even the most pro-Israeli administration won't go beyond certain limits in assisting Israel. These limits are dictated by budgetary concerns, other foreign policy priorities, and a virtual certainty that Israelis will ask for more than they realistically expect to obtain.

Nor have AIPAC's vaunted efforts to lobby the executive branch amounted to much. In fact, they have often proved counterproductive. When AIPAC becomes involved in an unfamiliar policy area or acts inappropriately, the result is trouble. The investigation and pending trial of two AIPAC staffers for allegedly receiving and passing along classified information on Iran to Israel is a case in point. While it is not true in every Middle Eastern issue such as the Iran Libya Sanctions Act where AIPAC's lobbying did not play a direct role, I cannot remember a single major decision on Arab-Israeli peace in which AIPAC, either directly or indirectly, prevented us from moving in the direction we wanted. We may have been constrained by Israeli prime ministers, by problems with Arab negotiating positions, or by our own fears of failure, but no explicit or implicit warning from AIPAC or any other Jewish organization ever blocked us. The pressures from the pro-Israeli community were significant but much more subtle, partly self-imposed, partly generated by what Wendy Sherman, former State Department counselor to Secretary Albright, called a "mantra of biblical proportions," which conditioned American officials over the years about what was acceptable and what was not concerning American policy toward Israel.

AIPAC's real mission and great success, Liz Shrayer, AIPAC's political director from 1983 to 1994, told me, "derives from its capacity to define what it means to be pro-Israel" and to galvanize the support, primarily in Congress and in the Jewish community. In this area AIPAC has no peer. The results during the past twenty years have been stunning. Today you cannot be successful in American politics and not be good on Israel. And AIPAC plays a key role in making that happen.

Tuesday with Morrie and Tom

I spent part of Tuesday with Morrie. A well-groomed, compact man, now nearly seventy, Morris Amitay, AIPAC's executive director from 1974 to 1980, is a Joe Pesci–like character whose smarts and acid wit are surpassed only by his commitment to Israel and a strong U.S.-Israeli relationship.

Educated at Columbia and Harvard, Amitay took over from the legendary Si Kenen, who created AIPAC in the early 1950s. Amitay took a small but committed organization, moved it from a crowded office at Thirteenth and G to Capitol Hill, tripled the staff and budget, and laid the foundation for the powerhouse that AIPAC would later become under Tom Dine.

Amitay's critical contribution, which led to AIPAC's success, was his decision to focus on Congress. Kenen's dictum had been that AIPAC's job was to "get the Congress to urge the president to overrule the State Department." Amitay took that dictum to its logical conclusion. By the end of the 1970s, particularly as Israel figured more prominently both in American cold war strategy and in peacemaking, Congress, with its fingers on the purse strings, became crucial. You could raise more money for Israel on the floor of the Senate in a single afternoon, Amitay realized, than Jewish philanthropists or United Jewish Appeal campaigns could raise in a year. Because AIPAC lacks the millions of grassroots supporters who back such lobbying giants as the NRA or AARP, Amitay explained, AIPAC must center its attention on Congress. Congressional action favorable to Israel amplifies the voice and power of the pro-Israeli community. When Presidents Ford and Carter took a stance in support of Israel, it wasn't because a "bunch of Jews wanted them to do it" but because "a bunch of people in Congress who they needed for the rest of their agenda were telling them what to do." Having a Hubert Humphrey, Scoop Jackson, or Jacob Javits make the case for you is much better than having Charlton Heston, Amitay concluded. Neil Sher, who ran AIPAC in the early 1990s, agreed: "A junior senator from anywhere is a much more influential lobbyist to the administration than five thousand billionaires going in to urge the president."

Amitay and Sher seem to have a point. Unlike the argument for oil, guns, or tobacco, the case for Israel was built on a strong moral, political, and even strategic foundation. AIPAC "is not selling heroin," declared Tom Lantos. "They're selling the desirability that the single political democracy in the Middle East be allowed to survive." "Israel is a giveaway," Amitay said, obviously wanting to wrap up the interview as he glanced impatiently at his watch. "Senator X says, here's another one of those pro-Israel things. Put me on; my constituents are for it; the public is for it; the Israelis are the good guys."

There was a lot Amitay didn't tell me, so I decided to check his views by visiting someone on the opposite side of the political spectrum. John Sununu Senior is a former New Hampshire governor, chief of staff to George H. W. Bush, father of Senator John Sununu, and an Arab-American activist who has strong views on the pro-Israeli lobby—but those views surprised me. "Look," Sununu said, "the American system is designed to be lobbied. And on Israel, the case is an easy one.

"It's like [having] a handful of pebbles in your shoe. It's there all the time. It's not just AIPAC, it's everywhere. Every congressman and every senator, before they win, is being soft-lobbied on this issue. Whether it's their friend who owns forty acres down the street whose grandfather happened to come from Kiev...it happens almost invisibly but across the board.

"Think of it this way," Sununu continued. "You are running in the third district in Iowa, and you have absolutely no interest in the Middle East. All you care about are farm prices, subsidies, and all your constituents care about is subsidies for corn, interest rates on loans, and inheritance taxes, so the kids and grandkids can get the farm. When somebody comes to you and talks about this great friend of the United States in the Middle East and how we've got to protect her...you accept the premise. Once you are lobbied on the premise, everything else is easy. It's not as insidious as people think it is. It's just the permanent presence of the pebbles, and it's not just one pebble but a whole shoe full of pebbles."

As compelling as the case for Israel might be, I wondered to what extent Senator X or Representative Y would be influenced by "pebbles" if he or she couldn't also discern strong political incentives and disincentives. Doug Bloomfield made clear that for most members of Congress, Israel is simply not a central issue, so why create a headache for yourself by opposing pro-Israeli forces? It's not "important enough of a concern to say no to, and there are clear upsides to saying yes."

Listen to former senator Kasten again. "Let's say Representative Sam Smith [from] western state X, from Wyoming or Utah, [becomes aware] of a letter condemning recent terrorist activity. He probably doesn't have many Jewish voters. There may be contributors to his campaign from places other than his state, and some of them might be pro-Israel or Jewish contributors. If he weighs the pluses and minuses, there's no down. He's got twenty senators in front of him and he could be the twenty-first. He sees something in there that's not going to bite him on a thirty-second ad at home."

And joining AIPAC's orchestrated initiatives has clear upsides. Graeme Bannerman recalls a conversation with a senator who was balking at sponsoring legislation to appropriate funds for absorbing Jewish refugees in Israel. "Why do they need that?" the senator asked. "They're going to get it, senator," Bannerman replied, "so you might as well be the sponsor of it and get credit for it because sometime in the future you're going to have an arms sale to an Arab country where you're going to get criticized, but you'll have this to hide behind." Bannerman also advised Jewish members to support a "good friendly little Arab country" so they could look balanced as well.

Changes in the campaign finance laws in the 1970s and the emergence of political action committees (PACs) meant that money, the mother's milk of politics, played an even more important role than ever before in the game of rewarding and punishing candidates. Neil Sher pulls no punches here: "If I were to walk into the office of a senator from Montana or South Dakota where there weren't Jewish voters, I'd get initial access and his vote not because the lobbyist is a nice Jewish kid from Brooklyn who's got something to sell. But behind me is the ability to raise political contributions plain and simple. That was the genius of expanding the range of AIPAC's influence politically, and Tom [Dine] deserves the credit for that."

I met with Tom Dine, when he was executive director of the San Francisco Jewish Federation, in a modest office rescued from plainness by a breathtaking view of the Bay Bridge. Dine, who ran AIPAC from 1982 to 1994, presents an image different from that of the hard-charging, fast-talking Amitay. Laid-back and intellectually expansive, Dine comes across as a policy wonk, attested to by years of working for Ed Muskie and Ted Kennedy, then USAID, and finally directing Radio Free Europe.

Despite my efforts to discuss money and PACs, Dine steered clear of the subject. He focused instead on information as power and getting "those forty-second bullet points" to elected representatives so they could argue cogently in advance of key votes. He envisioned AIPAC as an instrument to relieve Israel of American pressure, so offering the Israelis increased freedom of action to make decisions on the basis of their own best interests.

At the same time Dine left no doubt in my mind that he saw AIPAC as a powerhouse. The charge that the lobby controls U.S. Middle East policy is "bullshit," he said. But "AIPAC and the community can hurt you," particularly in Congress, where lobbies, not the administration, have the advantage. Being "the tough guy in the neighborhood" is still essential, since battles can't be taken for granted.

Dine's low-key manner should not mask the importance of the role he played in expanding AIPAC into a national organization, with dynamic reach and fund-raising capacity. A handful of wealthy Jewish businessmen and philanthropists drove the campaign to build on Amitay's foundation. These men, serving as AIPAC's lay presidents, set policy and established key conduits to mobilize big donors from around the country. District by district, state by state, AIPAC extended its information, educational, political, and financing capability in the service of a single issue: ensuring a strong and resilient U.S.-Israeli relationship. And it was Dine, Liz Shrayer asserts, who "created and built the organization into a dynamic pro-Israeli political machine." AIPAC is not a PAC; it funds no candidates; but its members, and those of loosely affiliated pro-Israel networks, do. Since 1990 pro-Israel interests have contributed $56.8 million in individual, group, and soft-money donations to federal candidates and party committees. Between the 2000 and 2004 elections the fifty members of AIPAC's board donated an average of $72,000 each to campaigns and PACs. One out of every five board members was a top fundraiser for either Bush or Kerry.

How important is Jewish money in the greater scheme of things? Because the overwhelming majority of seats in any congressional campaign are safe, contributions from any specific group no longer shape outcomes as they once did. But Norman Ornstein notes that in the small number of seats that are up for grabs, money takes on added importance: "If you're a strong supporter of Israel and you're in trouble, you've got enough Jews interested in politics generally that you can mobilize and raise money nationally." Conversely, if you adopt anti-Israel positions, "you can mobilize significant money against you." The reality, Graeme Bannerman points out, is that an opponent of a pro-Israeli candidate will find that "a ton of money can get poured in against you. It's not determinant, but you have to spend a lot more of your life countering the money that comes in against you." Bannerman concludes, "Frank Church...for whom I worked, went to New York, Miami, Chicago, San Francisco, and Los Angeles, to get reelected in Idaho. What happened to Pocatello and Boise? That's warping the system."

Can AIPAC actually defeat candidates whose positions on Israel it opposes? In most cases, Ornstein says, no. But in some well-known instances candidates who have adopted positions critical of Israel were hurt by money that American Jews raised for their opponent.

The two best-known cases are both Republicans from Illinois: Charles Percy, a three-term senator, and Congressman Paul Findley, a representative from Springfield, who served for twenty years. Both men frequently criticized Israel and issued statements sympathetic to Arabs and Palestinians. In their final losing campaigns (1984 for Percy, 1982 for Findley) both faced opponents financed in part with generous contributions from American Jews. Doug Bloomfield said flat out that AIPAC "loves taking credit for Percy." But by 1980 Percy already had lost credibility with his constituents. Mark Kirk, a fellow Republican from Chicago, says that Percy would roll into a Springfield town meeting talking about his latest encounter with this or that Saudi official. And people in Peoria would say, "We're in the middle of a Caterpillar strike here. What in the hell are you talking about?" It was the same with Findley, Kirk adds. "He lost because his constituents couldn't figure out why he was running around the Middle East and not in Springfield."

These defeats, as well as the more recent losses by Georgia congresswoman Cynthia McKinney and Alabama representative Earl Hilliard, both African-American Democrats, have a broader significance in the way the game is played in Washington. Abe Foxman concedes that pro-Israel Jewish organizations targeted Findley, but he says the community "made more of his defeat than was warranted." Whatever the actual reasons for their losses, and those reasons were complex, politicians have since seen the Percy and Findley defeats as cautionary tales about the danger of crossing the Israeli lobby. Findley played into this game and became the poster child for AIPAC's vaunted power. The more he spoke out, the greater the legend of Jewish power grew. When I interviewed him, Findley conceded that he could have run a better campaign, especially as his margin of loss was a scant 1,400 votes out of 200,000 cast. Still, Findley returned to his broader point: "Tom Dine claimed that I was his trophy."

The image of a defeated candidate can have a powerful impact. "So you shoot the dog dead, leave him on the front lawn," James Zogby, president of the Washington-based Arab-American Institute, quipped, "and these guys go walking by saying, 'That's going to happen to me too.'" Perception is reality. Abe Foxman told me flat out, regarding Findley, that there was a need to show a victory once in a while, "whether real or imagined." This sits fine with AIPAC. "If I were still running the organization," Sher told me, "I wouldn't say boo about Findley or the two professors' arguments about all this Jewish political power. It's bullshit, but let people think it." He asked me: "Why do you think that AIPAC announces every administration official and member of Congress who attends their annual policy conference? They don't give a shit whether you're there or not. It doesn't matter. It's that image of the eight-hundred-pound gorilla that matters."

Making the Case for Israel: The Arabs as Their Own Worst Enemy

At the end of June 2006, several weeks before the start of the Israel-Hezbollah war in Lebanon, my daughter Jen and I traveled to Liberty University in Lynchburg, Virginia, to interview the Reverend Jerry Falwell. (Falwell died in May 2007.) Falwell was preparing for the fiftieth anniversary of his ministry, so the interview was short. We actually spoke in his large black SUV. The reverend was behind the wheel, with the air-conditioning on full blast.

After laying out his case for supporting Israel, Falwell got to the main point: the entire Middle East "wants to see Israel in the Mediterranean." The Arabs, no matter what they say, have never accepted Israel's right to exist and never will. And then came the prediction, or perhaps I should say the prophecy: "In a matter of several minutes, any idiot in Damascus or Tehran could put a missile right in downtown Tel Aviv or Jerusalem."

Falwell's prophecy in this case was a bit off: the rockets used by Hezbollah two weeks later were supplied by Iran and Syria, and never reached Tel Aviv. But that didn't obscure his basic point, likely shared by millions of conservative Christians and a good many mainstream Christians and Jews as well. In the wake of 9/11 American perceptions of Arabs and Muslims as crazy Quran-thumping fundamentalists has only weakened their case and bolstered the arguments of those who want to make Israel's. As I drove back from Lynchburg to Washington, it struck me that Israel's case wasn't the only one being made. After 9/11 the perception was growing in many quarters that Israel's enemies—Iran, Hezbollah, Hamas—were now America's as well. The organized Jewish community was only too eager to make the connection.

Listen to Malcolm Hoenlein: "The American people understand that Israel fought the war on terrorism for us for fifty years. They were on the front line. Today we're all on the front line. For fifty years it was a war that nobody understood. Today they understand." Ralph Reed, former head of the Christian Coalition, makes much the same point: "On September 11 the horror of terrorism that Israelis had been living with for decades became a reality for a lot of Americans."

Jews and evangelicals are not alone in thinking that the case for Israel is made easier and more compelling by Americans' perception of Arabs and Muslims as radicals, extremists, and terrorists. If you're a politician in America today, you need to have good reason to argue against Israel's supporters. And these days there's not much in the Arab and Muslim world to make their case. Listen to Jim Bond, former Senate staff director of the Appropriations Committee: "Look at what's going on over there. There are these butchers killing people all over the place . . . Palestinians elect these guys from Hamas. It's just bizarre. Except for Israel, you look at that part of the world, and [you] got all these weirdos in the Gulf who are afraid to death of the terrorists, but on the other hand are giving them money ... Have you ever met the emirs of one of these places? I mean, they're creepy." Mark Kirk, comparing the cases for Israel and the Arabs, says: "The United States will get into a war over Kuwait. But the level of connection throughout the entire American body politic isn't there. Then one bad emir and the relationship could be ruptured." Americans perceive Israelis to be like them, said Ziad Asali, president of the American Task Force on Palestine: "What we've witnessed on the Arab side is a trend in the opposite direction, first by Arab nationalism, which was essentially anti-American and anti-Western, and then by an equally anti-Western and anti-American Islamic extremism."

There are no "Arab Abba Ebans," Norman Ornstein notes. The absence of such a polished spokesperson on the Arab side facilitates the presentation of the Israelis as the underdog, even as they remain the Middle East's preeminent military power. This is particularly true, David Saperstein, director of the Religious Action Center of Reform Judaism, says, when many knowledgeable Americans over fifty "think of Paul Newman in *Exodus* and not Menachem Begin when they think of Israelis." The last heroic Arab face America saw was King Hussein's, but even his image was undermined by Jordanian support for Saddam during the Gulf War; before him it was Sadat. Even at the height of the negotiations during the 1990s, what American elites and opinionmakers saw on the Arab side were the two Mr. A's—Arafat and Assad. Even in the best of moments, and there weren't many, neither leader generated much warmth or support. Now Arafat and Assad are gone, but there's a third Mr. A, Iranian president Mahmoud Ahmadinejad, whose anti-Israel, Holocaust-denial rhetoric and support for Hamas and Hezbollah make him a poster child for reasons to sympathize with Israel.

A conversation with Arab-American Institute president James Zogby reflects just how difficult and painful the challenge is for his community. Leon Uris's 1958 novel *Exodus* and the 1960 film version, he asserts, shaped American attitudes toward Arabs for years to come. To Zogby, *Exodus* essentially portrayed just another story of cowboys and Indians. The Israelis wanted nothing more than to carve out a place for themselves on the frontier, while the Arabs were identified as savages determined to stop them. The message to Americans was clear—and they got it. "I understand the Israelis," Zogby says. "They're just like me. But the Arabs, I don't get them. They're just too monodimensional. They just want to sit in front of the TV all day and hate America and Israel."

The images persist, he believes, not because there's some Jewish conspiracy to control the media but because the pro-Israel community simply plays the game better. Polling data reflect a desire among Americans for a more balanced Middle East policy, but the Arab-American community can't or won't capitalize on this opportunity.

Zogby uses American politics to explain the situation. A critical early requirement in any campaign is to define yourself and your opponent. The candidate who is first to win the contest of images, as Clinton did against Bush 41 or as Bush 43 did against Gore and Kerry, has taken a long step toward winning. "Israel [has] defined not only itself, but it also defined the Arab side," Zogby says bluntly, and the Arabs "never engaged in defining themselves. They didn't do shit." After the failed July 2000 Camp David summit, the only accounts sympathetic to Palestinians in the who-lost-Camp-David debate came from Israelis and American Jews. The Arabs were nowhere engaged in it. George Salem, a savvy, well-connected Washington lawyer and longtime Republican Party activist, makes the same point in regard to 9/11: "We missed a huge opportunity to try to cast this as an opportunity for the American public to understand that the reason Osama bin Laden can get away with something like this...is the Palestinian issue...We failed. Israel, far from being viewed as the cause of a lot of these problems, brilliantly cast themselves as fellow victims."

Israel certainly wasn't the cause of 9/11, but as I listened to these assessments, I realized what an uphill struggle Arab-Americans faced. The problem in trying to define the other guy negatively when your own image is worse doesn't give you much of an edge. In the days leading up to the September 1993 Oslo signing on the White House lawn, we worried about Arafat's image. "Can't you get him to wear a suit?" Secretary Christopher joked. His clothing was the least of our worries. We were concerned that Arafat would come packing a sidearm or would smother the president with kisses. Throughout the Oslo process Arafat remained a tough—if not impossible—sell for Arab-Americans. "Who wants to make Yasser Arafat the centerpiece of your citizen action program?" an Arab-American activist told me.

Doug Bloomfield makes the point another way. The strength of the pro-Israel lobby is that it stands positively for Israel, he says, and—with some exceptions, in the area of arms sales—"it didn't give a damn about what the Arabs got or didn't get." By contrast, the "pro-Arab" lobby was never really just pro-Arab; it was also anti-Israel, and its agenda was negative, in Bloomfield's words, having the negative goal "to pressure, punish and do damage to Israel." In Congress "members don't like that. They want to be everyone's friend."

Going negative against Israel or American Jews raises another problem. Without exception, every Arab-American I interviewed expressed serious and genuine concern that efforts to criticize Israel on policy grounds were conflated with anti-Semitism and, in the wake of 9/11, with anti-Americanism, to the point of discrediting Arab-Americans personally and chilling debate. I was branded the "lawyer for the terrorists," George Salem told me. "Everybody is scared," said Randa Fahmy Hudome, a close aide to former senator Spencer Abraham of Michigan and now a Washington consultant. "I think people are afraid of charges of anti-Semitism...whether [it means] losing a job, being closed out by their communities, or being taken off the A list of invitations to parties." How often such consequences happen is impossible to say. I never heard of a situation in which someone's anti-Israel views got them blackballed. At the same time, too many in the Jewish community do tend to conflate anti-Israel talk with anti-Semitism. I thought about my own case. If I was being accused of anti-Semitism and self-hatred, it wasn't much of a stretch to imagine what was being said about Arab-

Americans. "It's hard enough," Ziad Asali said, "to get my community engaged in politics within the system without the added burden of being accused of being an anti-Semite or losing your jobs or business."

The first axiom of American politics is that you can't beat something with nothing. Not only have Arab-Americans had trouble making their case, they've never been organized sufficiently to make it. In essence, they have been unable to mobilize a real counterconstituency to compete with the pro-Israel community, let alone offset it. "It's like Ohio State playing Harvard," one Arab-American activist told me. "There's just no competition."

Michael Suleiman, one of the country's leading scholars of the Arab-American community, leaves little doubt. "The evidence is overwhelming that the Arab-American lobby has little or no impact on political issues, especially those concerning foreign policy."[3] Unlike American Jews, who have organized around a handful of critical issues with Israel at the top of the list, the Arab-American community of roughly 3.5 million is decentralized, divided, and diverse. "We have organizations," Hussein Ibish of the American Task Force on Palestine told me, but "they're small, underfunded, and never supported or joined by the community at large. Over the past twenty-five years of Arab-American organizing, our entities have either gone bankrupt or they've had to turn to rich businessmen overseas and sometimes even to governments overseas, which is poison."

Not until June 1975 did a formal, official Arab-American delegation even meet with the president and secretary of state. A divided Arab-American community, Ziad Asali says, explains the slow start. "With twenty-two Arab countries, you're lumping Syrians, Algerians, and Iraqis with Palestinians. What do they have in common? They only internalize their state identities. And how do you bridge differences between the university professor and the autoworker?"

As Hussein Ibish asks, what is an Arab-American? That phrase meant little before 1967. Even today those Americans with Arab backgrounds can easily think of themselves as Lebanese-American,

Muslim-American, or Palestinian-American; some even identify with groups affiliated with cities, villages, and towns, like the Ramallah Federation, Bait Hanniyah, and the Bint Jubayl group in Detroit. John Sununu Senior tells the story of his efforts to organize a meeting at the White House between the first President Bush and Arab-American representatives. Having worked for hours to synchronize a unified script, he watched in consternation as one delegation member after another raised individual concerns. When the president rolled his eyes and asked for clarification, all Sununu could muster was "Mr. President, this is the Middle East."

The challenges confronting Arab-Americans in the wake of 9/11 may create new opportunities for more effective organization on critical matters closer to home, such as those relating to ethnic profiling and privacy, as well as a range of post-9/11 civil rights and security issues. But the obstacles to effective political organization run deep. Most Arab-Americans in the United States are not Muslim but Christian; most Muslims here are not Arabs but hail instead from Pakistan, Nigeria, Indonesia, and the Philippines. The differing agendas, social and economic backgrounds, and educational levels make organizing hard. Ibish, a sensitive and brilliant observer of the Arab-American scene, goes deeper still and lists several other obstacles: fear of engagement, that you'll somehow suffer at the hands of the Jewish or American establishment if you engage; the cynicism that comes from watching the betrayal, nepotism, and brutality of Arab politics; and defeatism that the obstacles arrayed against us are so great that "we can't make a difference." John Sununu Senior counters with the assertion that Arab-Americans, if they want to get heard, must engage and "put their tokens on the balance" and if necessary "plagiarize" rather than simply envy AIPAC's success. Ibish agrees that Arab-Americans won't know how effective they can be until they really try. But he's also harshly realistic. "If the Arabs got their act together, how much of a difference would that make? Can we hope to reverse things in the foreseeable future? I think the answer to that is no."

Conservative Christians: God Blesses
Those Who Bless the Jews

There's nothing quite like the "Night to Honor Israel" at the John Hagee Cornerstone Church in San Antonio. In October 2006 I flew down to Texas for the Sunday-night celebration, not knowing quite what to expect. I had heard about Pastor Hagee and Christians United for Israel, a kind of Christian AIPAC, and had spoken to him by phone. I'd learned that the pastor's feelings and support for Israel ran deep. Christians, he told me, had received a direct commandment from God to support and pray for Israel, the only nation the Creator had ever begotten. I also knew that Hagee had written in his 2006 book *Countdown Jerusalem* that Jewish sins and ungodliness would be ended by Jesus' return, so I figured Hagee's agenda was a bit more complex. Still, Hagee saw himself as leading American Christians toward full adherence to supporting Israel. The first pro-Israel night in 1981 provoked a threat against the church. "If these local anti-Semites think we're terrified and intimidated by what they've done, they're mistaken," he told me. "I'm going to do a Night to Honor Israel until they get used to it."

Hagee's intense pro-Israel activism (he raised $12 million to support projects in Israel in the last five years, including orphanages and schools) is not representative of the majority of American evangelical Christians. Hagee is a dispensationalist (roughly one-third of all evangelicals are) and subscribes to the view that God made certain promises to the Jews that the Lord intends to keep whether or not the Jews rejected Jesus or a new Israel emerged in the form of the Christian Church. Still, according to Timothy Weber, whose *On the Road to Armageddon* chronicles the rise of evangelical support for Israel, the vast majority of the community is strongly pro-Israel. Weber told me they have a "built-in, almost DNA feeling of support and propriety toward Israel because of the Bible. The Jews are there, Jesus was a Jew.

All that Holy Land stuff." When you consider that 28 percent of all Americans who voted in 2004 are self-identified evangelical Protestants, and of those half are traditional evangelicals (and 88 percent of those voted for George Bush), you must conclude that "all that Holy Land stuff" means a great deal to a lot of people.

Author and commentator Kevin Phillips claims that one of every four Americans is now affiliated with a self-described evangelical or similar church.[4] Richard Land, who heads up the policy arm of the Southern Baptist Convention (over 16 million members in 2006), isn't prepared to go that far. But he believes we're witnessing a "revolution" all the same. In 1960 mainline Protestants were 45 percent of the population; now they're 20 percent. America is more religious, Land asserts, and the nature of that religion is getting more traditional and evangelical.

Amid this changing religious-political landscape, support for Israel is a permanent fixture. When you talk to Land, a Princeton graduate and a walking encyclopedia (with maps) on changing demographics, you're talking to a believer, and you get a sense of just how strong this bond is. Land recalled as a boy watching a history program on the Allied bombing of Germany, and he remembers his mother saying: "Richard, that's what happens to countries who persecute the Jews." Simply put, Land was taught to believe the biblical injunction: "God blesses those who bless the Jews, and God curses those who curse the Jews." But his support for Israel is rooted in more than theology. "It's the only stable democracy in the Middle East, and there's a huge values issue here. We would be denying everything that we are and everything we have been, and everything we hope to be as a nation if we turned our back on Israel for reasons of self-interest. I could make this argument without even quoting a Bible verse."

Waiting for the Night to Honor Israel to begin in the Cornerstone Church's eight-thousand-capacity main sanctuary, I found myself seated next to Dina Shalit, a pleasant Canadian-born Israeli now living in Ariel on the West Bank. She was in the United States on a fund-raising tour with Ariel's mayor, who would receive a check from Hagee for $500,000 before the night was out. She was an avid Hagee supporter, but with a sense of humor and the absurd.

Dina, who offered to be my guide for the evening, had been to a "Night" before and seemed to know most of the players. This experience could be somewhat confusing for the uninitiated, particularly for Jews, she conceded. Here were six thousand Christians in a room together with a few dozen Israelis and American Jews singing Hebrew songs and moved to spiritual rapture by God's, Hagee's, and the assembled's commitment to the State of Israel, right or wrong.

In the beginning, Dina confided, Christian support had been confusing for her too. Living in Montreal, she had no Christian friends until she was thirty-five and no interest in or knowledge of evangelical support for Israel. But then she discovered Pastor Hagee, a Christian who supported Israel because God told him to and because it was the right thing to do. And this commitment, she continued, was "unconditional." He made no attempt to proselytize her, did not talk of Jews being saved or damned, and uttered no end-of-days mumbo-jumbo. "It's a learning process," she said, as we stood to sing both the American and Israeli national anthems, "for them and for us."

Clearly, I had a lot to learn. Sitting in that enormous hall facing an enormous dais backed by billowing twenty-foot blue curtains and flanked by two enormous video screens suspended from the ceiling displaying "Pray for the Peace of Jerusalem," I was ready for just about anything. Dina pointed out that onstage, in addition to Pastor Hagee, a large beefy man with a youngish face and baggy blue suit, were a couple of local San Antonio rabbis, a representative from Houston's Jewish Federation, and the regional directors who represented Hagee's newly created Christians United for Israel (CUFI). Each director was in charge of a region in the United States where smaller Nights had been held or were planned, including Las Vegas and Berkeley, California. CUFI's goal was to mobilize grassroots support for Israel in Christian America by raising dollars, consciousness, and ultimately an organization much like AIPAC. Richard Land of the Southern Baptist Convention of America had once remarked that organizing evangelicals was like "herding cats," but if anyone could do it, perhaps it was John Hagee. David Brog, CUFI's executive director, had no doubt. John Hagee wasn't an "important man" like all those people in Washington, he told the audience, to thunderous applause. Hagee was a "great man" who had anticipated and created a movement that "important men" would join.

The two-hour, largely musical tribute to Israel that unfolded was one of the more remarkable stage-managed productions I'd ever seen. The stately Cornerstone Church choir of about two hundred, clad in Israel's national colors, framed the dais and offered a veritable hit parade of Israeli and Jewish songs. Meanwhile a smaller and perkier group, the Cornerstone Singers, performed a variety of other songs, with moves I hadn't seen since the days of *The Partridge Family.* The outpouring of earnestness, professionalism, and genuine joy from the Christian assembly was powerful and evocative. Dina, who nudged me about an hour into the performance, speculated that about a third of those present were in tears. I couldn't tell. But at least three of the CUFI regional directors onstage were openly crying. John Hagee's Night appealed to a full range of emotions and then some. And the production managers played them all like a finely tuned violin.

For the young at heart, there was a rendition of the iconic "Hava Nagila" (Let's Rejoice). But it was performed Texas-style: the Cornerstone Singers donned cowboy hats, coonskin caps, and red bandannas and did a good old-fashioned hoedown mixed with line dancing. And as the country group Alabama sings, in Texas, "You gotta have a fiddle in the band," there was one of those too. I'd been to a lot of bar mitzvahs and Jewish weddings, but I'd never heard "Hava Nagila" done country-western style. The crowd loved it. For a little more gravitas, Hagee had brought in a choir of cantors from Israel. These guys had probably never been inside a church in their lives, and Dina (who seemed to have the inside scoop) told me they had been criticized in some Orthodox Jewish circles for participating. But we both agreed that when they performed their barbershop quartet rendition of "Adon Olam" (an important hymn praising God and a part of any synagogue service), they seemed happy enough. Who wouldn't be? These guys were cantors after all, and like rabbis, preachers, and imams, they loved big audiences.

On the serious side, Israeli deputy prime minister Shimon Peres sent a video message, as did former Israeli prime minister Benjamin Netanyahu, who twenty years ago saw the rising tide of pro-Israeli Christian evangelical support and, like the masterful politician he is, got on board early. There was no mention of Prime Minister Ehud Olmert or even Ariel Sharon, whose policies of disengagement from Gaza Hagee adamantly opposes.

Next came the gathering of the twelve tribes: a solemn procession of biblically clad figures who carried enormous cloth banners intricately stitched with the name of each Jewish tribe representing CUFI's twelve regional directors. The grand finale included a kind of martyrology, as the video screens depicted scenes of the persecution of the Jewish people from ancient times, including what looked to me like the Crusader sacking of Jerusalem, in which invading Christian forces had massacred thousands of Jews and Muslims. But this evening the sequence ended differently: two soldiers in full combat gear appeared, an American looking fierce and an Israeli with a prayer shawl draped over combat fatigues carrying a very good facsimile of an automatic rifle (in a church?) and looking even fiercer. Needless to say, the assembled went berserk.

The underlying message of the evening could have been summed up as follows: "We're sorry for everything and anything that bad Christians have ever done to you Jews. We'll never let this happen again." As Dina noted with great seriousness, "They feel they owe us for our history." This message of contrition and activism is precisely what John Hagee wants to convey. The Jews are God's chosen people; they've been persecuted for too long; we Christians, together with our Jewish brothers and sisters, will never be silent again; we will act to support them as God commanded us to do, particularly now with the new storm of radical Islam gathering in the East.

There were only two speeches that night, and they could have been interchangeable. Malcolm Hoenlein, like Netanyahu, had seen the Christian evangelical tide rising early and wanted to harness it in America's support for Israel. Hagee introduced him as a Jewish "champion of champions" as two enormous flags (Israeli and American) were unfurled behind him; then Hoenlein delivered a speech that would have made any evangelical preacher proud. His message was simple: America now stands on the front line with Israel, and together Jews and Christians, if not the entire civilized world, must stand shoulder to shoulder against Islamic extremism and terror, particularly against Iran. Hagee's speech, which drew the largest and most sustained applause, was much the same. The world must demonstrate the courage and intellectual honesty that it lacked in confronting Hitler. Dictators mean what they say. Iranian president Ahmadinejad's threat to extinguish Israel in a cloud of dust must be taken seriously, but so must God's desire to protect His chosen people. Hagee brought the hall to its feet when he warned the Iranian president that his own fate might be similar to the one he wished on Israel. The evening ended with the pastor making donations totaling $7 million to half a dozen Israeli organizations and communities.

As I left the hall that night, I realized that the evening had been about faith but also about politics and the temporal world. There was no talk of eschatology or Jesus Christ (not a single mention as best I could determine). This was clearly smart politics, but it also seemed to reflect that Pastor Hagee had found a way to marry deep-seated religious support for Israel with American values and security. Judging by the reaction of the thousands of Christians there that night, and the millions more whom Hagee plans to reach, it works.

I left San Antonio pretty confused but eager to learn more. If there was anyone who could explain to me the relationship between evangelicals and Israel, it was surely Yechiel Eckstein. The son of the chief rabbi of Canada, Eckstein is an ordained rabbi who worked for a time at the Anti-Defamation League. That is, until he discovered that perhaps the most pro-Israel community in America was evangelical Christians. He then made it his calling to engage them in dialogue and to create bridges and bonds with American Jews.

Eckstein has long been personally involved in these efforts between Israelis, Jews, and evangelicals: he brokered the first meeting between Israeli prime minister Menachem Begin and the controversial head of the Southern Baptist Convention Bailey Smith, and he is now Israel's goodwill ambassador to the world's evangelicals. He knows that American Christians had always felt a strong biblical connection to Israel. Indeed, religious Zionism among Christians predated political Zionism among Jews. The creation of the State of Israel and the unification of Jerusalem cemented these connections as "confirming signs" of biblical prophecy.

Fast-forward to the 1970s, Eckstein continues, and the emergence of Jerry Falwell's Moral Majority. For Falwell and later Pat Robertson, Israel, at least modern Israel, evolved from a religious to a political issue. The adoption of modern Israel as a cause was not only consistent with the evangelicals' religious teachings but was in line with their growing involvement in American politics. If you wanted to make a difference on issues like school prayer, Eckstein explained, reflecting the views of James Dobson, Ralph Reed, and others, you had to "get your hands dirty—enter into the political process."

The evangelical embrace of Israel took time to develop. A decade ago David Saperstein debated Ralph Reed at an AIPAC convention and pointed out to Reed that major Christian groups had issued not a single action alert on Israel. But in the last decade or so, Saperstein continues, evangelical involvement has mushroomed on issues such as religious freedom, Sudan, sex-trafficking legislation, debt relief, and global warming. And right up there on the list of foreign policy issues is Israel. More interviews with key evangelical figures confirmed Richard Land's idea that many have come to support Israel tenaciously not simply because of their theology and end-of-days view of the world. It has a lot to do with their view of Israel as a democratic ally in a dangerous world.

As I sat in Falwell's SUV in a parking lot in Lynchburg that day, I heard this view confirmed in spades. Referring to Israel and the Jews, Falwell noted that some evangelicals believe this is the end-time and that we're heading toward Armageddon. "That's not where I am," he said. "I have no idea when the Lord is coming." Others, he added, want to proselytize the Jews, but "that's not my chief motivation." There are three reasons we support Israel, he continued. "First, it's a biblical injunction to us. Second, Israel is literally America's best friend in that part of the world—maybe best friend period. And number three, forget the theology. If Israel were not there or were not our friend, we would be forced to maintain a very large contingency all over the Middle East. The few billion dollars we give to Israel are peanuts compared to what it would cost us to maintain a presence and at times, like now, to wage war." I asked him whether Israelis and American Jews had struck a kind of devil's bargain (forgive the choice of words I interjected) with evangelicals. Falwell smiled and without missing a beat said, "If I were an Israeli Jew, I would take all the friends I could get to help us get through today, tomorrow, and then we'll work that other thing out at the end of the world."

Pat Robertson of the Christian Coalition left me with the same impression. "My mother," Robertson recalled, "was teaching us to be nice to the Jews because God will bless those that bless them and He'll curse those who curse them. My father was a U.S. senator, so she had a profound influence on him." But values and national security reinforce the old teaching. Israel is "a land-based aircraft carrier in the Middle East. It is a democracy that shares our values in a sea of oppression and reaction."

Mike Pence, a two-term Republican congressman from Indiana, is perhaps the best embodiment of a traditional evangelical Christian involved in the modern give-and-take of American politics and policy. Where he stands on Israel may well reflect the views of millions of Americans.

I caught him on his cell phone traveling back home in Indiana. A week or so after 9/11, he said, twenty representatives had met with Condi Rice to express their outrage over leaks about the Bush administration's willingness to accept a Palestinian state. Pence told Rice, "I believe in the Book of Genesis where it reads, 'I will bless those who bless the Jews and curse those who curse you'...And I believe that America is in peril if we fail to vigorously defend Israel and her interests." Pence chuckled as he told me the story, recalling the raised eyebrows, but it reflected "the essence of my support" for Israel. "And I'm not uncommon. I'm driving across the cornfields of eastern Indiana right now," he concluded, "and I can tell you that what I just described to you would be at home in just about every buckboard church in every small town and hamlet in eastern Indiana."

Religious beliefs and common values, heightened by security fears in the wake of 9/11, provide a powerful bedrock support among millions of evangelicals (Falwell estimates 50 million, Weber 75 million) that is not going to change. The godless Communism against which Christian Americans railed during the cold war has now been replaced by the very real threat of radical Islam; and it is heightening common values with Israel at the expense of sympathy for or identification with the Arab and Muslim world, never all that strong in the first place.

No politician, certainly not in the Republican Party, can ignore that sentiment, and none will. Plenty of evangelical and mainstream Christians do not believe in Israel right or wrong and have been critical of Israeli policies toward the Palestinians, but they may no longer be the majority or, more to the point, a significant political force. Forty percent of George W. Bush's vote in 2004 came from white Protestant evangelicals, and 20 percent from conservative Catholics. What aspiring politician would want to risk alienating his or her base by adopting nuanced positions that would appear critical of Israel?

There are two issues that could cause George W. Bush to lose his evangelical constituency flat out, Richard Land said. "One would be to waffle on the abortion issue. Number two would be to be seen as pressuring Israel to give concessions that Israel felt endangered their national security." Pat Robertson was categorical: any effort by an American president to get Israel to give up any part of Jerusalem would cost Bush a huge part of his evangelical support. For the current administration, these contingencies are just thought experiments. George W. Bush's own religious beliefs (none of my evangelical interlocutors cared to comment on them), combined with his ideological support for Israel as a democracy under threat of terror in the wake of 9/11, would preclude real pressure on the Israelis anyway. As Land said, referring to the president's low approval rating, "Who do you suppose makes up most of that thirty-four percent?"

None of this, however, will affect support for Israel among millions of evangelical Christians. Regardless of who wins the White House in 2008, the pro-Israeli community will have a strong friend and supporter there. Luis Lugo, director of the Pew Forum on Religion and Public Life, observed, "How do I hedge my bets for Israel here, in a way that guarantees that everybody's got to pay attention, you couldn't imagine a better strategy." He was right. Jews have tremendous influence in the Democratic Party; evangelicals have it in the Republican Party. From an Israeli perspective, Zev Chafets, who directed Israel's Government Press Office under Prime Minister Begin, and whose book *A Match Made in Heaven* describes the ties between evengelicals and Israel, mused, "From an Israeli perspective, the Elders of Zion couldn't have cooked it up any better." He told me he had asked Reverend Falwell what would happen if Israel went after the Iranian reactor. "We'd stand up and cheer," Falwell replied. "That's seventy million people." "And the truth is," Chafets concluded, about Republican aspirants to the presidency, "you really can't get the nomination without the blessing of the evangelical wing of the party. That means a lot." Only half-jokingly, he concluded that the pro-Israel community has quite a lock: "If a Democrat's in, AIPAC owns the White House, and if it's a Republican, Falwell owns the White House."

Chafets sensationalizes his point. But it does reflect an underlying political reality: it's hard to compete and be successful in American politics without being good on Israel.

Do Domestic Politics Really Matter?

You bet they do. No president can ignore them, nor would want to rile up a powerful pro-Israel constituency without a reason. No administration I worked for went looking for a fight with the American Jewish community; some went to considerable lengths to avoid one. For good reason: Arab-Israeli diplomacy is hard enough without a domestic political handicap. "If the full force of the Jewish community comes down on you," Wendy Sherman said, "you're probably not going to accomplish your goals anyway."

At the same time the question of the influence of domestic politics on America's Middle East diplomacy is so rife with distortion and misconception that before we move on, it's important to straighten a few things out.

Lobbying by citizens or by groups pushing this cause or that is not some kind of dark cabal or even a necessary evil. It's the lifeblood of politics in a democratic system. There are excesses and not enough accountability, but the right to organize and make one's case within legal and ethical limits is basic to the American way of life. We may have no choice but to suffer its excesses. I certainly wouldn't want to see the lobbies disappear.

The same is true for the influence of Congress. Often my State Department colleagues, and occasionally a secretary of state, would rail on about the stupidity or ineptness of Congress when it came to foreign policy. At times they were right, but their arrogance was too much to take. "Who do they think they are that they know more about the national interest than we do?" one colleague almost shouted in response to a congressional letter about restricting aid to the Palestinians. Who elected him? I thought.

Some Arabists or Arabs saw Congress (and later the State Department) as "Israeli-occupied territory." A Saudi official once described Jewish members of Congress as the "little Knesset."

Arab contempt for America's system and politics, whatever its imperfections (and it has many), offended me and seemed to be as deep as their lack of understanding of the American political system.

I was no expert on American government, but I knew that the founders in their infinite wisdom had created three branches in order to maintain a system of checks and balances. I figured that this system, even with its drawbacks, was better than the alternatives. I no more wanted a bunch of guys at the State Department to define American interests than I did AIPAC or the Senate Foreign Relations Committee. If you want public support for your policies, then the political process has to be partly a collective enterprise. That the president has the authority to conduct the nation's foreign policy does not mean that everyone else should just sit around and watch from the sidelines. The dangers of that kind of passivity, or of leaving it to the experts or nonexperts, are all too apparent today.

"Read the Constitution," John Sununu Senior lectured me. "The system is designed to be lobbied." Sununu thought domestic politics weren't necessarily good or bad; they were just the way the system was made. When it came to AIPAC's influence or the Arab's lack of it, he was no naïf. Arab-Americans, he told me, have been convinced by the media that "lobbying is bad. It is not. Everybody needs to do it. Even our friends and foes across the oceans have an obligation if they want a response from our system." And the system must be played from the government end as well. "If you want a sustainable foreign policy," says Mara Rudman, a deputy national security advisor in Bill Clinton's National Security Council, "you better figure out what your politics are and who's with you, and who's against you, and how you manage those politics if you want your policy to work."

Domestic lobbying has its real impact on Congress, not on the executive branch. Certainly the president isn't immune to the not-so-subtle conditioning of a vibrant pro-Israeli domestic constituency, but more direct causality between lobbying efforts and results is evident on Capitol Hill in assistance packages, pro-Israel statements, resolutions, and legislation that tries to constrain, preempt, or counter efforts—real or imagined—to pressure Israel. Usually these congressional initiatives have little effect on diplomacy, and even Congress is reluctant to get in the way of a president's initiative on the Arab-Israeli issue. As George Stephanopoulos, a Clinton advisor and ABC commentator, told me, the "farther away you get from day-to-day work on the Hill, [and] the farther away you get from the campaigns, the less domestic political considerations dictate what is happening…Is it something that a president has to pay attention to? Yes. But does it determine the policy? Less so."

Still, political pressures have taken a serious toll by conditioning a key branch of the American government to be reflexively pro-Israel at a time when serious questions need to be asked and debated about Middle East policy. Congress has little stomach to serve as a forum for this dialogue and debate, let alone to play a role in seriously pressing an administration to pursue Arab-Israeli diplomacy. Some members in both the Senate and the House are willing to be critical of Israel or of AIPAC or to take positions that appear sensitive to Arab or Palestinian concerns, but certainly not many.

One who is willing is Chuck Hagel, the two-term Republican senator from Nebraska. Of all my conversations, the one with Hagel stands apart for its honesty and clarity. If I wanted to be in a safe business, he began, "I'd sell shoes." Hagel's logic chain is pretty compelling. America is Israel's best friend, but it also has key interests in the Arab and Muslim world that, particularly since 9/11, it must try to protect. Being too one-sided when it comes to the Arab-Israeli issue isn't good either for Israel or for America. And far too often Congress shrinks from making this clear.

"This is an institution that does not inherently bring out a great deal of courage," Hagel continues. Most of the time members play it safe and adopt an "I'll support Israel" attitude. AIPAC comes knocking with a pro-Israel letter, and "then you'll get eighty or ninety senators on it. I don't think I've ever signed one of the letters." When someone would accuse him of not being pro-Israel because he didn't sign the letter, Hagel told me he responds: "I didn't sign the letter because it was a stupid letter."

Few legislators talk this way on the Hill. Hagel is a strong supporter of Israel and a believer in shared values. "The Jewish lobby intimidates a lot of people up here," but as he put it, "I'm a United States senator. I'm not an Israeli senator." A handful of others, like Representative David Obie, are also prepared to speak out on the subject, particularly when it comes to criticizing Israel, but they are a very small group. And it's sad. The Arab-Israeli conflict is just too complicated and too important to American interests to have only one side presented.

Domestic politics does not invariably chill or prevent successful American diplomacy. But it does create obstacles that need to be negotiated. In the past, whenever a president or secretary of state engaged in successful Arab-Israeli diplomacy and actually brokered an agreement, U.S.-Israeli relations have always had a certain amount of tension which drew a domestic political reaction. Always.

The reason is stunningly simple. To mediate effectively, you sometimes have to push Arabs and Israelis beyond where they initially wanted to go. When that happens, as it did in the diplomacy of Henry Kissinger, Jimmy Carter, and James Baker, Israel mobilizes and pushes back on its own or through its supporters in the United States. This dynamic can be particularly messy when a hard-line Likud prime minister like Begin or Shamir faces off against a determined president like Carter or George H. W. Bush. And as Kissinger found out, the tough Labor prime ministers like Rabin pushed back plenty when they believed Washington was squeezing Israel. Rabin, who muzzled AIPAC in the 1990s, wasn't at all reluctant to mobilize it against Ford's reassessment tactic in 1975. Successful Arab-Israeli peacemaking causes bumps in U.S.-Israeli relations. That's why former AIPAC policy director Steve Rosen used to tell me how much he hated the peace process. It was one of the few issues that could cause serious, albeit temporary, divisions in an otherwise robust U.S.-Israeli relationship.

These domestic speed bumps do have an influence on the

pace of American diplomacy, and the executive branch is not immune to the influence of a well-organized, persistent pro-Israel community. My friend and colleague Dennis Ross, with whom I worked closely for almost a decade, wrote an eight-hundred-page account of U.S. policy and the peace process without discussing AIPAC or domestic political pressures. When I asked Dennis about it, he said that in his view the United States didn't do things simply because of AIPAC or the Jewish community. He's right. I can't remember a single decision of consequence American peace process advisors made, or one we didn't, that was directly tied to some lobbyist's call, letter, or pressure tactic.

But those of us advising the secretary of state and the president were very sensitive to what the pro-Israel community was thinking and, when it came to considering ideas Israel didn't like, too often engaged in a kind of preemptive self-censorship. That several of us happened to be Jewish was less important than the prevailing climate of pro-Israel sentiment that mushroomed under Bill Clinton as the new administration became determined to avoid what it believed to be the far too critical approach to Israel of its predecessors. The emergence of Yitzhak Rabin, and Clinton's unique relationship with him, Israel, and American Jews, contributed to sensitivity toward Israel. This affinity and the president's own empathy (he was remarkably sensitive to Palestinians as well) undermined our willingness to be tough with Israel on settlement activity and made it hard to say no to bad Israeli ideas or to adopt our own, particularly in brokering final status agreements, until too late in the administration.

Despite the influence of domestic politics and the strong case Israel's lawyers make, when the president makes Arab-Israeli diplomacy a top priority and pursues it seriously, domestic politics usually take a backseat. In the three cases where American presidents and secretaries of state actually succeeded in brokering agreements, they managed to bring the Israelis and their supporters along, though not without a fight and in certain cases with a political cost. When a president ties the pursuit of Arab-Israeli peace to a broader strategy as Nixon and Kissinger (U.S.-

Soviet détente) or Bush and Baker (stability in a post–Gulf War Middle East) did, they can be particularly persuasive in getting their way. But negotiating the bumpy road to successful Arab-Israeli diplomacy requires leadership, toughness, and smarts not only at home but in the tough-minded world of Arab and Israeli politics.

Part Two

AMERICA'S PROMISE KEPT

In 1995 Will Smith and Martin Lawrence starred in *Bad Boys,* a movie about two loose-cannon Miami narcotics detectives with reputations for being tough and persistent and above all for getting the job done. Its success at the box office spawned a forgettable 2003 sequel, *Bad Boys II.* Most likely Henry Kissinger, Jimmy Carter, and James Baker would neither understand nor appreciate being described as the "bad boys" of Arab-Israeli peacemaking. The tag may indeed seem a bit awkward, even disrespectful, for a former American president and two ex–secretaries of state. But it fits. These three were and are tough, and Middle East peacemaking is a rough-and-tumble busines. To stand even a chance of succeeding on the streets of one of the world's most dangerous neighborhoods, and to manage your own politics while coping with theirs, you must be strong-willed, hard, a bit devious, and smart.

What's more, to want to risk the effort and absorb the criticism, you need a big ego. Even if you accomplish something, few are likely to appreciate your efforts immediately or at all. The ink had barely dried on the treaty ending the 1905 Russo-Japanese War when Theodore Roosevelt received the 1906 Nobel Peace Prize for negotiating an end to the conflict. But Jimmy Carter had to wait almost a quarter of a century, until 2002, before picking up his medal for negotiating the Egyptian-Israeli peace accord and other accomplishments. More likely you'll be mercilessly attacked both at home and abroad, including by those you are trying to help. Nor is there any guarantee that your reputation will improve over time. Just ask Jimmy Carter, who lost almost 20 percent of the Jewish vote between his 1976 victory over Gerald Ford and his 1980 defeat by Ronald Reagan. Carter lost the 1980 election for reasons that went far beyond the Arab-Israeli issue, but many in the American Jewish community never forgave him for his tough rhetoric on Israel during his single term. After the publication of his 2006 polemic, *Palestine: Peace Not Apartheid*, those same elements subjected him to withering editorial fire, and his legion of critics stand ready to rebut any new criticism of Israel. James Baker is still viewed with great suspicion and mistrust by some in the Jewish community who thought he was unfairly tough on Israel and insensitive to its concerns.

The British historian A.J.P. Taylor once said that the only lesson of history is that there are no lessons. Taylor may be right. Looking for past patterns and precedents and applying them to our own time and circumstances is always risky, particularly in a matter as complex as Arab-Israeli peacemaking. Kissinger, Carter, and Baker had different styles and personalities, confronted vastly different challenges and conditions, and dealt with different Arab and Israeli leaders. To compare them to each other might seem a bit of a stretch; to make them the standard by which to measure their successors may be a bridge too far.

Still, whatever divided them in style and accomplishment, all three men combined common elements that helped them succeed. I call them the five T's of effective diplomacy: each man made the Arab-Israeli issue a *top priority*; each was *tough* enough to push back abroad and at home when Arabs and Israelis tried to push him around; each was *tenacious* in his effort; each gained enough of the *trust* of the leaders to do serious business; and each had an astute sense of *timing*, the capacity to divine what Arabs and Israelis could actually accomplish.

You also can't argue with success. And none of them did. When I interviewed Kissinger, Carter, and Baker and described the exclusive club to which they belonged and explained why, each of them quibbled a bit. With large egos and larger self-images etched in the public mind during decades in the political arena, their reaction was hardly surprising. None, I suspect, was used to thinking of himself or his diplomatic achievements as part of a broader design. Kissinger admired Carter but wondered whether he had a strategy; Carter questioned some of Kissinger's tactics; and both of them admired Jim Baker. But none of the three took issue with the basic judgment: in an enterprise so predisposed to false starts, failed initiatives, and broken dreams, these three American peacemakers, of all the many, had succeeded. And achieving that success—even with Arabs and Israelis who were prepared to make decisions—required a strong American hand.

Chapter Four

Henry Kissinger: Strategist

At eighty-five years of age, Henry Alfred Kissinger can still be pretty damned intimidating. On a sunny, cloudless day I met him in his surprisingly modest New York office on Park Avenue. I had met him only once before, thirteen years earlier, at a White House gathering the night of the Oslo signing on September 13, 1993. The Clintons had invited all the former secretaries of state, giving me a chance to talk to all of them. Everyone, that is, except Kissinger. He seemed uninterested in making small talk, or any kind of talk for that matter. I didn't take it personally. He was a busy, important man.

So on the morning of our interview in New York, I didn't quite know what to expect. "The only reason I agreed to see you," said the owner of the characteristically low, gravelly, and oft-parodied voice, "was because of Peter. I don't normally do this sort of thing. You have read my memoirs, haven't you?" Peter Rodman, for whom I had worked in policy planning at State, was a longtime Kissinger aide who had arranged the interview. But I was on my own now, and I wasn't off to a great start. Numerous colleagues had told me stories about Kissinger's bluntness and razorlike wit that in years past had sliced into more than one staffer and left him shaking.

But then I reminded myself that this was one secretary of state I hadn't worked for. It was a no-lose opportunity; so here I was, a student of the history of American diplomacy in the Middle East, sitting across from a guy who had made a fair amount of that history all by himself.

A refugee from Nazi Germany, Henry Kissinger had come to the United States as a boy of fifteen, then risen to become the president's national security advisor and secretary of state. He was the first naturalized citizen ever to do so, and the first to hold both jobs simultaneously. He had dominated American foreign policy for almost six years, shaping some of the most consequential events of our time, including the Vietnam War, Nixon's visit to China, détente with the Soviet Union, and war and diplomacy in the Middle East. That his ego equaled in size, if not exceeded, the magnitude of his accomplishments was no secret. When Marvin and Bernard Kalb published their 1974 biography *Kissinger*, reporters at the publisher's book launch party asked the secretary if he had read it. The Kalb brothers each told me they recalled Kissinger saying that he hadn't but that he loved the title.

In his fashionably tailored blue suit, starched white shirt, and subtly patterned dark blue tie, Kissinger looked remarkably fit for a man his age, especially one who had recently recovered from a bad fall. I reminded myself that he not only had been the master diplomat of the 1970s but had probably generated more genuine star quality than anyone else in Washington. Kissinger had accumulated an army of detractors because of his policies in Vietnam and Cambodia, but he nonetheless had emerged as a cultural icon. The cover of *Newsweek* depicted him in a cape and tights, soaring as Superman over the Middle East as "Super K." *Saturday Night Live* regularly spoofed his owlish gaze and Teutonic accent. The tabloids chronicled his alleged romances. The Republican Party considered him a potential candidate for governnor of New York. And in the ultimate tribute, from my perspective, Monty Python even wrote a song about him. "Henry Kissinger ... you're the doctor of my dreams/ with your crinkly hair and your glassy stare and your Machiavellian schemes."[1] The Kissinger-obsessed trivia freak could even learn that he was the only secretary of state since the Second World War not to part his hair.

Within the first five minutes of my hour-long conversation with Henry Kissinger, one thing became stunningly clear: here is a man who lives and breathes strategy. He has a coherent view of how the world works and what America should want from it. You could agree with him or not, but you could deny neither his passion nor his skill, particularly as he strove to fit means and ends together. The world of foreign policy, how nations behave toward one another, may be composed of separate bits and pieces, like a gigantic jigsaw puzzle on the living room floor; more than most secretaries of state, Kissinger not only saw how those pieces fit together but believed he was pretty good at assembling them.

When I asked him to identify the key to his success in the Middle East, he said simply, "We had a strategy." And that strategy was to wean the Arabs away from the Russians and to convince them—Egypt in particular—that they could not achieve their diplomatic aims with Soviet arms but "would turn to us." I noticed that Kissinger had used the word "us" quite deliberately, a reference to Richard Nixon. Not surprisingly, their views were quite similar. Clearly, there would have been no Kissinger strategy without the support of an empowering president. Alexander Haig, Nixon's chief of staff and later secretary of state under Ronald Reagan, had his own take. "Henry was a masterful tactician," Haig told me; Nixon, "who never got credit for shit from anybody," brought the strategic dimension to the policy. When I repeated that description to Kissinger, he wasn't so sure, but he did credit the importance of Nixon's being "on the same page with me." As Watergate consumed ever more of Nixon's time and energy, however, and particularly after the October 1973 war broke out, it was Kissinger who directed and implemented American policy in the region. Kissinger became strategist and tactician rolled into one, and that was just fine with him.

Before he became secretary of state, Kissinger claimed no Middle East expertise. He had been to Israel a couple of times but had never set foot in an Arab country. As a Harvard academic, he had specialized in the arcane and frightening area of nuclear war. Kissinger's first book, published in 1957, was titled *Nuclear Weapons and Foreign Policy*. During his service as national security advisor the president had purposely kept Kissinger out of Middle East policy. Nixon maintained that Kissinger's Jewish faith put him at a disadvantage with the Arabs. Nixon also didn't want to see his good friend and secretary of state William Rogers overshadowed. "You and I," Nixon told Kissinger, "will have more than enough on our plate with Vietnam, SALT, the Soviets, Japan, and Europe."[2]

Nixon was right. And although the Middle East experienced plenty of motion between 1969 and 1973, only a little was of consequence. Three State Department initiatives—including one, the Rogers plan, which carried the secretary's name—came and went, barely disturbing the puzzle pieces. Nixon had identified the Middle East as a key issue that the United States had to manage. At a National Security Council meeting in April 1969, with both Rogers and Kissinger present, Nixon, reflecting his own ambivalence, observed that "the United States must assume the leadership here— subtly...any settlement will have to be imposed—without calling it that." This process could take years, the president had said. Might it be possible to "slice off any part of it"?[3]

To Kissinger, the ultimate strategist and historical pessimist, the answer then was no. He derided the notion that a comprehensive approach or any Middle East initiative at all could succeed, so long as the Arabs relied on the Soviets, and simply wanted the Americans to pressure the Israelis into a settlement. He even made a private pact with himself to resign if Nixon supported an imposed solution. In 1972 Kissinger believed the Middle East wasn't ready for a breakthrough, and he reportedly remarked to a friend that "it isn't ready for me."[4]

Nixon, who saw the stalemate as a "fishing ground" for radicals and Russians, wasn't so sure. "I hit Henry hard on the Mideast thing. He now wants to push it past the Israeli elections in October," he noted in his diary in February 1973, and he con-

cluded that "Henry needs to have another great goal."[5] But
Kissinger saw little merit in trying to impose a settlement only to
convince the Arabs that "America was best dealt with by extor-
tion." Kissinger recalled that "the prerequisite to effective
Middle East diplomacy was to reduce the Soviet influence so that
progress could not be ascribed to its pressures."[6]

Anwar Sadat's expulsion from Egypt of fifteen thousand
Russian advisors and technicians in 1972 got Kissinger's attention, but not enough to respond seriously to the tentative signals
the Egyptian president was sending about the need for diplomacy under American auspices. The Americans did not understand that Sadat was also making plans to go to war.

By this time Nixon had taken the real responsibility for the
Middle East from William Rogers. On Vietnam or the Middle
East, Haig told me, Rogers "just didn't ring Nixon's bell."
Kissinger was now in charge of the Middle East. Without State's
knowledge he opened up a secret back channel with Muhammed
Hafiz Ismael, Sadat's national security advisor. Still, he was preoccupied with the Vietnam negotiations and unimpressed with
Ismael's proposals, so not much came of their secret meetings
throughout 1973. Sadat claims he made his decision to go to war
after the final inconclusive Kissinger-Ismael meeting. In any
event, Nixon had assured Israeli prime minister Golda Meir that
there would be no American initiatives until after Israel's elections, scheduled for later that fall. In August Nixon decided to replace Rogers with Kissinger as secretary of state. On September
22 the former teenage immigrant who had fled Nazi persecution
with his family took the oath to defend the Constitution of his
adopted country as its chief diplomat. By Nixon's specific order,
he retained the title of national security advisor.

Two weeks later, on October 4, Kissinger met in New York
with Abba Eban, Israel's UN representative, assuring Eban that
"nothing dramatic is going to happen in October."[7] At six o'clock
on a Saturday morning, October 6, Joseph Sisco, Kissinger's assistant secretary for Near Eastern Affairs, woke Kissinger from a
deep sleep in his suite at the Waldorf-Astoria to report Egyptian

and Syrian troop concentrations along the Suez Canal and Golan Heights. As Kissinger recalls somewhat melodramatically, when Sisco woke him there were just "90 minutes of peace left for the Middle East."[8] Lawrence Eagleburger, a key aide who would later serve his own brief term as secretary of state, remembers his boss still in "his shorts and socks" making futile calls to head off an attack that obviously had been planned for months. Only the day before, the president had been briefed that no war was imminent. Now war had come, and it would change the Middle East conflict in ways that not even Kissinger could imagine.

The October 1973 war (the Yom Kippur or Ramadan war, as the Israelis and Egyptians respectively term it) was perhaps the most consequential event in the Arab-Israeli struggle since 1948. In a 2006 poll Israelis ranked it the most important event in their history since the creation of the state, followed in significance by the 1967 war and Rabin's assassination in 1995.[9] During the three-week conflict Israel and Egypt fought the largest tank battles since the end of World War II. Both sides absorbed staggering losses: Egypt and Syria together suffered almost 15,000 combat deaths; the 2,688 Israelis killed were proportionately equivalent to an American death toll of 160,000.

Sadat had launched the attack to break the stalemate in the Arab-Israeli conflict, regain territory lost in the 1967 war, and win a strong position for Egypt in the negotiations to come. The situation on the Syrian front stabilized within several days as the Israelis pushed the Syrians off the Golan and moved within artillery range of Damascus. It was a different story in Sinai. Egyptian forces had quickly overrun Israel's Bar-Lev line along the Suez Canal, neutralized Israeli airpower with surface-to-air missiles, and secured a salient of land on Israel's side of the canal. As in Syria, Israeli forces counterattacked across the canal, this time pushing within one hundred kilometers of Cairo, and they were poised to destroy the encircled Egyptian Third Army. Nixon and Kissinger stopped them in order to preserve the possibility of postwar diplomacy. A successful canal crossing and limited military gains restored Egyptian pride. Israeli confidence had been shattered by a surprise attack for which Israel was not prepared and by a cease-fire that prevented a conclusive military victory; and American complacency about an unresolved and unmanaged Arab-Israeli conflict had been undermined. Unlike the 1967 war, which led to seven lean years for American diplomacy, the October 1973 war generated seven fat ones.

The 1973 war shattered almost every assumption that Henry Kissinger had held about the global jigsaw puzzle, especially the pieces in the Middle East. In 1970, during King Hussein's crackdown on the PLO, Nixon and Kissinger had counted upon Israeli military superiority to contain Syria from pressuring Jordan, but this time the Israeli military failed to maintain the status quo. Arab weakness, which Kissinger assumed would once again produce poor military and political strategy, had been replaced by bold and effective action. Soviet cooperation, which the secretary of state believed he had secured through détente, vanished amid threats from Communist leader Leonid Brezhnev to intervene in the war and to impose a cease-fire. And a steady oil supply, literal fuel of the American economy, came to a halt as Arab producers, angered over American support for Israel, imposed an embargo and cut production. All of this produced a crisis that directly threatened American interests.

That Kissinger had failed to foresee the October war wasn't all that surprising—after all, the vaunted Israeli intelligence establishment, located thirty minutes by air from Cairo, had missed the mark as well. Kissinger has been criticized for not making more effective use of the opportunities for diplomacy before the war, and especially for failing to take Sadat seriously. But neither Sadat nor Israeli prime minister Golda Meir would have been ready for serious diplomacy without the shock only the war could create.

The challenge of orchestrating America's response to the war during three short weeks would have daunted any president and secretary of state. When Israel's armaments dwindled dangerously, Nixon arranged a resupply airlift in the face of Soviet objections. When Brezhnev threatened to intervene directly to end hostilities, Kissinger with Nixon's authority raised the nuclear threat level and placed American armed forces on global alert. Nixon and Kissinger put heavy and continuous pressure on Meir and Israeli defense minister Moshe Dayan to refrain from destroying the surrounded Egyptian Third Army. Kissinger took the lead in dealing with the Soviets to facilitate a resolution by the UN Security Council ordering a cease-fire.

These accomplishments, which included addressing the impact of the oil embargo, are all the more impressive in light of Nixon's preoccupation with the Watergate scandal. During those same three weeks he carried out the famous "Saturday night massacre," firing Attorney General Elliot Richardson and accepting the resignation of his deputy, William Ruckelshaus; the House Judiciary Committee opened impeachment proceedings; and Vice President Spiro Agnew resigned to avoid indictment for corruption unrelated to Watergate.

Nixon believed a president's chief responsibility was to control the nation's foreign policy. Domestically, the country could get along well enough with little or no superintending. Though he was involved in making the critical decisions required by the 1973 war, Nixon's attention to detail naturally suffered because of Watergate. Kissinger's central role in making foreign policy became even more prominent. With Nixon's support, he demonstrated that the United States still could act boldly and decisively on the world stage.

Peter Rodman recalls that there was a "strategy every minute of the war." In a fast-moving crisis, adhering to a consistent and planned strategy was impossible. In 1967 Israel had struck first and rolled up its Arab opponents in an incredible six days. Like most observers, Nixon and Kissinger assumed the hostilities in 1973 would be something like a repeat performance, even though Israel first had to recover from a surprise attack. Continued Egyptian and Syrian advances exposed fallacies in the conventional wisdom but brought forth nimble responses from the two partners, as they made significant adjustments to strategy on the fly, including the resupply airlift and a different approach to a cease-fire. The gods, Kissinger knew, were offended by hubris. But Rodman's comment about strategy is still illuminating. From the moment war broke out, Kissinger knew where he wanted to go, and he got there by striving with remarkable effectiveness to bend and manipulate events.

As Haig observed, Kissinger's strategy, "directed and authorized by Nixon," had three basic goals. First and most vital, an Israeli defeat must be avoided, as such a result would validate Arab reliance on Soviet arms. By framing the goal in this manner, Kissinger could justify the refusal to sanction destruction of the Egyptian Third Army, since it would not radically change the outcome of the war. Second, American diplomacy, especially its postwar initiatives, must not be held hostage to Israel's needs, aside from the need to avoid defeat. In late October Kissinger told his staff that an entire Arab world that was radicalized and anti-American might be in Israel's interest, but such a turn of events would be a disaster for American interests.[10] Finally, the Soviet Union must not benefit from the crisis. The American strategy was dependent on *retaining* Israel's confidence while strengthening or creating trustworthy relationships with the Arabs, particularly Egypt.

Kissinger never would have succeeded without Anwar Sadat—and Kissinger knew it. "You made us all look good," he told Sadat years later. During our discussion about the Egyptian president's role in Jimmy Carter's diplomacy, Kissinger was quick to remind me that "I had Sadat, too." Kissinger played his Sadat card well, maintaining contact with the Egyptian leader almost from the beginning of the war and making Cairo the initial stop on his first Middle East trip in November 1973. He viewed Sadat, like himself, as a strategist with a broader grasp of international relations.

The key to gaining Sadat's confidence was to follow a course that no longer tied America exclusively to Israel's tactics and requirements, allowing America to appear more credible to the Arabs. But following any such course would mean treading a fine and narrow line, since the United States could not and would not abandon Israel, either hypothetically or in reality. "We can't make our policy hostage to the Israelis...because our interests are not identical in overall terms," Kissinger observed days into the war. In the typically blunt manner he reserved for private conversations, Nixon expressed the same sentiment to Kissinger on October 8, saying, "When the [Israelis] finish clobbering the Egyptians and Syrians...[they] will be even more impossible to deal with than before...We must not under any circumstances... have this thing hang over for another four years and have us at odds with the Arab world. We're not going to do it anymore."[11]

Circumstances have changed in the last thirty-five years, but it is hard to imagine Bill Clinton or George W. Bush talking as Nixon and Kissinger did, or being prepared to be as tough, independent, and balanced in their approach toward Israel. Significantly, at no point in the three-week crisis did any statement by American officials describe the Egyptian and Syrian attack as an aggression. In the 1967 war President Lyndon Johnson fingered Egypt as the aggressor, but neither Nixon nor Kissinger made an issue of blame for starting the war. In their view, the Arabs may have been foolish, but an attack on occupied territory wasn't immoral, or at least they felt no need to say that publicly.

Kissinger's strategy during the 1973 war had a single overriding goal: to make a credible America the dominant player in the Middle East at war's end. His balanced design to attain this goal included these particulars: Israel would win, but the scope of its victory would be limited to avoid the humiliation of Sadat; Sadat would be offered a seat at the peace table, but only if he understood that America sought an incremental approach rather than a comprehensive settlement; the Soviets would be engaged as a negotiating partner, but in a subservient role; and the Arabs would be persuaded to remove the oil embargo, with no appearance that America had submitted to blackmail to achieve this result. The Arabs, Kissinger hoped, would come to see that Washington, not Moscow, held the key to their region's future.

Kissinger endured bitter criticism at the time and afterward for what his detractors saw as Machiavellian and duplicitous manipulation. He was accused of delaying the massive resupply airlift to pressure Meir and Dayan. "It's a myth," Kissinger told me when I raised the allegation. (Alexander Haig only half-jokingly quipped that he himself had "run the goddamn airlift and the war with Nixon.") The Israelis accused Kissinger of negotiating secretly with the Soviets on the terms of a cease-fire without notifying them, and they vehemently attacked him for stopping them from destroying the Third Army. "We would have betrayed a cease-fire we had arranged. It would have worsened our relationship with the Soviet Union, ruined our relations in the Arab world...and [Israel] would have had a Saddam in Cairo," Kissinger told me. Destruction of the Egyptian forces, he noted, would have dealt Sadat a needless humiliation.

For all his detractors (and there are many) and for all his deviousness (and there was much), Kissinger deserves high marks for his efforts. On any number of issues related to the crisis, he could have stumbled badly. But with Presidents Nixon and soon Ford covering his back, he positioned America well for the postwar period and set the stage for perhaps the most consequential Middle East diplomacy ever conducted by a secretary of state.

Between November 1973 and September 1975 Kissinger undertook eleven trips to the region. Those journeys produced a series of agreements, some of them substantive, others mainly symbolic. Even the symbolism, however, drove Middle East diplomacy forward, creating an environment that Carter and Baker used to their advantage. On October 28, 1973, Egyptian and Israeli military commanders talked directly to each other. A largely symbolic but nonetheless unprecedented peace conference at Geneva in late December brought the foreign ministers of Egypt, Israel, and Jordan to the same table. One month later a disengagement agreement between Egypt and Israel ended ongoing military confrontation. A similar agreement between Israel and Syria in June 1974 stabilized the Golan front and had far greater importance for every American because it ensured an end to the Arab oil embargo. The climax of this Kissingerian whirlwind was a second Israeli-Egyptian disengagement accord, signed one month shy of the 1973 war's second anniversary. I believe this accord, with its provision for monitoring by American forces, locked Egypt and Israel into an American-brokered negotiation process. The agreement did not guarantee Carter's ultimate triumph, the Egyptian-Israeli peace treaty, but without it, there probably would have been no treaty, and almost surely a train of new and unfortunate consequences for the Middle East would have resulted. How Kissinger pulled all this off is worth a look.

"As a professor, I tended to think of history as run by impersonal forces," Kissinger mused to reporters during his first Middle East shuttle in January 1974. "But when you see it in practice, you see the difference personalities make."[12] Perhaps his comment referred to Sadat and Meir, but he may have been talking about himself as well. Some of the key reasons for his success were undoubtedly his willingness to place himself in the middle, his opportunistic risk-taking, and his ability to put each agreement together by manipulating (there are few better words) a combination of factors. Among those factors were a fortunate disposition among Arabs and Israelis to reach agreements; American carrots and sticks; circumstances; and the force of his own personality. The more people I interviewed who had worked for him and the more memoirs I read from those Arabs and Israelis who knew him, the greater my appreciation grew for the impact of his personal involvement. Sadat and Dayan may have encouraged him to undertake his shuttle diplomacy, but having managed the October crisis, Kissinger personally wanted to shape postwar diplomacy.

By putting himself in the middle, Kissinger ensured continuity and follow-up. He dealt with Sadat, Meir, Rabin, and Dayan personally and became the repository of their confidence. They grew to like him. He became Professor Kissinger, consultant, confidant, interpreter of one side to the other. On the Syrian-Israeli shuttle, Harold Saunders—a key aide to Kissinger, later assistant secretary of state for Near Eastern and South Asian Affairs, and most likely the author of the phrase "peace process"—recalled that Kissinger, in interpreting one side to the other, was veritably explaining to the Israelis and the Syrians what "life was like on another planet." "He would spend hours," Robert Oakley, who worked for Kissinger at State and the NSC and was later ambassador to Zaire, Somalia, and Pakistan, remembers Kissinger "talking to Rabin about Egyptian realities, and hours talking to Sadat about Israeli realities." Typical was Kissinger's tutorial to Rabin in an October 1974 meeting: "With Sadat...I thought he was trying to play us off against the Russians. He may still do it. But my impression is that he talks as an Egyptian nationalist. Can you be sure? No you can't. But you have to weigh it against what happens if there is no movement."[13]

Yet he always looked for the common thread of a strategic big picture. He would flatter Assad by asking him his views on the international scene, playing to his instincts as a strategist. He would always remind everyone of what the strategy was. When Meir got mired down on some particular point, Saunders noted, Kissinger would lean back and say, don't forget what the strategy is—we're going to "push the Russians back, get the oil embargo lifted, and then we'll demonstrate a bit of movement here and bring Sadat along, even Assad."

When Kissinger couldn't persuade, he would try to pressure or cajole. His doomsday scenario speeches were legendary, combining as they did reminders to the Arabs and Israelis of the real stakes, lessons in how cooperation produces achievement of national goals, and gloomy forecasts of the dire consequences if they failed the professor's final exam by refusing either to understand or to cooperate. Former Israeli prime minister Shimon Peres recalls that Kissinger would lay out "grim scenarios with enormous skill," warning that failure meant "disaster would follow."[14] During the height of the March 1975 negotiations over a second disengagement, Kissinger, according to Rodman, warned Israel that "if this thing breaks down all the shit is going to hit the fan and we're not going to be able to shield you from it."

My interview with Kissinger was about half over when I decided to take a chance and ask what he thought of my concept of the five T's of effective diplomacy. I expected the worst, a slashing tutorial on avoiding cute alliterations when analyzing a serious subject. To my surprise, not only did the Professor agree with the concept, but he elaborated on the first T, about making the Middle East a *top priority*. This point was essential for success, he argued, because unless the secretary of state can be sure the president is behind him, "he can't carry the political weight of major agreements or of major negotiations." (When I asked Haig why Kissinger was so effective, he was even more categorical: "Because he had a president who understood the issue as well as he did, backed him, and in some cases, directed him.")

In what must have been the understatement of the century, Kissinger noted that he had a "particularly complicated president to deal with." Kissinger's problem was not that Nixon didn't care but that he had such strong views, particularly with regard to being tough with the Israelis. A full month before the October war, Nixon wrote in his diary that "Henry has constantly put off moving on it [the Middle East] each time . . . but I am determined to bite this bullet and do it now."[15] Nixon may have been preoccupied with Watergate, but he was still involved in most major decisions regarding the October war. It was Nixon who broke the bureaucratic impasse over the airlift to Israel. And it was Nixon's name that Kissinger invoked with Arabs and Israelis to get things done. For Kissinger, the president had to remain in the loop. Toward that end he wrote a memo to the president every night explaining the state of negotiations.

Kissinger had full authority to act on an issue that was critical to the national interest and that Nixon cared about. This centralization of power over foreign policy, which would have developed with or without Watergate, not only accelerated decision-making at home but sent an unmistakable signal as well to the Soviets, Arabs, and Israelis. I knew from my own experience that the locals will play you big-time if they perceive there are significant differences between the president and the State Department. Kissinger delivered key demands and messages in Nixon's name and acted with the power of the presidency at his back. When he spoke, threatened, or reassured, he did so speaking for the president. Had Kissinger been secretary of state of Belgium or Holland, Dayan noted, he would never have accomplished such "striking feats."[16]

I asked Kissinger if the Israelis trusted him. "Rabin for sure," he answered. Golda Meir did too, "as far as she trusted anybody. She was always convinced that some secret deal was being cooked up between us and the Soviet Union, without a shred of evidence." Still, Kissinger, who worked closely with two Israeli prime ministers, Meir and Rabin, and a number of other senior officials, including Yigal Allon, Moshe Dayan, and Simcha Dinitz, probably understood Israelis better than any other secretary of state.

He would not have succeeded otherwise, for in the traumatic period following the October 1973 war, Israel's self-image and confidence were badly shaken. A sort of national suspicion and fear, never far from the surface, broke through to become the guiding national philosophy for years to come. Golda Meir, whose toughness and distrust of the Arabs were as deep as the lines etched on her face, was fundamentally opposed to trading territory for time to placate America, let alone making peace with Arabs she didn't like or trust. Above all, Kissinger understood and respected Israeli fears. A "small country's survival in a hostile world can turn on nuances not easily grasped by faraway nations with wider margins of safety," he recalled. "America could afford experiments; for Israel a single miscalculation could spell catastrophe."[17]

Kissinger genuinely appreciated Israel's situation but also understood that Israeli leaders were, at the end of the day, politicians as well as statesmen, ready to milk and exaggerate their plight to obtain better terms. Shortly after his first Middle East trip, during which he concluded a six-point accord to stabilize the cease-fire, he remarked to his staff that it had been "an easy agreement" to sell to the Israelis, "keeping in mind, however, that if the Israelis get only 98 percent of what they ask for, it proves that they have been utterly betrayed by the United

States."[18] He told me that "anybody who gets 100 percent of the confidence of the Israelis has discovered something that has not yet existed."

Kissinger found this obstinacy maddening, but he understood it, and in so doing he won the trust of the Israelis—insofar as they have trusted any American leader. At the same time he always sought a balance and was always conscious of what he needed from one side in order to produce from the other. Kissinger's talent, also displayed but not nearly as adeptly by Carter and Baker, was his ability to grasp the mediator's challenge: making sure that your sensitivity to one side doesn't preclude being sensitive to the other, and producing what both require.

Kissinger had Israel's confidence and managed to gain Sadat's as well. From their first meeting in Cairo in November 1973 the two hit it off. Sadat recalled that this meeting with Kissinger told him he was "dealing with an entirely new mentality, a new political method." And Kissinger made clear to me that he knew Sadat had a strategy "close to ours" and could see the broader international significance of his actions. We forget, but in these years the Egyptians were not interested in holding direct negotiations with Israel. "Never forget," Sadat told Kissinger in November 1973, "I am making this agreement with the United States, not with Israel." But Kissinger would take what he could get. "Confidence in America," Kissinger mused, "could be the bridge across the gulf of four wars."[19]

Trust and confidence were necessary but not sufficient. "You owe them the feeling, the sense that you've really understood them," Kissinger said, continuing our conversation, "but that your requirements go beyond this." At times every successful mediation requires toughness and resolve. Small powers, Kissinger asserted, must understand that if "you turn down an American proposal that's not free. And that challenging America in general has consequences."

Throughout his shuttle diplomacy Kissinger, either directly or in Nixon's name, applied plenty of pressure, most often on the Israelis. Rabin recalled that "Kissinger could be a tough and occasionally dangerous rival." Upon meeting him for the first time, Ariel Sharon half jokingly said, "You're the most dangerous man in the Middle East."[20] And at critical moments the rhetorical strategy worked, alerting the Israelis when they had drifted seriously offtrack, or when they were taking America for granted. Faced with Israel's plan to destroy the Egyptian Third Army, Kissinger called Ambassador Dinitz in Nixon's name, saying, "You will not be permitted to destroy this army. You are destroying the possibility for negotiations." Kissinger told me that it was "painful" when we "cracked down on Israel" over the Third Army. But with Nixon behind him, he knew it was necessary and that he could get away with it. While negotiating with the Russians in Moscow over the cease-fire, he'd received a message from the president: "I'm prepared to pressure the Israelis to the extent required, regardless of the domestic political consequences."[21]

Reassessment: "It's Only Theater"

At no time was Kissinger's toughness, tenacity, or even his ability to gain trust tested more thoroughly than in his bid to secure a second Sinai disengagement in the spring and summer of 1975. By summer 1974 his step-by-step diplomacy had reached a dead end. Rabin found himself in a much weaker position domestically than Meir, and particularly after the initial withdrawal from Sinai and Golan, he could not consider a disengagement from the West Bank. King Hussein of Jordan had been ready, or at least claimed that he was, but the Arab summit decision at Rabat that October, which designated the PLO as the sole legitimate representative of the Palestinians, made a West Bank option moot. In light of Sadat's exposed status as the leading proponent of peace, as well as the rapidly deteriorating situation in Vietnam, Kissinger and the new president, Gerald Ford, eagerly sought a diplomatic success. They had been signaling Rabin since the fall of 1974 that such a success might involve a second Sinai disengagement. That Kissinger turned to the Middle East for what he thought would be a relatively easy sell demonstrates either his self-confidence or his failure to read the situation correctly, or both. With all other avenues blocked, a second Sinai accord became the default position.

Kissinger's failure to reach an agreement during his March mission left him frustrated and angry, primarily with Israel. In late June Ford wrote to Rabin on American Middle East policy, assuming perhaps the most abrupt tone taken by a president toward an Israeli prime minister since Eisenhower's peremptory missive to Ben-Gurion during the Suez crisis. Ford's letter spoke of the need for "reassessing," a word that soon would take on a new meaning, but it produced no movement on Rabin's part. To make matters worse, March 1975 had witnessed a number of setbacks to American diplomacy around the world. The hopes and plans of a dozen years lay shattered in Vietnam; the Khmer Rouge threatened and soon would overrun Cambodia; in Portugal a left-wing government took power after the fall of the Salazar dictatorship; and in Saudi Arabia a member of the royal family assassinated King Faisal. Rodman recalls that "it looked like our whole foreign policy was collapsing. It was very emotional, and we were telling the Israelis that."

Rabin, however, had problems of his own. Never as strong or as self-confident as Meir, he faced pressure from his more hawkish Labor Party rival, Shimon Peres, and from the opposition, led by Menachem Begin. Peres and Begin circled, eager to pick up the pieces following a Rabin stumble. Rabin may have been open to a second Sinai disengagement but only in exchange for a political move from Egypt such as an end to the state of war. And in any event, he was not ready to withdraw from the Mitla and Gidi passes in Sinai, which, like Quneitra on the Syrian front, became the new nonnegotiable Israeli redline. (Both positions ultimately would be negotiated away later.) Sadat meanwhile refused to extend formal nonbelligerency to Rabin under any circumstances, offering only its functional equivalents.

Rabin's refusal to make concessions on his March mission angered and even hurt Kissinger. He believed that Rabin had misled him and attributed the Israeli decision to domestic politics, which, he observed scornfully, was really all there was to Israel's foreign policy. Having warned the Israelis that the step-by-step process could unravel, he couldn't understand why "for the sake of a few miles in the desert a hundred kilometers from its borders, Israel was willing to risk an American stake in the Middle East." Because of Israel's refusal to cede control of the Sinai passes not to the Egyptians but to UN personnel, Sadat would be endangered and the Soviets would benefit. In a last-ditch effort to save his mission, Kissinger met with the Israeli negotiating team and dragged out his best doomsday speech: "Ask yourselves what the position of the United States can be at Geneva without a plan, even for the most benevolent president. That is my nightmare—what I now see marching toward you. Compared to that, 10 kilometers in the Sinai is trivial."[22] Harold Saunders recalls that after Kissinger unloaded on the Israelis, the secretary of state confided that Israeli shortsightedness concerned him seriously: "Well, you know when they act like this I worry about the future of my son as a Jew in America."

Kissinger's attitude toward Rabin ranged from anger to genuine concern for a man he liked and respected. In an unusual gesture of respect, the prime minister personally escorted Kissinger to the airport, speaking emotionally of the responsibility he carried for every Israeli soldier, including his own son Yuval, who was then serving in Sinai. Kissinger admits to being greatly moved. In turn Rabin, who never had seen Kissinger so stirred, recalled beginning to cry. It was a very personal moment for two men who held great affection for each other but whose countries were entering the worst rift in their relations since Suez.

The next three months revealed both how acrimonious the U.S.-Israeli relationship could become, and the stake each side had in ensuring that the relationship experienced no permanent rupture. President Ford's affable nature hid a steely toughness and a determination to succeed in Middle East diplomacy. Ford remembers being "mad as hell" at Rabin, convinced that the Israeli leader was stalling, and planned to fight over "every kilometer."

The day after Kissinger returned from his March shuttle, he briefed the congressional leadership. Following that meeting, Senate majority leader Mike Mansfield informed the press that the president had decided to "reassess" American Middle East policy. Ford claimed the word as his own and told his press secretary, Ron Nessen, to let Mansfield's comment stand.[23] According to Saunders, credit for the phrase belonged to Kissinger. By the end of March, amid signs of displeasure with Israel, the administration had postponed consideration of all future economic assistance, frozen Israeli requests for F-15 aircraft, and delayed delivery of already promised Lance missiles. Spokesmen for the president also announced that the administration viewed with reluctance entering into new arms commitments to Israel while the reassessment was in train. In support of these sanctions, Kissinger began a round of consultations with foreign policy gurus about America's Middle East policy and recalled several of his Middle East ambassadors for consultation.

To nobody's surprise, reassessment provoked a furious response from the American friends of Israel. On May 21 seventy-six U.S. senators sent a strongly worded letter to President Ford, praising Israel as the most reliable barrier to domination of the area by outside forces and urging him to be responsive to Israeli needs. There is little doubt that Israel instigated the "letter of '76," and AIPAC almost certainly drafted it. Pete Lakeland, who worked for Republican Senator Jacob Javits of New York, recalls that AIPAC approached him (Lakeland) and "might even have presented me with a draft." "Morrie [Amitay] and AIPAC had determined," Lakeland notes, "that if this was arm wrestling and a political challenge, we can force you [the U.S.] to bend." "Seventy-six of us promptly affixed our signatures," Republican Senator Charles "Mac" Mathias Jr. of Maryland would later write, "although no hearings had been held, no debate conducted, nor had the administration been invited to present its views."[24] The letter produced the effect its signatories expected—real support in Congress. Rabin believed he could weather reassessment as long as he had congressional support. And Lakeland believes the letter had an impact in another critical area, adding, "I think it sobered Kissinger up."

Not according to Kissinger. "The letter of '76 was not a great thing for Israel to do," he told me. "It looked good on paper but didn't influence us much at all." Kissinger remembered that a couple of senators called to reassure him, telling him to ignore the letter. Ford seemed equally determined not to let it influence his decision-making. "The letter," he recalled, "really bugged me... I was not going to capitulate to it." President Ford told me that while he "caught hell" for reassessment, he had to "discount" politics, because American Middle East policy was more important.

In conversation, Kissinger readily dismisses the impact of domestic politics on foreign policy, but domestic politics, that is to say American-Jewish politics, clearly affected him personally. "With thirteen members of my family having been killed [in the Holocaust], I had a special feeling about Israel. So at the same time I found Jewish pressures more irritating than non-Jews would. I couldn't look at Jews as an outside group. I couldn't analyze them as a pressure group, as voters." Kissinger admitted that those pressures could "wound me more inwardly" in ways that a non-Jewish secretary—like Baker, for example—never would feel.

At the same time Kissinger insisted that the activity of the organized Jewish community did not affect his policy choices. It was almost as if he couldn't be bothered. "I didn't know enough about politics," he maintained, and Nixon had "nothing to gain" from catering to pro-Israel sentiment. According to Kissinger, Nixon had always said that only 25 percent of Jews would ever vote for him, and that those who would were the "crazy Jews." Still, Nixon respected Jewish political influence and often attributed it to Kissinger's reluctance to engage on the Middle East out of fear of tangling with American Jews.

Given how tough Nixon and Kissinger could be, it is not surprising that the American Jewish community found much in their policies to oppose. But just as Nixon appreciated domestic

Jewish power, he genuinely admired Israeli resolve and military skill and stood by the Israelis at key moments. Meir and Rabin knew and understood this. Through his close relationship with Ambassador Dinitz and his frequent meetings with Jewish groups, Kissinger often preempted and contained much of the criticism. And he was good at it, because he convinced all with whom he met that they had become, if only for the few moments of the meeting, fellow global strategic thinkers. Meeting with a group of representatives from Jewish organizations in December 1973, Kissinger observed that "it doesn't hurt me with the Arabs to have a certain aloofness from this community," later adding that what he really wanted from those Jewish leaders was "some confidence that we are not in an abstract exercise to pressure Israel."[25]

The issue of Kissinger's Jewishness had been the subject of a great deal of speculation. Two of the most significant events of Kissinger's later life—confirmation as secretary of state and marriage to his second wife, Nancy Maginnes—took place on the Sabbath. Kissinger neither practiced his Judaism in an observant manner nor attuned himself to Jewish tradition. None of this meant, of course, that he lacked a sense of Jewish identity. His comments to me suggested that identity meant something very important to him.

He could also use his religion to his advantage when he could gain an objective. His disparaging comments about Jews and Israelis during his meetings with the Arabs were legendary. Meir "doesn't like to yield territory," he told Sadat in May 1974— "she's a Russian peasant."[26] Golda Meir, who believed that Kissinger never let his Jewish identity affect his work, played on it anyway. Marvin Kalb, the veteran CBS newsman who traveled extensively with Kissinger, recalls the secretary pleading with the Israeli prime minister to stop referring to his religion. "Golda, you're killing me...you're ripping me to pieces. Don't you realize I'm supposed to be secretary of state for the United States of America. Forget the Jewish thing." One can only wonder who was playing whom. Dayan later would recollect that while Kissinger was "sympathetic" to the Jewish people, he "was not on Israel's payroll."[27]

Rabin believed Kissinger supported the Israeli people on an emotional level, but Rabin also noted that he could be cynical, manipulative, and detached when discussing American domestic politics and the American Jewish community. Clearly, Kissinger chose to be disingenuous when he said that he lacked familiarity with the politics of his adopted country. After all, the conduct of diplomacy in the middle of the nation's worst domestic political scandal required a quick study of domestic matters, and Kissinger was the very definition of the term. When meeting Arab officials, he always raised the complications of American politics, which not only bought time and provided an explanation of why immediate progress wasn't possible but also put some distance between himself and the Jewish community. In a meeting with the Saudi foreign minister a week after Nixon's resignation, he laid out the American political situation adroitly: "We need to get firm control here. The next thing is to avoid a confrontation with the Jewish community before the elections, because we would like to reduce Democratic gains in Congress."[28] In one of his most guileful performances he told Jordan's Crown Prince Hassan that President Ford could "contribute $100,000 to the United Jewish Appeal, condemn the PLO three times a day, and make [Democrat Daniel Patrick] Moynihan secretary of state, but the Jews will still work against him. Why? Because a new administration will need two years to learn about the subject and couldn't do anything."[29]

More than thirty years later Kissinger believes that the reassessment was "theater." It could only have been theater, he told me, because in the end "there was nothing to reassess." A useful tactic, reassessment served dual and closely related purposes: it reminded Israel that saying no to the United States came with a cost; and it functioned as an expression of frustration over shortsighted Israeli negotiating tactics at a critical moment, when America could find little of a positive nature in its worldwide diplomatic endeavors. Kissinger had no real alternative to his step-by-step approach: neither the Arabs, Sadat least of all, nor the Soviets conveyed a sense of urgency to reconvene the Geneva conference. In mid-1975 a comprehensive solution was too far a reach. Both Rodman and Eagleburger believed the reassessment to be theater, which drew a strong negative reaction from Congress, but succeeded in reinvigorating the step-by-step approach.

Theater or not, reassessment paradoxically strengthened Rabin politically, as a result of his tough stance with Washington. The reassessment drama left him better positioned to sell disengagement at home. Ford's angry letter in late June probably helped Rabin to win cabinet support. And an American promise of early warning stations (to be located in the Sinai and manned by Americans), and several separate U.S. assurances (including no recognition or formal negotiation with the PLO until it accepted UN Security Council Resolutions 242 and 338 and accepted Israel's right to exist) sealed the deal, which was signed by Egypt and Israel under American auspices in September.

Kissinger told me that he believed the second Sinai agreement was his most significant accomplishment. The accord committed both sides to resolve their conflict by peaceful means, abjuring the resort to force or the threat of the use of force against each other. Certainly Sinai II qualified as his most difficult agreement, both because of the American domestic blowback and because of the strain placed on the American relationship with Israel to achieve it. Kissinger would tell Jordan's Crown Prince Hassan—in part for effect, in part because he believed it—that for the first time an American secretary of state and American president "took the [Israelis] on for six months and made them go back."[30] The second Sinai disengagement may not have been "the forerunner of a peace treaty," as Kissinger described it to me. But no further progress could be achieved in this area by taking small steps. Only a giant leap would suffice now. For the time being the September agreement was about the best that could be accomplished and certainly the best that America could buy.

Kissinger the strategist was also Kissinger the historical pessimist, who dealt more in probabilities than in possibilities. Given the political landscape of the Arab-Israeli conflict in the early 1970s, he made caution a virtue and rightly refused to expose the United States to the chance of needless failure. Saunders, who was no shrinking violet when it came to American activism, reminded me that the Jordanian option, using King Hussein as Israel's major partner to resolve the Palestinian issue, was a nonstarter because of the king's weakness, the PLO's strength, and Israeli caution.

Saunders also reminded me that the agreements committed the parties only to small steps, not to the existential leaps that came later; still, existential or not, these were steps being taken by Arabs and Israelis for the first time. As I listened to Kissinger, I occasionally had to remind myself that during his day neither side negotiated directly in any sustained manner with the other, a roadblock our team never faced. Then, neither side possessed trust or confidence in the other; nor did they extend the benefit of any doubt. In such a claustrophobic environment, Kissinger correctly refused to make the unattainable the enemy of the attainable. He milked his negotiating position for everything he could get, neither over- nor underreaching.

That's not to say Kissinger wasn't prepared to take risks. He willingly placed himself at the center of events—an attribute rare for secretaries of state. The desire to be on center stage was accompanied by a thirst for success. These elements of the Kissinger persona created a persistence and stamina that became legendary. Meir commented on his ability to simply outlast everyone else at the table. Dayan, certainly no stranger to fatigue and battlefield pressure, noted during one early morning encounter that "I almost dropped from fatigue, but he appeared sprightly as ever." Rabin recalled that, no matter when he turned up, Kissinger looked like he "had just had ten hours of sound sleep."[31]

We can't leave the Kissinger story without mention of his thirty-four-day, two-thousand-plus-mile Israel-Syria "shuttle." The irrepressible Joe Sisco named this diplomatic style during the first Egyptian-Israeli disengagement negotiations, but it could have been born just as well in the sky between Jerusalem and Damascus. Not since Robert Lansing accompanied President Wilson to Versailles in 1919 had a secretary of state been out of the United States for such a lengthy period on an official mission. Dayan remembered that had Kissinger known the Syrian leg would require more than a month to conclude, he never would have gone. Married shortly before the trip began, he instructed his new bride, Nancy, who planned to accompany him, to "pack lightly." Having run out of underwear at the eight-day Wye River Israeli-Palestinian summit in October 1998, I knew the feeling.

But critical American national interests required an agreement between Israel and Syria. The Saudis had assured Kissinger that if he made the effort, the oil embargo would be lifted; Sadat needed it to reduce the propaganda attack against him by Arab extremists; and a resuscitation of step-by-step diplomacy depended on the cover of a success, either with Jordan or Egypt. "If we get a Syrian disengagement," Kissinger told Nixon in March 1974, "we can go back to Egypt for a territorial settlement because Syria will have signed a document with Israel." He warned the president, however, that "we could fail with Syria." As Kissinger later wrote, Hafez al-Assad had made "intransigence a national characteristic."[32]

Kissinger described Assad as a "first-class mind allied to a wicked sense of humor," and a man who negotiated "like a riverboat gambler to make sure that he exacted the last sliver of available concessions."[33] No wonder the two got on so well. Kissinger earned the distinction of being the first secretary of state to deal seriously with Assad, and like most of his successors and presidents from Nixon to Clinton, he found Assad a fascinating character, one with whom a deal could be struck. Kissinger may well have originated the American fascination with Assad. I met the Syrian president several times but never completely understood his allure for my colleagues.

Sadat, Arafat, and Hussein readily followed the same script: secret negotiations with the Israelis, coupled with public diplomacy to affect Israeli public opinion. Assad flatly refused to play this game. He wanted all of the Golan Heights to the June 1967 lines, not just to the 1923 international border, but he wanted it for less—that is, without participating in confidence-building or conducting both secret and public diplomacy with Israel, which made the others' success possible. If nothing else, Assad remained consistent. He would die in May 2000, remaining true to his principles but without much in his pocket.

But I'm getting ahead of my story. In the spring of 1974 Assad, who had been badly beaten by the Israelis on the battlefield, wanted an agreement to push Israeli forces back, but as Rodman recalls he wanted to make Kissinger "sweat for it," and he did. Assad refused to dispatch his foreign minister to Kissinger's Geneva conference in December 1973, and he opened negotiations by insisting upon the return of the entire Golan Heights, then magnanimously reducing his territorial claims for a disengagement agreement by half. Israeli reactions to Assad ran the gamut from suspicion to deep fear. Meir demanded that before any negotiation could begin, he submit a list of Israeli POWs. The Israeli political and military leadership never seemed to get over the fact that a man who had lost the war now preened and made demands as if he were the victor. And they dug in.

Hammering out an acceptable disengagement boundary required making sixteen stops in Damascus and fifteen in Jerusalem over a monthlong shuttle. Before success finally limped into view, Kissinger twice threatened Assad with a cessation of talks, and Nixon sent a letter to Meir threatening an aid cutoff if the Israelis did not come around. The agreement, signed June 4, 1974, provided for UN-administered buffer zones and demilitarized areas. It had taken thirty-four grueling days to conclude, but driven by Israeli and Syrian national interests, it has lasted for more than thirty-four years.

By now Kissinger's secretary was buzzing, and he was fidgeting. But I decided to ask one more question: "Do you think you positioned the United States well?" "You know, in retrospect," he mused, lifting himself with some effort out of his chair, "that one could do three disengagement agreements in eighteen months seems almost mythical." That Kissinger saw his accomplishments in mythical terms is not surprising. But he was right about the diplomacy. Today people tend to dismiss his step-by-step diplomacy as overly expedient, shortsighted, and ultimately self-defeating. His legions of attackers criticize him for ignoring the Palestinian problem and for refusing to go for a West Bank disengagement through talks with Hussein. But anyone who's ever been seriously involved in negotiations between Arabs and Israelis knows how hard it is to get anything done. In a two-year period Kissinger squeezed just about everything he could from new circumstances and very old rivalries. He became the first secretary of state to create an Arab policy for the United States; the first to prove that America's close ties with Israel could yield workable agreements with Arabs; and the first to create conditions in which the Israelis felt confident and secure enough to cede territory. He managed to retain America's special tie with Israel, so critical to achievement, yet still created a new, albeit different, special relationship with Sadat. Above all, he positioned the United States as the key mediator in the Arab-Israeli conflict.

By 1976, however, the maestro had run out of music. The master of the shuttle had flown about as far as he could go. The parties could disengage no further. Perhaps if Kissinger had been offered more time and a compatible president to advise, he would have taken a crack at the Palestinian issue. He knew America could not avoid it forever. But it was not to be. A new American president, with a far different style but an equally steely resolve, was about to take up the challenge and make his own unique contribution to American mediation and diplomacy.

Chapter Five

Jimmy Carter: Missionary

All Dressed Up but Nowhere to Go

Talking to Jimmy Carter about Arab-Israeli peace, or just about anything at all, means having a very serious conversation with one serious guy. You can be misled at first by the quiet demeanor, the soft southern accent, and the softer blue eyes. They mask a single-mindedness and self-confidence that don't stay hidden for very long. A man who starts a conversation, as the former president did, by recalling that "since I was three years old I've had the Holy Land as a focal point in the religious aspect of my life" is not fooling around. The intense conviction, tinged with moralism and a deep but unrealistic hope that the Arab-Israeli problem could be comprehensively resolved, drove Carter way offtrack for the first ten months of his presidency. But once he focused, under Sadat's lead, on what could actually be accomplished, that intensity enabled Carter to broker the first peace treaty ever signed between Israel and an Arab state.

The president met me in his spacious, rotundalike office at the Carter Center in Atlanta. I found him gazing out the floor-to-ceiling windows at the lush greenery of Freedom Park. He was a little shorter and slighter than I recalled. Carter was dressed in an outfit straight out of an L.L. Bean catalog—blue-and-green fleece vest, blue work shirt, khaki slacks, and outdoor shoes. He looked as if he had just come back from a long walk around his property in Plains, Georgia, where he spends at least three weeks a month when he's not traveling or in Atlanta.

I had met him only once before, at the Lebanese embassy in Washington during the 1980s. Then he had wanted to talk about the never-ending crisis in Lebanon, and he did, going on and on, seemingly impervious to the group of curious onlookers gathered around him. It was to be the same now as it had been two decades earlier: no chit-chat, no small talk. Passionate about the Middle East, Carter plunged in, eager to get going.

As we began our conversation, Carter's take-charge approach immediately struck me. He'd clearly been over much of this ground before, and despite my effort to inject a second question, he spoke continuously for a full five minutes. Carter knew precisely where he wanted to go and how he wanted to get there. This tendency to take the initiative and maintain control, arising from the conviction that he knew what was right or best, characterized our interview, much as it marked his Middle East diplomacy. "When I saw that I might be president," he observed in regard to the Arab-Israeli conflict, "I began to make plans on how I might make a consummate contribution." Whoa! What an opening! Nobody else I interviewed had talked this way. Kissinger and Baker saw the Arab-Israeli issue as a trap or a minefield to be avoided, or at best, a mess to be managed, but hardly as a land of diplomatic promise to wander in search of a solution.

As I listened to the president's monologue, I couldn't help but reflect on the often-expressed belief that Carter, a former engineer and submariner, had an instinctual need to plan, anticipate, and control all the details. After all, late in his term a story had gone public that he personally oversaw the use and scheduling of the White House tennis court. Rear Admiral Harold J. Bernsen suggested to me that Carter ran his Arab-Israeli policy like a "diplomatic submarine," running neither silently nor deep but always under his command. Carter clearly had the "con" and didn't want to relinquish it. His determination to place himself squarely in the middle of the Egyptian-Israeli mix, and to drive the diplomatic process, by now had assumed legendary status.

With some pride, he told me that he had written the first draft of the Egyptian-Israeli agreement on a "scratch pad" at Camp David.

Carter believed he had most of the answers, if only people would listen to him. They should listen as well, he declared, to one another. More than a quarter of a century after winning the White House, Carter still exhibited the naïveté and self-righteousness that allowed him to tell the American people in 1980 that "I will never lie to you." At eighty-four, after all these years, here was a former president who still believed that the Arab-Israeli conflict could be resolved and who very much wanted to be in the middle of efforts to obtain that resolution, because he had a solution in mind.

Not everyone admired Jimmy Carter's approach to diplomacy. Kissinger acknowledged his success but thought he'd gotten there "by accident." Many observers, following the line of the late Prime Minister Rabin, argued that Carter's zeal and passion for a comprehensive agreement had scared Sadat into concluding a separate peace. There's some truth here. But those who insist that Carter was lucky or wrongheaded miss the point: Carter took advantage of the opportunity Sadat handed to him, and admittedly picked the lowest-hanging fruit on the tree—an Israeli-Egyptian accord. At the same time, we forget too easily that even after Sadat's historic journey to Jerusalem in November 1977, one of the most audacious acts of statesmanship in the last century, Egyptian-Israeli peace still beckoned only as a possibility, not as an inevitability. Carter made it so through two key interventions: bringing Sadat and Begin to Camp David in September 1978 and traveling to Cairo and Jerusalem in March 1979 to close the deal. No matter whom I spoke to—Americans, Egyptians, or Israelis—most everyone said the same thing: no Carter, no peace treaty.

Carter stands out from Kissinger and Baker, not to mention from every other American president and mediator who ever dealt with the problem of the much too promised land, in that he decided, almost from the start of his presidency, to make Arab-Israeli peacemaking a personal mission. Why he did so, why he readily spent so much time, energy, and political capital, is not clear. In January 1977 the Middle East presented neither an immediate crisis nor an opportunity. It did offer many traps and minefields, particularly for a Washington outsider and peanut farmer from Georgia with no foreign policy experience. And in his first year in office Carter fell into or stepped on many of them.

Unlike Kissinger, Jimmy Carter was no cold war strategist whose primary view of the world was through an East-West great power prism. He was clearly aware of the Soviet angle and would become even more so after the Soviet invasion of Afghanistan. The Holy Land, he told me, was a tinderbox "for potential explosive relationships between us and the Soviet Union." Carter's Polish-born national security advisor, Zbigniew Brzezinski, did think in these terms. Unless the Arab-Israeli conflict was managed, he told me, the Middle East "might blow, and deliver" the region to the Soviets.

But Brzezinski made clear that he spoke only for himself, not the president. He attributed Carter's intense interest in the Middle East to other motivations. After all, the new president pursued Arab-Israeli peace tenaciously, publicly, and comprehensively, with little regard for domestic political costs or the fact that no immediate crisis or opportunity presented itself to justify his actions. And thirty years later he appears more committed than ever, leading election-monitoring efforts in the West Bank and Gaza and writing books with radioactive titles such as *Palestine: Peace Not Apartheid.* That essential commitment arose from a deeper place than concern about some future conflict with the Soviet Union.

I think Carter's intense interest can be attributed to a mix of his Southern Baptist upbringing and his moralism, married to an idealism and pragmatism that convinced him that problems could actually be resolved. Like so many of the evangelical Christians with whom I spoke, Carter's religious upbringing left him deeply affected by and knowledgeable about biblical Israel and God's promise to the Jews. His moralism and his perception that Israel, however small, was the stronger party and had to make concessions to the Arabs made him particularly sensitive to the suffering and homelessness of Palestinians with whom he would increasingly identify over the years. To me, Carter sometimes sounded like Rodney King: "Can we all get along?" He seemed unable to accept on an emotional level why Israel could not withdraw from the 1967 lines; why Palestinians could not have a homeland; and why the Arabs could not recognize Israel.

"I was familiar with the geography and history [of the Holy Land]...taught it, including on Sunday," Carter responded when I asked him why this issue was so important to him. Brzezinski speculated that Carter "thought that it was the right thing to do because he had a deep feeling for the Jews, particularly because of his Christian background and of course the Holocaust, but also because he thought the Palestinians deserved better than what they had." His interest was "biblical," Walter Mondale, Carter's vice president, told me. "There's a little bit of the prophet in him. He wanted to do noble work on his watch." And finally Carter again: "I would hope before I die that I can see an Israel that's at peace and that's accepted peacefully by every Arab country living side by side with Palestinian people who have justice and the right to be free, and I haven't given up on that."

Unlike Kissinger and Baker, who might give you a thousand reasons to avoid a full-bore effort to solve the problem, Carter really believed in the possibility of achieving a solution and in the need to try. This attitude, together with his view that Israel, as the stronger party, bore more responsibility for making concessions, guaranteed that when it came to the Middle East, his vocabulary would contain a lot of "shoulds" and that his style would alienate both American Jews and Israelis. Today Carter's "shoulds" seem shriller than ever.

In an age of cynical, manipulative politics and poll-driven priorities, it's hard to imagine a president not only talking as Carter did but actually acting on his convictions. I'm not sure that even Bill Clinton, another Baptist and moderate southern governor who was intensely committed, felt that strongly about Arab-Israeli peace. Untainted by Watergate and Vietnam, committed to an open, public diplomacy that gave high priority to human rights, and actually convinced that some problems could be resolved, Jimmy Carter came into office determined to pursue a new approach to foreign policy and to the Arab-Israeli issue, regardless of the cost or consequences.

As our conversation continued, Carter left little doubt about his determination. "Shortly after I became president," he asserted with great conviction, "I decided to address the issue both forthrightly and aggressively." Brzezinski played a major part in shaping Carter's views, at least for the first six months of 1977, until Secretary of State Cyrus Vance claimed a larger role. Brzezinski counseled the president to "move hard and fast" from the very beginning, on the assumption that domestic politics would increasingly intrude on foreign policy. Brzezinski told me that if Carter was to succeed, he would have to be prepared to bite the bullet and even go through a phase of confrontation with the leaders of American-Jewish organizations.

"Above all, not too much zeal," the French statesman and diplomat Talleyrand was reported to have advised about diplomacy. Talleyrand would not have gotten a job in the Carter administration. A review of the first ten months of Carter's presidency reads like a "how not to" manual for successful Arab-Israeli peacemaking. Rightly convinced that Kissinger's step-by-step, interim approach had reached a dead end, Carter wrongly came to believe that negotiation of core principles for a comprehensive settlement, including a solution to the Palestinian problem, made more sense. It was not that Carter analyzed the situation incorrectly: in fact, his view was really quite prescient. When finally signed, the Egyptian-Israeli peace treaty would indeed be based on core principles, including Israeli withdrawal, the nature of peace, and a framework—flawed though it was— for addressing the Palestinian issue. Step-by-step was indeed dead, but what Carter and his team hadn't banked on was that Sadat would be prepared to take a "giant" step by going it alone, instead of preferring a more comprehensive approach that might bog him down in Soviet-American or inter-Arab rivalries.

Carter intended to sign everyone—Israel, Egypt, Jordan, Syria, the Soviet Union, and even the PLO—to a grand design for a comprehensive peace. This focus, so ill timed and ill conceived, marked his first efforts for certain failure. Every cliché imaginable—a bridge too far, more than the traffic can bear—would be insufficient to describe the breadth of Carter's overreach in 1977, especially after the election in May of the hard-line, revisionist Menachem Begin.

Carter operated publicly and noisily, engaging in what Mondale charitably described to me as "thinking out loud." In March Israeli prime minister Rabin met Carter in Washington and came away dismayed by the new president's style. Rabin liked Carter's public airing of what the Arabs must do to obtain peace with Israel, but he reacted negatively to the president's unprecedented comment that Israel should withdraw to the 1967 borders with "minor adjustments," a controversy Rabin actually helped trigger by saying after his meeting with the president that Carter agreed with him on the need for "defensible borders," which the administration had not said.

Later that month Carter "thought out loud" once again during a speech in Clinton, Massachusetts, commenting about the need for a Palestinian homeland. Carter, the first American president to take the Palestinian issue seriously, proudly told me that within two months of becoming president, he had called for the establishment of a Palestinian homeland "without knowing the format it would take." That was precisely the problem. He introduced a new element, which today may be taken for granted. But then his trial balloon popped, lacking as it was in context, prepared public opinion, and thought-out strategy. And the president seemed to be operating on his own without consulting his foreign policy team. Brzezinski recalls that he and the secretary of state were left huddling "on how to handle this new development."[1]

Carter had at least half a plan. Given his view, backed up by his own experts, that the Palestinian issue was central to a comprehensive deal, the president wanted to do some conditioning. He wanted to "stir things up while he was fresh and new,"

William Quandt, the NSC's key Middle East hand, recalled. Sam Lewis, the U.S. ambassador to Israel, told me that Carter wanted to "overturn the frozen table."

When it came to Arab-Israeli peacemaking, Jimmy Carter was all dressed up but had no place to go. The president's grand plan, particularly on the Palestinian issue, exceeded both the means at his disposal to achieve it and the capacity of the Arabs and Israelis to execute it. Even the Jordanian option, which had the good King Hussein negotiating with Israel, either together with Palestinians or on their behalf, seemed too much for Rabin to handle. And if Rabin couldn't deal with the PLO, as he told Carter in Washington, Menachem Begin, waiting in the wings to assume power, neither could nor would. Quandt, who was as close to Carter's strategy as anyone, summed it up best: "We had a framework and some hopes." Unfortunately, implementing a sound strategy in Arab-Israeli peacemaking is hard enough. American mediators cannot expect progress, much less success, when their plan depends on a wing and a prayer.

Although Carter failed in his initial appearance in the Arab-Israeli arena, alienating just about everyone in his first ten months, this period still contributed to his later success. Whatever his blunders, he had put the United States in the middle of the Arab-Israeli mix, made Washington a focal point of the region's attentions, and began to meet and develop relationships with the key leaders. By May he had seen Rabin, Sadat, Hussein, Assad (in Geneva), and King Fahd. Carter was also becoming hooked on the Middle East, rare for a president so early in his first term. And his personal ties with these leaders was part of his investment. "The only way to resolve a major problem," he told me, "is to deal directly with the person responsible."

During these months Carter developed relationships with the two leaders who would later share a singular piece of history with him. In April, Anwar Sadat came to call, and as Carter recounted (as only he could), "A shining bright light burst on the Middle East scene for me."[2] Not until Bill Clinton fell under the spell of Yitzhak Rabin would a Middle Eastern leader so deeply enthrall an American president.

When I asked Carter about his relationship with Sadat, the floodgates opened: "Sadat had total trust in me. We were kind of like brothers." After the official state dinner at the White House, Carter took Sadat to the residence, where his conversation convinced him that Sadat was "something of a soul mate. He and I began to develop a strategy." The feeling was apparently mutual. Sadat recalled that he found Carter to be a man who understood what he wanted, "a man impelled by the power of religious faith and lofty values—a farmer, like me." Later Carter would confide to his wife, Rosalynn, that his meeting with Sadat had been his "best day as President."³ On substance, Sadat seemed to be in a hurry, interested in a strong American role and a strong American plan. For the first time he even hinted that normalization of relations with Israel could be on the table. More important, a relationship began, one that time and time again demonstrated Sadat's willingness to trust Carter and to give him his proxy.

Carter's relationship with Menachem Begin assumed an entirely different character. As the former president continued our conversation, he made it quite clear that Begin's election, as head of Israel's first right-wing government, left him "very discouraged." The administration's entire strategy, such as it was, had presumed a Labor victory. Now Begin's views on giving back territory, building settlements, and the PLO seemed to make any progress impossible. "I didn't think I had any chance with Begin for success," Carter concluded.

But the election of a tough prime minister and his Likud bloc would usher in a curious and somewhat paradoxical period in regard to the U.S.-Israeli relationship generally, and to Arab-Israeli peacemaking in particular. For the next fifteen years, until Rabin's election in 1992, Likud governments alone, in national unity partnerships, or in rotation with Labor, would dominate Israeli politics. Likud prime ministers signed two of the three American-brokered accords, including the first peace treaty based on Israeli withdrawal from Arab land. Given the centrality of security to Israel's regional view, tough conservative leaders are better positioned than more moderate or liberal ones to command the political power required to reach controversial agreements and to win over a dubious public. Americans know this reality as the "Nixon to China syndrome." The history of Arab-Israeli peacemaking really is a record more of transformed tough guys than of committed peacemakers. Abba Eban talked the talk, but Menachem Begin walked the walk. And of necessity, the history of American successes in Arab-Israeli negotiations is really a record of finding ways to work with Israeli hawks.

Carter's initial meeting with Begin at the White House in July 1977 went much better than anyone anticipated. Despite Brzezinski's advice to be tough, even confrontational, Carter took the high road, perhaps partly to repair some of the damage caused during and after Rabin's earlier visit. Carter may also have been influenced by the counsel of Ambassador Samuel Lewis, who read Begin better than anyone in Washington. Lewis urged Carter to try "guile and honey" before he used a two-by-four. Lewis's advice was simple. Treat Begin with respect, which is what a prime minister who had been on the outside his entire life wanted, to see whether there was some chance of progress.

And Carter played it that way. The meeting, Lewis recalls, was a "holding action." Seemingly on almost every issue—settlements, the PLO, the applicability of UN Security Council Resolution 242 to the West Bank—gaps between American and Israeli views yawned. Yet Begin seemed amenable at least to convening a symbolic Geneva conference. The visit probably succeeded in persuading Begin that Carter respected him and treated him as an equal. But the settlement issue was already complicating their relationship, a bad omen of things to come. Shortly after Begin returned home, the Israeli cabinet conferred legal status on three settlements created under the previous government.[4]

"Did Begin trust you?" I asked Carter midway through our interview. "I don't think Begin trusted anybody, certainly at

Camp David," the president replied. At the same time, Carter continued, Begin could be seen as "recalcitrant but courageous." The trust issue defined itself not as the ability to trust in the openhearted manner in which Sadat related to Kissinger and Carter, but as the capacity to work together and, for Carter, to gain enough of Begin's confidence to play the mediator. So began the complicated and contradictory relationship between two leaders whose religious faith and love of precision in words drew them together, but whose views on the West Bank and settlements split them apart.

The middle ground where both came to cooperate would be the need to achieve peace between Egypt and Israel. Shortly after Begin's visit Carter expressed the view that if the United States gave Begin support, "he will prove to be a strong leader, quite different from Rabin." Unlike Brzezinski and others who saw the Israeli prime minister as a warmonger, Carter, in Sam Lewis's recollection, seemed convinced that Begin really wanted an Egyptian-Israeli peace. And Lewis had put his finger on a critical element of the Begin personality: having been on the run much of his life, living in the shadow of the Holocaust, the British, and David Ben-Gurion, Begin indeed desired the respect and support of the American president.

At times their relationship was a volatile one. According to Brzezinski, Begin never quite learned how to deal with Carter's polite yet tough nature. Cyrus Vance's courtly manner and honesty appealed to the prime minister and helped cool things down and keep the relationship stable. In the end, Carter and Begin found a way to work together on their own. The prime minister saw Carter as an honest man committed to Israel's security and to peace. And Carter respected Begin's courage. In another revealing Carteresque comment, the president told me, "Begin was the one I felt was the most courageous and gave up more, because it was much more difficult for him to come from where he had been for an agreement than it was for Sadat. I was just the innocent."

Innocent or not, neither the president nor his Middle East team performed well in the period between Begin's July visit and

Sadat's historic decision in November to visit Jerusalem. Begin had agreed to hold a conference in Geneva but expected nothing of substance to emerge. Carter believed otherwise: he wisely concluded that negotiating in advance with Begin over any set of principles would almost certainly fail, yet somehow he believed that he could wring something out of the Geneva effort. I suspect that Carter, having invested so much in this effort, had no alternative but to press on toward a peace conference. And while a conference would only cover bilateral negotiations, the president's advisors really weren't at all sure how these could be launched. Unlike Baker, who would spend nine months seeking the parties' agreement on these points, Carter had no such plan. International conferences are good either for launching talks or for concluding them. Carter's conception of Geneva was unlikely to do either.

Sadat Makes the Party Possible

As often happens when America approaches the Middle East with a poorly designed strategy—or worse, no strategy at all— the locals make other arrangements, sometimes for war, sometimes for peace. In August and September Anwar Sadat concluded that the Geneva train was moving far too slowly to suit him and that the passengers, especially the PLO and Syria, might very well keep Egypt from reaching its chosen destination on its terms. Begin, while certainly not thinking about giving up all of Sinai, was interested in meeting with Sadat. And so, using the Romanians and Moroccans as intermediaries, Israelis and Egyptians quietly felt their way toward secret contacts. Carter seemed weak and adrift.

The two meetings in Morocco between Sadat's deputy national security advisor Hassan Tuhaimi and Moshe Dayan in August and September reminded me of a similar situation in the early 1990s. Frustrated with the slow pace and publicity glare surrounding the Washington negotiations launched in the wake of the Madrid peace conference, Israelis and Palestinians, working through Norway, initiated secret contacts. Those covert meetings led not only to a mutual-recognition agreement between Israel and the PLO but also to substantive accord on a declaration of principles. A similar set of secret meetings between Israelis and Jordanians in 1994 produced the foundations of a peace treaty that would be negotiated without American involvement. Such secret contacts preceded every successful Arab-Israeli deal but as Oslo demonstrated did not guarantee success.

By the fall Sadat was at a crossroads. He knew America must play a critical role in Arab-Israeli peacemaking. For one thing, he had never received a commitment from Begin that he'd get the whole of Sinai; nor did a process of secret, direct Israeli-Egyptian negotiations take place. At no point did Sadat envision direct talks with Israel without a strong American presence. In fact, in August Sadat had secretly passed to Secretary Vance the draft of a peace treaty with instructions that it be shared with Israel only when they presented their draft to the Americans. From the beginning Sadat believed that the agreement could be achieved only under American auspices and within an American framework. Reaching out to Israel offered an independent way to hedge his bets and to determine where he and the Israelis stood.

It may well go down as one of the great ironies of Middle East history: a clumsy bid by Carter to lay the basis for a comprehensive accord generated a counterbid by Sadat that, within two years, turned into a separate peace. On October 1, 1977, the careless, ill-advised American effort, cosponsored with the Soviet Union, to arrange a substantive Geneva conference that neither Sadat nor Begin really wanted finally died of a huge paper cut inflicted by a Vance-inspired joint U.S.-USSR communiqué.

Secretary Vance had put considerable effort into working with the Soviets on a range of issues. Since May he had been developing a text of terms for U.S.-Soviet cochairmanship of a reconvened Geneva conference. It wasn't so much the text of the statement that caused the explosion as the timing, the lack of preparation, and the negative interpretation quickly assigned to it. Carter, already being hammered by the Jewish community for chasing the PLO, faced accusations of inviting the Russians back into the process after Sadat had kicked them out. Dayan, who happened to be in Washington, was given an advance copy. He didn't react, but giving the text to him ensured that his government would alert Congress and the pro-Israel community.

The October 1 joint U.S.-USSR communiqué was clearly less than met the eye. It did not open the way for Soviet domination of Middle East peacemaking, arranged by a sinister or naïve administration cabal. Instead, it was a logical effort to use the Russians as cover, much as Kissinger had done to convene the 1973 Geneva conference. Brzezinski told me that Geneva was intended as pressure on the Israelis. Bill Quandt recalled it as an effort to squeeze the PLO and the Syrians. The fact is that no one knew precisely what it was intended to do; nor did anyone anticipate the reaction, a sure prescription for things getting out of control. Vance and the U.S.-Soviet specialists may have had a purpose, but it wasn't carefully coordinated on the Arab-Israeli side. Moreover, Carter's press secretary and political advisors—Jody Powell, Stuart Eisenstadt, and Mark Siegel— all told me they had no knowledge of it.

On October 1 Jimmy Carter celebrated his fifty-third birthday. Rarely has a president, Jody Powell, Carter's press secretary, recalled, had a more "unpleasant birthday surprise."[5] Congress, the media, and the Jewish community unloaded on the administration. The communiqué, which did not include the ritual reference to UN Security Council Resolutions 242 and 338 but did include a new formulation of Palestinian legitimate rights, drove the Israelis crazy, providing Begin and Dayan with new leverage and ammunition. On October 4 Dayan met with Carter and the president's advisors in what Brzezinski described as a "humiliating" session, during which Dayan went at Carter "hammer and tongs." Carter pushed back plenty, asserting that Israel "was an obstacle to peace." At another point in the meeting Dayan, in a rare, perhaps unprecedented reference to his physical infirmity, shot back, "Mr. President, I only have one eye, but I'm not blind."[6] The Israeli foreign minister threatened to mount a campaign within the United States critical of the administration if the president continued with his current approach. At the same time Dayan showed a conciliatory side, offering to come to terms on Israel's participation in Geneva.

By late October the president had run out of hope and ideas. After the joint communiqué episode, he told me, his efforts "could have been over." Instead he turned to Sadat, in a handwritten letter in which he appealed for the Egyptian leader's help. Sadat recalled in his memoirs that Carter's letter started him thinking about a visit to Jerusalem.[7] If so, that thought process cannot be credited to American skill or competence.

Sadat had mixed feelings about the joint communiqué and Geneva. He liked the idea of comprehensiveness in principle, but he also began to wonder whether Geneva, with its endless focus on procedure, might not be a straitjacket for him. He knew the Soviets could never deliver the Israelis and might enhance Syria's veto power over him. At the same time Sadat saw, as Brzezinski recalled, a good deal of American "wavering" under Israeli pressure without any real strategy to advance Egyptian interests. Sadat also read Begin much better than did Carter. There wasn't a shred of evidence that Begin would agree to give anything before, during, or after Geneva and a great deal of evidence to the contrary. As Sam Lewis recalled, right up to Geneva, Carter believed he could make his game plan work "whether they [the Israelis] liked it or not." Sadat knew better. Bill Quandt graphically summed up Sadat's thinking about the Americans: "Oh my God, you don't have a strategy, and in fact you're being jerked around by the Israelis. This guy [Carter] is really weak, and the lobby has him by the short hairs, and now I've got to do something to break the impasse."

On November 9, 1977, Anwar Sadat announced his epochal plan to visit Jerusalem. Slow to see that the Geneva conference was a dead end, Carter and his team were also slow to recognize the opportunities that Sadat's announcement presented. Invested in a comprehensive approach, genuinely persuaded that Sadat would expose himself unnecessarily, and clearly irritated by being sidelined, Carter was initially less than supportive. Stuart Eisenstadt, Carter's chief domestic policy advisor, remembers standing outside the Oval Office right after Sadat's announcement with a "very upset" president, who wanted to criticize the Egyptian president publicly for risking "ripping apart" the possibility of a comprehensive settlement. Both Brzezinski and Quandt worried that Sadat had essentially "jumped" without a safety net; soon the administration would get its bearings and join Sadat's cheering section. Even today Carter has a hard time admitting that the remarkable solo initiative caught him by surprise. During my interview with him, the former president studiously declined to claim credit for anything, but offhandedly observed that he and Sadat worked out the Jerusalem visit together. There is no evidence to support this claim.

On reflection, Jimmy Carter really had two presidencies when it came to the Arab-Israeli issue. The first, from January to November 1977, was an impatient, noisy, and hyperactive drive to put together a peace conference for a comprehensive solution that not only failed but did so embarrassingly. The intensity that produced failure in 1977 brought forth a stunning accomplishment in the second phase, in 1978 and 1979. Indeed, Carter's persistence proved invaluable, for even after the Egyptian president's extraordinary visit to Jerusalem and address to the Knesset, Begin and Sadat could not bridge the chasm on their own. They needed an American engineer to construct a road they could safely cross.

Carter Convenes the Party

In the several months after Sadat's trip, the president struggled to make sense of the remade Middle East. Any hope that Egyptians and Israelis could or would negotiate on their own vanished quickly. The gaps on key issues, including the extent of Israel's withdrawal, the nature of normalization, and the

Palestinian issue and settlements were huge. Sadat was under terrible pressure from the Arabs to justify what he'd done. And Begin, by announcing additional settlement activity, didn't make Sadat's life any easier. That December the two met together at Ismailia in Egypt and made no progress. By January 1978 Sadat had pulled out of any bilateral negotiations with Israel.

Sadat visited Carter at Camp David in February, and the two presidents began work on a complicated strategy to corner Begin. But this effort got sidetracked as the administration became entangled in a deeply divisive fight with Congress that spring over arms sales to Saudi Arabia. Around that time Carter began to realize that he would have to downsize his dream of a comprehensive peace if he was to have any success at all. He seems to have come to this conclusion well before his national security advisor, secretary of state, or Middle East team did. When I asked Carter whether he knew Begin's or Sadat's bottom line before Camp David, in particular that Sadat might accept a separate deal with minimum cover for the Palestinians, he confidently replied, "Yeah, I knew." While there's no evidence to suggest that Carter had such a commitment from Sadat, he may have heard something to that effect during their February meetings at Camp David. Bill Quandt recalls a conversation with Carter that spring that the former president won't acknowledge to this day. Carter apparently said, "Sadat doesn't give a shit about the West Bank." From that point Carter began acting as if an Egyptian-Israeli deal were possible.

Even under the best of circumstances that deal was only a possibility, not an inevitability. What Carter had to determine was whether Sadat and Begin could meet each other halfway on an Egyptian-Israeli accord and at the same time link that accord to a framework for the Palestinians. Sadat needed cover, but how much did he need, and would Begin agree to give it to him?

In July a three-way foreign ministers meeting at Leeds Castle in Britain had pointed up the obvious: if Carter wanted answers to these questions, he'd have to risk convening the leaders to get them. Most of his advisors opposed such a move; even Carter described it as an "all or nothing gamble."[8] Mondale told me he feared "we were betting the presidency" and exposing Carter to ridicule if he failed. After all, Carter was contemplating the first presidential summit between an Arab leader and an Israeli leader who neither liked nor trusted each other. After laying out for me his advisors' objections to the summit, Carter added, "But I thought better."

Carter's Camp David gamble paid off because two strong leaders participated and made the hard decisions. They resolved the issues before them in a way that met their respective domestic political requirements. And finally an American strategy drove the process to a successful conclusion. The tenacity and toughness that Carter showed during his first year, his determination to make Arab-Israeli peace a top priority, and his ability to gain sufficient trust from Sadat and Begin now combined with the right call on timing. Instead of pushing for a comprehensive deal, Carter focused on taking one giant step. Both Begin and Sadat expressed eagerness to attend the Camp David summit, and they both were in control of their politics. They had bottom lines that could conceivably be reconciled, and although they had little trust in or regard for each other, in the end both willingly took that giant step with Carter.

Camp David, September 1978: Jimmy Carter's Show

For two weeks in eastern Maryland's Catoctin Mountains, Jimmy Carter revealed his best qualities. The shrillness, moralism, and tendency to confront had diminished, leaving in their place a wiser and shrewder but still persistent and determined president. To be sure, Carter had help. If Begin trusted Carter not enough, Sadat trusted Carter too much, and he wanted an agreement to the point perhaps of being unwilling to leave Camp David without one. Carter's advisory team—Saunders, Quandt, Lewis, Roy Atherton, and Herman Eilts, the U.S. ambassador to

Egypt, most veterans of the Kissinger era—came to the summit exceptionally well prepared and served Carter ably. The Israeli delegation included authoritative figures such as Moshe Dayan, Ezer Weizman, and Aharon Barak, former attorney general, soon to be appointed to Israel's supreme court, whose creativity and flexibility could be used to influence Begin.

Still, Camp David was Jimmy Carter's show. He drove the summit from beginning to end. Listen to those around him: "This was his from start to finish," Stuart Eisenstadt recalls. "Carter was both the coach and quarterback," Sam Lewis remembers. "He gets ninety-nine percent of the credit," Brzezinski told me. President Carter didn't just run the summit, Aharon Barak recalled on the twenty-fifth anniversary of Camp David. "He was involved in every detail."[9]

Carter's centrality to the success of the summit cannot be overemphasized. Without Begin and particularly without Sadat, the historic treaty would never have emerged. Without Carter, however, the summit would not have occurred in the first place. Carter decided to bring the Israelis and Egyptians together against the recommendation of many of his political advisors. During the intense planning that preceded the summit, Carter pressed for a detailed agreement rather than settling for a general declaration of principles or a vague framework for future negotiations. "I rejected that," he told me as our interview continued, "because I thought it was a onetime make-or-break opportunity. So I went down the river of no return." Most of the president's advisors assumed the parties simply could not reach accord on any major issue. At best, Bill Quandt recalls, they might get a joint statement from the leaders that could guide the negotiations.

Building on what he sensed (or knew) to be the possibility of a separate Egyptian-Israeli deal that also afforded Sadat minimum cover on the Palestinian issue, Carter struck out in a different direction from that recommended by his team. In their thinking, an Egyptian-Israeli accord could be dangled before Begin as a carrot to obtain concessions on the West Bank. Carter agreed with his team as far as the bilateral treaty was concerned, but thereafter his thinking angled toward another approach. Sadat told him on the summit's first day, Carter averred, that he wanted only two results from the summit: the Israelis off his territory and a comprehensive statement on Palestinian rights. Carter long had understood, apparently better than his advisors had, that no force on earth would drag West Bank concessions from Begin. A bilateral agreement grounded on such unrealistic hopes would die an early and ugly death. Carter's proposal, a treaty combined with the best cover possible for Sadat on the prickly Palestinian issue, made sense. The American president worked on that basis, ensuring that the Egyptian president got everything he needed on the first element and as much as possible on the second. Bill Quandt reminded me again that Carter's assessment may have been based not only on what he heard from Sadat on the summit's first day but as well on a statement he might have heard earlier: "If all I can get is my own peace, that's better than nothing."

Achieving that goal, however, required an effective agenda and appropriate tactics. After only two meetings Carter came to the bleak realization that the two leaders could not work together. Rather than acting as a facilitator, the role he expected to play, he would need to be a mediator and a driver. "The two men were totally incompatible," Carter affirmed during our interview. "They never met face-to-face in the last ten days at Camp David. I went back and forth between them."

From the very start Sadat desired an American-made proposal, which became the quid for the quo of full American control over direction of the conference. The concept, which Carter now labels the "single negotiating text," actually made its first appearance as a draft agreement prepared by Harold Saunders the night after the Leeds Castle talks ended. This document, which would eventually go through twenty-three drafts, set forth the basic terms of the summit's end products. The U.S. proposal, a framework agreement on Palestinian self-rule and principles to govern an Egyptian-Israeli accord, enabled the sides to define both differences and common ground. The Americans retained ownership of the draft, incorporating changes from both sides, then issuing a new revision. In this way, working on different levels with Egyptians and Israelis, the Americans controlled the process while keeping both sides invested as if they owned it.

By the end of the first week the Americans presented the text to both sides. The Israelis hated it; the Egyptians reacted less harshly, although not positively. Carter weathered these initial reactions, largely to show that he would not allow either side to jerk him around. The American draft became the vehicle through which the parties achieved their substantive agreement. At the same time Carter introduced his own special project, a set of core elements to guide negotiations for the Egyptian-Israeli peace treaty. Working directly with Sadat, and employing Dayan, Weizman, and Barak to overcome Begin's objections, Carter found enough common ground and creative ambiguity to lay the basis of this first accord between two nations that had regarded each other as implacable enemies.

Carter's decision to hold the summit represented a very personal as well as a geopolitical gamble—a decision to trust Menachem Begin, even though the Israeli prime minister clearly mistrusted him. The trust gap did not keep the two men from working together. Jody Powell believed that there was "a little bit of Begin in Carter and Carter in Begin." Sam Lewis, whose ambassadorial duties included the difficult task of explaining Begin to Carter, believed that the president saw in Begin an honest man rough around the edges. Stuart Eisenstadt added that Carter empathized with Begin's Holocaust background and that his primarily generous treatment of the Israeli leader made Begin "more flexible than advertised." Their relationship would be strained and would never quite recover from a critical misunderstanding over settlements on September 16, the last night of the summit. Carter believed Begin had agreed to an open-ended freeze on building new West Bank settlements, whereas Begin claimed the freeze would last only three months. Even that shock to their relationship did not prevent them from finding compromise solutions leading to the peace treaty the following year.

In sum, Carter got the job done with persistence and toughness. He treated both sides equitably from his deeply felt moralism, and he convinced both sides to take an ownership stake in the long, laborious process. Carter clearly had earned Sadat's trust, could work with Begin, and could stand up to both when necessary. Brzezinski believes Carter prevailed on each to accept ideas they initially rejected. Unlike Nixon and Ford, Carter never threatened to reduce or cut off assistance, although he came very close during an incident involving Sadat. On the eleventh day of the summit the Egyptian president threatened to leave, after Dayan told him that Israel would make no further concessions.

Carter's reaction, detailed in his own memoirs and in Brzezinski's, mixed reassurance and steely resolve. He threatened to end the U.S.-Egyptian relationship and his own personal friendship with Sadat if Sadat left. Carter also promised him that he would not hold Sadat to any of the concessions he had made if Begin would not agree to his.

> *I was stricken, because Sadat had been my friend, personally. I didn't know what to do; Sadat was leaving, I couldn't do anything about it. And I went in a back room and I knelt down and prayed, and I asked God to help me. And then I walked over to Sadat's cabin, and he had all of his suitcases out in front, and all of his aides were there ready to load his suitcases into the helicopter. And I went in to his room, and I told everybody else to get out, and Sadat and I stood with our noses almost touching, and I told Sadat that he had betrayed me, and betrayed his own people, and if he left, our friendship was severed forever, and the proper relationship between the United States and Egypt would be dealt a severe blow. And he went over in a corner by himself and he came back and said, "I'll stay."*[10]

Such episodes only emphasize the point that Camp David verged on the edge of complete breakdown almost until the last moment. At one point, with hope of compromise apparently slipping away, Carter asked Quandt to draft a "failure speech," which would have placed most of the blame for the summit's failure on Begin.[11] Indeed, the principals struggled long into the last night of the summit before reaching final accord. On September 17 the parties concluded two agreements: a framework dealing with the Palestinian issue on the West Bank and Gaza, and a detailed formula for achieving an Egyptian-Israeli peace treaty. The parties gave themselves a ninety-day period, ending on December 17, to turn the framework into reality. Reality slapped back at them with painful rapidity.

Monday Morning Blues: Toward a Peace Treaty

It is difficult to describe the feeling of accomplishment after the successful conclusion of any meeting dedicated to the goal of reaching agreement between Arabs and Israelis. In the aftermath of the 1991 Madrid conference and the interim Israeli-Palestinian accords we helped broker in 1997 and 1998, I experienced an extraordinary sense of satisfaction and relief that we had actually achieved anything, anything at all. Carter realized objectives of far greater consequence. No matter the significance of the achievement, however, a sense of letdown creeps into your thinking within days, darkening the moment of satisfaction, replacing it with the somber reality that you have come only one step on a very long road.

To say the least, the onset of this Monday-morning syndrome is very deflating. Getting Arabs and Israelis to implement what they agreed to do, let alone convincing them to take a perilous next step, is often a brutal exercise. Domestic political combat takes a toll, as leaders seek to explain and rationalize the tough choices they've made. So too, American leaders have difficulty sustaining or re-creating the urgency and focus of an intense shuttle or summit. Of necessity, they turn their attention to other matters, allowing aides to clean up the details.

This is precisely the problem Jimmy Carter faced in the wake of his historic accomplishment at Camp David. He was in a hurry to expedite the process, yet Begin and Sadat, under pressure from various constituencies, seemed less so. Sadat wanted Sinai back, but he also needed movement on the Palestinian issue to justify what he'd done. Moreover, an enormous amount of negotiating remained to be done, including setting the timing of Israeli withdrawal from Sinai, deciding when the normalization process would begin, determining how Palestinian elections would be handled, and in effect defining the relationship between this issue and Egyptian-Israeli peace.

Moreover, in the Middle East one step forward always means several steps back. Begin, eager to demonstrate that he hadn't agreed to a settlement freeze, wanted to prove it on the ground. In May 1977 there were roughly eighty settlements on the West Bank beyond the green line, with a total population of about 11,000, not including about 40,000 Israelis who had moved into the Israeli-controlled portions of East Jerusalem. Begin's election had really accelerated an existing trend rather than creating an explosion of new settlements.[12] But even talking about settlement activity and Jerusalem undermined the Palestinian dimension of the Camp David accords and created additional pressure on Sadat. To add to his worries, the November Arab summit in Baghdad threatened, if Sadat signed a peace with Israel, to expel Egypt from the Arab League and move its headquarters out of Cairo.

By the end of 1978 Carter confronted the very real prospect that neither Camp David framework would or could be implemented. Ten days of intense talks at Blair House in October, including personal participation by the president, did not advance matters; nor did a December trip to the region by Secretary Vance. The Americans, Egyptians, and Israelis were still hashing out a draft text of a treaty, but many issues remained open, and the self-imposed December 17 deadline came and went with no agreement. Meanwhile Begin had adopted a minimalist view of Palestinian autonomy, which strained the U.S.-Israeli relationship, already stretched because of the continuing flap over West Bank settlements. In Cairo, Sadat was becoming increasingly critical of the entire process. Still, the ever-determined Carter made clear that he would continue to press for agreement and that Israel should be prepared to receive the bulk of the pressure. Brzezinski recalls that before Vance's December trip to the Middle East, Carter asserted that the secretary should lean on Israel, even though doing so might cost him the election and Jewish support. Shortly after Christmas the president confided to his diary that he would "not postpone the difficult discussions, even though they were costly to us in domestic politics."[13]

Carter's Middle East clock began to tick faster under the pressure of events in the region. Increasing unrest in Iran culminated in the overthrow of the shah in February 1979 and his replacement by an Islamic regime under the rule of Ayatollah Ruhollah Khomeini. Khomeini's rise, a clear threat to American interests, generated new urgency. Carter also recognized political realities at home. Although he had taken heat from the pro-Israel lobby, he realized that an Egyptian-Israeli peace might help him domestically. Tough private moments and angry talk notwithstanding, he did not want to pick a fight with Begin that would undermine his capacity to score a badly needed diplomatic triumph. Even in 1979 it was clear that Carter faced a reelection campaign with uncertain prospects; later he would have to overcome a challenge from within the Democratic Party by Senator Ted Kennedy.

In January, Defense Secretary Harold Brown went to the region, reporting that success in achieving Arab-Israeli peace would strengthen America's strategic position. The following month, as the shah fled Tehran, deadlock at a three-way U.S., Egyptian, and Israeli ministerial conference had convinced Carter that only his personal intervention could resolve the remaining issues blocking an Egyptian-Israeli treaty. After inconclusive (but slightly encouraging) meetings with Begin in the first few days of March, Carter decided on a risky but necessary course: to conclude the treaty by a presidential shuttle to Cairo and Jerusalem. Hedging his bets, he sent Brzezinski to give Sadat a "political" message. Carter won't or can't recall that fact now, but according to Brzezinski, the message he delivered from one president to another said, "If you don't help me, I'm going to be finished in America."

In his memoirs Carter writes that his decision was an "act of desperation." Vance described it as a "breathtaking gamble" and "an act of political courage."[14] Most of his political advisors were worried. Carter told me that he encountered their "most vehement opposition." His advisors, with the exception of Hamilton Jordan and Brzezinski, warned him that it would be a "devastating political blow if I ostentatiously went all the way across the world to be rejected." On balance, even though Sadat had assured him he'd do everything possible to make his mission succeed, Carter took another leap in the dark, as he had six months earlier in bringing Begin and Sadat to Camp David. But key issues remained to be resolved when Air Force One departed Washington for Cairo on March 7.

Stopping first in the Egyptian capital, Carter essentially received Sadat's proxy to negotiate the final terms. Carter talked about strengthening the U.S.-Egyptian relationship once the treaty came into force. Notionally he planned to fly to Israel, get Begin's agreement, and then hold double signing ceremonies in Jerusalem and Cairo.

Carter's brief visit to Egypt was thus easy, ceremonial, and in his word, "delightful." But the Israel stop must have seemed like a forty-eight-hour visit to his dentist. Begin was determined to give Carter a tough time, to fight for every last issue, and to drive home the image of a tough-minded Israeli prime minister resisting American pressure. Begin told Carter on arrival there could be no treaty signing without extensive cabinet and Knesset debate. Things got worse the next day during the two leaders' meetings with their full delegations. Begin rejected Sadat's proposals on treaty obligations, Egyptian liaison officers in Gaza, and the idea of granting autonomy first to Palestinians living in Gaza. Later that day Begin told Carter that Vance should return to Cairo and share his ideas with Sadat, and if everything could be worked out, perhaps the treaty could be signed in a matter of weeks. Because this was Carter's first visit to Israel as president, he visited Yad Vashem, which Carter recalled made him more understanding of Begin's mindset, and he addressed the Israeli cabinet and Knesset.

None of this seemed to matter much. The next day Begin informed Vance that there would be no more flexibility from Israel. Agriculture minister Ariel Sharon reinforced this position, declaring that Egypt wouldn't be allowed into Gaza under any circumstances. The prime minister then announced that the talks were over and handed Vance a joint communiqué that reported some progress had been made. Bill Quandt recalls that this example of Israeli chutzpah was apparently more than Carter could handle. The president instructed his staff to prepare for departure to Washington.

Carter's implicit threat to leave, to borrow Sam Lewis's elegant phrasing, "scared the shit out of the Israelis." Begin may not have been intimidated, but sitting around the conference room after the failed Vance-Begin meeting, Dayan and several other ministers began to worry about the consequences of sending the president of the United States packing without an agreement. After all, had Carter not come on a mission designed to help Israel achieve what it wanted most—a peace treaty with the Arab world's largest and most powerful country?

The absurdity and seriousness of the situation must have impressed itself on Dayan. Only two issues now barred the path to an accord. Dayan secured Begin's permission to see Vance, with whom the defense minister had become close. The two spent several hours developing possible fixes, which Carter and Begin agreed to the next morning.[15] With success in hand, Carter prepared to leave for the airport and Cairo—but not before suffering one final aggravation. The president recalls being trapped in an elevator with Begin—they extricated themselves by climbing up a ladder after the doors were jacked open by a six-foot crowbar. En route to Cairo Carter received the first congratulatory message from an unlikely well-wisher, Saudi Arabia's King Fahd. Speaker of the House Tip O'Neill added his kudos: "You're not just a deacon anymore, but a pope."[16] On March 26, two weeks later, as Begin had predicted, he, Carter, and Sadat signed the Israeli-Egyptian peace treaty in Washington.

Domestic Politics: "To Hell with It"

My interview with Carter almost concluded, I asked him what I had expected to be the toughest and most sensitive question: "What role did domestic politics play in your Arab-Israeli diplomacy?" I shouldn't have worried, for he spoke openly, without the lightest trace of hesitation or reluctance.

"I was thoroughly familiar, obviously with AIPAC, and with its enormous influence," Carter began. "It almost totally dominated the Congress and was a major influence in the White House and State Department. Formidable. And there were very distinguished members of the Senate, like Hubert Humphrey, who would come to the Oval Office and warn me of the adverse political consequences of calling for a Palestinian homeland or negotiating in a way that might result in Israel's withdrawal from the occupied territories. I understood that, and I just finally said to hell with it. I did what I think was best, and I think that if that gets a permanent peace for Israel, they will forgive. I lost support for the first time in history, certainly since 1948, from the Jewish community in 1980."

Jimmy Carter's answer, tinged with some sadness and more than a trace of resentment and frustration, seemed a true reflection of his views from the vantage point of thirty years' distance. When I saw him in early 2006, his latest book, *Palestine: Peace Not Apartheid*, hadn't yet been published, but it would only embroil him more deeply with a Jewish community with which, to use a word of my daughter's generation, he still had "issues."

Carter's rumination captured only part of the reality of his behavior and actions as president. By bringing Begin and Sadat to Camp David and then traveling to the Middle East in pursuit of the peace treaty, courting a real possibility of failure and embarrassment, he took enormous political risks. Given his tendency to put the onus for possible failure on Begin, he invited a confrontation with both Israelis and American Jews. Begin's policies, particularly in regard to settlements, doubtless ran counter to American interests, but Carter also brought on himself much of the domestic opposition, through missteps, misjudgments, and a tone-deafness that created needless tensions and confrontation. The missionary never seemed to be able to find his message or give a sermon that American Jews and the American public at large could hearken to or believe.

Part of Carter's problem with the Jewish community was the same one he faced with the entire nation: he was an unknown and had a hard time communicating. Ed Sanders, a former AIPAC president and White House liaison to the Jewish community, described Carter as an "unknown born-again Baptist from Atlanta," where the Jewish community numbered about forty thousand. Sanders joked, "I got more Jews on my block." Stuart Eisenstadt recalled that on the campaign trail, despite the candidate's delivery of some red-meat pro-Israel speeches, Jews manifested great suspicion of this "born-again" Christian. My own father echoed this feeling. At a fund-raiser in Cleveland, he approached Carter and, to the consternation of his security detail, put his hands around the governor's neck, saying, "I'll support you, but if you ever let Israel down, I'll never forget it."

Jody Powell believes that the Washington cocktail circuit had trouble adjusting to a "devout Southern Baptist from a small rural town in South Georgia" and the advent of his "Georgia boys." Soon after Carter took office, Herblock, the *Washington Post*'s nationally syndicated cartoonist, published a humorous but biting cartoon titled "Dog Patch on the Potomac". The illustration depicted the Carters as characters from Al Capp's *L'il Abner* comic strip.

Carter's plain-speaking, think-out-loud style didn't help matters. Mark Siegel, deputy assistant to the president for political affairs, who resigned after the Saudi F-15 sale, remembers the impact of Carter's Palestinian-homeland comment—it turned out to be a "red-hot, red-button term." Siegel claims the president simply did not realize the extent to which his rhetoric "would inflame." Things got blown way out of proportion. By the second call to the White House, according to Siegel, Carter was being accused of supporting the creation of a Palestinian state headed by Yasser Arafat.

After the Clinton, Massachusetts, remarks, Hamilton Jordan apparently asked Siegel to function as an informal "eyes and ears" to the Jewish community. Siegel did more than that: in June, Jordan sent a Siegel-drafted memo to the president, describing how nervous and suspicious the community was about Carter and calling for a number of steps the administration could take to build confidence. "If the American Jewish community openly opposed your approach and policy toward a Middle East settlement," a key sentence read, "you would lack the flexibility and credibility you will need to play a constructive role in bringing the Israelis and Arabs together."[17]

Siegel, through Jordan, offered sound advice, but it didn't seem to make much of an impact. The blunder of the October 1 joint U.S.-USSR communiqué finally prompted a change in decision-making, allowing for better coordination between policy and politics and laying the foundation for an outreach campaign to the Jewish community that depended on Mondale to play a key role. Still, according to Siegel, Carter looked on any effort at ethnic political outreach as "pandering and patronizing." In fact, had Sadat not undertaken his solo initiative—which forced Carter to invest in, rather than to confront, Begin—relations between Carter and the Jewish community, let alone with the Israelis, could have gotten much worse.

Part of the explanation was Jimmy Carter's philosophy of governing, which he seemed to believe should be as detached as possible from running for office or securing reelection. Just about everyone I talked to confirmed Carter's "to hell with it" approach. Stuart Eisenstadt made clear that it wasn't confined to the Middle East but reached across the board, including Carter's decision to ram the contentious Panama Canal treaty through the Senate during his first term. Carter persuaded himself that if you solved any problem "the right way," you'd reap the reward, but he wasn't "going to play the typical political game." Even after the joint-communiqué fiasco, Siegel recalls, Carter still believed that "domestic politics shouldn't be a part of the international foreign policy decision-making process." Even though Carter personally identified with Jewish suffering during the Holocaust, Siegel suggests, he initially rejected the idea of creating a Holocaust Memorial Council as "pandering." Brzezinski, whom critics labeled as the dark force behind the president's tough posture on Israel and Begin, admired Carter precisely because, as he told me, the president was "less inclined to accommodate or cater to domestic views." Indeed, Brzezinski often found himself pushing on an open door, which swung his way more in the early years of the term, but not always, as Carter's inclination to invest in Begin and a success in the Middle East demonstrated.

Stuart Eisenstadt discerns another dimension in Carter's stubbornness and rigidity. The president's advisor recalls that Carter was often mystified by the Jewish community's opposition, because he really believed that American Jews should trust him and that he had given them no reason not to. His conviction that he knew what was best, and above all was always doing the right thing, meant that others should see it his way as well. This moral rectitude, unaccompanied by any sense of doubt, made Carter determined but tone-deaf, eager to talk, but not necessarily to listen, to those who saw domestic politics as an inescapable reality. Mondale summed it up best: Carter felt that standing against the need to do the right thing "were politicians who were unaware or unwilling to accept the burden of higher service to the country who had to be humored and worked with on the side."

In the end, to get an Israeli-Egyptian treaty, Carter did precisely that: he adjusted to the hard, less noble realities of both Arab-Israeli and American politics. In the Middle East he lowered his sights from the unattainable (a comprehensive peace) to the attainable (a bilateral peace treaty). Instead of confronting Begin, he invested in him and banked on Sadat's being willing and able to provide the kind of cover on the Palestinian issue that Begin could accept. The missionary accomplished only part of his mission; he wouldn't have succeeded otherwise.

By the fall of 1979 domestic electoral considerations had begun to figure more prominently in Carter's calculations. Missteps continued to alienate the Israelis and the American Jewish community, including UN ambassador Andrew Young's unauthorized meeting with a PLO representative and the administration's vote first for and then against a tough UN Security Council resolution criticizing Israeli settlements. But most of Carter's high-profile thinking out loud on Arab-Israeli issues would have to wait for his postpresidency.

Like Kissinger, Carter had invested an enormous amount and accomplished something quite historic in the Middle East, but neither the region nor the American political calendar could accommodate much more. By 1980 he'd run out of both tiny and giant steps. The Camp David accords talked about resolving issues such as elections and Palestinian self-government, but the autonomy negotiations they called for were stymied by the most fundamental obstacles. Neither Jordan, nor the PLO, nor West Bankers and Gazans would join, putting Egypt in the untenable position of representing Palestinians. Meanwhile the Israeli and Egyptian conceptions of autonomy were quite far apart. Carter had little reason to invest in talks that wouldn't work and that could only provoke tensions with Israel. The choice of Robert Strauss as negotiator, the tough-talking Texan lawyer with a close relationship to Israel, indicated that Carter's advisors wanted to put some distance between the president and the Middle East. That Strauss left by year's end to return to Carter's reelection campaign further demonstrated the new priority of politics over policy.

At the same time the region's political center of gravity shifted both geographically and strategically. On November 4, 1979, Iranian students seized the American embassy in Tehran, taking hostage fifty-three Americans. At year's end Soviet troops invaded neighboring Afghanistan in support of an embattled puppet regime. The two crises morphed into a daily political and psychological nightmare. The president pledged to halt travel on behalf of his renomination campaign against Kennedy until Iran released the captive diplomats and Marines. But as Kennedy's political strength mounted and CBS anchor Walter Cronkite continued to end each night's news broadcast with the elapsed number of days since the embassy takeover, Carter was forced to abandon his promise under a shower of ridicule and anger.

Ridicule gave way to consternation and horror when an obviously exhausted president delivered an unprecedented early-morning address to the nation describing the failure of an ambitious hostage rescue mission on April 25, 1980, which had come to grief amid death and flaming wreckage of American helicopters at a secret desert site in Iran. Meanwhile the Soviet invasion of Afghanistan seemed to undermine Carter's pronouncements earlier in his term that Americans could begin to set aside their fears of Communism. By the summer Carter's image of competence and credibility lay in ruins. And the Arab-Israeli issue, so central to his presidential mission and legacy only a year before, all but vanished from sight. Ronald Reagan's crushing defeat of Carter in November would spell an end to serious American peacemaking efforts in the region for almost a decade.

Ezer Weizman—Israel's seventh president, former minister of defense, Camp David negotiator, and iconoclast par excellence—once said to me that there were two guys he'd never want to meet in a dark alley: Jimmy Carter and James Baker. Still, in his memoirs Weizman asserted that no American president had helped Israel as much as Jimmy Carter.[18] In 1981 Weizman's assertion would likely have started an argument in any Tel Aviv or Haifa café. Many Israelis might have preferred Harry Truman, for recognizing the Jewish state in 1948, or Richard Nixon, for ordering the emergency arms airlift during the Yom Kippur War. And yet, in terms of overall Arab-Israeli peace, perhaps Weizman made the right choice. Peace between Egypt and Israel—even a cold peace—still stands as an extraordinary accomplishment. Sadat and Begin made it possible, but Carter's single-minded effort delivered it. Carter's character came heavy-laden with moralism, naïve idealism, and self-righteousness, but fortunately that persona also included tenacity, toughness, and a grasp of timing that brought success in this historic endeavor. Whatever his detractors say about him today, he deserves enormous credit for what he accomplished then. The 1979 Egyptian-Israeli peace treaty was an accomplishment that remains unmatched by his presidential successors. Indeed, it would take another twelve years for an American president and his immensely talented secretary of state to chalk up another success in Arab-Israeli diplomacy.

Chapter Six

James Baker:
Negotiator

"Aaron, I was scammed." I couldn't believe what I was hearing. James Addison Baker III, the guy who left Arabs and Israelis checking their wallets after every Middle East trip, had been taken in by Sacha Baron Cohen, alias Ali G, alias Borat, alias gonzo rapper who devoured his victims on HBO in a frenzy of comedic shtick and left them confused, conned, and looking ridiculous.

Months earlier my daughter Jen, a fan of both Baker and Ali G, nearly brought the house down one night, yelling for me to turn on the television immediately. Baker was about to become Ali G's latest victim. Sure enough, there he was trying to answer Ali G's ridiculous questions. If Iran and Iraq both start with the letter I, why can't you have the same policy toward the two? Baker played along. And Jen made me promise I'd ask him how he got sucked in to begin with.

AG: Ain't they the same thing though?
JB: No, they're two different countries, Iraq and Iran.
AG: Do you think it would be a good idea if one of them changed they name to make it very different sounding from the other one?
JB: No, because "Iran" doesn't sound like "Iraq".
AG: Ain't there a real danger that someone

> **like gives a message over the radio saying
> "Bomb Ira..." and the geezer don't hear it
> properly and bomb Iran rather than Iraq?**
> JB: No danger.
> **AG: How do you make countries do stuff you
> want?**
> JB: You deal with carrots and sticks.
> **AG: But what country is gonna want carrots
> even if there is like a million carrots you be
> given over to them?**

"The guy came in wearing a dark blue suit and asked to set up in the conference room," Baker began. "He'd sent us a letter about doing an interview to educate the youth in Britain about American politics. But when I walked in, he'd changed into his jester suit. You know, the hip-hopper. 'Great respect, great respect, me mon.'" Baker was now doing his best Ali G impersonation. "I could have done what Marlin Fitzwater did and walked out. But when you're caught, you're caught." Could it be, as I listened to Baker's sorry tale, that the consummate insider and deal-maker, and arguably the most effective secretary of state since Henry Kissinger, was losing his feel for the con?

But my doubts were dispelled during my hour-long interview with Baker at his Houston law firm, Baker-Botts, which had seen several generations of Bakers come and go. I'd last seen him a year earlier, in Jerusalem at the tenth anniversary of Rabin's assassination, where he'd led the American delegation. Baker had always struck me as ageless; the hair was now a little whiter and gray. But he was trim, tan, and as always well tailored in a dark blue suit, pale green tie, and monogrammed shirt; his penetrating blue eyes could bore right through you. He could have been back on the secretary of state's aircraft, diet Dr Pepper in hand, taking off from Andrews Air Force Base on any of the nine trips that it took to pull off the historic Madrid peace conference in October 1991.

The interview was vintage Baker, carefully prepared, laced

with humor, and above all guarded. I had my five T's of diplomacy; Baker had his five P's of life, imparted to him by his father: "Prior preparation prevents poor performance." Preparation was clear here as well. Baker had seen my questions in advance and had meticulously prepared for them, referring me back to his published memoirs as secretary of state whenever possible.

Baker was careful in a way that Kissinger and Carter were not, particularly in his reluctance to talk about the current policies of the Bush administration. I was there to talk about history, not about Iraq, but Iraq was obviously much on his mind. In June 2006 Baker and Lee Hamilton were deep into their congressionally mandated Iraq Study Group. When I asked him about Iraq, he wouldn't talk about it on the record. As a close and loyal friend of the president's father, he wasn't about to engage in a lot of freewheeling criticism of the son's policies, certainly not in front of me, and not at a time when he'd signed up to produce recommendations by year's end.

And yet I understood from conversations we'd had that Baker was not at all comfortable with George W. Bush's Iraq policy or his approach to the Arab-Israeli issue. If you wanted Baker's views on Iraq, all you had to do was pull out his 1995 memoir *The Politics of Diplomacy*. In a couple of pages of prescient analysis eight years before the American invasion, he'd laid out the reasons why the first President Bush had decided not to march to Baghdad. Baker's own analysis, based on common sense and uncommonly good judgment, foreshadowed with a terrifying accuracy the consequences of Bush 43's fateful decision.

During our interview the subject came up only once. I asked Baker about relationships between presidents and secretaries of state. He certainly had a unique one with Bush 41. "I was the alter ego of the boss," he told me. "He'd back me up even if I was wrong. Look at poor Colin. It's almost tragic. I told him his first year, 'Colin, you need to go in there and say "Sir, this is not what I signed up for," ' because they needed him a lot more than he needed them. His problem was spelled D-I-C-K."

Baker had the negotiator's mindset, a tendency to see the

world of power and politics in terms of problems to be solved, managed, or deferred. Maybe it was the lawyer in him, or maybe the deal-maker, or maybe it was just the plain commonsense realization that American power and interests are multifaceted and complex and that the instruments needed to advance them require a careful, deliberate adjustment depending on circumstance. Not every problem can be solved, but in Baker's world you didn't want to make them worse and in the process screw up American interests. Baker seemed to subscribe to the diplomatic equivalent of the Hippocratic oath, "Above all do no harm," and always leave yourself a way out.

Baker was not a grand strategist, lacking Kissinger's view of the world and Carter's global moralism. But he recognized opportunities when he saw them, and as he told Prime Minister Shamir during their first meeting, principles are fine, but if you're going to succeed in carrying them out, you need to be pragmatic. In 1989, according to *Fortune* magazine, a Nexus search revealed 390 hits of post-1980 news stories and articles in which Baker's name appeared within thirty words of "pragmatic" or "pragmatism."[1] If pragmatism has to be based on real-world evidence—as William James, pragmatism's intellectual father, argued—then Baker was one pragmatic guy. When it came to the Middle East, Baker was cautious and deliberate and required real-world validation that American efforts could actually make a difference and that he could make a deal. The art of successful politics, he'd say to anyone who would listen, was how to exceed expectations. Never overcommit or overextend. If you fail, you're a goat; if you succeed, having not raised hopes, not only won't you disappoint, you'll be a hero.

Baker's single contribution to Arab-Israeli diplomacy—the Madrid peace conference—was very much an exercise in low expectations and surprise diplomacy. Still lowballing his own accomplishments in his latest book, *Work Hard, Study...and Keep Out of Politics*, Baker wrote that Madrid's real significance was that it happened at all.[2] But part of Baker's routine was a kind of occupational modesty that protected him against seeming to invest too much and that only highlighted his success when it came. Madrid surprised almost everyone in the press corps that had been traveling with Baker for almost nine months straight. I jokingly warned Tom Friedman, who was then the *New York Times*'s diplomatic correspondent, not to lose sight of the bigger picture or be blinded by Baker's low-key style. Unless he was careful, I told him, without much warning a ten-ton safe would fall out of the sky on his head.

When the safe fell, Baker's modesty notwithstanding, it had a consequential impact. Madrid was the first American-brokered success in the Middle East in twelve years. For the first time ever Israelis, Syrians, Jordanians, and particularly Palestinians sat at the same table and launched bilateral negotiations that broke taboos, legitimized Palestinians, and continued for the better part of a decade. The Madrid conference was not as significant as Kissinger's disengagement diplomacy or Carter's Egyptian-Israeli treaty. In almost ten subsequent rounds of talks in Washington that stretched on until December 1992, it resulted in no formal agreements. Some argue that it provided cover for the emerging secret Israeli-PLO dialogue known as the Oslo process; others suggest that its unproductive public, formal character pushed Israelis and Palestinians into that secret channel.

But there's no point in overclaiming. Baker didn't. He understood that the presence of Shamir, Assad, and Arafat (who was pulling Palestinian strings behind the curtain) made the chance of a breakthrough slim. That Baker paid little attention to the Madrid negotiations until Rabin defeated Shamir in Israeli elections in June 1992 was all you needed to know. At best, Madrid was intended as a stage-setter, an investment trap to keep Arabs and Israelis at the table in the first Bush administration and, with luck and reelection, to provide opportunities for serious breakthroughs in the second.

How Baker put it together—by exercising toughness, timing, tenacity, making it a top priority, and gaining enough trust to play his broker's role—contains important lessons for any future American success. Madrid also represents a fascinating chapter in the U.S.-Israeli story. Baker's success in gaining enough of Shamir's confidence to get him to Madrid, and yet to stand up to Israel on its settlement policies in a way no other administration had done previously, would contribute directly to Shamir's defeat in June 1992. This toughness, linked to an actual strategy to get something done, has not been seen in America's policies since Kissinger and Carter. And it would vanish with Bush's defeat in his 1992 reelection bid. In this sense James Baker was a wasted asset. He would never make this claim, but had Bush been re-elected, Baker, working with Rabin, a man he admired and re-spected, would probably have brokered at least one final deal either between Israel and Syria or between Israel and the Palestinians.

The Road to Madrid: Mr. Toad's Wild Ride

Working for Baker was exhilarating and fun. As I watched him do his Ali G act, I remembered why. It took him six months to get my name right and stop calling me Andy, but once you be-came part of the small team he'd put together on a specific issue, particularly on the Middle East, where he'd log more miles and hours than on any other issue, you got to see him up close. And what you saw was one smart, tough, colorful, and at times bril-liant negotiator. You realized he was using you for what you knew, and you couldn't get really close, but you were motivated nonetheless because you knew he was serious and had the presi-dent's confidence, a reputation for getting things done, and the respect of both Arabs and Israelis.

Baker was also a showman, an actor who sharpened his for-midable negotiating skills through humor, emotional reactions, and a tough, no-nonsense persona. He was physical and would grab you hard by the neck or shoulder, like a football coach in practice. He was earthy, with well-timed and well-chosen exple-tives to make his points and a colorful mix of Texas expressions to keep anyone off balance. What did Baker mean, the Israelis and Palestinians would ask me, by "pissing in high cotton"? I didn't know either. Hanan Ashrawi recalls the Baker meetings where the air was heavy with a combination of Texas-Palestine, or Texatine or Palexas, as she described it.[3] The PLO had enough trouble understanding basic diplomacy, she told me—imagine their difficulty with Baker's expression "Don't let the dead cat die on your doorstep." This phrase, whose origins Baker himself can't trace, means roughly, "If the process collapses, make sure the other side takes the fall." Indeed, dead cat diplomacy was one of Baker's central tactical instruments in getting Assad, Shamir, and the PLO to agree on terms of reference for Madrid.

The kicker of all Texas phrases occurred in a late April meeting between Baker and Hafez al-Assad, a man who loved to debate and to utter the words that went with it. The Syrian president was verbally off on some peripheral point, and Baker wanted to get him back on track. You know, Mr. President, he said, if a "bullfrog had wings, it wouldn't scrape its ass on the ground." Ed Djerejian, our ambassador to Syria, was so stunned, he stuck his hand in a bowl of hummus; Gamal Helal, our ace Arabic interpreter, told Baker he couldn't translate it into English, let alone Arabic. (Gamal would later tell me Baker had initially used "balls instead of ass," but that wouldn't have made much difference to Assad.) Meanwhile, the Syrian president was pressing for an explanation. Baker recovered by coming up with something like, if the dog hadn't stopped running, he would have caught the rabbit. Neither Baker nor Assad, I assure you, had a clue what that meant.[4]

Baker was a hunter, and sometimes I sensed that he looked at the road to Madrid as a chase, with Arabs and Israelis as quarry, to be pursued and bagged. I'm sure they often felt this way. The first time around, in 1989 and 1990, Baker had failed to put together an Israeli-Palestinian dialogue largely because, in his view, Shamir had walked away from his own initiative. And Baker was determined not to let Shamir slip away again. Early on *Time* magazine had done a profile on Baker and followed him on one of his wild-turkey shoots in west Texas. "The trick," Baker said, "is in getting them where you want them, on your terms."[5] I wasn't at all sure whether "them" meant the turkeys or the Israelis.

I saw this competitive edge and hunter's mindset during one of the early Baker trips. We were several hours out of Andrews Air Force Base, dreading the work that had to be done before we arrived in Tel Aviv in about ten hours. A large black fly had boarded the aircraft with us, seemingly determined to get to Israel. Looking for any excuse not to work, we were equally determined to stop it from reaching its destination. During one of my particularly futile and pathetic swipes, Baker walked by, en route to a press briefing at the back of the plane. Hours later, having tired of the fly, I was writing an arrival statement on a yellow legal pad. I sensed a presence and then a hand on my shoulder. As I turned, the hand opened and dropped one really dead ugly black fly on the pad in front of me. Without a word, Baker turned and left, his unspoken words hanging in midair: "Boys, that's how we catch flies in Texas. Don't you try to do it now."

Baker was tough, calculating, and determined, not just in catching flies but in hooking Assad as well. In a late-night meeting in mid-October in his suite at the Sheraton in Damascus, I saw the competitive edge again, this time in Baker the fisherman. Baker believed that in order to catch Shamir, he had to reel in Assad first, which essentially meant getting the Syrians to say yes to the terms of Madrid. Exhausted and ill, clad in a white terry-cloth robe, he gathered us around the table in an ornate dining room that was overdone even by Syrian standards. Lowering his voice, he raised his hands as if he were reeling in a trout and said he was going to "hook Assad." During that same encounter he tried to hook all of us as well. At one point during the meeting Baker looked at my colleague Dan Kurtzer and me and asked, "Are any of you boys taking notes?" We both turned a hundred shades of awkward, and before we could respond (fortunately), Baker laughed and said, "I hope so, because if this works, it's going to be one hell of a story."

Looking back at Baker's success at Madrid, I think several

factors set the stage for effective diplomacy in 1991. First, big changes in the region had altered the basic calculations of Arabs, Israelis, and Americans alike. Baker told me flat out that in contrast to the 1989–90 period, now "the stars were lined up to get something done." For the three key players, options had either contracted or expanded or both. The Gulf War and the ascendancy of America, combined with the collapse of the Soviet Union, had reduced Assad's and Arafat's room to maneuver and weakened the leverage of the Arab world's two most difficult peace-process actors. Jordan's King Hussein, eager to recoup American goodwill that had been lost through his fence-straddling in the U.S.-Iraq confrontation, was also more open to an American-brokered process. The Saudis and Egyptians expected an American-orchestrated peace initiative and realized, in the wake of the American victory over Saddam, that more was expected of them. Russia had lost the ability to compete with the United States in the region and seemed only too happy to settle for a symbolic cosponsor role. And the Israelis, now more secure with Saddam's defeat, would have to respond positively to any reasonable initiative.

For the United States, building the coalition in the wake of a tumultuous shock, and pushing Saddam out of Kuwait had been a rare opportunity to stabilize the region. The Americans, Baker in particular, had resisted formally linking the Arab-Israeli issue to Iraq in an effort to avoid playing into Saddam's propaganda game. And for much the same reason Baker had avoided visiting Israel before the war began in January 1991. The Americans wanted to keep the world's focus against Saddam and not convert Iraq's invasion of Kuwait into an Arab-Israeli issue. That same logic would motivate President Bush and Secretary Baker to persuade Shamir, in an act of remarkable political courage, to refrain from responding to Iraq's January 1991 SCUD attacks against Israel.

At the same time, linkage delayed was not linkage permanently deferred. Everyone anticipated that should the Americans prevail quickly and decisively in the war, there would be a serious effort toward Arab-Israeli peace. America had a unique moment.

"The way we conducted the war and the way we did what we said we'd do," President Bush told me, "helped us with the other Arab countries when we went to go do the Middle East peace conference. They were all relatively enthusiastic about it." The Gulf War, as Richard Haass, then Bush's Middle East point man at the NSC, recalled, "put tremendous resources in our political account, and we thought we could do something dramatic." Haass, an academic and longtime veteran of government service, was tough, smart, and emerged as a key player, particularly in reflecting NSC and White House interests.

Baker's relationship with Bush, and the president's willingness to empower Baker to make peace a top priority, was indispensable. As Bush's friend of thirty-five years and political counselor, Baker could rely on, argue with, and probably influence the president in a way that was unparalleled in American diplomacy. And the affection and trust were mutual. In my interview with him the president spoke about Baker ("Jimmy") as if he were a younger brother, praising his remarkable efforts to produce Madrid. In his memoir Bush recalled that asking Baker to be his secretary of state was like a "gimme" in golf—an easy shot, a no-brainer. The reason was not just their Houston connection: Baker, the president said, was a "tough trader and strong negotiator." And Baker made it clear that he wasn't about to disappoint. Instead of being State's man at the White House, Baker made it known he'd be the president's man at the State Department.

Middle East peace is hard enough without having to watch your back at home and to persevere in the face of tough-talking lobbies or turf-conscious bureaucrats. Unless you have the confidence of the president or are the president, neither Arabs nor Israelis will take you seriously. Kissinger, Carter, and Baker all had that. Secretary of State Powell, in his last Middle East trip, was badly undercut and embarrassed by a White House that was unwilling to support him at a difficult moment. Such a possibility would have been unimaginable with Bush 41 and Baker.

"People have to know," Baker told me, "that when you speak, it carries the imprimatur of the president."

George H. W. Bush empowered Baker and was present at Madrid, with Gorbachev, to launch the conference. But Baker put it together. He did so with no process, no inheritance, no ready-made, agreed-upon framework other than UN Security Council Resolution 242, which meant vastly different things to Assad and Shamir and failed to include even a reference to Palestinians or their issue. Baker made up much of his diplomacy as he went along.

Like Kissinger and Carter, Baker drove the diplomacy; unlike his two predecessors, he had no Sadat, no willing partner to help him. Intellectually he never seemed taken or compelled by the region's history or culture. To use Margaret Tutwiler's phrase, he did little "touring around" on his diplomatic shuttles, lest it be a sign that he was not serious. Dan Kurtzer and I would be asked to do short two-page papers on relevant issues. I can't remember Baker ever asking us for anything that went beyond the current procedural issue at hand.

That would not have been Baker's way. But no one in my view was a better negotiator-politician with a more intuitive sense of how far he could push Assad and Shamir without, as he termed it, producing "deal-breakers." Baker was a tour de force operating in an environment where the laws of gravity were heavily weighted toward pulling you and your proposals into a black hole of failure. We forget—procedural breakthrough or not—that Madrid came out of an environment in which the sides had no contact, no trust, no agreed-upon anything. In fact, they were openly hostile and disdainful.

Baker used to talk about the importance of using parallel and reciprocal confidence-building measures, but they never really worked. The truth is, Baker was the only confidence-building measure we had, and with his negotiating and people skills, he was the only one we needed. Don't get me wrong. Baker, as Tutwiler explained, was not "an empathetic guy." He didn't feel

your pain. What he felt and intuited was your politics, your weak-
nesses, and how to play them. With Shamir he gained points by
fencing the PLO out, yet he did not allow Israel to impose conditions that would make it impossible for us to control the process.
With Assad, he gained points by giving on symbols of an international conference and the promise of a robust U.S. role, yet he
emptied them of real substance. Baker's negotiating world was
defined by redlines, deal-breakers, and dead cats. He knew how to
respect the first two and wasn't afraid of using the third. Larry
Eagleburger, who was Baker's deputy and would become acting
secretary when Baker left State in August 1992 to head up Bush's
reelection campaign, told me that Baker was one of the "most superb negotiators" he'd ever seen. His ability "wasn't intellectually
driven," Eagleburger recalled, "as much as it was a physiological,
psychological something."

At the same time Baker emanated a sense of fairness, toughness, and honesty. Madrid was stacked toward the Israelis on substance (for them it was a conference made in heaven really), yet
he kept himself honest with the Arabs by using tough rhetoric
against settlements and issuing give-up-the-dream warnings
about Israel holding on to the West Bank. Much as Kissinger had
done, he would criticize the Israelis in his meetings with
Palestinians and then reverse direction when he met with
Shamir. Baker also used both incentives and disincentives to cajole and persuade both Arabs and Israelis to buy into the Madrid
format. To Assad, he dangled the prospects of an improved U.S.-
Syrian relationship and an American security guarantee on the
Golan Heights. To the Palestinians, he promised that only a U.S.-
sponsored negotiating process with Israel could limit settlement
activity (something he probably never believed). And to the
Israelis, he promised a faux international conference with no
PLO. And with all sides, he dangled the unsightly image of leaving a dead cat on their respective doorsteps, should they not agree
to this Baker idea or that.

The fact is that in the spring of 1991 Baker saw an opportunity and took it. Bush, Cheney, and Powell had run a successful

war; Baker was now determined to play a leading role in pushing ahead on some kind of postwar peace. Using his ties to the president and generating just enough comfort, unease, and pressure, he drove and sustained a diplomatic process that could never have succeeded without him. After all, this was not Oslo, which was sustained by Israelis and Palestinians who were seriously invested in their own diplomacy. This time Shamir, Assad, and the PLO authorized a conference because they couldn't afford not to, and they weren't happy about it. Their concessions were made not to one another but to America, and to Jim Baker.

Baker's success was also facilitated by the team he gathered around him. Not that Baker's advisors had some sort of inordinate influence on him—they didn't. In fact, Baker's team worked precisely because he was in charge of guiding and shepherding them at critical decision points. But as both Kissinger and Carter told me, a good team, balanced, smart, and creative, was essential to generate ideas, plan strategy, and handle follow-up. Baker had long before realized that succeeding meant getting the best people to support you. Some of his predecessors advised him to use the Foreign Service without allowing the "building" to control the policy. And he didn't. He used Larry Eagleburger, his deputy secretary, to deal with Brent Scowcroft and to manage issues in which he wasn't all that interested or that he simply didn't have time for. He deployed Robert Kimmitt as undersecretary of state for political affairs to manage the policy process and the department. He relied on Bob Zoellick for big ideas particularly on trade and economic matters, and on Dennis Ross, his director of policy planning, for advice on Soviet and Middle East affairs. Margaret Tutwiler, a longtime advisor and confidante, handled press and public diplomacy and was Baker's eyes and ears on political matters.

The core Middle East team at State that staffed and supported Baker on the road and at home was composed of four people: Dennis Ross, Bill Burns, Dan Kurtzer, and myself. It's worth saying a bit about each of them because they'd all continue to hold key positions on Middle East policy for the next decade or more.

And although the core Middle East team worked exceptionally well under Baker, it didn't operate nearly as well under Clinton.

Dennis Ross was clearly first among equals. As head of policy planning, Dennis, along with Tutwiler and Zoellick, was part of Baker's inner circle on whom he relied for actual policy execution. A Soviet specialist by training, Dennis had served at the Pentagon, the State Department, and the NSC. He'd gotten to know Bush 41 as vice president, joined his 1988 presidential campaign, and become head of Baker's policy planning staff, with operational responsibilities for Soviet and Middle East affairs.

I first met Dennis in the 1980s. I liked his accessibility, his analytical and intellectual bent, combined with his practicality. During our first meeting we got into a heated discussion about Jordan, and we have been arguing ever since. I admired his prodigious memory, his creativity, and his remarkable ability to synthesize and summarize the different positions of Arabs and Israelis. For almost a decade I think I spent more time with Dennis than with my own family.

Beneath Dennis's boyish accessibility lay a driving ambition to succeed and to exert control, a fact that would become increasingly clear as he began to dominate policymaking during the Clinton administration. For an academic, he also had uncanny survival instincts. His capacity to survive the transition from Bush 41 to Clinton flowed not only from his expertise but also from his willingness to play the political game. After all, he'd worked to reelect George H. W. Bush. And yet within six months—having convinced Tom Donilon, Warren Christopher's key political advisor, of his indispensability—Dennis emerged into a position of influence on Middle East policy that lasted well beyond the Baker years.

Dennis, like myself, had a inherent tendency to see the world of Arab-Israeli politics first from Israel's vantage point rather than from that of the Palestinians. Not that he didn't understand Arab or Palestinian sensitivities. But his own strong Jewish identity and his commitment to Israel's security combined with something else: a deep conviction that if you couldn't gain

Israel's confidence, you had zero chance of erecting any kind of peace process. And to Dennis, achieving this goal required a degree of coordination with the Israelis, sensitivity toward their substantive concerns, and public defense of their positions. Baker's good judgment and toughness balanced and controlled this inclination, which was not the case under Clinton.

If Dennis emerged as manager of the Israeli account, Dan Kurtzer's role was to try to keep the process level and honest. Dan was one of the smartest and most creative people I'd ever met. As an Orthodox Jew who for a time had been a dean at Yeshiva University, he combined the best of the academy (a Ph.D. from Columbia's Middle East program) with the Foreign Service. Having done tours in Egypt and in Israel (he'd later go on to become ambassador to both countries), Dan had an acute appreciation of regional politics. He'd helped George Shultz craft his 1988 initiative and was a major force on the road to Madrid. Dan would leave the peace-process team in 1994, when it became increasingly clear that Dennis was shutting him out. More than a little tension existed between the two as a consequence of disagreements over style, substance, and of course influence. Dan's departure in my view was a major loss. We needed his honesty, balance, and creativity, particularly during the mid-1990s and in the run-up to Camp David.

Bill Burns, who would later go on to serve as ambassador to Jordan, then to Russia, and as assistant secretary for Near Eastern Affairs at State under Colin Powell was Dennis's deputy at policy planning. I first met Bill during a temporary tour at our embassy in Amman. He was incredibly creative and talented. Bill had it all—a Ph.D. from Oxford (where he had been a Rhodes scholar), a deep appreciation for Arab-Israeli politics, an inherent sense of fairness about it all, and a quiet strength that enabled him to detach himself from the whirlwind at key moments and offer sound judgment about policy and politics.

Baker's team worked well because Baker himself, as a strong secretary of state, provided the adult supervision required. He benefited from our small group discussions and was confident enough to let us argue among ourselves in front of him. Frankly, I think he enjoyed it, particularly when Dan and I argued with Dennis. Bill Burns believed that Baker "held the reins just right"—loosely enough to encourage creativity and constructive differences, but firmly enough to ensure that policy was disciplined and precise.

At the same time, Baker's inherent sense of balance and fairness with regard to Arabs and Israelis kept all of us honest. Margaret Tutwiler put it best: "Baker one hundred percent understood where everybody's natural bias was coming from." When he didn't like the advice he was getting, he rejected it, or when he thought we were veering too much to one side, usually toward the Israelis, he'd say so. "There were a hundred times," Tutwiler told me, when "Jim Baker completely, and one hundred percent politely, overruled Dennis." This dynamic, in which Baker was open to hearing diverse points of view but was possessed of his own judgment and intuitive feel for what was necessary to make the deal, produced better policy.

Shortly before the Madrid invitations were to be issued, the Palestinians had not yet provided a formal list of names for their delegation. Together with the Russians, Baker was having second thoughts and had decided to postpone the announcement.

Dan and I pushed Dennis hard to get a meeting with Baker, who was then literally in a discussion with the Russian foreign minister. We were absolutely convinced that postponing the announcement by even a day could lead to the collapse of our effort. With both the Russian foreign minister and the American secretary of state in Jerusalem, it was now or never, and we knew it. Baker was annoyed at being pulled out of the meeting. Led by Dan, we made the case. "You'll never get all the details nailed down," Dan said. "The invitation itself will be the tie that binds." I added, "If you don't move now, the Israelis and Palestinians will take a powder." Baker agreed. Within hours he and Soviet foreign minister Boris Pankin convened their press conference, and Madrid was born.

One additional aspect of Baker's Middle East team needs to be mentioned because it would also carry significance for the Clinton years. Of Baker's four core Middle East advisors, three were American Jews. If you added Richard Haass at the NSC, that would have been four of five. I never asked Baker about this fact. Margaret did and told me flat out that for him it didn't make a damn bit of difference. But as tensions mounted between a tough Likud prime minister and an equally determined Bush and Baker, largely over settlements, others seemed to care a lot. Some of Shamir's advisors called us Baker's "Jew Boys." PLO officials in Tunis called us the "Three Rabbis." And angry right-wing Israeli settlers and some American Jews called us "Jewish Benedict Arnolds." In the end, however, it all amounted to a kind of inside Jewish baseball. Bush and Baker set the policy guidelines, and on the road to Madrid, Baker's inherent fairness and determination to find a balance between Israeli and Arab needs were all that mattered, not the predispositions of any of his advisors.

On balance, if the Jewish background of Baker's advisors affected anything, it was paradoxically a tendency to be less sensitive to Israeli concerns, particularly when it came to public diplomacy. Baker's speech at AIPAC in May 1989, which Dan Kurtzer drafted and which all of us loved and approved, contained one line: "Now is the time to lay aside, once and for all, the unrealistic vision of a greater Israel." That line would set people's hair on fire. Part of the problem was that Baker had taken out all of the "we love AIPAC" language from the speech's introduction which Baker's savvy speechwriter, Harvey Sicherman, had added. Even so, Tom Dine told me he thought it was a fine speech when he heard it. After the active pot-stirring by Steve Rosen, then AIPAC's policy director (who hated the speech), as well as by Shamir and Arens, Baker's address became a clarion call to the Israelis and the Jewish community to mobilize. By early June ninety-four senators had sent a letter to the president expressing support for Israel.

The AIPAC speech didn't buy us much and in fact was probably gratuitous. We reveled in having Baker speak out against settlements, but we could have made the same point without the give-up-the-dream language. Predictably, the Arabs applauded.

The tension between the Jewish community and the administration deepened. But to what end? On the way to Madrid tough talking in public to both sides made sense to me; in 1989, four months into a new administration, and with no real strategy, unnecessarily angering the Israelis didn't make sense. Dennis believes that Bush and to some extent Baker believed that Reagan had been too solicitous of the Jewish organizations. And Baker did seem to enjoy the controversy. Looking back, however, I'm not sure we served him well on that occasion by pushing language that was certain to provoke.

Four Plus Ten Plus Five Equals Zero

Jim Baker's initial foray into the wilds of Arab-Israeli diplomacy failed. To his credit, his initial instinct to avoid the Arab-Israeli issue (Nixon had told him it was "insoluble") was right. We encouraged him to visit the region; after all, what secretary hadn't in his first year in office? "Bullshit," he'd say. "The only way I'm going anywhere is if there's a point." And frankly there wasn't one.

Between 1989 and 1990 Baker agreed to use a combination of telephone diplomacy, secretarial letters, and meetings in New York and Washington. The objective was to gain Arab, Palestinian, and Israeli agreement on key points to start an Israeli-Palestinian dialogue. Given the prospects for success, this relatively hands-off approach was about right. Largely under pressure from a Palestinian intifada, Israel had articulated a four-point initiative, one of whose points called for Palestinian elections in the West Bank and Gaza. Largely because Rabin, Shamir's defense minister, had pushed for it, we urged Baker to build on the Israeli plan and try to reshape it around an Israeli-Palestinian dialogue on elections and hopefully other issues.

After almost a year of effort—which included persuading Baker to put his name on a five-point formula, to bridge the gap between Israel's four-point plan and an Egyptian ten-point proposal—Baker ended up with no points. Shamir correctly assessed that the American effort, however reasonable it may have been, was in fact designed to change his own plan. He voted against Baker's compromise formula in the Israeli cabinet. Within weeks the national unity government collapsed, and Shamir was able to form a new coalition in June. Recalling Kissinger's advice about Israeli foot-dragging, Baker lamented that he should have listened to "his advice and my own instincts."[6]

For well over a year, until Desert Storm succeeded in pushing Saddam Hussein out of Kuwait and generating new possibilities for Arab-Israeli peace, the secretary did precisely that, listening to his own instincts. Baker hated to fail, let alone be diddled or outmaneuvered. Next time—if there was a next time—Baker would not make the same mistakes. That earlier period carried some important lessons that would be critical to Baker's success at Madrid and that are worth pointing out.

If anything was to be achieved, it became clear, Yitzhak Shamir was going to be either the central player or the obstacle. He'd have to be engaged, or confronted, or both. Built like a small refrigerator, with a striking resemblance to the comedian Jerry Stiller but without his sense of humor, Shamir was a hard-line revisionist and underground fighter whose Stern Gang, during the 1940s, had practiced its share of terror, violence, and assassination against the British and the Arabs. Shamir was quiet and secretive, a tough political insider who (we now know) had carried on a fair amount of quiet diplomacy with both King Hussein and the Moroccans.

That Shamir was willing to negotiate peace with Jordan should not mask his determination—like Begin's—to hang on to the West Bank and Gaza. Unlike Begin (Shamir had voted against the peace treaty with Egypt), the Israeli prime minister had a love affair with the status quo and no real sense of how to manage his relationship with the United States.

In early April Shamir came to Washington, his four-point initiative in hand, and had what could only be described as a disastrous encounter with the president. This meeting would set the tone of their relationship until Shamir's defeat by Rabin in June 1992. Rarely have two leaders been so different physically, politically, and emotionally. I asked President Bush about their relationship. "Chilly," he responded. "We had to lean on him a lot." Bush was being kind. Both the president and John Sununu, his chief of staff, had taken to calling Shamir "that little shit." Scowcroft said that Shamir and the president just didn't get along.

Richard Haass recalls preparations for the first visit. Egyptian president Hosni Mubarak had visited several weeks earlier, and the president had taken him to a Baltimore Orioles game. The Israelis, particularly Shamir's advisor, Eli Rubenstein, were looking for a parallel confidence-builder. Apparently Shamir had no hobbies, so the president and prime minister settled for a walk around the White House Rose Garden and an excursion to the Air and Space Museum, where the two watched a film on the U.S. space program. "You treat Mubarak like your *bubala*," an annoyed Rubenstein told Haass, using the Yiddish word for baby or sweetie pie, "and all you can offer the prime minister is a walk around the Rose Garden." Shamir found Bush "courteous, if cool."[7]

But what really ruined their relationship was an exchange, in their meeting in the Oval Office, on settlements. President Bush doesn't recall the scene, but Haass, who was briefed by the president after the meeting, will never forget it. The ghost of the Begin-Carter disconnect on settlements at Camp David seemed to be haunting the White House. Bush raised the issue of settlements, indicating how much of a problem they were for him personally and for American policy. Shamir told Bush that settlements "wouldn't be a problem," waving his hand dismissively in the air. "Well, good," the president replied, convinced the matter had been resolved. Within ten days Shamir announced two new settlements in Gaza. Unquestionably Shamir never intended to mislead the president—under no circumstances would he ever have agreed to a settlements freeze. It hardly mattered. Bush believed he'd been lied to. Even though Shamir's courageous decision to absorb SCUD hits during the first Gulf War would draw Bush's respect, their relationship, such as it was, never recovered. The settlements disconnect in April, together with Israel's continuing settlement activity on the ground, would pave the way for Bush's determination, in the fall of 1991, to deny Shamir billions in loan guarantees.

Ironically, while Bush was disconnecting with Shamir, Baker was trying to forge something of a relationship with the prime minister. As we've seen, where you stand is always a function of where you sit. Charged with the diplomacy, Baker knew that if he wanted to stand a chance of succeeding, he'd have to create some basis for trust and confidence with Shamir. And he did. He prides himself on forging that relationship.

"People never understood," Baker told me, "that I had a very good personal relationship with the man." As he recalled, Shamir never "lied or leaked." For his part, Baker promised only what he could deliver. Yossi Ben-Aharon (head of the prime minister's office) and Zalman Shoval (Israel's ambassador to the United States), neither a Baker fan at the time, both told me that Shamir had confidence in Baker and doubted that Madrid would have happened otherwise. Like Carter in 1978, Baker made a decision to invest in Shamir and to respect his redlines, particularly when it came to fencing out the PLO. In 2005 Baker, who had long been touched by Shamir's gesture in planting trees in honor of his mother—she died while the secretary was in Jerusalem in 1991—called Mrs. Shamir to ask about her husband, who now had Alzheimer's. Personal relationships, Baker told me, really are important to effective diplomacy.

The collapse of Baker's initial effort to forge an Israeli-Palestinian dialogue in March 1990 would leave him, in his own words, "beaten, battered, and betrayed." The fact is, Baker hadn't even started yet. He'd been sucked into the wonderful world of Israeli and Palestinian politics without ever leaving Washington. In June 1990 Shamir formed a very hard-line government with Sharon, Levy, and Arens in the cabinet.

Nor was the administration's dialogue with the PLO going anywhere. In fact, a month before, a small Iraqi-backed Palestinian group that sat on the PLO's executive committee launched an unsuccessful attack near a Tel Aviv beach. Arafat wouldn't expel those involved in the operation, or disassociate or even distance himself from it. I was in the unenviable position of drafting the instruction to our ambassador in Tunis authorizing a suspension of the U.S.-PLO dialogue that had begun in 1988. I took it to Baker's office, sat down, and waited for his approval. I saw the frustration mount, the narrowing eyes. Baker threw the cable into the air. As I watched it descend, in a near state of shock, Baker looked at me, saying: "I want you to know, Aaron, if I had another life, I'd want to be a Middle East specialist just like you, because it would mean guaranteed permanent employment."[8]

As I walked back to my office, I realized that, as frustrated as he was, Baker hadn't even met a Palestinian yet, let alone gotten involved in negotiations. An Israeli-Palestinian dialogue was small-stakes poker. Hooking Shamir, Assad, and Arafat would require something bigger, but I didn't know what. Six weeks later, in August, while hiking in Switzerland with my wife, Lindsay, I turned on CNN in the hotel room and couldn't believe what I was hearing. Saddam Hussein had just invaded Kuwait.

Getting Serious

Wars change things. As I sat watching Saddam's forces devour Kuwait, I felt the same sense of unpredictability and uncertainty I had experienced in Jerusalem in October 1973. Would this conflict alter the landscape of a region that seemed to prefer the sclerotic status quo that it knew over the dynamic changes it didn't? It turned out that Iraq's invasion of Kuwait and the American effort to throw Saddam out would impress even a region inured to violence and instability, rearrange the political furniture, and shock Arabs and Israelis who believed they'd seen just about everything.

I saw some of these shocks in early 1991, on Baker's Middle East trips after the war. That spring I had a front-row seat for the human and environmental destruction that Saddam had wrought. I'm not a religious person, but as we flew over the remains of Kuwait's burning oil fields and wells, which had been destroyed by Iraq's retreating forces, I had a vision of what religious people must imagine when they think of purgatory. It was early afternoon, yet the desert sun had been obscured by billowing black smoke and a gray and black haze. Vast fingers of flame shot skyward, puncturing the smog blanket that hung over everything. When we landed and approached the burning fields, black soot, flakes, and film from roughly five hundred oil well fires covered everything. The heat was as intense as anything I'd experienced. This was as close to a living hell as I'd ever want to be.

I also had a chance to see the human misery of Kurdish refugees forced by Saddam across the Iraqi border into Turkey. After a helicopter ride over some of the most breathtakingly severe mountains and depressions I'd ever seen, Baker and his staff set down at the Turkish village of Çukurca, close to the Iraqi border. The rest of the trip was made in four-wheel-drive vehicles up to a height of about ten thousand feet. It was a stunningly beautiful cloudless day. As we came up over a ridge nearing our final destination, I'll never forget the scene. Across the ridgeline and into the valley, a sea of humanity surged—fifty thousand in all, we were told. Thousands of refugees lacked adequate clothing, food, and clean water. Mothers sheltered babies from the cold and washed clothes in fetid streams. Baker was mobbed. The visit lasted less than ten minutes. Despite an American airlift of food and supplies already under way, several days later we were told that thirty-seven Kurdish refugees had died from exposure, most of them children.

The war was a human and environmental disaster but also began to change the political calculations of those in the region and outside, certainly when it came to possibilities for Arab-Israeli peacemaking. For the Kuwaitis and Saudis, the war had demonstrated their vulnerability and deepened their dependence on and debt to the United States. At the same time, long convinced that an unresolved Arab-Israeli conflict would give Saddam and others much to exploit, the Arabs began to press the United States for a postwar initiative. The Arabs, including Egypt, had bought the administration line about postponing linkage, but not forever.

For Syria, soon to become the linchpin in Baker's strategy, Saddam's defeat had weakened its Iraqi enemy but also further narrowed options that had been diminishing for some time. Assad's quest to gain strategic parity with Israel meant he was heavily dependent on the Soviet Union, an ally that was itself in the throes of change. Patrick Seale, Assad's biographer and perhaps the Westerner closest to him, told me that as early as 1987 the Syrian president was considering options other than reliance on the Soviets, whose reforms under Gorbachev made him increasingly nervous. The collapse of the Soviet Union, as well as America's victory in the Gulf War, gave Assad, a man slow to change, no other option. Baker's first visit to Syria in the fall of 1990 allowed Assad to begin a relationship with the United States and with Baker personally. Eventually he would join the allied coalition against Iraq, sending Syrian troops to Saudi Arabia, but not to Kuwait to fight.

Baker recalls that Assad's decision to join the allied coalition was a strategic one. If that's accurate, then it was based on his shrinking options, not on any commitment in 1990 to make peace with Israel. Syria could not afford to be outside an Arab coalition on which Assad depended for support, particularly at a time when his Soviet patron was collapsing. Assad was ambivalent about America. He liked Kissinger and confronted Shultz but never trusted the United States. Patrick Seale told me he did admire Baker's honesty and would come to place "tremendous hopes on him." For Assad, Shamir could never be brought around; instead Madrid was all about developing ties with America. It would take Rabin's election to start Assad thinking about the possibility of dealing seriously with the Israelis. And even then he looked toward the United States as the key instrument to deliver the Golan Heights to Syria.

For the Israelis, at least for Yitzhak Shamir, America's war against Saddam created both risk and opportunity. In January and February 1991 Israel had been attacked by thirty-nine Iraqi

SCUD missiles. Two Israelis had died, eleven had been seriously injured. Baker believed that Shamir had made a decision not to respond to the conventional attack out of a practical calculation that there was little Israel could do against this missile threat that the United States could not. But the fact remains that practical considerations during a crisis mix with political and emotional ones. Shamir's restraint, which Bush, Baker, and Scowcroft all applauded, was itself remarkable under the circumstances.

At the same time Shamir looked at the future with some trepidation. In the face of an expected American initiative, he knew his restraint on the SCUDs might not buy him much. As Efraim Halevy, deputy Mossad director, recalls, Shamir wasn't against engaging the Arabs—he had at least three secret meetings with King Hussein during this period. But he was adamantly opposed to an international conference or any dealings with the PLO. Shamir couldn't be certain where America was heading. As Baker recalls, the prime minister seemed to be interested in "doing something and scared to death at the very prospect."

As for Jordan, the weakest party in the neighborhood with a long border with Iraq, the war had left King Hussein in a very tight spot. The king's survival instincts had told him he had to hedge his bets, so he couldn't sign up for the anti-Saddam coalition. Fence-sitting, however, had made the Americans angry, and the king, once America's darling, had to find a way back from the dark side. Hussein was not a major player in the run-up to Madrid, but he willingly accepted the idea of a joint Jordanian-Palestinian delegation and supported Baker on the Palestine issue when he could. It would take his own peacemaking directly with Israel in 1994 to finally let him find his way back to America's good graces and to the economic and political support that came with it.

Not surprisingly, with a history of making bad choices, Palestinians suffered most from the Gulf War. Like Hussein, Arafat wouldn't choose sides. But his pro-Saddam rhetoric and his unwillingness to speak out against the Iraqi aggression against

Kuwait drove the Gulf Arabs to take action against him and the PLO. Kuwait expelled thousands of resident Palestinians; the Saudis cut Arafat off financially. For the Israelis, who watched too many Palestinians in the West Bank cheer Iraqi SCUDs, the prospect of finding a Palestinian partner now seemed more remote than ever.

The PLO had already been caught off guard by the 1988 intifada. Cut off financially and isolated diplomatically, with the collapse of the Soviet Union, its stock had fallen to its lowest point in a decade. As the run-up to Madrid demonstrated, Palestinian leverage and capacity to block a U.S.-orchestrated process declined as well. The delegation that finally showed up at the conference was a joint Jordanian-Palestinian one with no Jerusalemites, outsiders, or PLO officials. Still, the PLO would retain control over the Palestinian delegation, pulling every string from behind the curtain in its Tunis headquarters. Madrid proved to be the one lifeline to maintaining Palestinian political relevance and an important stage for highlighting the Palestinian narrative before an international audience.

For us, the war looked like a huge opportunity. As early as October we'd been tasked by the secretary to look at options for postwar Arab-Israeli diplomacy. It was already an open secret that the president had committed himself to some kind of initiative as a way of mobilizing the Arab coalition against Saddam. At the United Nations the president had spoken about "opportunities" for states in the region to "settle the conflicts that divide the Arabs from Israel."[9] Bush made clear to me that postwar Arab-Israeli peace was a "priority worth devoting some serious time to." In the spring of 1991 the only question was how to fashion an initiative that would avoid our previous mistakes and take advantage of new postwar realties.

When I asked Baker where the strategy for Madrid came from, he generously said, "Well, it was mine, plus you guys." True, his peace team did have a role in shaping a two-track approach involving the Arabs and Palestinians. But it was Baker who sold it to a skeptical Brent Scowcroft. And he laid it out to his good friend the president. "Look what we've done for the Arabs and the Israelis," Baker said, recounting his conversation with the president. "We have a window of opportunity." There was more than a little ego here. Baker, who had assembled the coalition in the run-up to the war, had watched Bush, Cheney, and Powell lead a successful military effort. I think he was eager to get back in the action.

The loosely fashioned concept we outlined for Baker, which he would amend and revise as he went along, was a two-pronged initiative designed to get both the Arab states and West Bank/ Gaza Palestinians into a negotiation with Israel. The vehicle was to be a peace conference, properly structured, that would meet the Arab world's need for an international symbol but assuage Israel's concern about its having any real authority or power. Getting the Arabs, particularly Syria, to participate was critical to hooking Shamir; structuring the conference and getting the Palestinians were essential to hooking the Arabs. Multilateral negotiations between Israel and Arab states on issues of water, refugees, economic development, and regional security were added to sweeten the deal for the Israelis.

Beyond that we thought very little about the future. And if Baker's own peace processors weren't focused on a future after the conference, he certainly wasn't. He saw Madrid as a way to break taboos and create an investment trap that would keep Arabs and Israelis at the table for a long time. It wasn't about reaching agreements or wrestling with the tough issues. In fact, Baker tried to finesse or kick down the road every contentious issue that might constitute what he called a deal-breaker. If the conference had been left to his experts and advisors, who knew way too much about Middle East history and politics, Baker might never have gotten to Madrid. But the secretary was like a laser beam. "Boys, you need to crawl before you walk and walk before you run," he'd say when we confronted him with this or that political complication. For Baker, the goal on this hunt was to get them to the table. As it turned out, it took nine months, nine trips, and sixty thousand–plus miles to put the Madrid conference together.

Baker's game plan for a Madrid peace conference had three elements tied together by one overriding asset—himself, backed up by the president. First, put Shamir in a position where he couldn't say no. This meant getting Assad and Arafat to say yes and offer Israel the first formal negotiations with Syria and the Palestinians. Second, put together a conference that had enough symbolism for the Arabs but not too much substance for the Israelis. And third, come up with a fix to a problem that had eluded all of his predecessors: how to get "non-PLO" Palestinians to sit at the table with Israel. Baker achieved these aims by using diplomacy to coerce, to reward, and to embarrass. If you said no, not only would you take the fall, but you'd be saying no to the United States. In the spring of 1991 no one from Tunis to Cairo to Damascus to Jerusalem wanted to be in that position.

In March 1991 Baker made his first official visit to Israel. He'd avoided a trip there for almost two years, but his tough public diplomacy and reputation had preceded him, so no one was expecting much in the way of warm and fuzzy bonding with the Israelis. Traipsing behind him at Yad Vashem, I sensed he was genuinely moved. I went back and found what he'd written in the museum's guest book: "A chilling reminder of a tragedy that must never be repeated. With great respect and affection for the Jewish people." The Israelis took him on their standard helicopter tour, along with a special guide, Major General Yossi Ben-Haran, an Israeli war hero in the 1973 battle for the Golan Heights. Baker seemed impressed by Israel's vulnerability but drew the opposite conclusion than the Israelis intended. In an age of missiles, Baker recalled, territory was much less important. Still, his private dinner with Shamir began to create some mutual trust. Shamir seemed open to Baker's initiative and even amenable to the idea of a U.S. security guarantee on the Golan should Syria and Israel reach a deal. That sense of trust would prove critical in persuading Shamir that Baker was "not trying to cut our balls off," as Foreign Minister Arens had feared.

In the next several months Baker worked hard to gain Shamir's confidence, both on a conference and on Palestinian representation. In 1989, Baker had opened himself up to charges of playing internal Israeli politics by dealing with Rabin; this time around he focused on Shamir alone, usually with no note-takers. Shamir probably never really trusted Baker, but he came to believe that the secretary was not interested in forcing the PLO on Israel or in embarrassing him. And that belief proved enough to create a bond that enabled the two to work together successfully.

At the same time Baker was honest and tough enough not to allow the Israelis to ask for things that pushed over the limit. When Shamir demanded that West Bankers and Gazans publicly distance themselves from the PLO, Baker said no. During a meeting in April Baker exploded at Shamir over Israel's unreasonable positions on conference modalities. "I'm working my ass off, and I'm getting no cooperation from you...I'm hardly inclined to come here again." En route to the airport he'd quip: "I'm going to leave that dead cat on Shamir's doorstep."[10] Still, by early May Baker had made considerable progress with Israel. The combination of honey and vinegar seemed to work. Baker was tough, Yossi Ben-Aharon, Shamir's tough office director, told me: "No sentiment there." But he succeeded in winning "a degree of confidence" from Shamir; "otherwise Madrid would have never materialized," Ben-Aharon concluded.

Central to Baker's efforts to produce Madrid was the challenge of getting Syria to participate. Baker's calculation here was much like Kissinger's. Syria was the hardest-line Arab state sharing a border with Israel; hooking Assad would therefore make it easier to get the other Arabs, and maybe even the Palestinians, to the conference. Ed Djerejian, who was closer to Baker on Syria strategy than anyone else, made clear to me that the only way Baker saw Madrid working "was to get the big guy on the block to the north of Israel to say yes."

Baker tried the same honey-and-vinegar approach he had used with Shamir. In late April it was on display. To gain Assad's confidence, he'd stress the honeyed possibilities of an improved U.S.-Syrian relationship; he'd also play to Assad's obsession with a central American role in the negotiations. To gain concessions on the conference, he'd trade a U.S. role in security arrangements on the Golan. By criticizing Israeli settlement activity and Shamir's intransigence, he made Assad feel as if Syria were a privileged partner in American strategy. Much like Kissinger's, Baker's trash-talking to the Arabs about Israel helped build confidence in him.

At the same time Baker was prepared to be tough with Assad. I asked Baker about this, and he said, "You've got to be tough as nails. I remember telling Assad at one point, 'Well, fine. If you think you can get your Golan back, you go get it.'" At least twice en route to Madrid, Baker threatened to break off negotiations with Assad. On one occasion he slammed his leather portfolio shut and said, "If I get the right answers...I'll be back in Damascus... If I get the wrong ones, I don't expect to see you again for a long time."[11]

At the end of May, Baker had made some progress; but frustrated that he hadn't yet gotten either Israel or Syria to sign on, he decided to turn up the heat. In an effort to force the Arabs and Israelis to consider saying yes or no to the president, he had Bush send a letter asking for a positive response to his terms of the conference. Shamir came back with a studied "No, but," raising objections to almost every issue but not closing the door. The Israelis clearly were in a holding pattern, waiting to see what Assad's response would be. Six weeks after the president's message was sent in late July, Assad finally replied with a yes. Even with all of his bravado and self-confidence, I think Baker was surprised he got it. It would take Shamir another two weeks to recover from the shock of Assad's yes and to confirm that he'd agree to a conference. When Baker arrived in Jerusalem to confirm Israel's participation, he recalled that Shamir looked "as if he'd just bit into a green persimmon." The roller coaster to Madrid was not yet over, but Baker had succeeded in making

Assad and Shamir offers they couldn't refuse. Don Vito Corleone would have been proud.

Strangely perhaps, the issue that had absorbed almost all of Baker's attention during his first foray into Arab-Israeli diplomacy in 1989–90 was not the major focus of his second. Baker's relationship to the Palestinian issue flowed from two realities that would give it a peculiar character. The PLO in Tunis was making the decisions for the Palestinians, using West Bankers and Gazans as proxies. But since Baker wouldn't meet with the PLO (and neither would Israel), the U.S.-Palestinian process had an artificial character. In all, Baker met with Palestinians eighteen times in nine months. The dynamic was pretty much the same: they'd complain to us, we'd try to empathize but would also make clear what they'd have to do and the costs (to them) of not doing it. Hanan Ashrawi got it about right: "Israel got all the carrots and asked for more. We got all the sticks in the form of morbid forecasts about the consequences of saying no." In Baker's first meeting with Palestinians in Jerusalem, the dialogue was pretty predictable. When they pleaded with Baker to deal with the PLO, he said, "You're lucky I'm talking to you. Your guy [Arafat] backed the wrong horse." With regard to Palestinian complaints about settlements, Baker said, "I'm not going to send in the Eighty-second Airborne. The only way we can address Israeli settlements is to get you in a political process with Israel."[12]

I felt bad for the Palestinians, and I believe that after several meetings so did Baker. Challenged by their own hard-liners, constrained by the PLO, and undermined by Israel, they were exposed and vulnerable. Baker got a firsthand account of the Palestinian narrative, and through his relationships with Faisal Husseini and Hanan Ashrawi, he came to see them as individuals caught up in very tough circumstances. They respected Baker and admired his toughness and honesty. "He was open, willing to engage, to discuss, negotiate, to get angry and accept other people getting angry," Ashrawi told me. "He could influence policy and had the ear and confidence of the president."

Maybe so. But Baker could do little for the Palestinians except offer them a process that might, over time, address the Israeli occupation and their national aspirations. Keeping Shamir on board while he went fishing for Assad meant that the Palestinian delegation could have no PLO association, no Jerusalemites, and no diaspora Palestinians. "Our policy," Baker told me, "was a charade. Shamir knew it. We knew it. We'd go to those meetings, and they'd read their scripts sent from Yasser." With the PLO in a weakened state and Assad on board by July, Arafat had little choice but to accept Baker's terms—participation in Madrid by a joint Jordanian-Palestinian delegation. It wasn't much comfort to the Palestinians that one of the members of the Jordanian side of the delegation had roots in Jerusalem.

Still, pinning down the terms and participants for a Palestinian delegation came down to a nail-biting finish. On October 17, the day before the announcement of the Madrid invitations, the PLO had not yet agreed on the list or formally given it to Baker. We had agreed to Israel's request for a letter of assurance outlining previous U.S. commitments. And we had finalized a similar letter to induce Palestinians to join the Madrid process as well. All that remained was to receive the Palestinians' list.

What we didn't know was that Arafat was worried that the West Bankers were acting too independently and was determined to let everyone know who was in charge; he had told Ashrawi, hours before the Baker meeting with the Palestinians at the U.S. consulate in East Jerusalem, that under no circumstances were they to turn over any list to Baker.

The secretary was in no mood for what he perceived to be Palestinian games, at least on the part of Hanan and Faisal. "You better get your act together or you'll prove Abba Eban right," I recall him saying. "If you don't like the terms, tough. The souk is closed. Have a nice life." Hanan pushed back, accusing Baker of insulting the Palestinians by his use of Israeli expressions. But Baker had clearly had it. Partly for effect but mainly out of exhaustion and frustration, he slammed his notebook shut and stormed out of the meeting. Whether motivated by genuine frustration or not, this was great theater. When Baker came back almost fifteen minutes later, the Palestinians agreed to provide an informal list.

The next day Baker received the Palestinian delegation and was given an informal list. Having just blasted them the night before, he now gathered the Palestinians around him, much as a football coach would huddle with his players for a pregame pep talk. The yelling had stopped; the reassuring now began. It was a difficult moment for the Palestinians, and Baker knew it. "We can now do this," he said to them, "because you've made a correct and courageous decision."[13]

Loan Guarantees, Domestic Politics, and Endgame Diplomacy

One other piece of business had to be taken care of before Madrid, and that was the issue of U.S. loan guarantees to Israel. The road to Madrid was not just about diplomacy; as Kissinger's and Carter's experiences had revealed, it was also about the interaction of foreign policy and domestic politics.

The issue was straightforward enough. In September 1991, faced with the prospect of absorbing hundreds of thousands of Russian Jews, Israel formally requested $10 billion in loan guarantees from the United States. These were essentially American guarantees with commercial banks, so that Israel could borrow funds at favorable interest rates to handle the costs of absorption. The problem was that money is fungible. Funds freed up for the absorption of immigrants could be used, for example, to expand settlement activity. Against the background of Shamir's aggressive settlement policies and the absence of any real trust between him and the president, as Madrid approached, the administration was determined at least to delay Israel's request. When I asked President Bush whether domestic politics had influenced his Arab-Israeli diplomacy, he said, "No. Look at loan guarantees." At eighty-four he still remembers the fight and the emotions it conjured up. "I didn't ride in here on a watermelon truck," he began. "I know how the powers that be work, and I knew that when the head of AIPAC came down that we were in for a fight. I felt the politics would be tough. On the other hand, the American people supported us, so maybe the politics weren't as detrimental. Some people have said that this cost you the Jewish vote. I don't know if that's true or not, and I can't whine about that."

If Bush, at a key moment in Arab-Israeli diplomacy, wasn't about to give in on loan guarantees to an Israeli prime minister whom he didn't trust, Baker was even more dug in. Contrary to the public image, for the previous two years, when it came to Shamir and settlements, he had been the pragmatist in an effort to create a relationship with the prime minister and get something done on the diplomacy. It was Baker who pushed back against a White House inclination to declare settlements illegal. It was Baker who told Bush he'd "fucked up" when he talked about opposing settlements in East Jerusalem and thereby given Shamir more ammo, in internal Israeli deliberations, to defeat the American initiative in 1990. And it was Baker who in the fall of 1990 worked out, with then Israeli foreign minister David Levy, a deal that granted Israel $400 million in loan guarantees with the understanding (never honored by Israel) that the United States would receive information on Israeli settlement activity (to assuage American concerns). In the fall of 1991 Baker had already seen the Israeli settlements movie too many times. On the eve of his effort to put together an Arab-Israeli peace conference at Madrid, he was not going to allow even the appearance that America was subsidizing Israeli settlements with big money to stand.

I asked him about loan guarantees. "My philosophy is that you achieve political power," Baker began, "in order to accomplish results, and that you of course have to weigh the domestic political consequences of what you do. But we had political support from all over the country that said, 'No guarantees unless you agree to stop settlement activity.' " Baker, now talking about politics, made clear that Jewish votes and financial support were simply not that important to Bush's reelection strategy. "We didn't lose in 1992 from any adverse consequence from [the loan guarantees]." Unlike Carter and even Ford in 1975, Bush and Baker were playing with a very strong political hand, even with a Democratic Congress. And on Arab-Israeli peace, which both the president and the secretary of state were convinced was a key American national interest, they played that hand well with Congress, Israel, and the American Jewish community, and they won.

The messy fight that broke out over loan guarantees for a few weeks in September might have been avoided altogether had Israel accepted Baker's proposed 120-day postponement. But a perfect storm was brewing that made compromise highly unlikely. Baker's determination was matched by Shamir's determination to fight and win; Shamir's miscalculation was fed by some of his advisors and by AIPAC's equally wrongheaded view that the president would have no choice but to compromise on what the American Jewish community came to see as a humanitarian issue—the rescue of Soviet Jews.

For Shamir, the loan guarantees became a matter of entitlement. Having absorbed Iraqi SCUDs and having agreed to go to Madrid, he believed that the administration owed him, and that the humanitarian character of emigrating Russian Jews would carry the day both in Congress and with the American public. Some of his advisors, including his finance minister, Yitzhak Modai, had told Shamir that Israel didn't need the guarantees on economic grounds. But according to Yossi Ben-Aharon, who initially pushed Shamir to press ahead, the prime minister wanted to prove a political point that the Bush administration supported absorption. Arens and Zalman Shoval would later advise Shamir to postpone his request, but the prime minister figured he could prevail. When Baker told Shamir that the administration would have to oppose his request, he recalls Shamir saying, "I am told we can get them anyway."

AIPAC's calculations were equally off base. Buoyed by congressional support for postwar aid to Israel and by the power of the Soviet Jewry issue on the Hill, the pro-Israel lobby seemed to believe that the president would have no choice but to compromise. AIPAC and others deeply mistrusted both Bush and Baker and felt that the Jewish community needed an issue around which to mobilize. "Nobody ever thought that Bush or Baker were good buddies after five P.M.," Tom Dine, AIPAC's executive director at the time, told me. There was a perception, he continued, that "these guys wanted to stick it to Shamir." Well before Israel presented its formal request for the guarantees on September 6, the Jewish community had organized an "education day" to bring people to Washington to highlight for Congress and the administration how much they cared about loan guarantees and implicitly to make clear that opposing them would have political consequences. "It wasn't meant to be anti-Bush," Malcolm Hoenlein, who played a key role in organizing the effort, told me. It was a "humanitarian" issue, not a political one.

What made the loan guarantee fight even messier were the president's comments at a September 12 news conference, the very day the Jewish community's education day was unfolding on the Hill. That day, the president had a meeting with key AIPAC supporters, one of whom, Baker recalls, all but said that Bush would be hurt politically if the guarantees were not approved. After a staunch defense of his efforts to help Jews leave the former Soviet Union and his support for Israel, Bush was asked about the "powerful political forces" he'd referred to that opposed him on the issue. He answered by describing himself as "one lonely little guy down here against something like a thousand lobbyists on the Hill working the other side of the question."

That remark, against the backdrop of rising American Jewish anxiety on loan guarantees and Bush's and Baker's views on Israel, set off a bombshell. "Oh shit," Tom Dine blurted out, watching the press conference in his office. "Here's a real confrontation. It's a total distortion. Bush is trying to play the victim." With those remarks, Hoenlein recalled, the president turned "education day" into an "anti-Bush event." The organized Jewish community interpreted the president's remarks as a direct assault on its right to lobby for Israel and aroused fears that the president was implying that Jews were not loyal Americans.

The Jewish community had only itself to blame. Shamir and AIPAC had both miscalculated badly. One veteran AIPAC lobbyist told me that the Israelis had misread American politics and believed "Congress was so strong with Israel, it didn't matter what a president thought. You could just keep going, run it through." In late August Baker had begun some preemptive lobbying of his own, sensing that even among some Democrat senators like Vermont's Patrick Leahy and House Speaker Tom Foley, there might be some potential support. Pro-Israel senators like Kasten and Inouye were initially more inclined to fight, but ultimately they concluded that the votes might not be there to override a presidential veto. Jim Bond, who worked for Kasten, recalls a meeting he attended with pro-Israel senators and AIPAC officials in which it was clear there wasn't much stomach for a fight. "I think I'm going to convert because at least then there will be one Jew that's got balls," Bond said. "You guys are just going to give in to this crap." The fact is that the settlement issue was not worth risking a messy fight with the president. "A lot of us in Congress agreed with Jim Baker at that time," Bob Kasten recalls, "but...we didn't feel it would be helpful coming out and saying, 'Okay, the Congress says no aid.'" Postponement of a decision on loan guarantees was the best alternative.

By late September that was precisely what had happened. Taking on a president in the middle of a diplomatic initiative on the settlement issue—which many senators already opposed, particularly when the decision involved only postponement of Israel's request, not cancellation—made no sense. Shamir agreed to postponement. On October 2 the Senate voted to postpone it for 120 days as well. When the issue of loan guarantees was joined again in February, Israeli elections had been set for June, and there was no way Bush or Baker would give Shamir an edge as he squared off against Rabin. Baker had worked out with Congress a compromise for conditionality—a dollar-for-dollar deduction from guarantees for any money spent on settlements. Shamir would not accept the compromise. Clearly Shamir's loss to Rabin was partly driven by the former's mismanagement of loan guarantees and his bungling of the U.S.-Israeli relationship. After some tough negotiations in August, the new prime minister accepted the dollar-for-dollar provision, and the "other Yitzhak" received an initial tranche of $2 billion in loan guarantees from America.

Like Kissinger and Carter, Bush and Baker were tangling with a tough Israeli prime minister and a determined pro-Israel lobby and Jewish community. It was for them—as it had been for their predecessors—an occupational reality. Those who argue that Bush and Baker lacked the kind of gut pro-Israel affinity of a Reagan, Shultz, or Clinton are absolutely right; those who argue that Bush and Baker were anti-Semites or unreasonably harsh on Israel are wrong. When Richard Haass told the president that his "one lonely guy" remark could set off a firestorm, Bush didn't believe it. He may have been tone-deaf to Jewish sensibilities, but he wasn't anti-Israel. Several months later, during a mend-the-fences meeting with the Conference of Presidents, Hoenlein recalls Bush, with tears in his eyes, apologizing for the way his September remarks were construed. Hoenlein would tell me that the president was just "trying to implement a policy and now Congress and everyone was trying to undermine it." To be blunter: long opposed to Shamir's settlement policies, both Bush and Baker were determined not to grant Shamir loan guarantees and to avoid both the appearance and the reality of subsidizing settlements.

Were Bush and Baker too tough on Israel? In the first year, some of their public comments were gratuitous, brought them little from the Arabs, and cost them the confidence of Israel and the American Jewish community. Planning for Madrid using tough public rhetoric, while coordinating closely with the Israelis on substance, was a fair trade-off and gave Baker the image and credibility he needed to sell his ideas to the Arabs. On balance, the Madrid conference was a great deal for the Israelis.

On loan guarantees, let's not forget that Shamir was asking the United States for political backing without extending much reciprocity, particularly given Israel's stonewalling on providing credible information on settlement activity. When it came to an Israel led by Yitzhak Shamir, Bush and Baker were not sentimental guys. Rabin and Peres, the president said, concluding our interview, "were two great leaders. I think if we had more of them we'd be farther along the road to peace."

Still, as I sat in Madrid's Palacio Real, the official residence of the king of Spain, as a member of the American delegation to the Madrid peace conference, I knew the president and the secretary of state had accomplished a great deal. The drama of the moment was undeniable. In the ornate and spacious Hall of Columns, at the top of one of the most spectacular staircases I'd ever seen, the Spanish had constructed an enormous T-shaped table covered in white linen beneath half a dozen dazzling crystal chandeliers.

At the top of the T, Presidents Bush and Gorbachev, flanked by Baker and Russian foreign minister Pankin, looked across the table at the prime minister of Israel, the foreign ministers of Egypt, Syria, and Jordan, a joint Jordanian-Palestinian delegation, and representatives from the UN, the European Union, and the Gulf Cooperation Council. With the exception of ours and Russia's, flags, nameplates, and other assorted national trappings had been prohibited. That didn't stop Saeb Erekat, always willing to push the envelope, from wearing a black-and-white Palestinian *hatta* or headdress that draped over his shoulders. That and his pre-Madrid interview with CNN, in which he linked the Palestinian delegation with the PLO, would put him on the wrong side of Jim Baker for months. The only other bit of pre-conference controversy was a minor tiff with the Spanish over whether to remove the enormous oil painting of Charles V killing the Moors. They moved it.

Not surprisingly, the conference had as much warmth and good feeling as a shotgun wedding. No one knew precisely how to react or behave. When Shamir entered the hall looking awkward and uncomfortable, I went over to him to see how I might help. "What should I do now?" he said. Other than take his seat, I didn't know what to tell him. Finally, I blurted out: "Why not go over and kibitz with your new friends?" The remark was too flip by half. Sitting between the Lebanese and the Egyptian foreign ministers, both of whom gave very tough anti-Israel speeches, Shamir was not happy. His own remarks, laced with grievances against the Arabs, were hardly uplifting. After all, in the words of former Israeli foreign minister and Madrid delegate Shlomo Ben-Ami, Shamir had come to Madrid to "protect his possessions, not to negotiate them away." When Ben-Ami asked the prime minister what he thought of Gorbachev's speech, Shamir, honest to a fault, replied, "I don't know, I fell asleep." Eli Rubenstein, himself a Madrid delegate and close advisor to Shamir, had once quoted to me the remark of an African king: "Sometimes I sit and think, sometimes I just sit." At Madrid, Shamir, who left the conference early, claiming he couldn't be out of Israel on the Sabbath, was just sitting.

For Palestinians, despite all the conditions and constraints on their participation, Madrid was a significant moment in their national life. The conference did nothing to change the reality of life under Israeli occupation, but it offered them, for the first time, an American-produced international forum to highlight the Palestinian narrative. Here Palestinians emerged not as hapless refugees or bloodthirsty terrorists—images fixed in America's mind—but as articulate, responsible political interlocutors. Haidar Abdul Shafi, a tough ex-Communist with impeccable nationalist credentials, gave perhaps the best speech of all in a series of speeches in which everyone else took the low road. Abdul Shafi was tough, blasting Israeli practices in the West Bank and Gaza, but he also reached out to the Israelis: "We wish to directly address the Israeli people with whom we have had a prolonged exchange of pain. Let us share hope instead...your security and ours are mutually dependent, as entwined as the fears and nightmares of our children." More important, from Baker's perspective, Abdul Shafi didn't advertise what everyone knew: the PLO was calling the shots.

The surreal theater that surrounded the Palestinian representation at Madrid really was surreal. The delegation's members and the opening address had been approved by Arafat personally. Numerous PLO officials descended on Madrid. Ashrawi admits that the PLO leadership had no real strategy either for Madrid or for the talks that would follow. What mattered was that the PLO was in charge and that everyone knew it. I learned later that the night the conference opened, Arafat had secretly arranged for an aircraft to transport a hundred Palestinians to Algiers for meetings with PLO officials.

But the prize for chutzpah, even by the low-road standards of Madrid's speeches, had to go to Syrian foreign minister Farouk Shara. Shara really annoyed Baker, and Baker thoroughly enjoyed beating up on him. In a meeting shortly before Madrid, Baker pushed Shara so hard Shara felt like throwing up. "You must be on drugs," Baker exploded, in response to another of the Syrian's unreasonable demands.

Shara was a man of small stature and even a smaller worldview. Admittedly, given Assad's hard-line views, he wasn't interested in reaching out. As I watched him on the conference's final day, standing at the speaker's podium. I couldn't believe what I was seeing. Shara had given a tough speech at the first session. Now he was in overkill mode. "Let me show you an old picture of Shamir when he was thirty-two years old," Shara began, holding up an old British "wanted" poster of a much younger Shamir from his days in the Stern Gang. "He kills peace mediators and talks about Syria, Lebanon terrorism."

We never really called Shara on his antics. We were prepared to beat up on the Palestinians and Saeb's *hatta*, but we acquiesced in Syria's refusal to engage in any serious public diplomacy. On reflection, I think this willingness to tolerate from Syria what we wouldn't accept from the Palestinians proved costly. It only reinforced Assad's belief that he could do peacemaking his own way, without the public diplomacy that the Egyptians, Palestinians, and Jordanians had so effectively used with the Israelis. And it set a pattern, which began after Madrid, that we could be jerked around. Unhappy with

President Bush's use of the phrase "territorial compromise," Shara was now balking at allowing the delegation to sit with Israel in what was to be the first bilateral Syrian-Israeli negotiation. The two sides met on November 1 in Madrid, but it would take Baker's intervention with the Saudis to make it happen. For both Shamir and Shara, I thought that we should have had T-shirts made with the words "I survived Madrid." That's about all either of them did.

Madrid was really the end of Jim Baker's sustained involvement in Arab-Israeli diplomacy, and he knew it. Coming back on the plane, he said that this would be his "last trip." Actually he would travel to Moscow in January 1992 to launch the multilateral negotiations and would take one final trip to the Middle East in July. Baker's remark partly reflected the reality that given the intransigence of Assad, Shamir, and the PLO, there wasn't much chance for serious progress in the post-Madrid negotiations. And he was right. Between December 1991 and December 1992, ten rounds of negotiations were held in Washington. More taboos were broken, ideas were exchanged, and an agreement on an Israeli-Jordanian agenda was concluded, but the public, formal character of the talks, and the yawning gaps between the sides, meant that Baker wasn't about to invest much in Washington talks that couldn't produce much.

Looking back, I have little doubt in my mind that Baker saw Madrid as a way of setting the stage for Arab-Israeli diplomacy in the first Bush administration that might have led to a possible breakthrough during the second. Denying Shamir loan guarantees in the fall of 1991 may not have been designed to help defeat him, but it had that effect. Rabin, who defeated Shamir in June 1992, exploited Shamir's mismanagement of the U.S.-Israeli relationship. Bush and Baker, who both thought the world of Rabin, were only too happy to see Shamir go. And in July Baker found in the "new Yitzhak" a serious partner for moving ahead with Syria and the Palestinians.

A new chapter was about to open in Arab-Israeli peacemaking, but Baker would not be part of it. In August he resigned his position as secretary of state to run the president's reelection campaign. As I listened to Baker's emotional departure speech, together with hundreds of my State Department colleagues, I realized that the wheel was turning once again. That fall, even with Rabin as prime minister, the negotiations in Washington dragged on, now burdened by an approaching American presidential election and by their own internal contradictions. That December, in the wake of Rabin's decision to deport 415 Hamas members to southern Lebanon, negotiations broke down. They continued off and on for the next seven months until the secret Israeli-PLO Oslo breakthrough in August 1993 rendered them completely obsolete.

The significance of what Baker accomplished at Madrid is mixed, as is revealed by his own ambivalence. Its real significance was that it "took place," he said to me in Jerusalem in 2005. But six months later, when I interviewed him in Houston, he said that there would have been no Israeli-Jordanian peace treaty without it. Both judgments are right. Madrid produced no agreements, but it broke taboos, legitimized Arab-Israeli negotiations, and provided political cover, time, and space for secret diplomacy to work. The 1992 Washington talks also helped prevent an escalation of violence and confrontation, particularly between Israelis and Palestinians.

On balance, and with some perspective, Baker's accomplishment at Madrid was more about the process of diplomacy than about results. The 1991 Madrid framework was the last significant American-brokered agreement between Arabs and Israelis. Since then the United States has not mediated a single agreement of consequence that has actually been fully implemented. The skills that James Baker demonstrated to pull off Madrid— the toughness, tenacity, timing, and trust—were the same ones Kissinger and Carter exhibited. To his credit, President Bush made Arab-Israeli diplomacy a top priority and backed up his secretary of state.

Unfortunately, those same skills, needed so badly to confront the next phase of peace-process diplomacy, when in fact there were real opportunities, were by then not nearly as evident. Had there been a second Bush administration with Baker as secretary of state, "I know we would have reached one agreement, probably with Syria," Dennis Ross told me. "With Rabin," Baker told me at ceremonies in Jerusalem marking the tenth anniversary of the prime minister's murder, "I know we could have got something done." Having watched James Baker operate for four years, I had not the slightest doubt.

Part Three

AMERICA'S PROMISE FRUSTRATED

"Have you seen Dennis Ross?" I asked the White House staffer standing outside the conference room door. "It's really important that I talk to him." It was January 2000, and we were winding down a week of Israeli-Syrian negotiations in Shepherdstown, West Virginia. I was headed to Israel, the West Bank, and Gaza for more talks with the Israelis and Palestinians and had to discuss a minor but urgent travel issue with Dennis. "I think he's in with the president," the staffer said.

I stuck my head in the door, hoping to catch Dennis's eye. Instead I saw President Clinton in a typical informal pose: feet on the conference table, chomping on an unlit cigar. He was chatting with Secretary of State Madeleine Albright, National Security Advisor Sandy Berger, and several others as he attacked a crossword.

The president looked up. "Aaron, maybe you can help me. None of my other advisors can seem to figure this one out." Expecting some detailed question on the Golan Heights, I was thrown more than a little off balance. "What's a seven-letter word for a shoulder-launched antitank weapon?" he asked me. *Is he kidding?* I thought. Drawing on my vast knowledge of World War II weaponry, which rested on careful research in comic books and television programs, I responded with the only answer that came to mind: "Bazooka, Mr. President." "That works," Clinton replied, filling in the boxes. Glancing at Albright, he added, "Madeleine, maybe we should give Aaron a raise."

In retrospect, if we had been as good at giving the president sound advice on Arab-Israeli negotiations as we were in providing answers to crossword puzzles, we might have gotten a good deal further than we did. Bad advice, however, was only one of the problems that plagued the Clinton years, and it was not the one that contributed to our lack of success.

Bill Clinton inherited the most promising environment for Arab-Israeli peacemaking in the history of America's involvement in the issue. In August 1993 Prime Minister Yitzhak Rabin told Secretary of State Warren Christopher that he was ready to withdraw fully from the Golan Heights if Syria would meet Israeli needs. Israel and the PLO, negotiating secretly, agreed not only on mutual recognition but also on a series of implementing agreements that quickly became known as the Oslo accords. In October 1994 Jordan and Israel, negotiating secretly, once again on their own, signed a full treaty of peace. By the time of Rabin's assassination in November 1995, Arabs and Israelis, with American support, had created an unprecedented network of contacts and ties: with the exception of Iraq and Libya, every member of the Arab League (even Mauritania and Djibouti) had some form of contact with Israel.

Unlike Kissinger, Carter, or Baker, Bill Clinton and his team had the advantage of working with three Israeli prime ministers—Rabin, Peres, and Barak—who wanted to do serious peacemaking. The fourth, Netanyahu, began his term as an intractable foe of any pact with the Palestinians but finally succumbed to Clinton's appeals, even agreeing to redeploy from the West Bank city of Hebron—something too difficult for his Labor rivals to implement. We also dealt with two Arab leaders, Arafat and Assad, who, while difficult in the extreme, possessed the authority and weight to conclude agreements, and a third, King Hussein, who rivaled Sadat as an attractive and compelling Arab leader. Finally, we had Bill Clinton himself, the first American president to wrestle seriously with the most difficult issues in the Arab-Israeli problem. That each could be described with the word *final* demonstrated the mortal nature of the stakes for all concerned: the final status of Jerusalem as the capital of two states; the final delineation of borders between Israel and a new Palestinian state; and the final resolution of the

Palestinian refugee problem. Clinton made Arab-Israeli peace a top priority, gained the trust of the parties, and pursued his goal tenaciously right up to the end of his term.

Yet with all these advantages, when Bill Clinton left the White House eight years later, the Arab-Israeli peace process lay in ruins, bloodied, battered, and broken. Israel and the Palestinians had plunged into a crisis of confidence and a paroxysm of violence and terror from which they have not yet fully recovered. What happened? How was such an extraordinary set of opportunities lost? And what role did the president and his advisors play in this tragic turn of events? This last question is particularly important. Given the stakes for America, we need to take a hard, honest look at what we got right and wrong. Michael Jackson, a guy who doesn't usually impart much wisdom in his lyrics, had this one about right: if you want to make a change, "start with the man in the mirror."

Chapter Seven

Caterer, Cash Man, and Crisis Manager, 1993–99

Sometime in the fall of 1992 I called Dennis Ross, who'd left the State Department to join James Baker in his effort to manage President Bush's reelection campaign. I told him I had some good news and some bad. On the positive side, Rabin's election earlier that year had created some possible opportunities in the negotiations; on the negative end, given Bush's prospects for reelection, we wouldn't be around to work on them. As usual, we laughed about it.

It didn't take a brilliant political analyst to sense that Bush was in trouble, particularly in a three-way race, or that the transition to a Democratic administration would mean our exclusion from the peace process. All life begins with the personal, and even though I was a tenured civil servant, the new guys weren't likely to want the old around. After a twelve-year drought, a line of experts a mile long with solid Democratic connections had formed, eager to do foreign policy.

But the need to manage and succeed can trump politics. Rabin's deportation of 415 Palestinians tied to Hamas, after a spate of terror attacks in December, triggered a suspension of the Madrid negotiations, and the new secretary of state, Warren Christopher, asked Dennis to stay on for a brief period to help out. Ambassador Sam Lewis became the new director of policy planning and asked me to join him in working on the Arab-Israeli issue. And there was more. Tom Donilon, Christopher's key advisor, got to know Dennis and decided that since he "was one of the smartest guys in the whole friggin' building," he should stay permanently to coordinate all Arab-Israeli negotiations, which is what Dennis wanted if he had been asked earlier to remain. In June 1993 the president created the Office of the Special Middle East Coordinator (SMEC) for this purpose. Dennis asked me to join him as deputy coordinator.

On balance, the creation of the SMEC was great for me but not entirely positive for management of the negotiations. Like almost all of its predecessors stretching back to Nixon's day, the Clinton administration created a small and highly centralized structure to deal with the Arab-Israeli issue, reporting directly to the secretary and the president. Because of the sensitivity of the issues, particularly in a fast-moving negotiation, you needed a small, dedicated team. But you also needed transparency, supervision, and balance, all of which appeared to be increasingly lacking as time passed. Our office accorded subordinate or derivative roles to the Near East Affairs (NEA) Bureau and to our ambassadors in the field. We failed to brief them on many of the conversations we were having with Arabs and Israelis; nor did we give them time or opportunity to provide a useful critique of our tactics and strategies. A tight circle formed. We included NEA but could exclude it inadvertently and at will in the inevitable process of modification and adjustment of our approach. Ambassador Bob Pelletreau, who would become assistant secretary of the NEA bureau in 1994, observed that the "whole show" was pretty much run out of Dennis's "hip pocket."

NEA naturally complained about this process—or lack thereof—but I dismissed most of the complaining as sour grapes motivated by the oldest bureaucratic grievance of all: they weren't in charge. I was partly right, as I was to find out when I tried to make my way in the second Bush administration eight years later. You can't run the peace process by committee. But we kept few detailed records and did not share information with the goal of producing the best policy. We should have maintained a comprehensive negotiating record of the historic Camp David summit. A historian by training, I should have pushed harder for such a record but did not. In September 2000, when Israel's lead negotiator, Gilad Sher, discovered that no detailed account existed of what Israelis and Palestinians had said to each other, he was stunned.

These imperfections caused more than minor bureaucratic snafus. Toni Verstandig, the smart, politically savvy NEA deputy assistant secretary covering the peace process and economic issues, pleaded with me to understand that a tight circle was no way to run a railroad, particularly given how much work we faced. Bruce Riedel, the president's senior advisor on Arab-Israeli negotiations, told me that we lacked the necessary support for major presidential involvement. The structure for making foreign policy decisions, he said, was "completely null," and we rarely "talked to anybody outside."

The lack of balance, particularly when we began to dig into permanent status issues, became an even more glaring problem. Baker had retained a firm hand on his advisors and experts, providing the necessary balance and direction when he sensed we were veering too much in the direction of either the Israelis or the Arabs. Given the close ties between Rabin and the president, and given the administration's desire to eliminate the American-Israeli tensions of the Bush-Baker years, our lack of balance meant that we tended to see things mainly from an Israeli perspective.

When Israelis and Palestinians were negotiating on their own as they groped toward the Oslo accords, our bias toward Israel did not seem consequential. Indeed, Kissinger and Baker had also worked from an Israeli script at times, but ensuring the Arabs got things too.

The Clinton administration eventually would come to understand the need for balance in its policy toward the parties, when it made a presentation in December 2000 on parameters for permanent status. But by then it was far too late. If the president wasn't going to be tough with Rabin or Barak on the issue of settlements, and he wasn't, he'd hardly push them on the even more explosive issues of Jerusalem and borders. Oddly enough, we did display balance by the unfortunate fact that we failed to press Arafat sufficiently either. By any standard, we should have been far tougher with the Palestinian leader on violence, terror, incitement, the absence of rule of law, transparency of governance, and honest fiscal management of Palestinian institutions.

Clinton's choice of Warren Christopher as secretary of state embodied our tendency to move away from the forceful diplomacy of the Baker years. Christopher's first substantive meeting with Arafat, in Amman at the end of 1993, said it all. Arafat was on one of his more outrageous rants, literally screaming at the secretary as the Palestinian leader cataloged real and imaginary Israeli abuses against Palestinians. Christopher sat frozen, almost sphinxlike, not moving a muscle. He was firm but polite with Arafat to a fault. Dennis recalls the secretary saying after the meeting, "I never want to deal with him again."

Christopher was laser smart, politically savvy, and had a fine hand for drafting, a skill honed during his years at the prestigious L.A. law firm O'Melveny and Myers. Kind and considerate, he was the most decent person I ever encountered in almost twenty-five years of government service. I never heard him use profanity or lose control. In my effort to break the ice and create a relationship, I gave him a copy of the first book I had written, on the origins of America's special relationship with Saudi Arabia, in anticipation of his first trip there. He presented it to King Fahd, introducing me as the "distinguished Professor Miller."

Looking back now, when it came to the Middle East, I think Christopher was trapped in a three-cornered box, hedged in by Clinton, Rabin, and America's pro-Israel community. Having been deputy secretary of state during the Carter administration, he was no stranger to the Arab-Israeli issue. He knew how hard it was to make progress and how tough you had to be to do so. At the same time he was now dealing with a president who wasn't going to push the Israelis around and who had a stake in repairing ties with an American Jewish community that felt kicked around by Bush and Baker. Christopher was never quite sure how far he could push

Rabin, whose "forbidding" persona, to use the secretary's own words, made pushing no simple matter. Between Clinton, Rabin, and American Jews, Christopher didn't have much choice but to hold back and pull punches. Given our role as a facilitator rather than broker, his personality suited the moment. Still, there were times when I sensed that the inner man wanted to yell and explode. It would have helped us if he had.

In the early years the other senior advisors only reinforced the understandable pro-Rabin sentiments. Sam Lewis, who had enormous experience with the Israelis, liked and respected Rabin and would no more have second-guessed him than would any of us. Martin Indyk's emergence in 1993 exemplified the Clinton administration's desire to ease tensions with Israel and the American Jewish community. Indyk also favored pursuit of an agreement on the Syrian track first. He'd go two out of three. A smart, tough Australian national who was close to AIPAC and ran a pro-Israel think tank in Washington, Martin became an American citizen and ultimately served as the NSC's senior Middle East expert, as assistant secretary for Near East Affairs, and twice as ambassador to Israel. Martin and I argued constantly about everything from settlement activity to the wisdom of putting Syria first. His views on Israel toughened considerably over the years, but in the early 1990s he helped shape and reinforce a trend that was already clear: Bush and Baker had needlessly alienated and antagonized Israel and American Jewry. Serious movement on the peace process required America to regain Israel's confidence before all else.

Whatever else we disagreed on, Dennis, Martin, and I brought a clear pro-Israel orientation to our peace-process planning. Dennis often told me that Israelis saw him as the Palestinians' lawyer, and I know he believed it, but I chuckle now when I think about it, because the Palestinians never regarded him that way. In truth, not a single senior-level official involved with the negotiations was willing or able to present, let alone fight for, the Arab or Palestinian perspective. Under Bush and Baker, the administration's four key peace-process advisors were also American Jews, but the secretary and president provided the necessary checks and balances to ensure that policy remained fair. At Camp David in 1978 Sam Lewis, then ambassador to Israel, presented Begin's perspective when necessary, and people listened. The Clinton administration offered no comparable voice for the Arabs.

Different points of view always coexist in a close-knit team. Not everyone bought into the groupthink on how sensitive we should be to Israeli needs. Dan Kurtzer, who had left the peace process in 1994 because he felt shut out by Dennis, had always argued for balance, and as a career Foreign Service officer, he pushed hard to factor in the views of our ambassadors and embassies. During the Camp David period Dan was in Cairo as ambassador, and we should have given greater weight to his views, as well as those of Bill Burns, our ambassador to Jordan. Our entire approach would have gained considerable credibility had we simply listened to these two exemplary public servants.

Rob Malley, one of the most thoughtful people I ever worked with, also took a dissenting line. He'd grown up in France, where his father had been a prominent journalist covering the Middle East, and acquired rigorous intellectual standards through his own education: a Ph.D. from Oxford and a law degree from Harvard. He was only one of two Americans in the inner circle who argued that the two Mr. A's would not accept much less than 100 percent of their demands. But he couldn't push the envelope too far, since he worked directly for Sandy Berger and the president.

Gamal Helal was one of the most remarkable people I'd ever met. Originally from Assiut, south of Cairo, Gamal came to America in the 1970s, specializing in cross-cultural communication, and in the mid-1980s joined Language Services at the State Department as an interpreter. I met him for the first time on one of the Baker trips.

To say that Gamal served as an interpreter is like saying that Cal Ripken played baseball. By the mid-1990s Gamal had emerged as an analyst, advisor, and at times confidant not only of President Clinton and his secretaries of state but also of Arafat, the Palestinians, and the Saudi and Egyptian leaders as well. The Israelis loved Gamal in particular for his language skills and original analysis. Rarely if ever has anyone at his level been willing to speak as openly and honestly to presidents and foreign leaders. And Gamal did so with respect, humor, and a capacity to teach that generated real trust. His relationships in mid-2007 with President George W. Bush, Secretary Rice, and Vice President Cheney attest to the fact that he's a nonpolitical national asset.

If only we'd listened to him. He consistently came down hard on Arabs and Israelis alike and derided any sentimentality. In Gamal's dry-eyed view, we were dealing with a tough neighborhood in which the Syrians, Palestinians, and Israelis, were often duplicitous. We must convince ourselves that no peace could be bought on the cheap, and we had to let the Arabs and the Israelis know in straight talk that they'd have to respond to each other's needs if they expected to reach agreements. If either side snookered us, Gamal told me repeatedly, we had only ourselves to blame.

With all its imperfections, the Clinton administration's Middle East negotiation team consisted of talented, creative, and dedicated people. Had I not been so caught up in the "being there" phenomenon, I might have tried harder to address the key flaws in our operation. As an academic with ties to outside experts, I should have pressed for the inclusion of other views, particularly in the run-up to critical meetings. And being inclusive by nature, I should have fought more tenaciously to open our tight little circle.

But hindsight's always twenty-twenty. I could barely keep up with my own schedule and had to spend much of my time trying to obtain as much information as possible from an all-too-often tight-lipped Dennis. The peace process didn't fail because we lacked an adequate management strategy. Still, a better structure would have enabled us to more effectively advise the secretary and the president, as would freer discussion and debate in front of the decision-makers. We had argued in front of Baker, who took what he wanted from the exchanges but benefited, I am sure, from hearing the give-and-take. This freewheeling style of discussion stopped under Christopher, who became uncomfortable with a lot of chatter and made Dennis the point man for all briefings. I quickly realized that discretion was the better part of valor and did not argue for a return to open debate. Neither I nor the peace process benefited from argument with Dennis in front of the secretary.

Madeleine Albright told me that one of her "great joys" had been watching Dennis and me argue about peace-process matters great and small, but I think she was being kind. Jamie Rubin, her press spokesman, probably had it right when he compared our arguments to the bickering of an old married couple about the best route to get to the movies. Decision-makers don't need a cacophony of discordant voices, but they do need time to listen to different options before key actions are taken.

From Mediator to Facilitator

Having been through four presidential transitions, I knew that every new administration comes to Washington with the intent of reinventing the wheel in some policy area. The Clinton administration was no exception. But when it came to the Middle East, the Democrats who arrived in 1993 inherited something that they needed to nurture and protect. Bush 41 and Baker had done remarkably well in passing on a set of Madrid negotiations that, while ultimately unproductive, still resulted in Arabs and Israelis talking to each other. The new administration wanted to keep the conversation going. One of the few senior officials to survive the changeover was Ed Djerejian, who stayed on as assistant secretary for Near Eastern Affairs, serving as a symbol of Clinton's commitment to Madrid.

New strategies, Anthony Lake once told me, are greatly overrated. President Clinton's first national security advisor went on to say that events usually lead to adjustments or fresh ideas. Bill Clinton had as much foreign policy experience as Jimmy Carter, the last southern governor to reach the White House. But it didn't take a Henry Kissinger to figure out that in the Middle East, particularly in Arab-Israeli negotiations, at a minimum the new administration must preserve the gains of the old. If a foreign policy construct was developing for the Middle East, it could be loosely described as dual containment—an approach designed to check both Iranian and Iraqi ambitions. For the peace process, this construct produced one very important consequence—it made Syria a key priority. Bush and Baker had also focused on Syria, but now, instead of having to push futilely on a door that the first Yitzhak (Shamir) slammed shut, Clinton's team had merely to knock on a door that the second Yitzhak (Rabin) had already opened. The notion of Syria first dovetailed with the thinking of the new Israeli prime minister, whose own strategic goal would be to make peace with the inner circle (Syria, the Palestinians, and Lebanon) so as to counter more forcefully the strategic threat to Israel posed by the outer circle (the acquisition by Iran and Iraq of weapons of mass destruction and by Islamic extremism).

Indeed, Rabin's accession to power represented the single biggest change in the Arab-Israeli arena during the Clinton years. His policies and presence influenced the American approach more than any strategy we developed. Clinton now had a historic opportunity: Rabin's desire to do serious peacemaking, gradual and cautious though it was, fundamentally reoriented America's thinking. In his second incarnation as prime minister, Rabin became the first Israeli leader to commit his government to a strategy based on peace. And we would do everything possible to support him and his commitment. The operating logic was clear: Israel needed American support to move ahead, and that meant strengthening Israel's confidence wherever and whenever possible.

The transition from Shamir to Rabin and from Bush to Clinton also ushered in a new style of operating toward the American Jewish community. "We were determined," Tom Donilon recalled, "to take an entirely different approach." Dennis, who'd helped Baker run Bush's reelection campaign, remembered how the Democrats had used the president's antisettlement policy against him. The new administration now made a determined effort to ensure that the tensions with Israel and the Jewish community would become vestiges of the past. "They were going to show they were different," Bruce Riedel recalls. "Bringing in Martin Indyk was a signal." Some elements of the community expressed concern about the appointment of Warren Christopher as secretary of state, because of his association with the Carter administration. I asked Christopher about this. He said that he had met early on with Jewish leaders and "gave them the reassurance that I would make myself accessible."

And we did, reaching out to the organized Jewish community with conference calls, meetings, and briefings, not only Christopher, but the president as well, and on down from him. As a result, Bill Clinton faced less pressure from domestic politics than any other president engaged in serious Arab-Israeli diplomacy. In fact if there was any pressure from the Jewish community it came from groups like Peace Now and the Israel Policy Forum that were pushing him to go fast. At times, there were hiccups, especially during the Netanyahu years, and we had to deal with standard bumps in the road, such as the perennial legislation to move our embassy from Tel Aviv to Jerusalem. But as Christopher recalls, at least during Clinton's first term, "I can't remember a specific issue on which we took a decision or didn't take a decision because of fear of the so-called Jewish community."

There were two reasons for this harmonious relationship. First, of the four prime ministers with whom we worked, three were proactive in peacemaking and had exceptionally close ties with the administration. Good relations with Israeli prime ministers engendered good relations with the American Jewish community. In fact, not long after becoming prime minister, Rabin warned AIPAC to stay out of Israel's business on the peace process, and after the Oslo accords were revealed, he appealed for the organization's support, according to Steve Grossman, former AIPAC president and DNC chairman.

But most of the credit belonged to Bill Clinton who, as a natural politician, understood the importance of cultivating one of the Democratic Party's natural constituencies. Clinton, as Maria Echaveste, his domestic policy advisor and later deputy chief of

staff, told me, was very much aware of "who his donors were...
If the Middle East was on their mind, they'd talk to him and they
had lots of access." Steve Grossman, also close to the president,
put it another way: "Here was a guy who built deep relationships, valued those relationships, and was eminently comfortable
with the Jewish community and his Jewish friends." Clinton
wasn't pandering. Reaching out and bonding were fundamental
components of his DNA. "He was the first Jewish president and
the first black president," John Sununu Senior mused. After all,
with Israeli prime ministers pushing for peace, a Jewish community (Republican Jewish activists notwithstanding) following
their lead, a Democratic Party in love with its first president in
twelve years, and that president eager to do everything he could
to support bold Israeli moves, why should any domestic tensions
over Arab-Israeli negotiations erupt?

The real problem during the Clinton years was not pandering
to the Jewish community or even domestic constraints: it was the
change in America's perception of its role in Arab-Israeli peacemaking. The combination of the "do it themselves" Oslo process,
Rabin's reflexive opposition to a strong American role, and Clinton's
"reverence" for the prime minister, as Dennis put it—conditioned
us in the early years to act as a very cautious and deferential facilitator. "Rabin didn't want a mediator," Dennis recalls. "He wanted
us to be the facilitator or the intermediary," at least with the
Palestinians. This seemed to make perfect sense then. Oslo was
their breakthrough, not ours. We participated neither in the negotiating history nor, at least in the early years, in the implementation
process. And wasn't Oslo an American negotiator's dream come
true? Sadly, it wasn't. Within two years the Oslo vision was coming
apart, and America was in no position to save it.

Clinton and Rabin: Friends Forever

"Yitzhak loved America, and he loved Bill Clinton," Leah
Rabin told me, sitting in her living room in Tel Aviv a year after

her husband's murder. "He felt America was part of him, and he knew how important it was to the State of Israel." Rabin thought strategically, and whether as chief of staff of the Israeli army, ambassador to Washington, minister of defense, or prime minister, he knew that intimate ties with America were critical to Israel's survival. But the bond between Rabin and Clinton—so critical to understanding the early years of the Clinton administration—was far more than just about strategy.

All you had to do was see them together to understand that there was a deep bond of partnership. But what an odd pair. In 1993 Rabin, now seventy, more confident and mature than in his previous stint as prime minister, was a genuine national leader, a founding father, soldier, and politician. He could be crusty and short-tempered and was always unwilling to engage in meaningless small talk or to suffer fools. Bill Clinton, a young, untested president, a man of great appetite who knew little of war and conflict and whose strength was the art of the political and personal conversation and of building relationships, seemed his polar opposite.

When the two first met in the summer of 1992, this gap seemed very apparent. Eitan Haber, a longtime Rabin advisor, described that meeting as a "real disaster." Rabin gave a long and boring lecture about the Middle East while, according to Haber, everyone else talked quietly about the weather and Broadway plays in order to avoid listening to Rabin's "long, long and boring lecture." Everyone except Bill Clinton, who looked at Rabin the entire time like an adoring student with a brilliant professor. Haber recalls Rabin's saying, "He's too young to be president."

Talk to anyone around the president, and the perception of Clinton's reverence for Rabin endures. "He's everything Clinton would like to be. He's a soldier, a statesman, he's experienced everything there is to experience—none of the things Clinton has," Dennis Ross observes. Rahm Emanuel, who taught Clinton the Hebrew word for balls—*baytzim*—said that when Rabin came up in conversation, Clinton would often say that the prime minister had "an incredible set of brass *baytzim*."

And the bond was a mutual one. Haber believed that Rabin, who confided in few people, was incredibly open and honest with Clinton. Not only could Rabin tell that Clinton understood his politics, but he thought Clinton was a "great leader." It's fair to say that with the exception of Sadat and Carter, no American president was ever as close to any Middle East leader. In a statement that still amazes me every time I read it, Clinton recalled in his memoirs, "I had come to love him as I have rarely loved another man."[1]

If Rabin's persona impressed Clinton, his policies, particularly Oslo, sealed the deal. Not only did the historic signing and handshake on the White House lawn make Clinton a partner in the enterprise, it elevated him into the history books. "Clinton loved it. It appealed to him and gave him a kind of standing on the world stage," Tony Lake recalled. When I asked Sandy Berger where Clinton's interest in the Middle East came from, he said the president knew it was a "critical area" but urged me not to forget "the glorious opportunity of 1993." Oslo fell into the administration's lap, and the president was smart and ambitious enough to know that he couldn't let it go. For a young and inexperienced president, the chance to be associated with a solution to a very old conflict was the stuff of history. Carter recalled that meeting Sadat in April 1977 was his greatest day as president; September 13, 1993, may have been Clinton's.

The upside of the Clinton-Rabin bond was clear, but the downside, rarely acknowledged, was also evident. Some of the people I interviewed believed Clinton saw in Rabin the father figure he'd never had. Others thought the professor-student relationship was more accurate. I'm wary of psychobabble interpretations. Clinton was an astute politician and president of the United States, after all, not a twenty-something hanging on every word of a wise and brilliant lecturer. But most of us, when we're dealing with someone far more experienced, in this case one of the founding generation of the Israeli state, have a tendency to listen, learn, and not push back, let alone confront. And let's face it, Rabin was not one of the warmest personalities. In my experience, he could be incredibly intimidating. Clinton saw Rabin as "a monument of experience," Dennis Ross recalls. "So if this guy says something, it must be right."

None of us ever gave much thought to challenging the prime minister. Clinton was a quick study on the Middle East, but what did he, or any of us, know about matters relating to peace and war? And however much regard the prime minister had for America, he was never comfortable with letting us get too close to the negotiations unsupervised. Rabin was worried that if America got involved, we'd level the playing field at a time when he wanted to keep the pressure on Arafat. Dennis recalls now that one of our "main failings" was not to challenge Oslo's logic and Israel's actions. So we never had a tough or honest conversation with the Israelis on settlement activity. (The Israeli population of the West Bank and Gaza would grow by 46 percent during the Rabin years.) Long after Rabin's death, the pattern set by Clinton in the early years would continue, with Peres, even Netanyahu, and certainly Barak. We were very uneasy about any sustained challenge or second-guessing of Israeli prime ministers, what I've called the "Jewish lobby of one," at the end of the day the most effective pressure point on our policy.

Syria First, or Maybe Never

"It doesn't mean a damn thing who rules in Ramallah. What matters is the strategic importance of an Israeli-Syrian agreement." Martin Indyk's Australian accent was thick with sarcasm, and Dan Kurtzer and I, sitting in Ed Djerejian's office, were in the middle of a doozy of an argument with him in the first month of the Clinton administration on what our peace-process priorities should be. The two of us felt strongly that the real urgency and volatility for American interests lay in the untended Palestinian problem. And if the Arab-Israeli conflict had a core issue, this was certainly it. Others such as Martin, Ed Djerejian, Dennis, and ultimately the president saw a real chance with Syria.

It wasn't that I was opposed to the logic—at least on paper—of making Syria a priority. The case was really quite compelling. Assad was a strong leader. Syria was a real state, or close enough when compared with the Palestinians. The longevity of the 1974 Israeli-Syrian disengagement agreement had shown that Assad could abide by his agreements. And a deal for Golan would also mean an Israeli-Lebanese peace all without the political ferment that an Israeli-Palestinian agreement would bring. Sure, there were 20,000 settlers on the Golan, largely put there with Labor Party support. But there were 200,000 on the West Bank, some of whom were willing to fight rather than leave should an agreement be reached, and then there was Jerusalem. I also knew that Assad had fascinated every president since Richard Nixon and that this administration would be no exception, especially in light of the notion of dual containment, which sought to draw Syria into the peace orbit to make containing Iran and Iraq easier.

It all seemed to make so much sense, if (and this was a big if) you could get Assad and the Israelis to play along. I had watched Baker, a master negotiator, deal with Syria and wasn't all that certain the new negotiators could. To me, Assad, whom I dubbed "the Frank Sinatra of the peace process," wanted to make peace "his own way." This meant getting more than Sadat and giving less. The Egyptian got the international border; Assad wanted the June 4, 1967 lines.

I admit to a real bias here. The Syrians could demand their 100 percent, but they'd also have to give as much as they got. And they didn't give much of an indication in Madrid that they were prepared for this. In ten rounds of post-Madrid negotiations, there were no relaxed coffee breaks, few handshakes, and no quiet bilateral meetings, let alone consequential secret or public diplomacy. Assad seemed to want us simply to deliver the Golan to Syria. Forget cold peace—in 1993 his idea of the future with Israel looked like a blizzard. That and the fact that neither Rabin nor Assad seemed to be in a hurry strongly suggested that a Syrian-Israeli deal would be a long slog, at best a waste of time and at worst (and my fears came to be realized) a waste of an opportunity with the Palestinians.

But my argument with Martin and my views about Syria hardly mattered. When Rabin came to Washington in March 1993, he already had a plan for Syria. Tony Lake recalls how impressed he and the president were with the prime minister and his preference for at least testing whether he could do a deal with Syria first. Ed Djerejian had made a secret visit to Damascus in April that had produced very little from Assad regarding his views on normalization or setting up a discreet channel with the Israelis. And by May Rabin, playing two tracks at once, had authorized Israel's "official" involvement in what had been an internal back channel with the PLO under Norwegian auspices.

Early in August, with the Oslo channel near a breakthrough, Rabin made a startling offer to Christopher in a final effort to achieve a deal with Syria. Rabin conveyed to the secretary the famous "pocket" or deposit. Israel would commit itself to "full withdrawal" from the Golan Heights as long as Syria would meet Israeli needs on water, security, and peace. Christopher was authorized to tell Assad it was his understanding that Rabin would agree to these terms. The secretary recalled that en route to Damascus he was so excited that he could "barely contain my usually very containable self." Assad took note of Rabin's obvious move but not surprisingly raised issues with timing of withdrawal and normalization, signaling the long and never-ending story that would become the Israeli-Syrian negotiation. Disappointed in the extreme, Rabin stood down on Syria and consummated the Oslo deal. The first of three openings that might have, with heavy American lifting, led to a breakthrough entered the black hole of lost Arab-Israeli opportunities.

The August 1993 episode reflected the "ships passing in the night" problem that would define the Israeli-Syrian peace process during the Clinton administration. Never has so much time and energy been expended on a process that produced so little in the end. Clinton would see Assad in Geneva and Damascus (January and October 1994); two sets of unprecedented talks would take place between Syrian and Israeli chiefs of staff (November 1994 and June 1995); the Israeli and Syrian ambassadors would hold hundreds of hours of quiet discussions in Washington under

American auspices; and in the wake of Rabin's murder real progress would be made in two sets of negotiations at Wye River, during which Israelis and Syrians actually lived and negotiated together (December 1995 and January 1996).

Watching and participating in this process (although admittedly as a naysayer), I began to see early on that several major problems made chances of a deal slim to none.

Unlike the Israeli, Egyptian, Jordanian, and Palestinian breakthroughs, no one seemed to be in much of a hurry. Without urgency, where was the incentive to make a deal? Assad, cautious by nature, figured he'd hold out for the June 4, 1967, border. The only time he seemed to want to speed things up was in late 1999, as he contemplated his son's succession. After 1993 and 1994, with two agreements with the PLO and Jordan under his belt, Rabin was more likely interested in a process with Syrians that would protect his gains on those two fronts rather than in pushing hard for an agreement to surrender the Golan. Rabin understood what Barak didn't: negotiating deals with Syria and the Palestinians together, or even in close proximity, would mean that he'd have to confront two settler constituencies and contemplate two withdrawals from territory that had huge religious, emotional, and security implications. For this reason, after the Oslo breakthrough the possibility of Israeli withdrawal from the Golan went way down.

The Israeli-Syrian peace process was also all wrong. If Assad wanted 100 percent, then he'd have to do more than rely on the Americans alone to deliver it. And yet he wouldn't contemplate secret diplomacy (quiet talks at the Hyatt in Bethesda, Maryland, under our auspices in September 1999 were not consequential enough) or any public diplomacy, at any point. He was determined to outdo Sadat, Arafat, and Hussein by giving less and getting more. In the end, all he accomplished, nine years after negotiations began at Madrid, was to price himself out of the market.

So too we and the Israelis never faced up to the cost of doing a deal with Syria. Assad's requirements on territory never changed. He said from the beginning that he needed the June 4, 1967, line, where Israeli and Syrian forces were deployed on the eve of the

1967 war, not the international border defined by the French in 1923. The difference included three salients totaling no more than twenty square kilometers, one of which put the Syrians off the waterline into the Sea of Galilee. The Syrian ambassador to Washington, Walid Muallem, now Syria's foreign minister, told me repeatedly that he knew the difference in these borders was not great but that the issue was "Syrian sovereignty" and "every inch is sacred to us." As far-reaching as Rabin's August 1993 offer was, it wasn't enough for Assad; not for another year would the prime minister accept a June 4, 1967, line again provided that Israeli needs on water, security, and peace were met, not to mention agreement on a timetable to determine withdrawal and normalization. This would have still required an agreement to define a mutually acceptable border. No amount of finessing could change the fact that Assad wanted Syrian feet in the water where he claimed to have gone swimming as a boy. Barak would later insist that he could not sell any settlement that took away from Israelis the capacity to drive around the lake, which would have eliminated Syria's sovereignty on the waterline, and ensured Israel's water needs.

Some argue that Christopher should have taken Rabin's deposit of full withdrawal that August and shuttled until he got an Israeli-Syrian accord. I think that's right. But in any event, Rabin's Oslo deal in the fall of 1993 made any agreement to withdraw from Golan almost unthinkable while Israel was giving up territory to the Palestinians. Prospects of a warmer peace process with Jordan the next year further reduced incentives for a deal with a cold, withholding Syrian leader. Two years later, after Rabin's murder, another small opening for an agreement appeared, but Shimon Peres was fearful (probably rightly) that without a summit with Assad, even with the legacy of a murdered prime minister, he couldn't sell the deal.

The third and final opening to achieve an Israeli-Syrian breakthrough came late in 1999, when Barak seemed ready and Assad, concerned about his health and paving the way for the succession of his son, appeared serious as well. Looking back now on our approach to the Israeli-Syrian deal, even with all of its difficulties, I think we developed a way of operating that made it almost impossible for us to close a deal in Clinton's second term.

We were never honest with ourselves or with the Israelis about what it would take to close a deal. I think Assad could have gotten June 4, 1967, had he been prepared to do a Sadat, but he wasn't. Instead of dragging the process out by engaging both sides with ideas that wouldn't work, in the hope of finding a way to finesse the border issue, we should have made clear to the Israelis that it would take a 100 percent (June 4, 1967) to close a deal. If they committed to it, we'd try to get them what they needed. And we should have made it clear to Assad that if he wanted 100 percent (and we'd support that), he'd have to meet Israeli needs, including meeting directly with Israeli leaders. Otherwise we should have said to both sides, Don't waste our time. The fact is we didn't know how to close the deal. Nor were we willing to walk away, even though both sides needed us more than we needed them.

Palestinians and Jordan, Now

"Dad, Dennis is on the phone. He says it's important," my thirteen-year-old daughter, Jen, was calling. *What now?* I thought. We'd just gotten back from a Middle East trip with Secretary Christopher. Dennis was in California on vacation. I was with my family on the west coast of Florida. Nothing ever happens in August, I reassured myself. As I reached for the phone, the image of Saddam's August 1990 invasion of Kuwait suddenly flashed into my mind. "Aaron, you won't believe it." Dennis sounded tired but excited. "They've reached an agreement: you might think about heading back to Washington. There'll be work to do."

The Oslo breakthrough in August 1993 didn't come as a total shock. For months we'd known that the Norwegians were hosting quiet discussions between Israeli academics and PLO officials. Their focus had been a declaration of principles involving interim

Palestinian self-government on the West Bank and Gaza. In May the unofficial talks had become official and were now under the control of Peres and Rabin. But no one, from Secretary Christopher, who had been "briefed" by Norwegian foreign minister Johan Jørgen Holst, to Dan Kurtzer, who'd served as our informal contact point and had been kept informed, realized that the "discussion" channel was really a decision-making channel and that it would produce historic agreements on Israel-PLO mutual recognition and a declaration of principles that would transform the Israeli-Palestinian conflict.

Hearing the news from Dennis, it occurred to me that when Arabs and Israelis really wanted to do serious business, cutting the Americans out, at least initially, was nothing new. The Egyptian-Israeli breakthrough had come via secret talks between Dayan and Tuhaimi, and so would the agreement leading to an Israeli-Jordanian peace treaty. Israeli law forbade official contacts with the PLO, so it was no surprise that Oslo had been done quietly. After all, our initial reaction to Israeli-PLO contacts when we first learned about them in late 1992 had been cool, mainly because we didn't think they were doable. Why would the Israelis and Palestinians want to embarrass a new administration that was busily hosting post-Madrid negotiations in Washington between official Israelis and West Bankers and Gazans who hadn't a clue about what the Oslo channel was producing? Rabin, as late as August, wasn't even convinced himself that a deal was coming; otherwise why empower Christopher with the "pocket" on Syria?

Had we been more open to the reality that the Madrid talks were failing, we might have seen the Israeli-PLO deal coming. As early as March, during Rabin's visit to Washington, the prime minister scheduled a rare breakfast meeting with his team and ours, minus the secretary of state. I'll never forget the meeting because Rabin was at his analytical best. Smoking, gesturing, and unusually relaxed, he delivered a brilliant analysis of the threats and opportunities that Israel faced. The prime minister went on to say that he couldn't see how a negotiation with weak and unempowered West Bankers and Gazans could work and that Israel wouldn't deal with Hamas. That logic left few alternatives. Sam Lewis, the most senior American in the room, who knew Rabin well, said, "Sounds to me like you're talking about dealing with the PLO as your only alternative." Rabin's answer was noncommittal, but his analysis and body language (and we all talked about it afterward) seemed to indicate he was thinking about it.

It's important to point out that Rabin was not chasing the PLO. The Oslo talks, begun by two creative Israeli academics, Yair Hirschfeld and Ron Pundak, were being shepherded by Yossi Beilin and Peres, who in the spring of 1993 were much further along on the need to cut a deal with the PLO than Rabin. In a way, Oslo and the PLO were the prime minister's default position. "I don't like them," he had grumbled to me in August. This ambivalence stayed with him. He'd even had his own back channel that July to check up on what both Peres and Arafat were doing.

But Rabin's analysis of the limitations of the Madrid talks (too public, too formal, too much American input) and his view that West Bankers and Gazans would not act on their own, coupled with Assad's disappointing response to his August offer, persuaded him that a deal with the PLO was the only recourse. Israel could never solve the Palestinian problem militarily, and the continuation of the occupation threatened Israel's well-being, security, and democratic character. Rabin thought strategically. And Oslo seemed to be the first step in a strategy to end the Israeli-Palestinian conflict.

"What the hell do we do with the Americans?" Terje Larsen, the indefatigable Norwegian intermediary, said to Foreign Minister Johan Jørgen Holst after Israeli-PLO representatives signed their agreement in Oslo on August 19. The answer was to get on the plane and fly to California, where Holst and Peres briefed Secretary Christopher and Dennis Ross. Rabin called Christopher and in a "no frills" tone passed on the good news. When Peres suggested that the United States take credit for the negotiations, Christopher wouldn't hear of it. The compromise was that the agreement would be officially signed in Washington at a ceremony hosted by President Clinton.

As I sat with Lindsay and my kids, Jenny and Danny, on the South Lawn of the White House on a brilliant sunny day watching an uncomfortable Rabin, a smiling Arafat, and a beaming President Clinton clasp hands, I was convinced we'd reached a point of no return, and that with all the problems ahead, there'd be no going back. If I had been buoyed by watching Baker and Pankin announce the invitations for Madrid two years earlier, I was over the moon now. After all, this wasn't just a process. It was Israeli-PLO recognition, and agreement on a negotiating process that would not only change realities on the ground but pave the way for permanent status talks within five years on issues such as Jerusalem, never before agreed to by an Israeli government. As Warren Christopher recalled that day, "Anything, everything seemed possible." And that's the way I felt. Caught up in the moment, the three articles of faith that had moved me before now seemed validated in ways I couldn't even begin to imagine: the Arab-Israeli conflict could be resolved; negotiations were the only way; and America had a key role to play.

The good news about Oslo was that the Israelis and Palestinians had done it themselves. For the next two years their negotiators solved problems. They lived, laughed, yelled, and cried together against the backdrop of missed deadlines, terror, violence, and continuing mutual suspicion. They became friends. I saw security officials from both sides with Israeli and Palestinian blood on their hands come together on the basis of profound respect and even affection. At one session at Jerusalem's Laromme Hotel, I saw West Bank security chief Jabril Rajoub and IDF central commander Shaul Mofaz jokingly lie down to pretend to take a nap in the same bed. With remarkable stamina, creativity, and courage, Israeli-Palestinian negotiators Uri Savir and Abu Alaa, themselves fast friends, negotiated agreement after agreement (Gaza-Jericho, May 4, 1994; the Interim Accord, September 28, 1995), which pushed the Oslo process uphill against the laws of political gravity, as terror, violence, settlement activity, and their own suspicions of each other threatened to drag it back down.

But the bad news about Oslo was also that they had done it

themselves. The solutions they found simply could not be sustained, given the realities on the ground and the expectation gap that divided the two sides. The logic of Oslo seemed sound on paper. The concept of interim agreements was based on the sensible notion that territory would be transferred gradually to the Palestinian Authority, in exchange for assumption of security responsibilities by its security forces. That gradual process would enhance confidence and trust and lead to a situation where within five years Israelis and Palestinians would be able to address the harder permanent status issues. This never happened. By 1999 not a single deadline had been met; permanent status talks had actually begun three times (May 1996 and October and December 1999), but they were neither serious nor sustained. Neither Israelis nor Palestinians could see where the endgame was heading, and both grew tired and wary of an interim, salamilike process.

Ending the Israeli occupation over time, while Palestinians were still under occupation and while Israelis remained the occupier, was simply not practical, according to the terms they set. Even while they negotiated as friends, partners, and equals, the sides were forced to play their respective roles as occupied and occupier. Israeli settlement activities, closures, land confiscation, and the construction of bypass roads to accommodate settlers and the military continued. Palestinians saw Israeli confidence-building measures as bargaining chips that Israelis played in return for getting their own needs met. On the Palestinian side, Hamas and Islamic Jihad, operating outside the Palestinian Authority, continued to attack and kidnap Israeli soldiers and civilians. And Arafat—who never abandoned violence as a potential tool and could never do enough to arrest Palestinians engaged in terror, crack down on infrastructure, or collect weapons—acquiesced. Palestinian Authority media continued to generate anti-Israeli and anti-Semitic propaganda. These unilateral acts competed with the goodwill and problem-solving capacity of the negotiators and undermined some of the real gains made on the ground, particularly Israeli withdrawal from six West Bank cities and towns by the end of 1995.

Finally, the Oslo process come up against a huge gap in Israeli and Palestinian expectations that could never be overcome. For Palestinians, and certainly for Arafat, Oslo subordinated all the things they had wanted—statehood and self-determination—to an interim process in which they had little faith and great suspicion. For Arafat, interim phases were part of his struggle for independence, a necessary concession to gain legitimacy from the two parties, America and Israel, that had never given it to him. Oslo was his final major concession on the way to either quick independence or a prolonged struggle.

For Israelis, Oslo was essentially a probation period to test whether Palestinians were ready for independence. The sentiment may have been understandable given their deep mistrust of Palestinians, but it guaranteed tremendous animosity on the other side that no amount of goodwill could overcome. And despite Oslo's secondary gains for Israel—a peace treaty with Jordan, growing ties with the Arab world, a booming economy, particularly an increase in direct foreign investment—poor Palestinian security performance and Arafat's unwillingness to control Hamas and Islamic Jihad persuaded most Israelis that he could not be trusted and that without reciprocity on security, Israel had no partner. These mindsets produced an insurmountable barrier. As Uri Savir, Israel's top Oslo negotiator, recalls, "Each side wanted to extract the maximum from the other, rather than exploit the advantage of a partnership."[2]

Starstruck with both Rabin and the Oslo breakthrough, Bill Clinton and the rest of us on his team never thought about imposing ourselves on a process we hadn't negotiated. The night before the signing ceremony Clinton was so excited he'd stayed up reading the Book of Joshua. He chose a tie with trumpets, in what Sidney Blumenthal, then a Clinton advisor, called a "sartorial reference to Jericho."[3] The president had said the week before that Oslo felt "like a gift." George Stephanopoulos recalled that "the whole peace thing fell into everyone's lap." Under these circumstances no one was going to ask tough questions or challenge concepts. Why spoil the party? Even with all its bumps, Oslo seemed to be working.

The United States, having inherited a set of secret negotiations we couldn't alter, been kept out of the implementation process largely by Israel, and relegated to an important but derivative role as caterer, cash man, and crisis manager, was not in a position to change the contours of the Israeli-Palestinian peacemaking process. The problem was not bilateralism as such but the absence of any mechanism to monitor, let alone ensure, compliance. As a third party, Avi Gil told me, America could have seen the problems better than either Israelis or Palestinians at the time. Part of the problem, to be sure, was that we were too enamored of the process, too persuaded of the virtues of bilateral talks, and not enough focused on the flaws. I lost count of the number of times when one side would complain about the other's behavior, and I'd say, "You'll find a way to work it out. You always do." We took on plenty of problems during those first two years, but we couldn't effect a change of behavior on those that really counted. None of the Oslo accords strictly prohibited settlement activity, and despite Rabin's decision to stop it in densely populated Palestinian West Bank areas, significant construction continued in Jerusalem, along with continued closures and checkpoints. I don't recall a single tough, honest conversation in which we said to the Israelis, Look, settlements may not violate the letter of Oslo, but they're wreaking havoc with its spirit and compromising the logic of a gradual process of building trust and confidence.

On terror and violence, we pressed the Palestinians plenty. But when Arafat indulged Hamas and Islamic Jihad, we were never prepared to impose costs of our own. We lauded Rabin's policy of fighting terror as if there were no peace and pursuing peace regardless of the terror. But although this approach allowed the process to continue, it created too many loopholes and allowed too much tolerance for lapsed Palestinian security performance. Arafat could control Fatah (or at least most of it), but he would not act as Israel's policeman in the West Bank and Gaza, particularly against Palestinian opposition groups who were criticizing him constantly for agreeing to Oslo without ending settlements, let alone the Israeli occupation. We could talk to him all day long about his responsibilities, and how he really needed to do this for Palestinian national interests, not Israel's, but it was like punching a bowl of Jell-O. All politics are local, and Arafat (at least in 1995) was not going to risk a violent split within the Palestinian community without a huge payoff. The sad fact is that Israel (and we) were trapped in a peacemaking process that was fundamentally flawed with Arafat but nonexistent without him.

Maybe we couldn't have solved this conundrum, but we didn't try very hard. Each side wanted us to be a kind of judge in their corner, carrying their water, lambasting the other side. What we needed to be was a tough, honest friend, telling each side what they needed to do to make the process work better and cajoling both with threat of public criticism or worse if they didn't. They had almost no accountability, at least from us, in those early years. Dennis Ross now admits that "we allowed the parties to get off on the wrong foot and there was no accountability because of that." Could we have imposed any? The truth was that neither Israelis nor Palestinians wanted their policies on security or settlements to be monitored by America or anyone else. Dennis Ross again: "Clinton sensed that Rabin doesn't want us doing this, so you don't go in and do things he doesn't want you to do."

By the summer of 1995, as Palestinians and Israelis continued to wrestle with the contradictions of the Oslo process they had created, two trends were evident. First, the complaint ratio by each side had skyrocketed. Rabin complained to Christopher in March that Arafat was doing little to fight terror, citing statistics about the scores of Israelis killed in terror attacks. Unless Arafat improved security, there'd be no further redeployment of Israeli forces from the West Bank. Later that same week Arafat pressed the secretary hard, saying that Israeli closures and checkpoints were strangling Palestinians. Israel also needed to turn over Palestinian revenue from taxes that Israel had collected according to prior agreement.

The second trend was that by the summer Israeli and Palestinian negotiators continued to hammer out the last two agreements flowing from the Declaration of Principles. It was as if they had no alternative, despite their suspicions and complaints about each other. That fall Rabin summed up Oslo and Arafat best for me: "Once you start dancing with a bear, you can never let go." It was as if the Israelis and Palestinians, driven by their proximity problem, were prepared to press on regardless of their mistakes, transgressions, and screwups.

That summer, in another heroic demonstration of creativity and commitment, the Oslo negotiators hammered out the details of a two-hundred-page (with annexes) agreement detailing further Israeli redeployments, Palestinian-Israeli security cooperation, provisions on a Palestinian port and airport, and further economic cooperation. The agreement, signed on September 28 in the presence of President Clinton, King Hussein, President Mubarak, and Rabin and Arafat, was a stunning demonstration of both hope and experience. If there was a high point since the original Declaration of Principles, this was it. The next month Abu Mazen and Yossi Beilin would actually conclude an unofficial and secret agreement on how to handle the permanent status issues; and in late October the second Middle East North African Summit would open in Amman. Stopping off in Jerusalem en route from the summit back home, Dennis and I had a meeting with Rabin. On the way out of his office, I mentioned to the prime minister how amazed I was at the tenacity and durability of the peace process. With a dismissive wave of the hand, he said, "I hope so."

On a rainy first Saturday afternoon in November, I was driving to the dry cleaners in Chevy Chase, addicted to the local all-news channel as usual, when I heard a sketchy report that Prime Minister Rabin had been shot. I immediately called the State Department Operations Center. They confirmed that Rabin had been shot in the back by an Israeli leaving a pro-peace rally in Tel Aviv. Within hours State Ops called me to say that Rabin was dead.

That afternoon I thought about the Kennedy assassination, where I was at the time, and how profoundly shocked and saddened I was, even at thirteen. For me, Yitzhak Rabin, like John F. Kennedy, was a historic figure and a great leader. He combined courage, caution, and pragmatism, just the right mix to lead a country and to try to make peace in a dangerous neighborhood. Sometimes I thought of him, to use the words Kennedy allegedly used to describe himself, as "an idealist without illusion." But maybe this was a stretch. After everything Rabin had experienced, could he really have been an idealist?

I had known Rabin since my early twenties. He was a friend of my parents, was especially fond of my father, and I had gotten to know him as a real person. On one of Christopher's first trips to Israel, at a Friday night Shabbat dinner that Rabin hosted for the secretary in his Tel Aviv apartment, the prime minister had asked me to chant the traditional Hebrew blessing over the wine. I was a little uneasy. Christopher didn't know me well, and he hadn't a clue why the prime minister of Israel had turned to one of his staff to recite a Hebrew blessing. As I held up the wineglass, I looked at Rabin, and he smiled and winked at me as if to say: "What are you worried about? It will be okay."

By every account, President Clinton, though he had known Rabin for only three years, was devastated by the assassination. Clinton recalls being told by Tony Lake that Rabin had been shot. He remembers calling Hillary, who came down from the residence and held him, while they talked about the prime minister. Lake recalls that telling Clinton that Rabin had died was the hardest thing he would ever do: "It was as if someone punched him in the stomach." Rahm Emanuel told me that, seeing Clinton later, "he was white" and "stricken beyond politics." But Steve Grossman put it best: "Something in Clinton died when Rabin died." Watching Clinton in the days afterward, particularly at the funeral in Jerusalem, there was no doubt. Rarely had the death of any foreign leader affected an American president so deeply. Clinton's speech was powerful and passionate, a tribute not just to an Israeli prime minister but to a friend and partner.

Part of Clinton's motivation to achieve a breakthrough on Arab-Israeli peace in the next several years was surely shaped by his desire to sustain Rabin's legacy.

Rabin's murder did not cause the collapse of the Oslo process, but it did accelerate its demise. The Palestinians and Israel would conclude three more interim accords, but removing Rabin dealt their relationship a huge blow. Rabin did not like Arafat, but he came to respect the hard decisions Arafat had made, and the two had developed a working relationship based on a semblance of partnership. Rabin had always tried neither to surprise nor lie to him.

The next two elected Israeli prime ministers had little patience with or understanding of Arafat. Moreover Netanyahu had opposed Oslo, and Barak had withheld his support in Israel's parliament. Both tried to put their own stamp on the agreements either by whittling down Israel's interim obligations or, in Barak's case, by backtracking on what was promised, or by trying to move too quickly to permanent status talks without an understanding of what was required to conclude them. Don't get me wrong—Arafat bears a huge responsibility for Oslo's demise and for the failure at Camp David. But with Rabin's death, particularly between 1999 and 2000, the gradualism to which he and Arafat had grown accustomed was replaced too abruptly with a totalism that lacked the sense of confidence and partnership required to sustain it. Had Rabin lived, the crisis triggered by Oslo's flaws would still have come, but it would probably have been less severe.

The six months from Rabin's murder to the election of Benjamin Netanyahu as prime minister in May 1996 was a frenetic period of American activity as we tried to make progress between Israel and Syria, defuse crises, and frankly do all we could to ensure that Shimon Peres, heir to Rabin's legacy, won the election. The idea that America doesn't sometimes interfere in Israel's politics is about as absurd as the notion that Israel doesn't meddle in ours. Much of what we did during that period was designed to support Peres and in so doing save Arab-Israeli diplomacy.

Unfortunately, successful implementation of the Interim Agreement, in which Israel withdrew from six West Bank towns, and two rounds of very productive Israeli-Syrian talks, could not trump terror or the perception that Shimon Peres was weak on security. Four suicide attacks in nine days by Hamas and Islamic Jihad that left more than sixty Israelis dead capped a growing unease about Palestinians and Oslo. Nor could President Clinton's effort, at Sharm el-Sheikh in March, to bring the Arab states together with Israel, and his follow-on visit to Tel Aviv and Jerusalem, help Peres much. A serious Israeli-Hezbollah confrontation across the Lebanese-Israeli border further unsettled the Israeli electorate; and Israel's Arabs—who were angered by Peres's tough response, particularly the deaths of more than a hundred Lebanese and Palestinians by an errant Israeli artillery shell at Qana, Lebanon—stayed away from the polls and supporting the Labor Party.

Only intense shuttle diplomacy by Secretary Christopher ended the Lebanese crisis. And in April, as we sat in Peres's office celebrating the U.S.-brokered agreement by drinking champagne out of plastic cups, I thought maybe we'd actually succeeded. But Peres ran a mediocre campaign. Netanyahu, the master politician, ran a better one and eked out a slight victory by sixteen thousand votes in the first direct election of an Israeli prime minister. On election night all I could think about was how we were going to save the Oslo process from extinction. But I didn't get it. Oslo, as Israelis and Palestinians had known it, was already dead.

Fighting Fires: The Netanyahu Years, 1996–99

For the next three years we tried to rescue an Israeli-Palestinian negotiating process that was already deep in what Gamal Helal once called in Arabic a *raibooba*, or political coma. We had a fair measure of success. We helped Israel and the PLO reach two interim agreements, and although neither was fully implemented, the process kept things from exploding and no doubt saved lives on both sides. For a time we even succeeded in making the Oslo enterprise the property not just of the Israeli Labor Party but of the Likud as well. Having pledged never to meet with Arafat, Netanyahu not only shook his hand (Ariel Sharon as foreign minister would not, a sign of things to come) but also withdrew from most of the West Bank city of Hebron.

The Netanyahu years were filled with paradoxes. The tough Likud prime minster, wary of America's involvement, allowed the United States to get closer to an Israeli-Palestinian negotiation than any of his Labor predecessors. The broken negotiating process still produced agreements. Despite tremendous mistrust among the leaders, Israeli and Palestinian negotiators worked well together, and Palestinian terror, which skyrocketed when the peace process was producing, plummeted when it wasn't, partly because of our more intense focus on Palestinian security performance and partly because of improvements in Israeli intelligence and counterterrorism tactics.

At the same time these years generated a sense of confidence, false on reflection, that if we just kept the process going, we could create momentum and get back on track. It was a reasonable conclusion, drawn by a team of negotiators with a sense of mission to preserve what we could against collapse. We understood that not much more than interim issues could be worked through with Netanyahu and Arafat. But at the same time we lost sight of the fact that we were expending enormous effort on those interim issues. It took us four months of continuous shuttling to produce the Hebron agreement, which facilitated Israel's withdrawal from Hebron, a leftover obligation from the 1995 accord.

After three years of watching a functioning process from the sidelines, we were playing the mediator's role now, trying to correct the defects of a process that was long since broken and probably beyond repair. I was as gung-ho as anyone, perhaps more so, touting our new-found intervention. It was the American-drafted Note for the Record that sealed the Hebron deal in 1997; the CIA's trilateral meetings that helped cement Israeli-Palestinian

security cooperation; and President Clinton's masterful performance at Wye River that made the summit succeed. In short, we
were holding the whole process together like some modern-day
Dutch boy with his finger in the dike. We brought way too much
hype to these accomplishments and began to believe our own
press, and in doing so, we generated a false sense of confidence
that with the right leaders we could do bigger things. In fact, the
president's role was so impressive at Wye that he may well have
come away with the sense that if he could solve interim issues,
maybe he could address the big ones as well.

Small Frogs

"We succeeded," Yitzhak Molkho, Netanyahu's personal attorney and top negotiator, recalled, because "you can swallow
twenty small frogs, but you cannot swallow one big frog." Molho
was referring to efforts to reach two agreements during the
Netanyahu years, and he was right. Small pieces of West Bank
land for assumption of Palestinian security was the quid pro
quo—a no-nonsense, unsentimental trade-off. In many ways, the
Wye process was more honest than Oslo. Both sides had few illusions and no expectations, perhaps with the exception of those of
us who saw this period as a way station on the road to a more ambitious bit of peacemaking.

For the most part, the tiny-steps approach was consistent with
the tiny feet of Arafat and Netanyahu when it came to the peace
process. It reflected each leader's estimation of his own needs and
view of the other. Netanyahu, a brilliant politician with a hard-
line strategic vision to fight terror and Islamic extremism, had
little sense of how to get things done. He had, to be sure, inherited a peace process that he and his Likud party had aggressively
opposed. But now as prime minister he pledged to continue, trying to implement agreements that previous governments had accepted.

For the first several months Netanyahu drifted, and then in

September 1996 he made the situation worse by opening up an archaeological site to the public, a tunnel actually, that in Hasmonean times had run adjacent to the Western Wall. Given the Palestinian and Israeli sensitivity regarding Jerusalem, it set off the worst Israeli-Palestinian confrontation since Oslo, particularly between the two sides' security forces. The crisis now had to be managed. Netanyahu couldn't do it on his own, so we ended up in the bizarre situation of a hard-line Likud prime minister meeting with Arafat in Washington in October to launch a U.S.-brokered agreement that on Netanyahu's watch provided for Israeli redeployment from part of the historic city of Hebron, a redline for the Israeli religious right. Trapped by his own mistakes and Israel's commitment to Oslo, Netanyahu's mindset, in the words of one of his closest advisors, seemed to be "I'll be more grudging and it will take longer, but I'll hold my base because they'll see how hard I can resist." This tension between the politics of the "tribe" and the peace process also created the one-step-forward, one-step-back problem. A European ambassador would describe Netanyahu's behavior as a "drunk lurching from lamppost to lamppost." Not long after the Hebron Protocol was signed, Netanyahu announced a ground-breaking for Har Homa, a major new housing project southeast of Jerusalem.

For Arafat, master politician and manipulator, Netanyahu presented both a challenge and an opportunity. Arafat had picked up points in Washington even before Netanyahu's election by launching a major crackdown against the Hamas infrastructure (something he would never do again), in the wake of its suicide attacks in Israel that spring, that included massive arrests and going into mosques and threatening Hamas's economic and social infrastructure. He was still a maddening partner to deal with. I'm certain he came to an understanding with both Hamas and Islamic Jihad to ease up on the terror to position himself well with the Americans. And in the face of Israel's settlement activity, Arafat's anti-Israel rhetoric and his willingness to give these groups leeway escalated.

At the same time Arafat clearly made a decision that with

Rabin gone, his real partner was America, not Israel. He welcomed our role in the negotiations even while his behavior—particularly an unwillingness, up to the very end, to close on the Hebron deal—drove us crazy.

Looking back now, I'm struck by the fact that we saw Netanyahu as a short-timer with a natural limit on how far he could go in the negotiations; we saw Arafat, on the other hand, as a permanent fixture whose bottom lines were still not clear and worth testing. Not coincidentally, these years witnessed the creation of a U.S.-PLO joint committee, the first American assistance package to Palestinians in the wake of the Wye accords, and the president's historic visit to Gaza in 1998, as a quid pro quo for Arafat's amending the Palestine National Covenant. Our focus on security performance would also witness the CIA's open involvement in the peace process. And we milked this aspect of our relationship with Arafat for all we could get. "For whatever reason," George Tenet told me, "the CIA meant something to Arafat. It was a back door into the government." Tenet and Arafat developed an unusually close relationship that not only helped produce the Wye accord but contributed significantly to giving Arafat a stake—at least during those years—in delivering more than he'd ever done and would do again on security.

Working with Netanyahu, Not Against Him

I'd never entered a foreign country secretly before, certainly not one that was so small that within hours of arrival I was certain to bump into someone I knew. The July 1997 secret mission to Israel was a first for me and an example of how far we were prepared to go in working with Netanyahu, and not against him, during those years. We had made a decision to lay out American ideas on the extent of Israel's further redeployment from the West Bank as well as on security performance for Palestinians, and as usual we felt obligated to run our ideas by Israel first. This "no surprise" understanding actually went back to Kissinger, and

even Baker had abided by it. But agreeing not to surprise Israel
didn't mean giving it a veto over our ideas. The July trip was designed to share our views with Israel quietly, to highlight the importance of what we were doing in Bibi's mind, and to avoid the
appearance of collusion, although collusion was precisely what
we were doing.

We flew on an unmarked plane from a Virginia airport with
no passports or other identification other than a small white card
with an alias handwritten on it. Dennis chose Harvey T. Long; I
picked John Anderson. When we landed in Scotland and the airport authorities boarded the aircraft, I gave them the card and
said my name. I was nervous but also feeling pretty ridiculous
about the whole thing. And it required every ounce of concentration to stop myself from laughing out loud.

When we arrived at Ben-Gurion Airport, we were driven to
the Mossad facility for our meeting with the prime minister. Like
so many of our best-laid plans, this one didn't turn out the way
we expected. Bibi was nervous. He liked the steps on security
we'd laid out for Palestinians, but he wasn't happy about what
we'd asked him to do on redeployment from the West Bank. So
instead of going ahead, we vacillated in an effort to try to get the
Israelis to agree. As so often was the case, delay was our enemy.
On July 30 Hamas pulled off a double suicide attack in Jerusalem
(the first in a year), and any notion of playing hardball with the
Israelis was now out of the question.

The president really didn't like Netanyahu, at least in the beginning. During their first meeting in the summer of 1996 Bibi
lectured him about the Arab-Israeli issue, prompting Clinton to
ask his aides when it was over, "Who the fuck does he think he is?
Who's the fucking superpower here?" Secretary Albright and
Sandy Berger, frustrated by Netanyahu's erratic and often obsti-
nate policies, particularly on settlements, urged a much tougher
line. But over time the president came to believe that the only
way to get anything done was to work with Netanyahu, not
against him. True, all of us saw Bibi as a kind of speed bump that
would have to be negotiated along the way until a new Israeli

prime minister came along who was more serious about peace. But we also sensed that what little progress could be made needed the prime minister's cooperation.

Not everyone shared this view, especially the secretary of state. Madeleine Albright was the only secretary of state I could dance with (and did). Smart, irreverent, and at times profane, she cared deeply about Arab-Israeli peace and worked for over a year to lay the groundwork for the president's successful summit at Wye. I know she felt patronized by Bibi, whom she would have loved to rough up, and I sensed her tremendous frustration with Barak and Arafat during the three days Clinton left her at Camp David to manage a summit that by then had probably already failed. In her office she had two small rubber look-alike figures of Arafat and Netanyahu. I could imagine her squeezing the hell out of them when she got frustrated. But being tough on them in the real world was another matter. I know Albright sensed that if she went too far, Bill Clinton might not be there to cover her back.

That she was the first woman secretary of state was simply not relevant to our successes and failures. It took me about ten seconds to understand that I was working for the sixty-fourth secretary of state, not the first woman to hold the job. Whatever their cultural bias, the Arabs and Israelis understood this as well. They had no choice because they knew they were dealing with the president's personal representative. If they didn't take Albright seriously, it wasn't because she was a woman. It was because they believed they could push America around and get away with it. And that had more to do with the president and our approach than with the gender or personality of America's top diplomat.

The president would get angry and blow up, but he'd never maintain or channel the upset into a sustained toughness. Dennis recalled that Clinton was not "keen to have a confrontation with Bibi, or with anybody. That's who he is." Baker had cooperated with Shamir, an even harder-line prime minister, but had also challenged him and pushed back hard when he believed the Israelis had crossed the line. We would never do that on any sustained level with

Rabin, Netanyahu, or Barak. The reason was not domestic political pressure. Much of the Jewish community had problems with Netanyahu, and (in contrast to their feelings toward George H. W. Bush) they loved Clinton. No, the reason was the impact of the "Jewish lobby of one" and the president's unwillingness to push back against any Israeli prime minister out of concern that if he pushed too hard, he might not succeed in Arab-Israeli peacemaking, and because of Clinton's nonconfrontational nature. With Rabin and Bibi the die had been cast. By the time it came to dealing with Ehud Barak, Bill Clinton was simply being Bill Clinton.

Wye Not: I Can Do a Presidential Summit

Looking back now on President Bill Clinton's brilliant performance at the Wye River summit in late October 1998, where he brought Arafat and Netanyahu to sign an agreement on interim issues, I thought about the *Seinfeld* episode where George and Jerry set out to write a pilot for a television show "about nothing." At the time I saw Wye as a tremendous accomplishment. Two weeks before congressional elections, the president, capping almost a year of preparation, brought two unlikely leaders, filled with mistrust and a fair amount of mutual loathing, together at a summit for the first time and hammered out an agreement on Israeli redeployments and Palestinian security cooperation. It wasn't pretty. The Israelis put empty suitcases outside their quarters in a bluff to leave, and Sharon, there as foreign minister, refused to shake Arafat's hand. But we did broker an agreement.

The problem was that Wye produced a memorandum and a timeline that remained stillborn. In November Netanyahu's government went into crisis. I was sent to Israel and the West Bank to monitor the implementation of the first phase of the agreement. (One Israeli pundit described me as a "kosher inspector.") But on December 6 Bibi resigned and a year's work went into oblivion. It was a summit about nothing, not because the issues weren't important—"land for security" was essentially the core Oslo trade-off—but because a year had been spent on this agreement, and eight days of the president's time brokering an accord between two leaders who could never implement it, all against a backdrop of a peace process that had been kept on life support by the United States. Arafat and Bibi were making commitments not to each other but to us. And despite all the trilateral mechanisms the summit created, we couldn't guarantee implementation. It may well be that Wye's greatest consequence was to bring about, quite unintentionally, the demise of Netanyahu's government, which broke apart over the agreement he signed.

Far more significant than the substance at Wye was the president's performance there. The best of Bill Clinton was on display at Wye. Even with a year of preparation, there was no guarantee of success, yet the president made it a top priority anyway. He was tenacious, hammering out the details of the final accord in a marathon fifteen-hour day-and-night session; he won Arafat's trust promising aid and a Gaza visit to the Palestinians. He had gained Netanyahu's by ensuring that the 13 percent of the West Bank from which Israel would redeploy was known well in advance; he was even considering a pardon of the American spy Jonathan Pollard, until George Tenet's threat to resign stopped him. Finally, at times he was tough, yelling at Bibi when he retracted an earlier pledge on Palestinian prisoners: "This is just chicken shit. I'm not going to put up with this kind of bullshit," the president snapped.[4]

Wye worked largely because Arafat and Bibi could "swallow small frogs" and because neither wanted to be blamed by Clinton or lose credibility with America. Bill Clinton's hands-on approach and interpersonal skill brought it all together. "He was like a psychiatrist," Madeleine Albright recalls, "trying to get his patients to drop their defense mechanisms." Clinton could "really get into somebody's head," Maria Echaveste recalled about the president's performance at Wye. With the Palestinians, he genuinely made them feel like a "partner, albeit a weak one." And that empathy would again be on display a couple of months later at the Shawa

Center in Gaza, when Clinton addressed the Palestinian National Council. Sitting there, I was moved and chilled by the power of the president's words: "I am honored to be the first American president to address the Palestinian people in a city governed by Palestinians, for Palestinians." "He should be our president," one Palestinian participant said to me afterward.

On reflection, I'm now more convinced than ever that Bill Clinton's performance at Wye, and the power of his personal skills, gave us a sense that if we got into a real negotiation over the big issues, the president could pull it off. Wye was very emotional. A dying King Hussein came to encourage the participants, and Clinton doubtless grew more committed to doing something big on Arab-Israeli peace as domestic scandal threatened to drag him down. "Wye created the perception in the president's mind that a deal was possible between Israelis and Palestinians," Bruce Riedel, the president's Middle East point man at the NSC, observed. "I think the president probably thought he could apply the same skills in Camp David," Sandy Berger told me. "If I could do that with Netanyahu," Maria Echaveste believed the president reasoned, "what could I do with Barak?" Madeleine Albright recalled that Wye convinced both herself and the president that agreements could be reached if "we pushed long and hard enough."

Clinton later observed about Wye that he was "eager to hold it" and always preferred "failure in a worthy effort to inaction for fear of failure."[5] Wye was a masterpiece of diplomacy by a guy with extraordinary confidence in his own personal skills. Mara Rudman recalls hearing the president say many times, and not just about the Middle East, "Let me get into a room with them. I know I can convince them." But as Netanyahu gave way to Barak, and as interim issues gave way to big-ticket items like Jerusalem, borders, and refugees, we would soon see that personal skills, confidence, and commitment alone would not be enough to trump the complexity and power of issues seared deep into the identity, politics, and security of Israeli and Palestinian leaders—and their publics.

Chapter Eight

Mr. Nice Guy: Bill Clinton and the Arabs and Israelis He Loved Too Much, 1999–2001

On May 17, 1999, Ehud Barak was elected the tenth prime minister of the State of Israel with an impressive victory in excess of 56 percent of the popular vote. Barak's coalition, composed partly of the ultra-Orthodox Shas Party and the very secular Meretz Party, left him a bit weaker than his popular mandate implied but did not undermine his confidence, particularly in his plans for Arab-Israeli peacemaking. Barak may have fashioned himself Rabin's heir, but he had in mind a far bolder peace agenda than the fallen prime minister.

The Norwegian peace intermediary Terje Larsen tells a story of being invited to the new prime minister's house shortly after Barak's election. "What are you going to do on the peace process?" Larsen asked Barak. "I will do the opposite of Oslo" came the reply. "You see, Terje, we have a dog in front of us, and this dog is very ugly. Why is it ugly?" Barak questioned his bemused visitor. "Because it has an ugly tail. If we take the tail away, the dog would be beautiful. You Oslo people would chop the tail off like salami. I will chop it off." Larsen is now imitating Barak's diplomacy by karate chop, making cutting motions in the air. "I'll make peace with Syria, Lebanon, the Palestinians," Barak concluded. "I will have the end of conflict, totally in one go."

Had any other Israeli political leader announced such a grandiose scheme, Larsen would have dismissed him as a dreamer who might imagine it, but could never implement it in the real world. To Larsen's credit, he repeatedly warned us of the dangers of such totalism. But Ehud Barak did not see himself as ordinary; nor did others. A decorated war hero and commando who in April 1973, disguised as a woman, had assassinated Palestinian terrorists in Beirut, a concert pianist with an M.A. from Stanford in systems analysis, Ehud Barak saw himself elected to perform a mission: to end the Arab-Israeli conflict or else to make clear to the world that Israel had no Arab partners worthy of the name. "He was so courageous, you can't imagine," Amos Gilad, head of the IDF's production branch in military intelligence, told me. "He lacks the sense of fear." It was Gilad who would brief Barak before the July 2000 Camp David summit with the bad news that Arafat would ask for 100 percent of the West Bank and Gaza plus East Jerusalem. "It's difficult when you deal with determined leaders," Gilad recalled. "With Barak, he knew everything."

I liked Barak and had first met him during the early 1990s, when he was at Georgetown's Center for Strategic and International Studies in Washington. He was bold and decisive, with an analytical mind that I imagined whirred like a computer. As I got to see him in action as chief of staff, as foreign minister, and later as prime minister, he also seemed somewhat inflexible and always in a hurry. Ephraim Sneh, Israel's former deputy defense minister, who knew Barak well, described him as "too hasty in rendering judgments," believing that his "logic prevails over everything." Somehow this mindset seemed to me at odds with the skills required for battle, the capacity and flexibility to deal with new variables and surprises by the other side. If Barak somehow believed that his "logic" carried such power that it subsumed everyone else's, then he might also have thought that through force of will he could shape or even control their actions. Thrown together with the two Mr. A's, who were determined to hold out for their own brand of "logic," I couldn't have imagined a worse combination.

If Rabin, in the words of the Israeli novelist Amos Oz, was "a cautious engineer and a precise navigator" wanting to solve discrete problems, Barak was out to explore bigger horizons and make a much bigger story.[1] Sneh believes Barak saw himself as a man upon whom history had imposed a mission. In a conversation in 2003 Barak said to me that, like Churchill and Ben-Gurion, he wanted to lead. After the small-frog approach of Netanyahu, Barak's boldness was invigorating and courageous. Like a "rooster at dawn," Madeleine Albright writes, Barak entered office.[2] Sandy Berger described Clinton's excitement after his first phone call with Barak. "He really wants to go for this. He really wants to get a comprehensive peace," the president exulted. Barak's first visit to Washington left no doubt of his intentions. Publicly he laid out a vision to end the Arab-Israeli conflict by reaching accords with Syria, Lebanon, and the Palestinians by the spring of 2000, well before Clinton left office. The two leaders spent the weekend at Camp David and were up talking until three in the morning. Clinton showed the new prime minister the cabin where Sadat and Begin had met and recalled that Barak was interested in doing "something substantive" at Camp David.[3]

We all were impressed with Barak. The president described the new prime minister as a "brilliant Renaissance man." Secretary Albright, who would discover Barak's difficult side at Camp David, reminded me how "fascinated we all were by how smart he was: clock maker and classical pianist, and blah blah blah." We wanted to like him because "all of a sudden we had another chance with somebody we thought we could work with." And in a remarkably honest admission, she added, "We went to Camp David on his word."

Albright was right, and in her no-nonsense assessment she captured Barak's strengths and our ineffectual proclivities. Despite his grandiose objectives, Barak's risk-ready nature appealed to the president and to the rest of us, deeply committed as we all were to Arab-Israeli peace and to getting something done in the fifteen months that remained in Clinton's second term.

Frankly, I was a little more Dr. No on this one than my colleagues. I was glad Barak had won, but I was skeptical of his "two-for" (Syria and the Palestinians) and worried that the president, risk-ready himself, would follow Barak's lead without asking the tough questions about his tactics and strategy. Barak dealt only with the president, whom he'd call frequently, sometimes daily. We didn't help matters any by installing a secure phone in the prime minister's home to make those contacts easier. Bruce Riedel recalled that Clinton seemed thoroughly taken with this military hero "who loves to transmit but didn't listen a lot." Clinton would later sour a bit on Barak's erratic tactics at Shepherdstown and Geneva, but in 1999 his big ideas appealed to a president who had begun to think about his legacy. We never received a detailed briefing on the Clinton-Barak meetings at Camp David, but the prime minister had undoubtedly captured the president's imagination. In the process he would also capture American tactics and strategy on the peace process and, for the next year, push a boom-or-bust approach to Syria and the Palestinians that showed little understanding of the issues and less regard for the consequences of his actions.

One other point about Barak is worth noting, especially because we didn't realize it until much later. Barak's bravado, confidence, and boldness concealed more than a little uncertainty, as well as great sensitivity to his domestic position. He may not have been the manic poll-driven politician portrayed by his critics, but the idea that he took his gambles with no thought to his own politics is untrue. At Shepherdstown and Camp David politics and polls constrained him. And despite his "can-do" image, Ehud Barak did not have a clear sense of how to accomplish his goals. Nahum Barnea, veteran columnist for the Israeli daily *Yediot Aharonot*, had the best read on Barak that I'd ever heard: "He's a gifted, brilliant sober observer who can analyze the political and security situation better than anyone else, but he does not have the patience, ability to engage in dialogue, or understanding of people to change the situation for the better. His mind is long; his arm is short."

None of this mattered in 1999. Barak was our guy. In July he began negotiations with Arafat. By September he had reached an agreement to continue with further redeployments, and he added to the mix a goal of reaching a framework agreement on permanent status issues within six months, the first of so many unrealistic Barak deadlines and objectives that were never realized. We all attended the signing at Sharm el-Sheikh hosted by President Mubarak where Barak smiled, gave me the victory sign, and told me that things were back on track. I believed him.

Arafat and the Palestinians remained suspicious. Saeb Erekat wondered at Sharm el-Sheikh whether Barak was trying to evade the interim issues by focusing on a permanent status agreement so quickly and without adequate preparation. Unlike Rabin, who had taken Arafat into his confidence on occasion and tried not to surprise him, Barak was inaccessible. Gilead Sher, who would emerge as one of Barak's two key negotiators with the Palestinians, saw trouble coming. Palestinian cooperation couldn't be achieved, he would later write, "with an edict from the conqueror to the conquered."[4] I reassured Saeb Erekat: Barak understood the importance of the Palestinian issue, but like Rabin he needed time to create a relationship with Arafat. I spoke too soon. In the fall of 1999 the prime minister was thinking about a final agreement, but it wasn't with the Palestinians.

Syria, Again

Ehud Barak's decision to make Syria a priority was not a surprise. He had told the president at Camp David that this was his plan. On paper a Syria-first strategy still appeared to make sense, as Rabin had thought six years earlier. Now that Barak had publicly committed Israel to withdraw from southern Lebanon in 2000, a deal with Syria seemed imperative. Without it, unilateral withdrawal from Lebanon might dissolve into violence and chaos. Barak had promised Clinton a Palestinian deal in 2000. Hadn't he started to make good on that promise by concluding an interim agreement with Arafat? In any case, none of us moving down the Syria-first track in the fall of 1999 believed that the Israelis and Palestinians were anywhere near ready for a final deal.

Syria-first made sense from Clinton's perspective as well. With his remarkable political instincts, the president knew Barak could sell a Syrian deal to the Israeli public more easily than one with the Palestinians. Reinforced by almost all his advisors, the president also knew that a great deal of work had been done previously, and a Syrian-Israeli agreement was doable by the end of his term. Madeleine Albright recalled that "we were a little seduced by Assad." The president, who'd seen him twice and had long phone conversations with him, before and after Barak's election, felt that he had developed a relationship with Assad. I'm sure Kissinger and Baker, both fascinated by the Syrian president, felt the same way. But there was no sweet-talking Assad, as Barak and Clinton were to find out yet again.

There are moments when you really know that the course you're pursuing is wrong and likely to fail, but you can't do much about it. In the fall of 1999 I felt that way. Barak had put the Palestinian track on ice, it would take him a full two months even to announce a lead negotiator, and even then the talks were not productive. And with our full backing Barak went off to pursue Syria in a way I thought was doomed to fail. I'd seen this movie at least twice before, and I was convinced we were wasting time we didn't have.

I got an opportunity to make the case to Secretary Albright in November. Assad wouldn't be so easy. He would demand 100 percent, and in his Frank Sinatra role of doing it his way, he wasn't prepared to meet Israel's needs. Besides, I had been arguing for years that the Syrian-Israeli process was all wrong and that we were coddling Assad by enabling him to avoid secret or public diplomacy. What's more, with about a year to go in Clinton's term, we had time and political space for only one deal, not two. Yes, Arafat was impossible, a liar and a conniver, but the problem he represented—a Palestinian problem without a status quo— was a far more urgent and critical matter.

I think that the secretary was sympathetic, but she had

limited options. It was pretty hard resisting, she recalls now, when Barak said, "I want to do Syria first." It wasn't just Barak. The president was on board for the Syrian option. So was Dennis, who had invested enormous time on this issue, and whose voice could persuade others. Gilead Sher now says that we should have questioned Barak hard on Syria and made clear that we were uneasy about putting the Palestinian track in the deep freeze. But then again, Sher didn't grasp the extent of the problem. Conditioned to accept the counsel of an Israeli prime minister without pushing back, there was no way—at least in late 1999—that Clinton would put the brakes on Barak. That he couldn't move an inch on Syria without our auspices or that we saw him treading water on the Palestinians didn't seem to matter. For Clinton, the Jewish lobby of one was a powerful persuader.

With Rabin, Syria-first was perhaps a missed opportunity; under Barak, it became a weight that would drag down both the Syrian and the Palestinian opportunities. The problem was time. As Sher recounts, Barak set a deadline of September 13, 2000, for reaching an agreement with the Palestinians in the Sharm el-Sheikh accord, then deviated from that course by chasing Syria for six months, half of the time that Clinton had left in office.

But it was not just that. I recall sitting with the Palestinians in Ramallah when CNN made the announcement that the president was inviting Barak and Syrian foreign minister Shara to Washington for talks in December. I happened to be sitting next to Arafat. Some of his colleagues became excited. Now that Syria was in, pressure from the Syrian-backed Palestinian groups Hamas and Islamic Jihad would lessen. I asked Arafat what he thought. For a guy who never said much in large gatherings, his response spoke volumes. Squeezing my hand until it ached, Arafat simply said, "Barak shouldn't take me for granted." Seven months later, in July 2000, now at Camp David, I thought about Arafat's remark: Barak, desperate for an agreement, now faced a Palestinian leader who wasn't in such a hurry.

Albert Einstein said that the definition of insanity is continuing to try the same approach to solve a problem but expecting different results. As the clock ticked down on the Clinton presidency, pursuing Syria was bad enough, but how we went about it ensured that we would fail. I'll say in the interests of full disclosure that I'd basically checked out of almost anything to do with Syria by this time. My colleagues, Dennis in particular, got tired of my complaining, so I watched the next period unfold more or less from the sidelines.

But sometimes that view is clearer than the one from the middle of the field. I had participated in the earlier 1993–96 effort on Syria, and it seemed to me we had learned nothing from our previous experiences. On this one I sympathized with the Israelis. Assad's refusal to do anything "human," including allowing Shara even to shake Barak's hand at Blair House, meant to me that he didn't deserve what he was asking for. Still, this was the guy we were dealing with. He'd made it clear what he needed, yet we seemed unable to internalize it, let alone make it clear to Barak in a way that counted. Sandy Berger believed that Barak thought Assad would "take less than the 1967 lines." If the prime minister wanted to bargain, fine, but not with the president's credibility and reputation. And that was precisely what happened.

What's more, we couldn't find a way, or didn't know how, to get into an endgame. We had been working the Israeli-Syrian process off and on nearly six years, and had not once—even though the issues were well defined and the gaps clear—tried to put it all together. We got blinded by process and sidetracked by events. And instead of telling Assad and Barak what it would take to do the deal, we allowed their bargaining positions to set the agenda and shape our tactics.

And so between January and March 2000, largely at Barak's insistence, we chased an agreement between Israel and Syria with almost no chance to succeed. In eight days at the Office of Personnel Management's training facility and at the U.S. Fish and Wildlife Center outside Shepherdstown, West Virginia, large Israeli, Syrian, and American delegations negotiated, living in separate wings with separate hours for dining. Barak, who had pushed hard for the meeting, now wasn't so sure he was ready for the endgame. He simply didn't want to put June 4, 1967, on the table. The Syrians had made moves in his direction on both normalization and security. But the prime minister was probably worried that he couldn't defend withdrawing beyond the international border to a skeptical Israeli public. Later he would tell Sandy Berger that he didn't want to succeed on the "first try" and look "overeager." Fair enough. But if the prime minister wanted a "kabuki" meeting, he should have told the president. Instead—in Dennis's and Madeleine Albright's views, driven by polls in Israel—he got cold feet. The leak of the agreement we had drafted to help the two sides bridge gaps embarrassed the Syrians, and Assad's declining health ensured that the Israeli-Syrian track was heading south.

Shepherdstown wasn't a total loss—at least for the Syrians. Every night we provided a van for the Syrian staff to travel to the local Wal-Mart where, in the words of Pat Kennedy, head of the State Department's Administration Bureau, they would "buy and buy and buy." The Golan Heights may not have been on the table, but at least the Syrians got great bargains at America's premier discount store.

In the wake of Assad's decision to resume negotiations at the level of his foreign minister, it was certainly possible to rationalize presidential involvement at Shepherdstown; not so for the president's March 30 meeting with Assad in Geneva. Rarely has an American president been set up or allowed himself to be set up for failure. At Barak's urging, the president agreed to meet Assad in Geneva to present Barak's final offer on territory. That offer was supposed to be communicated to Clinton a week before the Assad meeting. Barak declined to have Secretary Albright go out to Israel to receive it and then to Syria to test it. The call never came, and we were told that Barak would phone the president in Geneva before the meeting. Geneva, to use the words of Clinton's chief of staff, John Podesta, was "a shocking disaster." Clinton arrived in Geneva from India, physically ill and exhausted. Sandy Berger remembers being "stunned" when the call finally came and Barak told the president what he had in mind. In fairness to Barak, no one on our side expected him to agree to June 4, 1967, allowing a Syrian presence in the Sea of Galilee. But once again we continued to ply the same waters and somehow expect different results. Rationalizing the Geneva meeting, we could argue that the president had to try, that Barak's "final" offer of the Golan Heights minus four hundred meters off the shoreline of the lake was worth the effort, and that he wouldn't move on to the Palestinians unless he was convinced a deal with Syria was impossible. With Barak's planned Israeli withdrawal from Lebanon fast approaching, it was clearly in Barak's interest to try one more time with Syria. But not at our expense. Not only did Barak's offer have zero chance of working, it wasted valuable time and again eroded American credibility. Another failed meeting—now two in a row—could only make the president look bad and weak.

"It's over. It was a giant flop," Gamal Helal said on the phone. He had done the interpreting for the Assad-Clinton meeting. He sounded exhausted but not terribly disappointed. Gamal had been one of the few who had argued all along that chasing the Syrians without June 4, 1967, in our pocket was a waste of time and would hurt our chances with the Palestinians. When his call came, I was in Washington managing the public front channel of Israeli-Palestinian negotiations at Bolling Air Force Base. Gamal told me that eight minutes or so into the meeting Assad heard the president say "mutually agreed borders." At that point the Syrian president essentially rejected Barak's offer. I wasn't all that surprised. I never liked to see America fail, but this failure seemed so inevitable and unnecessary. And at least now, I reasoned, we could concentrate on the negotiations that made sense. The timing of Gamal's call couldn't have been more appropriate. Lindsay and I were hosting a reception at our home for Israeli and Palestinian negotiators. We had decided to do it because morale on both sides was pretty low. Israeli and Palestinian negotiators knew they were a sideshow to the Syrian track. But that was about to change. I'd gone to the backyard to take Gamal's call. Muhammad Dahlan, Arafat's security chief for Gaza, was outside smoking. "What's up?" he said. "We're on your track now," I replied with a smile.

I should have controlled my enthusiasm. We were now, I was convinced, focused on the right track, but our six-month ride on the Syria express had created three new realities that minimized the prospects of an Israeli-Palestinian accord during President Clinton's remaining time in office. First, we had lost time. In April and May, when Israelis and Palestinians really energized their back-channel talks, we had eight months left in the president's term, but given the fall campaign plans, we really had much less time if we wanted full use of Clinton's time. Second, we had lost trust. Barak's chasing Assad angered Arafat in the extreme. Barak's inability or unwillingness to deliver on any of the interim issues he'd promised Arafat further damaged his credibility on permanent status talks. Saeb Erekat, Yasser Abd Rabbo, and just about every other Palestinian asked us and the Israelis how, if the prime minister couldn't transfer to Palestinian control three West Bank villages in the Jerusalem area because of political pressures, he could meet Palestinian needs on East Jerusalem as the capital.

Finally, there was the precedent set on territory. Assad died in May, going to his grave with the sacred mantra of June 4, 1967. He therefore set a standard that Arafat would have to match. None of us knew how much less than 100 percent of the West Bank and Gaza Arafat could accept. At the time I thought he had flexibility on territory, if some of the other issues broke his way.

But that wasn't the point. Assad's demand and Barak's offer of almost 100 percent of the Golan Heights minus four hundred meters or so off the northeastern portion of the lake made it impossible for any Palestinian leader to accept much less. Barak's 90 percent offer on territory at Camp David might have been the most generous in the history of negotiations from his point of view. But given the fact that he had offered Assad—a man whose view of peace was essentially nonbelligerency, who wouldn't allow his foreign minister to shake Barak's hand, and who was running a proxy war against Israel in southern Lebanon using

Hezbollah—99 percent of the Golan Heights, Arafat expected considerably more. With or without Syria, the Palestinians would have pressed Israel for close to what Sadat got, but the Syrian offer killed what flexibility they had. That first week in April, as we talked about how to handle the new opportunity and challenges of a Barak now energized on the Palestinian track, I thought to myself, *Don't ever pray for anything you really don't want.*

Going to Camp David: Let's Go Out and Do This Thing

"What do you think?" the president asked, peering over the top of his glasses during the second briefing on the approaching Camp David summit. "Do you think we made the right decision to go to the summit?" By then it was an academic question. We had issued the invitations, and Arafat and Barak would arrive in a week. But I admired him for his honesty and his expression of his uncertainty.

If Clinton was looking for dissenters, he wouldn't find them in this room. We were a committed bunch. Albright, Berger, Ross, Riedel, Malley, Gamal, and I gave almost identical answers. Our replies boiled down to *Yes, Mr. President, it's worth the risk. If you don't go, there will be violence, and you may be blamed for not grasping a historic opportunity to make progress on an issue you really care about.*

I followed suit and believed what I said. But I should have added (and to this day regret not saying), *Mr. President, you need to go, but don't turn it into a make-or-break moment, because you won't reach an agreement on the big issues—Jerusalem, borders, and refugees—in a week or so. We need a plan B, a postsummit soft landing to maintain hope and high-level interest.*

Two weeks earlier I'd floated the idea of a second backup summit and got yelled at by Sandy Berger. It would happen again at Camp David, this time by John Podesta. So I wasn't about to try it out again, especially a week before a historic meeting where Clinton was hoping to succeed. Besides, only a limited number were allowed on each delegation, and I worried that this kind of talk might cost me a seat at the table. I had heard the answer anyway. You don't plan a presidential summit and set up a crucible of decision-making by signaling anything less than the objective of reaching an agreement. Only in the heat of a summit would decisions be made.

Fair enough. But those assumptions (Barak's in the main) really wouldn't reflect the gathering we were about to sponsor. Ehud Barak, with a shrinking parliamentary majority, a disappearing Bill Clinton at the end of the year, and a failure with Syria at his back, was desperate for a historic deal to end the Israeli-Palestinian conflict but lacked a real grasp of what it would cost him. Yasser Arafat, on the other hand, angry at Barak for ignoring him but sensing his desperation, wary of U.S.-Israeli pressure but unwilling to stiff the president, wasn't in a hurry. And no one from Clinton on down thought success likely. Why then did we go? Why was the president with all his doubts willing to risk a high-level summit and go out and "do this thing," as he said to us at the end of the briefing?

Within two weeks of the Clinton-Assad meeting in March, Barak arrived in Washington with his next project: a fast-track Israeli-Palestinian negotiation to end the conflict. The January deadline for the framework agreement set in the Sharm el-Sheikh accord had already lapsed, and soon the September 13, 2000, deadline for a final deal would be upon him. Besides, as he told Gilead Sher, a deal with the Palestinians would require billions from the U.S. Congress, mandating an early breakthrough. And during that visit I'd also heard Barak's analysis that Israel was approaching "an iceberg of violence" unless something wasn't done quickly with the Palestinians. Dennis recalls seeing Barak at Blair House looking "like a mad scientist, up all night, there's yellow pages spread all around. He's disheveled, hasn't slept, and he's figured out what will work," and of course he wanted to see the president.

In the wake of the Geneva debacle there was enormous skepticism about another Barak extravaganza. Rob Malley recalls that he wrote memos for the president laying out what we'd need from him if he pushed again for high-risk presidential involvement. What's more, much of the prime minister's approach didn't add up. He wanted an end of conflict but couldn't come up with Israeli concessions to produce it. He wanted to focus on the big issues but yet was having trouble delivering on commitments he had made to the Palestinians on the small ones. He was thinking about a summit but wasn't into a hard sell with us yet. His lead negotiator told him in April that chances of an agreement were less than fifty-fifty.[5]

If Barak was in high energy mode in April, May would produce overdrive. Two things happened that month that would add to the case for considering a summit and create the urgency for doing it. In April the prime minister had authorized back channel Israeli-Palestinian talks that really were serious. And in mid-May severe Israeli-Palestinian confrontations occurred in what analysts would later describe as a kind of dress rehearsal for the September intifada. Opportunity and crisis are a powerful combination, and it made the Israeli case for a summit more compelling and our reaction more sympathetic.

The second time in my life I entered a country incognito was Sweden in the first ten days of May. Israelis and Palestinians had asked us to join them in their secret channel talks (they leaked the first day), hosted by the Swedish government at the prime minister's country residence at Harpsund, a sixteenth-century estate—complete with its own lake, manor house, and in May, at that latitude, almost continuous daylight—about an hour or so from Stockholm. Just what the Israelis and Palestinians need, I thought to myself, a 24/7 work environment. When we arrived the Palestinians, led by Abu Alaa, seemed generally upbeat about the atmosphere. The Israelis, Shlomo Ben-Ami in particular, were genuinely impressed by the substance of the discussion. For the first time there was some discussion of the "taboo issues," including refugees. And the Palestinians seemed to accept Israel's idea of settlement blocs, which would mean that some percentage of the West Bank would be annexed by Israel. In talking to Ben-Ami now, he says that Israel came away from the Swedish talks with the impression that the June 1967 border was "not sacrosanct."

Maybe it was the weird light of the Swedish summer, but I could never quite figure out why Harpsund created the degree of optimism it did. When Gamal asked Abu Alaa that last night, as only he could, what kind of movement there had been on the Palestinian side, Abu Alaa just laughed. The discussions had been good and productive but had produced no breakthroughs appreciably narrowing the gaps on borders, Jerusalem, and refugees. That false sense of confidence on the Israeli side, combined with the leak of the secret talks (most likely by Abu Mazen, erstwhile rival of Abu Alaa), showed the real problem underlying every negotiation leading up to the summit in July. Whether they were secret or public, regardless of their location—at Harpsund, Eilat, Jerusalem, or Washington—the negotiations presented several huge problems in trying to narrow gaps.

Neither Arafat nor Barak would really empower his negotiators to reveal much about bottom lines, and given the sensitivity of some of the issues, like Jerusalem, key aspects were never even discussed in detail. Inter-Palestinian rivalries, which Arafat encouraged, often threatened the discreteness of the channels and confused matters further. Abu Alaa, so "flexible" in Sweden, would be much tougher at Camp David. And finally, because the issues were so politically explosive, we monitored and asked questions but wouldn't dare suggest fixes on issues like Jerusalem or borders. Those who argue that Camp David wasn't well prepared miss the point. Israeli and Palestinian redlines, the lack of trust, and the explosiveness of the issues made conventional preparation impossible.

All of this would strengthen Barak's argument that only a leaders' summit could hope to produce an agreement. As I explained to Secretary Albright in the wake of the Bolling negotiations, traditional prenegotiations wouldn't work under these circumstances. "Brainstorming," which is what we asked the two sides to do on an issue like Jerusalem, was simply not possible. I passed on to the secretary Yasser Abd Rabbo's comment that "brainstorming" was about as natural to him as "walking down the streets of Ramallah in a dress." Don't get me wrong—there were countless hours of good, creative presummit discussion. But as Sher said, at the negotiator level, "We'd exhausted our mandates."

The problem was that Barak's logic was both right and wrong. Only leaders could decide these issues. At the same time the gaps separating the parties were enormous, and the political and psychological constraints on each to close them were exceptionally heavy. Nor was the absence of trust the key problem. Even had Arafat and Barak been the best of friends, it probably wouldn't have mattered much. In the summer of 2000, having only begun to discuss the core issues of their conflict, Israelis and Palestinians were not close to understanding or acting on what it would take to do a deal. Amnon Shahak, a former Israeli chief of staff, minister, and back channel negotiator himself, recalled that Stockholm produced no "big achievements" and what had been achieved was "far from what was necessary to start final negotiations."

From opportunity at Harpsund, we flew to Israel and directly into crisis. Palestinian demonstrations to mark the *nakba* had already begun. The clashes went on for almost five days in the worst fighting since the September 1996 Hasmonean tunnel crisis. By the end, six Palestinians had been killed and hundreds were wounded; on the Israeli side, there were no fatalities but about sixty soldiers and civilians were injured. What was new and menacing about the *nakba* demonstration was the degree of organization on the Palestinian side and the involvement of the Tanzim, Fatah activists under Marwan Barghouti, and the firing of weapons by the Tanzim behind demonstrators thronging at Israeli checkpoints. The Israelis, employing tactics that foreshadowed those used in the second intifada, responded disproportionately to make their point on deterrence. Both sides believe these tactics foreshadowed the approaching conflict in September, which some Israelis have concluded was preplanned with the *nakba* as a testing ground.

True or not, the May violence had a major impact both on Barak and on us. Barak now became even more determined to focus on the diplomatic endgame. He negotiated the transfer of the three villages through the Knesset but then wouldn't transfer them because of what he perceived to be Arafat's role in the violence. As we departed Israel for Washington, all of us felt a real sense of foreboding. Barak would tell Dan Meridor, a Likud politician, minister, and Camp David delegation member, that the horizon appeared very much as it had in the days before the October war: "The sky's blue, the sea is blue. Except that I see the iceberg we're going to hit. We need to divert the ship in time."

Beginning in June, I would wake up most mornings with a knot in my stomach. I was convinced we were headed for a summit whose outcome was stunningly uncertain or at some point a collapse of the negotiations in the face of violence. The president resisted Barak's call for an early June summit when they met in Lisbon. He told Arafat during his visit to Washington that if he called a summit, he wouldn't blame the Palestinian leader for a failure of the meeting and would support the Palestinian call for a further Israeli deployment from West Bank territory as a safety valve, should a final deal appear unattainable. To his great credit, in a last-ditch effort to protect the president, Sandy Berger asked the toughest questions of both Gilead Sher and Barak, but by June we all knew this was not going to end anywhere else but at Camp David. We bought a little more time with Secretary Albright's trip in late June to assess the situation. She found an eager Barak, a reluctant Arafat, and no real information on what either would give on substance once they got to a meeting with the president.

If historic decisions are made on the basis of the information at hand, then the decision to go to a high-risk summit probably made sense. The three advisors who sat with the president at Camp David on the July 4 weekend before the summit, when the decision was finally made, thought so. "We saw things unraveling on the ground," Sandy Berger recalled. "By July we had six months left...I think it was the right thing to do." Madeleine Albright: "Barak had some very bold ideas and wanted to use the last months of the Clinton presidency." As far as Clinton was concerned, she observed, he was "reluctant to substitute his judgment for that of an Israeli prime minister so determined to make history."[6] And Dennis Ross: "If you don't do this and you've got a guy who's prepared to make unprecedented moves and you're afraid violence is coming, then history also judges you for not being willing to risk to find out."

As risky as he knew the business was, Bill Clinton wasn't going to pass up a historic opportunity on the issue he cared about, particularly against a real possibility of violence. In the end, it wasn't the Lewinsky scandal or the memories of Rabin or King Hussein that drove him. It was Bill Clinton now, and the inherent optimism deeply encoded in his political DNA, and his confidence that maybe, just maybe, he could pull this off. He also knew that the clock was quickly winding down on his presidency. "The president was determined to get a success after two failures," Bruce Riedel recalled. "We were basically told, 'Put on your jogging suit. We're going to Camp David.' "

Lost in the Woods

If you take U.S. route 77 west out of Thurmont, Maryland, a small town of six thousand nestled in the foothills of the Catoctin Mountains, seven miles or so up the road you'd find yourself very near the presidential retreat of Camp David. It's not visible from the main park road or marked on any map. Sixty miles or so from Washington, D.C., the retreat, originally dubbed Shangri-La by Franklin Roosevelt after the magical mountain sanctuary in James Hilton's 1933 novel, *Lost Horizon,* and renamed by President Eisenhower after his grandson, is secure and secluded in the five-thousand-plus acres of Catoctin Mountain Park.

On a mild spring, summer, or fall day, exploring the hiking

trails of the mixed hardwood forests with their scenic views and high gradient streams can be great fun. You'd have no reason to be on the park's winding roads at night, unless you lived in the Thurmont area or had special business there. The night of July 10, 2000, we did. Our team was driving up to Camp David for a historic Israeli-Palestinian summit meeting with the president of the United States. Nervous and excited, with no need to hype the drama of what was about to unfold, I wondered, as the government driver negotiated the park's winding roads, what the actual negotiations would be like. This was not Madrid or even the Wye River summit. We weren't coming to discuss a process or Oslo's interim issues. Pushed by Ehud Barak and driven by his own commitment to reach a final deal, Bill Clinton was convening a presidential summit to reach a final agreement, only the second such effort in forty years of American peacemaking.

I'm not superstitious by nature. But that night, driving up to Camp David, we got lost. It was dark the way it doesn't get in the city. The roads were winding and narrow, and we'd clearly missed a turn somewhere. We stopped at a ranger's station, only to find it closed. There was a pay phone, so I called the State Department Operations Center. We eventually got our bearings and good directions. We joked about getting lost and agreed it wasn't a great beginning. If we couldn't find Camp David, I kidded Dennis, how would we know what to do once we got there?

But the humor couldn't alleviate my unease. I'd argued for the summit and even a second one, worried that a make-or-break approach in one meeting wouldn't work. But if we couldn't succeed in Israeli-Syrian talks at Shepherdstown, where the gaps had been well defined and clear for several years, how would we manage here, where they weren't? One thing was clear: if we wanted to have any chance of succeeding, the Americans, meaning the president, would have to take charge—and quickly.

Let's get something straight from the beginning. In the summer of 2000 the chances that Arafat and Barak would reach an agreement to solve or end the Israeli-Palestinian conflict were pretty close to zero. And each in his own way bears responsibility for what happened at Camp David. Bold, brave, and reckless, Barak wanted an end to conflict and all claims with the Palestinians, but in the words of his top negotiator, Shlomo Ben-Ami, the prime minister's idea of the concessions required of Israel for such a sweeping accord "fell far short of even modest Palestinian expectations." With no parliamentary majority (Barak lost a no-confidence vote shortly after he arrived at the summit), the prime minister was desperate, a man in a hurry whose only salvation would be a breakthrough. This urgency caused Barak's redlines to turn pink time and again, signaling a weak and wily Arafat that he could get more from the Israelis simply by holding out for more. How could the summit be a "moment of truth," Ben-Ami observed, when "every redline was changed in favor of the next one?"

Arafat was in no hurry to make concessions that fell short of what Sadat had received on territory and what Assad had pressed for. The notion that Arafat was dragged kicking and screaming to the summit is an exaggeration. I saw him the night he arrived, smiling, his kaffiyeh flapping in the evening breeze. He might have been nervous, but I also had the feeling he believed he'd finally made it—arriving on the president's helicopter at a place usually reserved for heads of state. He was wary of finding himself in an Israeli-American pressure cooker, but he couldn't say no and keep Bill Clinton in his corner. At the same time he came neither to make sweeping concessions nor to negotiate in any meaningful sense of the word. At a minimum, to maintain his street cred back home, he came to show that he would not give in easily in defending Palestinian interests. On the max side, he wasn't going to settle for much short of June 4, 1967, and sovereignty over most of East Jerusalem and the Haram al-Sharif. "We weren't prepared for making a historic deal," Yasser Abd Rabbo, one of Arafat's five or six negotiators, recalls. Muhammad Rashid, a key Arafat advisor and Camp David participant, was more blunt: "We just didn't engage" at Camp David. Arafat came to Camp David with no real strategy, little flexibility, and a suitcase full of complexes, including fear of an Israeli-American trap and a desire to get even with Barak for chasing Syria. At summit's end we should have had a special T-shirt with an "I Survived Camp David" logo. That's essentially what Arafat did.

I need to be equally clear, however, about the American role at the summit. The Clinton administration convened Camp David with the best of intentions, but the president and the rest of us who counseled him bear significant responsibility for what transpired there. Probably no American mediator could have overcome the problems we faced. At the same time our approach virtually eliminated any chance of success and left us poorly positioned to pick up the pieces. Without a strong American hand and strategy, the summit would be at the mercy of a hyperactive Barak and an aggressively passive Arafat. But that was how Bill Clinton approached the summit and acted throughout the two-week conference: he never developed or asked for either a strategy to maximize the chance for success or a backup plan to minimize the impact of failure; nor, I might add, did we give him one. We can blame Arafat and praise Barak all day long, but that doesn't address our share of the responsibility once we got to the summit. We didn't run the summit; the summit ran us.

Before we take a look at the American role at Camp David, I'll say a word or two about the place itself. There's no question we picked the right spot. High in political prestige, a place of historic importance in Arab-Israeli peacemaking because of the celebrated meetings of the first Camp David summit, the setting was also casual and low key. Isolated and secluded (we blocked all cell phone use and permitted the leaders' use only of outside hard lines), Camp David was a mix of a summer camp and a nice Marriott. Jackie Kennedy had described the decor of the cabins as "early Holiday Inn." They bore names such as Holly, Aspen, Laurel, and Birch. The place seemed like the ideal location to calm people down. The dress code was informal, with no ties or uniforms, except for Arafat, who wore his standard Che Guevara outfit. Meals were casual, no formal seating, usually buffet. No matter what the leaders' moods, Israeli, Palestinian, and American negotiators usually sat together and relaxed and mixed easily and effortlessly. I'd

seen Israeli and Palestinian negotiators just about everywhere—
first- and second-class hotels on four continents—and it was always
the same. Their humanity—joking, laughing, crying, arguing, and
fighting—was always on display. These people liked and respected
one another, and despite the many tensions, it showed.

We made clear from the start that there would be no coming
and going until the summit concluded. We made an exception for
Abu Mazen to attend his son's wedding. Akram Haniya, one of
Arafat's key advisors, would later complain that the Palestinians felt
like prisoners. But it sure looked to me like they were having a good
time. Some of the negotiating sessions were marathons, but no one
on either side worked themselves to death at the summit. Maybe
this was part of the problem. There were also plenty of recreational
activities—bowling, tennis, basketball, video games, pool. The food
was delicious. And both sides loved the golf carts, which they used
continuously and at high speeds, careening around the walking
paths chattering in Hebrew and Arabic. When one of the carts disappeared at the end of the summit, we joked that maybe one of the
Israelis or Palestinians had tried to drive it back home.

While the president was gone, Secretary Albright heroically
played the roles of entertainer and camp director. We showed two
movies—*Gladiator* and the World War II submarine movie *U-571*.
Curious choices. Wasn't this a peace summit? But the Israelis and
Palestinians loved them. One Israeli said after the U-boat movie
that it was a good thing that we showed it, because it reminded
him of the need to put submarines on Israel's wish list of military
hardware that it planned to request from the United States in case
we reached an agreement. In order to lighten the mood, the secretary took Barak to Gettysburg and Arafat to her farm in Loudoun
County, Virginia, where he posed poolside for pictures with her
children and grandchildren.

For all the drama anticipated at the July 11–25 summit, Camp
David proved a surprisingly undramatic event. There were moments of tension: Clinton shouting at Abu Alaa and storming out
when the Palestinian negotiator wouldn't even discuss anything
other than the June 1967 borders; Barak's nearly choking to death

on a peanut, saved only by Gidi Grinstein, the youngest member of Israel's delegation; and the final early morning effort by the president to persuade the Palestinians not to reject his ideas.

But the rhythm of the summit, particularly our erratic tactics, made sustained pressure or drama difficult. The president's trip to the G8 summit meeting in Japan deflated both expectations and Barak's mood. Like a modern-day Achilles sulking in his tent at Troy, he retreated to his cabin. Not even the secretary's offer (which he didn't take her up on) to move a piano into his cabin brightened his mood. In a way, our familiarity with Israelis and Palestinians (and theirs with us) made our ties a bit too comfortable and made the environment at the summit one more gathering of good friends. The tone was set by the president's accessibility, his openness, and his willingness to do just about anything to succeed. We could never summon up the toughness, focus, or distance we needed to create a more serious tone. "Rather than running the conference, you let it run itself," Shlomo Ben-Ami told me. Nor could you impress on either side that "there would be a cost to failure." America didn't intimidate at Camp David—"we were humbled," he concluded.

Our approach to the summit was flawed in critical areas that made success impossible. These problems did not emerge de novo. They were ingrained in our attitude and actions toward Arab-Israeli diplomacy during much of the Clinton administration. At Camp David they became magnified because the summit dealt for the first time with the big issues and carried profound consequences for Barak, Arafat, America, and the future of the entire Middle East.

No Sustained Strategy

Only a "comprehensive package" designed to address all the issues would stop the erosion in Israeli-Palestinian negotiations, Gilead Sher remarked to his colleagues on the eve of the summit. Maybe the Americans will "surprise us."[7] We didn't. Rob Malley described our behavior at the summit like the amusement-park ride bumper cars. When we hit an obstacle, we'd turn some other way and try something new. It actually wasn't quite that bad. Usually we'd stay with our tactic for a couple days. After pulling our negotiating text off the table on day four because neither side approved, we scrambled for an organizing approach, vacillating between encouraging direct talks between the two sides, and then small meetings between the negotiators and the president without the leaders. While no summit can be prescripted, and this one was especially challenging, we let far too much simply drift. "There were so many times at the summit," Maria Echaveste recalls, "where literally we sat around the table going, what do we do next?"

Listen to Gilead Sher, who was expecting a stronger American hand and who was a great admirer of President Clinton: "There was no negotiations schedule. There was no timeline for follow-up. There was no proposal or counterproposal, checking on the advancement or progress." Or to the words of Yasser Abd Rabbo from the other side: "It was total chaos. Every day a different meeting, committee, and issue. We didn't know what were our aims, to succeed, to fail, to escape."

As both Sher and Abd Rabbo knew well, part of the problem lay in the negotiating tactics of Barak and Arafat. Barak had his own strategy and timetable: keep his cards close, avoid letting Arafat pocket any of his concessions, build pressure, and wait to see where the Palestinians were going. Arafat's strategy was to be hyperpassive and see what was on the table but never authorize his negotiators to lay down authoritative positions. Barak would not meet directly to negotiate with Arafat in the presence of Clinton, out of concern that the Palestinian leader would use the president to extract something from him. And Barak wasn't interested in seeing Arafat alone, even though some on his own team encouraged him to do so. Not having the leaders negotiate directly wasn't necessarily fatal. At the first Camp David, Carter made a judgment early on that Begin and Sadat were too combustible. This put a premium on a firmer American role in July 2000, which wasn't there.

No Negotiating Text

Samuel Goldwyn, the great Hollywood producer, once joked that a verbal agreement isn't worth the paper it's written on. We needed a draft text for some kind of agreement to organize the summit. Otherwise, what exactly were we doing there? Barak objected not just to the substance of our text but to the kind of bridging exercise we employed to define, identify, and narrow the gaps. We changed our initial text to accommodate him, then pulled it off completely when the Palestinians hated the new version. I knew we were in deep trouble. At a summit like this, where the leaders weren't meeting and where the gaps between them were not defined, we desperately needed an organizing instrument—in this case, as Jimmy Carter had insisted at the first Camp David, a text that we could control. Without it we could not hope to structure the summit and thereby improve the chances for a substantive agreement.

The problem lay not in our showing the Israelis the text first. It was our standard practice and the Palestinians expected it. On the afternoon the Palestinians were expecting our text I saw Saeb Erekat on one of the walking paths. He asked me when it would be ready. After I said I wasn't sure, he rolled his eyes and gave me a look I had seen before that meant: *I wish the Israelis would hurry up and finish with it.* Had we gotten Barak's comments, taken what we thought appropriate, argued about what was not, and pushed back when the Israelis went too far, we might have preserved our integrity as a mediator. But we caved to Israeli objections. We had a substantive approach, Dennis recalls, but "Barak says no, so we back off." The president, to use one of his favorite words, was simply not prepared to "jam" the Israelis. This wouldn't have been jamming at all—it would simply have been smart negotiating. The framework agreement that produced the first Camp David accords went through twenty-three drafts, and the Americans, working closely with the Egyptians and the Israelis, controlled and managed the text. Looking back now, I think we probably lost control of the summit by day four, having blinked when both Barak and Arafat said no.

Not Enough Time

At Camp David I never saw so many people in such a hurry. Barak was in a rush, the president was impatient, Sandy Berger wanted quick progress. The summit had been scheduled in mid-July to avoid any conflict with the political conventions. In fact, far from being a strictly political calculation, the date set for the summit was based on Clinton's concern that he might upstage either convention by appearing to insert himself and a high-stakes summit into the mix. But there was understandably a concern about not having the president bogged down in this issue. "I want the shit dry by September," he joked as we left the briefing before the summit.

Far more problematic was the scheduling of the president's trip to the G8 in Japan, which created an artificial deadline for his departure seven days into the summit on July 18. I sympathized with the dilemma. He wasn't going to cancel his participation in that summit meeting. And maybe if he reached a quick breakthrough at Camp David, he could use the G8 to sell it and marshal the necessary financial and political resources. What's more, maybe the president's departure could create some urgency with the deadline hanging over Israeli and Palestinian heads.

All of this proved too clever by half. Barak didn't even begin to play his bottom-line cards until day eight; Arafat wasn't going to fold under pressure; and the idea of getting a quick breakthrough was frankly ridiculous. When Clinton left for Asia, leaving Secretary Albright in the unenviable position of trying to hold things together, it seemed a bad omen. We had told both sides that they could not leave Camp David until it was over. We should have followed our own advice. Clinton's coming and going did little to increase the pressure and urgency to make decisions;

certainly it had no effect on the Palestinians. Time was not our ally, but we made it more of an enemy by thinking we could crack these historic issues quickly. Carter had come to the first Camp David with a "we'll stay as long as it takes" mindset. The Egyptian-Israeli breakthrough came on the summit's thirteenth and penultimate day. Our "let's get it done yesterday" approach was out of touch with the issues, the leaders' own sense of timing, and the gaps that separated the Israeli and Palestinian bottom lines. Building pressure on Arafat to make major moves on Jerusalem quickly without Arab support, even in the face of Barak's bold decision to give sovereignty over the Muslim and Christian quarters, wasn't going to work. Arafat's need to show he was fighting hard on Jerusalem and not give in quickly precluded any fast compromise, even if the substance had been right, and it wasn't.

Illusions About Closing

The president and his team deserve the benefit of the doubt for many things—risking the summit, putting historic issues on the table, and wrestling with them for the first time in the history of the Israeli-Palestinian conflict. Where we ran off the highway was in our assessment of what was required in July 2000 to actually reach an agreement. We had been off with Assad, but not by nearly as much as we were with the Palestinians. In part, our inaccurate assessment was based on our belief (perhaps our optimism and pragmatism worked against us here) that the two Mr. A's would settle for something less than June 4, 1967, lines on territory (probably the easiest issue!) and our predisposition to consider Israeli needs and requirements as the standard by which to judge what we could live with. I remember in early 2000 how impressed I was by Barak's willingness to consider 80 percent withdrawal from the West Bank. No Israeli prime minister had ever even contemplated such an offer. As an initial bargaining position and the first step in the Israelis' own education about

Palestinian needs, it was credible. The president was excited to get Barak's offer of 90 percent at Camp David. But we never seemed to grasp that we couldn't do this on the cheap. I sat in the same lodge where Begin and Sadat had met. I could sense what both Arafat and Barak must have felt as the ghosts of two assassinated peacemakers, Sadat and Rabin, hovered about them. If you were Barak, offering 90 percent was plenty risky politically and, given Rabin's murder, even personally; if you were Arafat, accepting it would have been fatal. Instead, most on our side saw his demand either as unreasonable or as a contrivance, a negotiating tactic. And it proved to be a very wrong and costly assessment.

This kind of thinking, which Shlomo Ben-Ami described as marked by delusion and self-deceit in the case of Israel, clearly shaped Barak's approach. "When we came to Camp David," Ben-Ami reflects, "we were very far away from assuming the scope of the concessions that were needed to reach the endgame." What Barak offered was bold and unprecedented (and Arafat should have counteroffered), but in the summer of 2000 no Israeli government could have accepted much more than Barak put on the table and certainly not what Arafat was pushing for. Nor would Arafat budge so early in the negotiating process from his 100 percent position. Part of Barak's bitterness in the wake of Clinton's departure for Asia was his anger at Arafat's lack of responsiveness, but he was also beginning to realize that the price for a deal was much higher than he was willing or able to pay.

No Arab Support

If there was a no-brainer in preparing the summit, it was lining up the support of key Arab states to back our efforts. This was supposed to be an end-of-the-conflict summit, after all, which meant that Jerusalem would have to be part of any solution. Barak knew this and so did we, but he opposed coordinating with the Arabs out of fear of leaks and out of concern that it would weaken American and Israeli pressure on Arafat. The other problem was that we didn't know until late in the summit that Barak was prepared to make a bold move with regard to Jerusalem, agreeing for the first time to concede Palestinian sovereignty over part of the Old City. Had we known, Sandy Berger observed, "we could have gotten some Arab buy-in."

There was no way Arafat or any Palestinian leader could have signed off on any solution to Jerusalem without Arab support. So, too late in the day, we found ourselves in the bizarre situation of scrambling to mobilize the Arabs. Berger recalls the president trying to describe on the phone to Saudi crown prince Abdullah a complicated fix on the Jerusalem issue, only to find out later that "Abdullah had never looked at a map of Jerusalem in his life." Ned Walker, NEA's assistant secretary of state, who would be sent out after the summit to brief key Arab leaders on the results, believes the worst mistake we made was "not to go to every Arab and talk about the issue of Jerusalem before Camp David." When Walker saw Abdullah, the Saudi leader told him flat out that Arafat couldn't make a decision on Jerusalem without the Arab world's support. Egypt's President Hosni Mubarak, who knew less about the details of modern Jerusalem than Abdullah, told Walker that his response to President Clinton's request for help with Arafat was to wonder how he could support a proposal he really didn't understand.

Only a coalition of Arab moderates lined up behind an American bridging position on Jerusalem would have given us any chance of reaching an agreement. Amazingly, we just didn't plan for it, particularly because we had no idea where the Israelis were on the issue, and Barak wouldn't tell us. We couldn't bring in the Arabs, Madeleine Albright recalls, because Barak "didn't tell us what was going on and didn't want them to know." Sher thought that Barak erred badly in "not telling you that you need to do it." But since when did we need the Israelis? Why couldn't we figure this one out on our own? One guy who got it was John Podesta: "To think that regarding the Old City [of Jerusalem] you could just pull it out of your ass; I don't think we respected the panoply of players that might have been helpful there." And since after day nine of the summit the Jerusalem issue became critical to any progress, our inability to use the Arabs to either pressure or persuade Arafat to make a deal became fatal.

No Plan B

Once the decision was made to try for an end-of-conflict agreement, the odds of what Sandy Berger called a "soft landing" (preserving a real sense of direction, hope for a solution, and high-level follow-up) declined considerably. Toward the end of Camp David there was serious discussion of a "partial deal" that would have deferred Jerusalem. But for most of Camp David's thirteen days, Barak wouldn't hear of it. Once Jerusalem became a focal point, Arafat had to fight to defend Arab rights there and couldn't accept an agreement without it. The issue for us—when we considered it—was how to ensure an end to the summit that created a sense of momentum, preserved hope, and sustained reasonable ties between two leaders who were suspicious and angry. As it turned out, we ended up with the worst of both worlds.

Once the summit ended, Barak's make-or-break mindset faded. In late September, before the outbreak of the second intifada, he would have his best meeting with Arafat ever, and negotiations continued; Barak and his nonexistent redlines continued to move toward Palestinian positions. At the same time Barak blamed Arafat for the summit's failure and cajoled an already sympathetic Clinton into doing the same. Barak's and Clinton's anger were understandable, and the politician in Clinton was eager to do something for the bold and beleaguered prime minister. But I can't help thinking our behavior in blaming the Palestinians and facilitating Barak's campaign to delegitimize Arafat as a partner was immature and counterproductive. Sher now admits that whether or not Arafat deserved it (and in Sher's view he did), "the finger pointing" at the end of the summit was "completely contrary to what was needed then." And in any event we just kept dealing with Arafat anyway. Indeed, the president's presentation of his parameters on final status in December 2000 moved toward the Palestinians on every issue.

The last two nights of the summit, when it became pretty clear it was going to fail, I rushed around trying to sell what was deemed the "marshmallow option." This was, in essence, a statement that would have been more than the "commitment to continue negotiating" communiqué we issued after the final three-way Arafat-Barak-Clinton meeting, and less than a substantial agreement. It laid out a set of principles that Israelis and Palestinians could rightly claim represented real progress in their historic first cut at the big issues, such as Jerusalem, borders, and refugees. But this option was DOA on our side. And Barak, eager to unmask and reveal Arafat's perfidy, would never have accepted it. In the absence of a soft landing, the summit, in Berger's words, "just fell off a cliff."

Could a different outcome at Camp David, short of an agreement, have preempted the second intifada? It's impossible to know. Some, like Moshe Ya'alon, former head of IDF intelligence, argue that Arafat, under pressure from the Hezbollah model, planned the violence for months and, once fingered for Camp David's failure, sought to distract attention, regain the strugglers' banner, and demonstrate to those who blamed him the cost of doing so. Others, including Ami Ayalon, former head of Shin Bet, say a planned intifada is nonsense. But all agree that once the tiger of Palestinian violence was out of its cage, Arafat rode it, did little to moderate it, and in fact fed it to improve his own legitimacy.

Looking back now, the only course of action that might have preempted the violence would have been a decision by Clinton, Arafat, and Barak at the summit to develop a coordinated strategy and pursue Israeli-Palestinian negotiations for the next six months, including attending to the bubbling tensions on the ground. A positive end to the summit could have been a three-way meeting in which the president, flanked by Arafat and Barak, would have issued the following statement: "What we have witnessed here in the past two weeks was a historic departure in Israeli-Palestinian negotiations. For the first time Israelis and Palestinians discussed the core issues that drive their conflict. On every issue I believe there were significant openings that need to be explored. I am leaving here today with a commitment from Chairman Arafat and Prime Minister Barak to work on both the permanent status issues and the security and economic situation on the ground. I will be working closely with them until the end of my administration to maintain the progress made here today and to reach an agreement." A statement like this, followed by nonstop talks at the foreign minister level, another summit if needed, and a 24/7 American-orchestrated timeline to address issues such as terror, violence, settlement activity, prisoner releases, economic activity, and movement of Palestinians, would have made a difference. But like a big red balloon with a tiny pinprick hole, the Camp David enterprise started to leak air the minute we left the summit.

The President's Persona

There's no other way to say this: when it came to Arab-Israeli peacemaking, Bill Clinton was not the son-of-a-bitch he needed to be. Whether anyone could have closed a deal between Israelis and Palestinians there is an open question, but without toughness— the capacity to walk away and impose costs for saying no—it was never going to happen.

The first time I met Bill Clinton, he was dressed in jeans and an open shirt, chewing on the now-famous large unlit cigar. I introduced myself. Squeezing my hand (a Clinton trademark), he looked at me intensely and said, "Aaron, you don't have to introduce yourself. I know who you are. I want to thank you for your years of hard work on the peace process." His intellect, warmth, and accessibility captivated me. When Bill Clinton talked to you, you felt as if there were no one else in his universe, and he also told you—perhaps with the best of intentions—what you wanted to hear. But in the world of Arab-Israeli peacemaking, eagerness to please and the inability to stand your ground and say no are serious liabilities.

Bill Clinton cared more about and invested more time and energy in Arab-Israeli peace over a longer period of time than any of his predecessors. He impressed Arabs and Israelis alike with his mastery of detail, commitment, political instincts, and empathy. Clinton's empathy gave us a superb opening to build trust with the parties. Arabs and Israelis were blown away by his capacity to intuit the existential pain and practical politics of both sides. "Is he for real?" Dahlan asked me at the Wye River summit, as Clinton reeled off the number of Palestinian prisoners held by the Israelis and the names of the many Palestinian factions. Hanan Ashrawi recalls that no other American leader before him seemed able to see her people "as human beings." Clinton confirmed this impression for me during his remarkable December 1998 speech to the Palestinian National Council in Gaza city. Sitting in that crowded hall among more than four hundred representatives of the Palestinian national movement, listening to the president speak to them about their aspirations as if he were speaking to a Democratic National Convention, his power and passion amazed me. "He wore the yarmulke better, felt their pain better, shed a tear better," John Sununu Senior, chief of staff to the first President Bush, told me. President Clinton would always say, Madeleine Albright recalled, that you needed to "put yourself into the other person's shoes."

But empathy alone was not enough. Clinton lacked Kissinger's deviousness, Carter's missionary focus, and Baker's unsentimental toughness. It wasn't that he couldn't get angry. He told Barak he made him feel like a "wooden Indian" at Shepherdstown and that he had better not do it at Camp David, and he had Arafat close to tears in a tough tirade. But like an intense summer storm, the president's anger broke hard, passed quickly, and left a calm blue sky.

Dennis Ross, whose admiration for Clinton was unrivaled ("I wish he were still president"), believed he lacked "an intuitive toughness." Comparing Clinton with James Baker, he asked,

"Would Baker have gone to Shepherdstown and acted the way we did? Not a chance in the world. Same with Camp David." We needed the president to dish out "tough love." Instead the tough part got dropped. Dennis Ross again: "Every time in the last year we wanted to be tough on Barak, he'd just call the president and go around us. I'd say to Sandy [Berger], he can't take every Barak call, and Sandy would answer, 'I can't stop it.'" Ben-Ami now laments that Clinton needed to "crack heads" and tell leaders that their approach and ideas weren't working. Both sides learned that our anger was "short-lived."

Part of being tough is not being available all the time and being willing to walk away or impose a cost when you are being diddled. The president's own love of detail and mastery of the material worked against him. "Why is the president of the world," Ben-Ami recalls thinking, after one negotiating session at Camp David, "dealing with such minute details, like he was just like any other negotiator?" The president was trapped by his own nature. He loved the details, wanted to engage, and was good at it; and the Arabs and Israelis loved him for it. His availability made him (and us) part of the furniture, taken for granted and unable to intimidate. "We were sensitive to every little thing and forgot that we were the United States," Madeleine Albright lamented. Joe Lockhart, the president's press secretary during the critical last years of his second term, and a great admirer, recalls: "There were times when it would have been better to say 'Fuck you guys, I got better things to do.'"

Slouching Toward Bethlehem

After twenty years of working on the Arab-Israeli peace process, I suppose I should have come to believe in Hail Mary passes, but I don't. In the five months that followed the Camp David summit, more substantive and productive work was done on final status issues than in the previous five years. It was as if Camp David, in breaking the conventions against discussing the "taboo" issues, opened the floodgates on creativity and even some compromise. The approaching end of both Clinton's term and Barak's (he would resign in December) focused the minds and energies of the negotiators in a desperate last act to get something done before the final curtain came down. And Clinton deserves enormous credit for that. The parameters he laid out to Israeli, Palestinian, and American negotiators in the Cabinet Room two days before Christmas were the first comprehensive set of American ideas on how to end the Israeli-Palestinian conflict. As the president talked, never in my life had I seen a group of grown men copy anything down so fast.

Still, this period, particularly the nine weeks between the end of Camp David and the outbreak of the al-Aqsa intifada in late September (probably the only window during which any agreement could have been reached), unfolded in a strangely quiet and relaxed fashion. Scores of Israeli-Palestinian meetings and negotiations took place in these weeks, and we undertook a considerable amount of activity to better understand where the two sides now stood on the key issues, with a goal of developing new American ideas. The president, ever committed to finding a solution and to encouraging both sides, spoke to Arafat and Barak after their late September meeting. But it was as if we weren't reading our own talking points about the dangers of violence looming ahead. Bruce Riedel recalls a meeting with the president at the end of August where Clinton, looking directly at him, joked, "All you guys said if we went [to Camp David] and failed there it would be a great disaster, violence would break out, the Arabs would be mad at us. We went and we failed and nothing happened."

The absence of urgency wasn't the president's fault. It evolved from circumstances created by the summit's outcome. Barak's (and our) "make-or-break" Camp David moment had vanished. Arafat, having escaped one summit, certainly wasn't interested in being pressured at another; and in any event he wasn't going to invest much more in Clinton as the clock ticked down on his presidency. Barak blamed Arafat for the failure at

Camp David, yet he continued to negotiate with him. We, attached as ever to process, contended with the identical problem of negotiators who couldn't or wouldn't provide bottom lines. Some argue that we should have put the Clinton parameters on the table much earlier, and we thought about it. But they misunderstand who we were and how we operated. Although Barak was warming to the idea of a U.S. proposal, he wasn't there yet, and as ever, Clinton wasn't going to push him. If we couldn't compel Arafat and Barak to agree even on a set of principles to guide negotiations in the heightened atmosphere of a presidential summit, we certainly couldn't do it in the freewheeling and distracting political world that was challenging us in the fall of 2000.

In any event, the beginning of the Palestinian intifada in September and the three months of continuous confrontation that followed destroyed the chance of reaching any agreement. Had Bill Clinton transformed himself into the world's toughest negotiator, it still wouldn't have mattered. As the Israelis and Palestinians struggled on against a backdrop of shootings, lynchings, and demonstrations, Arafat's incentive to make any deal and Barak's capacity to sell one plummeted.

The cycle of funerals, violent demonstrations, and more funerals made the idea of any Palestinian flexibility laughable. Arafat wanted to use the violence to improve his negotiating position, not to close a deal. Israel's angry, fearful, and powerful response to what many Israelis came to believe was an intentional Palestinian campaign of violence, particularly after Barak's bold moves at Camp David, precluded solid support for further concessions. Our failure to broker a cease-fire in Paris and in Sharm el-Sheikh in October revealed how marginal we had become to affecting the situation on the ground. As usual, Barak was in a hurry to conclude something, but attaching his political future to an agreement seemed only to further erode his credibility with the Israeli public. His qualified acceptance of the Clinton parameters and the perception that he had offered Arafat concessions under the pressure of Palestinian terror sealed his fate. In

February 2001 he lost to Ariel Sharon in the worst defeat of any Israeli prime minister in the country's history. As for Arafat, to use Baker's words, he had no dog in this fight. Clinton was out; he would take his chances with the next president.

What then is the final judgment on Bill Clinton in the arena of Arab-Israeli peacemaking? Without question, he receives high marks for extraordinary commitment and caring and for nurturing a process of peacemaking that includes gains lasting to this day, including an Israeli-Jordanian peace treaty. And he deserves great credit for being the first American president to wrestle seriously with the core issues that await Israelis, Palestinians, and Syrians in the final status negotiations. If Arab-Israeli agreements ever emerge, it is almost certain they will be based on the concepts and ideas of the Clinton years.

But Clinton's record is a poor one in the critical area of understanding what it would take to close the deal and how to do it. Jon Schwartz, our immensely talented deputy legal advisor, was right when he said we didn't have enough respect for the issues. Had the president been more realistic and less willing to be enlisted in the service of well-intentioned but grandiose schemes, we might have pursued other goals that were less politically sexy but also contained fewer dangers to our national interests and credibility. Perhaps the task at hand was simply too difficult. It may well be that the mutually exclusive requirements set forth by Barak, Arafat, and Assad came at too high a price. It's an eminently fair issue to explore.

But it's equally fair to question whether Bill Clinton had all the qualities required to succeed in bringing peace to this particular troubled corner of the world. He had the empathy, intellect, and commitment. But the president and his advisors lacked the capacity to understand what was required to reach an agreement and the toughness to stay with American bridging proposals even if they had. Finally, to hold three summit meetings within six months and fail at every one is not an easy task. The notion that trying and failing is better than not trying at all is no substitute for developing and executing careful, measured policies and approaches by the leader of the world's greatest power and his advisors. In this case, the old college try, together with the Hail Mary pass, however noble, proved costly. Lacking Kissinger's deviousness, Carter's obsessive focus, and Baker's no-nonsense toughness, Bill Clinton was in no position to help close a deal unless Barak and Arafat were literally ready to do it themselves. And they weren't. Sadly, however well-intentioned, simply trying without a well-defined strategy left a costly legacy of failure that made it easier for Bill Clinton's successor to walk away from both the process and the substance of an issue that, tragically, was about to become more important than ever to America's security at home and its stake in the Middle East.

Part Four

AMERICA'S
PROMISE
ABANDONED?

In August 2004, a year or so after resigning from the State Department, I was in Washington for a meeting with President Bush. In the two years I had worked for Colin Powell, I had never met the president, so I really was looking forward to the opportunity.

I was now head of Seeds of Peace, a nonprofit conflict-resolution organization that brings young Arabs and Israelis, Indians and Pakistanis from the region into leadership and coexistence programming in the United States. We had arranged for the entire group of almost two hundred, including staff, to see the president. These Arab and Israeli teenagers had just finished three weeks at the Seeds of Peace camp in Maine, where they lived together, argued about their conflict, and broke down barriers of suspicion and mistrust. Now they were on their way home with a good deal more hope than when they arrived. Bill Clinton had met frequently with Seeds of Peace graduates. President Bush had seen them the year before. It must have been one hundred degrees as we waited—and melted—on the steps of the Old Executive Office Building, facing the White House's West Wing.

The president appeared in about twenty minutes, strode toward the group, shook my hand, and posed for a photo with the kids. I asked him if he could spare a minute to offer a word or two of encouragement to these remarkable young leaders who, given the grim realities on the ground, really represented a human road map toward Middle East peace. Unfortunately, the president filled my request to the letter. "Gotta go, gotta go," he answered in four words, and briskly began to walk away. Then, looking back over his shoulder at two hundred young Arabs and Israelis in their trademark green T-shirts sweating in the midday sun, he stopped suddenly as if jolted by a flash of insight and called out, "Gotta implement that road map, gotta do it." Without saying another word, the president turned and walked away.

Chapter Nine

The Disengager: George W. Bush and the Pursuit of Arab-Israeli Peace, 2001–2007

George W. Bush inherited a bad hand on the Arab-Israeli issue, and he knew it. Whatever the new president's limitations in the area of foreign policy, he understood from his days in the Texas oil business and as a part owner of the Texas Rangers that you don't throw good money after bad. And the "peace process" (the new administration would soon ban the phrase from its vocabulary) was definitely bad money. Hadn't Bill Clinton himself warned the new president on Inauguration Day that Arafat was a liar and to stay away from the PLO leader? In case Bush missed the message, his new secretary of state, Colin Powell, didn't. Powell remembers Clinton calling him on January 19 "ranting on the phone" about how Arafat had ruined everything.

Bush believed that he didn't need advice from Clinton on the Arab-Israeli issue—or on any other issue, for that matter—to determine the seriousness of the situation. All he had to do was read a newspaper or watch CNN. The Palestinian intifada had been raging since September 2000, and by early 2001 whatever "popular" character it had assumed at the beginning had vanished. It was now a bloody confrontation between Palestinian suicide bombers and the Israeli military. In 2000 there were four unsuccessful suicide attacks. By the end of 2001 the number would rise to 35, killing 85 Israelis. By September 2001, 714 Palestinians had been killed in Israeli-Palestinian confrontations.

If his predecessor had faced Arab and Israeli leaders who seemed ready to do serious business, Bush looked at a landscape hardened by confrontation and driven by angry and fearful publics and leaders who reflected their mood. A month after the president's inauguration, Israel elected as prime minister the tough-minded architect of the nation's settlement enterprise, Ariel Sharon, aka Arik, alias the bulldozer, in a landslide victory over Ehud Barak.

Sharon's campaign slogan said it all: "Sharon alone can bring peace." After six years of two young and inexperienced Israeli prime ministers (Netanyahu and Barak), the Israeli public had had enough, deciding to deliver its future into the hands of the battle-hardened, courtly, and grandfatherly Sharon. The people looked to him to end the violence, produce normalcy, and put an end to the erratic lurches that characterized the years under his two immediate predecessors. Sharon's comeback was one of the most dramatic in the modern political history of any nation. Disgraced by his responsibility for the 1982 Lebanon War, and barred by the recommendations of a State Commission of Inquiry from holding the defense portfolio, Sharon now had a chance to remake himself, ironically because of an intifada that he had helped to ignite by his September 2000 visit to the Haram al-Sharif/Temple Mount.

Ariel Sharon hadn't changed his strategic assessment of the Arabs: he still saw Israel embattled in a hundred years' war with its neighbors. But he had learned some things from the Lebanon experience that made him smarter and tactically more agile. He would try to stake out the center of Israeli politics, reflect the public's mood, and if at all possible, avoid alienating the United States.

If one old warrior, Sharon, had learned from his mistakes, Arafat, the other, kept repeating his. He rode, exploited, and milked the violence to enhance his image, maintain his street cred, and demonstrate to Arab, Israeli, and Western leaders that he could neither be taken for granted nor be blamed for Camp David without serious cost. Had he accepted the parameters Bill Clinton had offered him in December 2000, he could have even argued that his use of violence had forced an improvement upon the American and Israeli proposal at Camp David. But late in the day, reveling in his role of victim and struggler, he chose to take his chances with a new president and a new Israeli prime minister. I interviewed several Palestinians who claimed they had had contact with members of the "Bush family" after the November elections, who had assured them that the new president would be tough on the Israelis, like his father. I very much doubt these contacts were authoritative. In any case, Arafat guessed wrong on both counts.

But it really didn't matter to Arafat. He was in his element. I saw him four times during those years; on three of those occasions an automatic weapon would be lying in plain view on the table. "He got lionized," George Tenet recalls, "for being in that hole in Ramallah." Later he added, "I think he thought he was going to heaven because he didn't compromise on Jerusalem and his principles."

All of these nuances and complexities may have been lost on George W. Bush. But the main message wasn't: stay away from this issue. It's a loser. This was not George Bush Senior, whose views on the Arab-Israeli issue were shaped by a career as CIA chief, UN ambassador, and vice president, and by an unsentimental sense of realpolitik. Shortly before 9/11 the new president would, in response to Saudi pressure, undertake a momentary foray into the Arab-Israeli issue. But in the main the younger Bush was driven by his instincts, his emotions, and a strong pro-Israel orientation that only became stronger after 9/11.

In December 1998 Mel Sembler, a Republican committee finance chairman, personal friend of the president, and strong supporter of Israel, organized a trip to Israel for Bush and three other governors. That trip, which both Bush and Sembler described as "historic," included the standard helicopter tour with none other than Ariel Sharon, then foreign minister, as tour guide. I'd been on this ride with Sharon before, and I knew there was nothing standard about it. Bush was blown away by how small and vulnerable

Israel was. As they flew up north along the coast, where Israel narrows to about nine miles in width, Sembler recalls the future president exclaiming "We got driveways in Texas longer than that." He was also greatly impressed with Sharon, a man who had been fighting for his country since he was eighteen.

Bush, like Clinton, was deeply influenced by an Israeli prime minister. This time it was Ariel Sharon, whose life experiences as a pioneer, soldier, and farmer he could only imagine. Dov Weisglass, Sharon's key political and foreign policy advisor, thought Bush loved Sharon's stories, which could range from "the last thirty years to the third millennium." Colin Powell thought the president admired Sharon's toughness and no-nonsense manner. Bush also visited Egypt on that 1998 trip, but in a speech he delivered upon his return, Israel, especially its security, dominated the text. Visiting the Golan Heights, the governor of Texas ran into a transplant from Laredo and remarked how interesting it was to "hear the human side of what it's like to love a country as much as she does and yet have the concerns about living so close to a border of a nation [Syria] that often posted [*sic*] a real threat to their way of life."

Already inclined to see things Israel's way, persuaded that there was little he could or should do by getting in the middle of a white-hot conflict, and determined to be different in as many ways as possible from Bill Clinton, George W. Bush came into office with a mindset already predisposed to disengaging America from the Arab-Israeli issue. After 9/11, with Afghanistan under his belt and Iraq on the way, the predisposition to steer clear of the issue became a willful and purposeful policy during the administration's first term. Forget trying to solve it; the administration didn't believe it was even worth trying to manage the Arab-Israeli issue in a serious or sustained manner. Colin Powell summed up the president's view best for me: "I don't want to do what Clinton did because it takes a lot of time. The prospects of success, rather than fear of failure, are really quite low... and I got two wars going on. Why am I going to fuck around with these people?"

Other forces drove and sustained disengagement, ruling out

traditional diplomacy during these years. The ABC syndrome (anybody or anything but Clinton) clearly impelled the administration during its first year. The shock and changing priorities of 9/11 dominated during the second, and the calculation that they would likely fail if they tried always hung overhead. But trumping all these other considerations was the emerging view, even before 9/11, that the Arab-Israeli issue was neither key nor even important to protecting America's interest in a highly turbulent region. Nor would conventional diplomacy to divide up territory or solve the problem of Jerusalem lead to a settlement, let alone peace. The Arab-Israeli conflict continued because the Arab side had a leadership and democracy deficit. Israelis might be difficult, but they were our democratic allies, while Assad and Arafat were not.

The 9/11 attacks intensified the tendency to see the Middle East problem as a clash of values rather than as a contest of interests over occupied territory, Jerusalem, water, or settlements. Peace might be possible, but only when the nature of the region's regimes changed and when terror and violence no longer could be employed as instruments to gain what negotiations could not win. The failure of Oslo and Camp David, and the outbreak of the intifada, seemed to confirm all this to an administration already prone to see itself as identified with big and transformative ideas.

September 11 converted these ideas into an almost religious code, and practically every foreign policy initiative now flowed from a new post-9/11 agenda. If George H. W. Bush and Bill Clinton had seen the Arab-Israeli issue as a key center of gravity in protecting American interests, the Bush administration viewed it as subsidiary to a far more important struggle between democracy and authoritarianism, moderates and extremists, and terrorists and antiterrorists.

During its first four years, the administration would not just disengage from Arab-Israeli diplomacy; it would reframe the entire problem and reorient American policy in a different direction. To varying degrees, the small group of advisors around the president (Rice, Rumsfeld, and Cheney) and Bush himself shared this mindset. Powell never quite saw it that way, but by 2002 he'd run out of arguments and maneuvering room. The president's June 24, 2002, speech, in which he laid out his vision of two states, dependent on a new democratic Palestinian leadership, was not just an effort to park the problem until the Iraq file was closed; it marked the beginning of the entire reframing process. Doug Feith, who had a ringside seat at the bureaucratic battle that produced the speech, left no doubt of its purpose: "The president took the horse, this old nag, and shot it in the head and said we don't want this goddamn Arafat, PLO, antidemocratic, violent, terroristic, receiving arms from Iran nag. Screw it. Bang."

The truth is that some of these views were right. In the Clinton administration we had ignored pushing the Palestinians to reform, had tolerated Arafat's state security courts and one-man rule, and didn't do nearly enough about corruption and terror, largely to keep the peace process going, and partly because the Israelis tolerated it all as well.

But the Bush administration overdid it in the opposite extreme. The pendulum swung too far in the other direction. Resolving the Arab-Israeli conflict may not have been possible. But for Bush's first term and much of his second, managing this crisis was relegated to the back burner. Instead of making it a priority, the administration subcontracted it out to a series of talented but unempowered envoys, who couldn't make much of a difference. Arab-Israeli peace was not the key to protecting America's interests in the wake of 9/11, but abandoning it wholesale weakened our friends, emboldened our enemies, and undermined our image and credibility when we needed them most. While Arafat lived, there were probably few opportunities to do much, but even his death in November 2004 and the election of Mahmoud Abbas in January 2005, perhaps the best and last chance to do something serious, did not move the administration to act. Never, in the words of one senior official, has one administration missed so many opportunities "to turn chicken shit into chicken salad." Only in the summer of 2007, with the Palestinian national movement badly split (Hamas in control of Gaza and Abbas nominally in control of the West Bank), did the administration seem to get serious about Arab-Israeli diplomacy. Their newfound interest was driven largely by Secretary of State Rice, who seemed eager to demonstrate that she could do consequential diplomacy before her time ran out, rather than by the president's view that Arab-Israeli peace was now a key American priority in the Middle East. That American effort would produce at the end of November 2007 a conference at Annapolis, Maryland, attended by more than forty countries, which would trigger the formal resumption of permanent status negotiations between Israelis and Palestinians. After almost seven years, the administration seemed to have accepted that any chance of realizing President Bush's vision of a two-state solution would require not only a Palestinian Authority committed to security but the resolution of the core issues that drove the Israeli-Palestinian conflict.

The ABC Syndrome, January to September 2001

"That was a great briefing," I said to Dennis as we walked down the State Department's first-floor corridor, generally used by transition teams to prepare the new secretary of state for the confirmation process. It was January 2001. We had just spent almost four hours with Colin Powell, telling him about eight years of Arab-Israeli diplomacy under Bill Clinton. I thought we'd struck the right balance between assessment and prescription, even though I felt we should have taken more responsibility for what had at times gone wrong. But it's tough to admit that you screwed up so soon after the fact. "I'm really looking forward to working for Powell," I said. "He asked all the right questions and seems to get it." "He's a great guy," Dennis shot back, "but don't get your hopes up. I'm not sure the new team is all that interested."

That proved to be the understatement of at least the decade. It didn't matter as much to Dennis as it did to me. He had left. I was staying. As a career civil servant who had worked for

Democrats and Republicans, particularly for the new president's father and for Jim Baker, I assumed that I'd be staying. After all, we were facing the worst Israeli-Palestinian confrontation in fifty years. Powell seemed to understand the need to do something about it, and I figured that the new administration, after taking its own turn at reinventing the wheel, would come to believe in the value of seriously working the issue. Thinking back now on our briefing, I'm sure Powell was impressed by the level of our commitment and expertise, but I also believe he probably wondered, *What planet did these guys come from? Do they think we're going to invest in this issue the way Clinton did?*

Henry Kissinger exploited diplomacy to become a media superstar while secretary of state. But Colin Powell was the first secretary of state who was already enrolled in superstardom. Handsome and engaging, with a smile and charisma that charmed and captivated, Powell seemed to float free of partisan politics and could be imagined just as easily as secretary of state in a Democratic administration, or so it seemed to me. Powell was as comfortable and relaxed with himself as anyone I'd ever met. And he made you feel that way. He was a master at communicating, and under the right circumstances he could have been a great negotiator. It had taken Baker six months to stop calling me Andy and get my first name right; Powell learned my name, maybe a military habit, and never forgot it.

Powell had all the right instincts on the Arab-Israeli issue. He knew it was important, recognized Israel's security needs, and would come to empathize with the plight of Palestinians under occupation. A master at dealing with the Israelis and American Jews, he had acquired a stock of Yiddish expressions and an intuitive familiarity with Jews from his years growing up in the Bronx. Perhaps his African-American ancestry convinced Palestinians that he had special insight into what it was like to suffer discrimination and a denial of rights. More than once he would use a civil rights analogy when making a point to the Palestinians.

At the same time Colin Powell was a survivor with an innate sense of caution, sharply at odds with his enormous self-confidence. With his track record of stellar success in the military and political arenas, he had little to prove and not much desire to risk. Lawrence Wilkerson, a longtime friend and colleague who joined Powell at State as a key aide, recalls that Powell "had an uncanny knack for reading the tea leaves ahead of time. He would not invest a lot of personal energy and capital if he saw failure."

And what Powell saw in 2001 was Arafat and Sharon engaged in a kind of death tango, with neither leader interested in much more than getting rid of the other. In Washington he rightly assessed a hostile environment among the president's other foreign policy advisors toward Arab-Israeli initiatives. Let's be clear. In 2001 Arab-Israeli violence was on the radar screen, but not as an issue the Bush administration believed it could do much about. When discussions at the first NSC meeting in January 2001 turned to Arab-Israeli matters, Ned Walker, the State Department's assistant secretary of state for Near Eastern Affairs, clearly remembers the key message was "We're not going to do it the way Clinton did." Powell argued that the administration couldn't adopt a completely hands-off approach, but according to Paul O'Neill, the president made clear his intent to correct the imbalance of the previous administration, tilting back toward Israel. And besides, he said, "if the two sides don't want peace, there's no way we can force them."[1]

Powell gave Clinton high marks for effort but clearly believed he had expended too much energy on a hopeless cause. As we prepped the secretary for his first Middle East trip in February, he told me, "I'll be damned if I'm going to allow my young president to be dragged to a high-level summit with Arafat." When I interviewed Powell three years later, he seemed even more certain. "We started out with a predisposition not to get pulled into the same merry-go-round with the Israelis and Palestinians that took so much of Clinton's time and produced no particular results." The administration had a bias, he concedes, against Arafat, but also against "getting sucked into the same maelstrom that Clinton did...George Bush is not the kind of person, nor do I think I am, to go sit at Camp David for a month with Arafat or Barak. Can you imagine that? I think only Bill Clinton and Madeleine Albright could have done that."

The ABC syndrome was very much the Bush administration's operating software on the Arab-Israeli issue, and on many others. Whether it's true, in the words of one senior administration official, that Bush thought the former president was "Satan's finger on earth" isn't clear, but the new administration clearly believed that the old had made a mess of things on foreign policy, not least in the Middle East. "The whole White House vibrated in harmony with the president's emotions on this," Powell told me. "Don [Rumsfeld], who's a former negotiator, used to talk about 'so-called occupied territory,' so we knew his position." Cheney's position was "pretty well laid out." With these heavy hitters lined up against serious involvement, there wasn't much to be gained from swimming upstream. Powell was the only advocate in the administration for doing anything on the Arab-Israeli issue, and he tried. But the constraints and costs of failing or going too far were clear.

I'd been through several presidential transitions, but none so hostile and uncomfortable as the one from Clinton to Bush 43. It was ABC in spades. "Bill Clinton was viewed," a senior Foreign Service officer recalled, "as the incarnation of all that was morally corrupt, politically incompetent, and misguided on earth." Powell didn't share this view, but it reinforced his hesitancy about getting too close to any of "Clinton's issues." Along with almost all of the other special coordinators who had originated in the Clinton years, the administration decided to dismantle the SMEC Office. And Powell, who wanted a more vertical management style, also set out—as Shultz had done before him—to empower the Foreign Service and work through the regional and functional bureaus.

This new state of affairs created a radical change in my own circumstances. I soon experienced what it meant to be frozen out of the diplomacy about which I'd come to care so much. I moved from a large seventh-floor office to a small space on the sixth, overlooking the department's heating and cooling systems. I had a great-sounding title—senior advisor on Arab-Israeli negotiations. The only problem was that there were neither negotiations nor anyone all that interested in being advised, at least by me.

Several of my new colleagues in NEA, the bureau to which I was now assigned, kept wondering why I was still around and periodically would invoke the name of some unidentified White House official who they claimed was wondering the same thing. That politics extended down to my level showed how deep the antipathy to Clinton and any "holdovers" had become, including my new colleagues in NEA, who seemed determined to make sure that managing the peace process (such as it was) never migrated out of their control. I had to fight my way onto the secretary's first Middle East trip in February. That July, full of self-righteous indignation about how I had been exiled to the bureaucratic gulag at a time when the administration needed all the help it could get, I convinced myself I'd had enough. I tried to see Powell to let him know I intended to resign. Instead I descended upon Deputy Secretary Richard Armitage. Armitage, as only he could, told me to cut the "melodramatic shit" about resigning and assured me that he and the secretary would find a role for me. But he reminded me in no uncertain terms that the old days were over. There wasn't going to be a whole lot of peace-process activity.

Armitage had a point. For the first nine months the administration did very little. Powell's first trip convinced him, rightly, that Arafat and Sharon were mountains that couldn't be climbed. I suppose I didn't help matters when, in Jerusalem, I told him the parable about the shark. When you're swimming away from a shark, you don't have to swim faster than the shark, just faster than your friend. He laughed at the point. Sharon and Arafat appeared to be actively plotting, not to find common cause, but to create circumstances designed to gobble up the other.

Powell visited the Middle East again in June, but by then he had no intention of getting into the middle of what he now referred to as "the mess." Instead, we subcontracted. In April the Sharm el-Sheikh Fact-Finding Committee had published its report. Initially set up by the Clinton administration to look into the

causes of the ongoing Israeli-Palestinian confrontation, the group
was chaired by America's go-to guy for crises, former senator
George Mitchell. To his credit, Powell got the administration to
endorse its tough and sensible recommendations (end the violence,
ban settlements). But no one in Washington really wanted the responsibility for implementing the report. Senator Mitchell told me
that the administration "expected the recommendations to be self-
implementing." Someone, he continued, should have been over
there the day after it was announced "pushing to implement it."

In June CIA director George Tenet—next subcontractor in
line—would try to get the Israeli and Palestinian security services to agree to a work plan that aimed at a cease-fire. Tenet,
who was good at this kind of thing and loved doing it, actually
got both sides to agree. But focusing on security alone wasn't sustainable. And there was no way the president or anyone else was
going to push for a political track, out of fear of giving in to terror, alienating the Israelis, or bucking up Arafat. As Tenet recalls,
"There was no corollary political or incentive process. There was
no other channel. So I come out. Big fucking deal."

Before continuing, we need to be clear about something: in the
spring and summer of 2001 the administration had no good options for stopping the violence. The Israelis and Palestinians were
in open war; neither Sharon nor Arafat was willing (even if they
had been able) to pay the price for a sustainable cease-fire. Arafat
was in full duel mode, acquiring arms, lighting fires while talking
peace. Sharon's goal was to break the intifada without paying for
it politically or diplomatically. His demand for seven days of quiet
(which we implicitly endorsed) wasn't going to happen. To bridge
these gaps would have entailed a huge commitment by the administration and a plan to incorporate both security and political
incentives for both sides, if not in parallel, then in a closely
worked-out sequence. Given the animus toward Arafat (on June 1
a suicide bomber would blow up a Tel Aviv disco, killing twenty-
one Israelis) and our unwillingness to tangle with Sharon, no one
in Washington was willing to do it. Still, Powell, encouraged now
by his new, indefatigable NEA assistant secretary Bill Burns, con-

tinued to push for some initiative. In July Burns asked me to begin drafting a major Powell speech on the Arab-Israeli issue. After
all, if we couldn't act, we could always talk.

In August we also felt pressure to get more involved from a
familiar quarter. Colin Powell might not get the Disengager to
engage, but the Saudis might, in what was to become a familiar
pattern. In response to a particularly violent surge in the Israeli-
Palestinian confrontation, Crown Prince Abdullah, already angered and frustrated by the administration's hands-off approach,
sent the president one of the toughest messages in the history of
the American-Saudi relationship. In essence, the message threatened that the Saudis would no longer take American interests
into account unless the administration took their views on the
Palestinian issue more seriously. Prince Bandar, the Saudi ambassador to Washington, reportedly told Condi Rice, "This is the
toughest message I've ever delivered."

The president's response, drafted by the NSC's Bruce Riedel,
broke new diplomatic ground. Not only did Bush commit himself
for the first time to a "viable independent Palestinian state," but
he offered up language on Palestinian self-determination that no
previous administration had ever used. Riedel recalls that the purpose of the letter was to prevent the U.S.-Saudi relationship from
"tanking" and to appease Abdullah. No one I talked to believed
that the president had any real sense of what he was endorsing. It
was the first of many "if I do this on the peace process, don't bother
me again" moments. But the Saudis loved it, took it literally, and
shared the contents of Bush's letter with their Arab brothers.

The August episode is a curious one and reflects a couple of
points worth noting. During its first year the administration's policy toward the Arab-Israeli conflict was not necessarily fixed in
stone; far from deferring to Israel on all matters, the president had
more independent instincts and was willing to express them. Dan
Kurtzer, our ambassador to Israel, briefed Sharon early in
September on the president's growing inclination to focus on the
Middle East. And Kurtzer recalls that "Sharon's temperature went
from zero to a thousand." One letter does not a change in policy

make, and it's hard to determine in what direction Bush intended to go. In any event, there wasn't time to find out. Days later another Saudi sent another kind of message to the United States that transformed America's policy toward the entire Middle East.

9/11: A World Transformed, September 2001–June 2002

On the morning of Tuesday, September 11, I was driving down the Rock Creek Parkway listening to country music and mulling over Secretary Powell's speech when the local news intruded with a report that a small plane had collided with one of the towers of the World Trade Center. About thirty minutes later, now in my office, the reports about what actually had occurred came pouring in, and within the hour I was told, along with thousands of my colleagues, to evacuate the building immediately. Two months later Powell delivered his speech, but under radically altered circumstances. The 9/11 attacks permanently changed America, its role in the world, and its view of the piece of foreign policy that had consumed my career for two decades. In fact, from the administration's perspective, the attacks, following a short burst of activity, world reduce the Arab-Israeli issue to an even smaller priority.

For Arab-Israeli diplomacy 9/11 created a paradox: the attacks triggered the administration's most serious foray into the problem while planting the seeds of neglect and abandonment in its first term. Between September 2001 and April 2002 the president and secretary both publicly endorsed American support for a two-state solution, launched another envoy on a four-month mission to secure a cease-fire, and concluded the effort with a trip by Powell and a major speech by the president. By the spring of 2002, however, Palestinian suicide terror and Israel's reoccupation of much of the West Bank totally undermined the American effort. Powell, the last and only defender of serious American involvement, became a casualty of that failure, and the White House, never having taken the post-9/11 initiative all that seriously, dropped all pretense of concern as Iraq loomed larger in its strategy. Indeed, 9/11 generated considerable American diplomacy, particularly as the need to build coalitions among the British, the Europeans, and the Arabs for campaigns in Afghanistan and Iraq and the war on terror intensified, but it left a legacy of assumptions, convictions, and other unfinished business that made Arab-Israeli peace derivative of more important issues.

The emerging 9/11 paradigm would shape the future, reinforcing support for disengagement from Arab-Israeli issues. Powell made the point well. The attacks "changed the whole frame of reference in that we now, within a week, are engaged in a global war against terrorists, all terrorists . . . Hamas is a terrorist; Arafat's a terrorist. And if there's any doubt in our mind, Sharon will remind us on a regular basis that he is." Creation of a standard of moral clarity and consistency with respect to terror and its state sponsors comprised the first key element in the paradigm.

George W. Bush now presented himself as a war president, not a peacetime leader. America had been attacked. The tools required to protect the nation and strike back were military power, preemptive and preventive war, counterterrorism, and good intelligence. Diplomacy—at least as a tool of conflict resolution, already a suspect notion (at least à la Clinton)—would find no real place in this mobilization. States that sponsored terror, like Syria, Iran, and Iraq, needed to be contained and pressured, not engaged diplomatically. The notion that the nature of the regime determined its policies on peace and war took on new meaning as the administration came to believe the key to protecting a threatened America from rogue states could be found not only in containment but in the overthrow of authoritarian regimes, if required. Afghanistan, Iraq, and the West Bank and Gaza would become vital laboratories for these experiments in traumatic but necessary transformation.

Finally, the administration accorded like-minded democracies such as Israel, engaged in similar struggles against terror and extremism, high value and wide latitude of action in the common battle. That the president liked Ariel Sharon wasn't the point.

Indeed, Bush would bristle at the prime minister's public comments in October 2001 comparing the United States to Neville Chamberlain and Israel to Czechoslovakia, amid fears that America would sacrifice Israeli interests to secure Arab support in the war against terror. Nor did Sharon's repeated public rejections of the president's calls on Israel to stop settlements or incursions into the West Bank sit well. But these differences didn't matter all that much against the backdrop of the broader struggle America was waging against terror. When it came to fighting terror, seeking peace, and promoting democracy, Israel was on the right side of the line. Arafat and the others had chosen the wrong side.

The assumptions behind the new 9/11 paradigm made America's Arab-Israeli policy a derivative of the broader objective of war on terror and took America out of any position to play an active role during the president's first term. Even managing the Israeli-Palestinian conflict would have required dealing with Arafat, crafting an approach that dealt with security *and* political issues, managing Syria, and pressing Israel. It was probably too much, even a year after 9/11, to expect the administration to plunge into Arab-Israeli diplomacy. But the aversion to Arab-Israeli diplomacy would shape its views throughout the first term and well into the second. Richard Armitage, never one to mince words, called it "lazy diplomacy." "We don't like Chavez, so we're just not going to speak to him. We don't like these Hamas leaders, we won't speak to them. We don't like North Korea, we don't speak to them. We don't like Iran, we don't speak to them. Pretty soon we won't speak to Peru...Guess what? Pretty soon you're not speaking to more people than you're speaking to."

Still, by the fall of 2001 the White House had realized that mobilizing coalitions to fight the war against terror might be easier if the United States signaled interest in Arab-Israeli peacemaking. After all, some of its most vital allies, particularly Tony Blair and the two Abdullahs, the king of Jordan and the crown prince of Saudi Arabia, cared a great deal. Powell persuaded the president to include a reference to Palestinian statehood in his annual UN General Assembly speech. And despite an effort by the White

House to dissuade Powell from giving his own speech, the secretary delivered it in Louisville, Kentucky, in mid-November. I had written it. The White House vetting ensured it would break no new ground, but Powell used it to announce that Anthony Zinni, former head of the Central Command (CentCom), would now serve as the secretary's special envoy to the Middle East.

The Zinni mission emerged out of the curious yin and yang of Bush policy in the wake of 9/11. "I had to keep coming up with these ideas," Powell recalled, "knowing that we weren't likely to see a Camp David summit." Powell persuaded the White House to accept the idea of an envoy. Given the White House aversion to high-level envoys, candidates such as Baker or Mitchell were ruled out quickly. I didn't know Zinni, but Powell, Armitage, and Bill Burns did and had "high confidence" in him.

I had a personal interest in the Zinni mission because Bill Burns recommended to Powell that I serve as the advisor to the advisor. I'd never met Zinni and didn't know quite what to expect, but I liked him from the get-go. Anyone who was willing to do Arab-Israeli peacemaking without demanding money, title, or publicity in return was a guy worth knowing. We couldn't have presented an odder pair, and Tony joked that a smart Hollywood producer could make a few bucks by doing a Middle East version of the original *Odd Couple*. Why we clicked, I don't really know. Zinni was a no-nonsense, heavily muscled, buzz-cut Marine, a highly decorated vet who had seen service in Vietnam and Somalia and had risen to head CentCom, which included the Middle East. He'd talk to me about the Marine Corps's three basic food groups—red meat (on the bloody side), Cuban cigars, and long-neck bottles of Bud. In return, I'd brief him on the history of the Oslo peace process and teach him well-practiced but never terribly successful techniques about how to avoid getting kissed by Arafat.

Tony would later tell Tom Clancy, in their jointly authored book *Battle Ready*, that the reason we got on so well was that, despite all my Middle East experience, I'd let him reach his own conclusions and encouraged him to think out of the box. But I think more was involved. I respected Tony for his honesty and guts, and

I think it showed. Zinni was a thinking man's warrior, if there ever was one, and he often presented his views in language that was brutally frank and honest. But he also listened, because unlike some in the administration, he knew what he didn't know and wanted to find out. I reciprocated, and he respected that. We quickly developed a no-bullshit policy. During his first briefing at State in late November, I asked him directly why he wanted to ruin a brilliant career by taking on a mission that was more likely than not to fail. "No one ever lost money betting against Arab-Israeli peace," I told him, and he probably wouldn't lose money either. Zinni laughed and said he was used to hopeless causes. In that case, I told him, "he had come to the right place."

The Zinni mission, which lasted from November 2001 until April 2002, was the Bush administration's next effort to subcontract out Arab-Israeli peacemaking to an outstanding American with absolutely no chance to succeed. The mission underscored Powell's larger predicament. We needed to do something, but not too much; we would focus on security, but leave political issues out of our charge; we were to beat up on Arafat, while going easy on Sharon. Arguably, sending Zinni was better than doing nothing. Of course, he had no mandate to do anything.

That became clear in meetings with Powell and the president before we left for the region, shortly after Thanksgiving. "Get the Tenet plan into play," Powell told Zinni; beyond that "use your imagination out there and see what the opportunities are." Tony later described this idea to me in military lingo as the "recon pull." See what you can develop, and we'll follow up. If no mandate was better than a tight set of instructions, we were in good shape. Reflecting either how well briefed he'd been or how much he cared, the president, during his meeting with Zinni in the Oval Office, asked him: "What's your mission?" If Bush wasn't clear about what Zinni was going to do, he was, in Tony's words, very clear about something else: if this failed, it wasn't going to be on the president's head. Leaving the Oval Office, Zinni recalls the president saying to Powell, "Colin, this is your baby."

Zinni doesn't recall that Powell told him that he should

watch his step with Sharon, but I do. Even before our departure some in the American Jewish community had expressed concern that Zinni's Middle East experience might make him less sensitive to Israeli concerns, so we arranged a lunch for him with Mort Zuckerman, chairman of the Conference of Presidents of Major American Jewish Organizations, at which Zinni allayed a good many unfounded suspicions. It was already clear, and Powell made it even more plain, that Zinni was to steer away from peace plans and focus only on security. The secretary understood that discussing security without dealing with the political issues wouldn't work, but he too was on a very short White House chain, which could be jerked at any time, as he would find out on his April 2002 Middle East trip. When we tried to push the security envelope into political areas, Powell said to Bill Burns and me, "You don't get it; we're not stretching this; do the best with what you've got."

With no mandate to "stretch things" and no support from the White House, the chances of success weren't great. Had we entered a violence-free environment, succeeding would have been hard enough.

We spent December becoming familiar with a security situation that was spinning out of control. Targeted killings of Hamas leaders and suicide terror defined the landscape. We held productive meetings with Israeli and Palestinian security officials, and Arafat and Sharon said all the right things to Zinni. But despite almost three weeks of reasonable calm, neither leader really wanted an agreement so much as they wanted to place blame on or to get rid of the other. Giora Eiland, head of the IDF's planning branch, reminded me that "Zinni was caught in an historic situation that couldn't be prevented." Sadly, neither Israel nor the Palestinians had yet tired of conflict and were, in Eiland's words, "determined to show the other side they could prevail." To have any chance of securing a sustainable cease-fire, Zinni would have had to pressure Arafat to truly crack down on Hamas, assert greater control over Fatah, and then push Sharon to move on a political process involving redeployment from the West Bank and freezing settlements.

Obtaining any of these concessions would have involved wrenching negotiations with the parties that would have gone nowhere without solid support from President Bush.

By early 2002 the Israeli-Palestinian problem had turned into a giant game of "gotcha" with Tony Zinni in the middle. Two events early in the new year brought Sharon and the administration to the edge, then would help both push Arafat over. Returning to Israel on January 3, we were met planeside by Ambassador Dan Kurtzer and rushed to a Shin Bet briefing. Avi Dichter, head of Shin Bet, told us the Israelis had been tracking a ship, now in the Red Sea, carrying tons of weapons from Iran via Hezbollah destined for Gaza and Arafat.

The next morning we helicoptered down to Sharon's farm at Shikmim, south of Ashkelon, expecting to hear the worst. Instead, we found a smiling, relaxed prime minister. The scene was reminiscent of any spider-and-fly story. Sharon briefed us on the ship, called the *Karine A*, and made clear that the Israelis intended to board it the next day. Instead of threatening our mission, he urged Zinni to confront Arafat with the information, but not before noon the next day. After the meeting Zinni and I agreed that Sharon believed he had Arafat "by the balls," and instead of rushing to finish the matter, he wanted to play it out to position Israel well politically and diplomatically in the final push to destroy him. During lunch the next day we raised the *Karine A* with the Palestinians. They were just getting word of Israel's action. Arafat, for whom dissembling and lying was second nature, predictably dismissed the matter as an Israeli plot to destroy him. A gleeful Sharon ordered the seized weapons to be displayed as proof of Arafat's treachery.

Arafat vowed to "investigate" the *Karine A* affair, but no one took him seriously. In late January President Bush delivered his "axis of evil" State of the Union address. For many in the administration, particularly Don Rumsfeld and Dick Cheney, *Karine A* pulled all the pieces together. Not only did Arafat endorse suicide terror; now he was in cahoots with Iran, Hezbollah, and Syria. *Karine A* may well have focused the administration on regime change in Palestine. David Satterfield, a senior State Department official deeply involved in peace-process matters, remembers that he'd been given wide latitude to meet with younger Fatah officials. Then National Security Advisor Condi Rice told me that as early as February the administration had begun to talk about supporting new elections in the West Bank. Doug Feith remembers that the ship incident "was a very big deal, especially with the vice president." Cheney, Feith continued, saw *Karine A* as showing that Arafat "was part of the global terrorist network." And "if he became a head of a state that it would not serve American interests."

If Arafat set himself up for a fall with *Karine A*, the Hamas attack on the Park Hotel in late March was the proverbial last straw. The violence had been escalating for weeks. Returning to Israel in March, we continued our kabuki peace effort. Indeed, against Zinni's better instincts, I pushed him to put a set of bridging proposals on the table that were meant to produce a security performance plan acceptable to both Israelis and Palestinians. I should have known better. Now under "house arrest" in his compound, Arafat was focused much more on trying to get the Israelis to let him out so he could attend the Arab summit in Beirut and meet with Vice President Cheney, then traveling in the region, than he was on saying yes or no to Zinni's ideas. In an interesting and counterintuitive twist, Cheney was quite amenable to seeing Arafat if it would advance our efforts. Surprisingly, the Israelis accepted the Zinni plan without modification, a historic first, while the Palestinians dithered.

The night of March 27 Zinni and I were attending a Passover seder at the home of one of Sharon's younger advisors, a Canadian-born Israeli named Shalom Lipner. Zinni, a Roman Catholic, had never been to a seder before and very much wanted to participate.

In the middle of the service our security detail called me out to take a call from the State Department Ops Center. A suicide bomber had blown himself up at a large Passover seder in the Park Hotel in Netanya, north of Tel Aviv, killing 28 Israelis and wounding 120. When I returned to the table, Zinni knew by the look on my face "that it was over."

We returned to our hotel to start making calls, including one to Arafat to condemn the attack and a second to the prime minister to express condolences, but this was all beside the point now. As I sat watching Tony on the phone to Washington, flipping channels between CNN and *The Simpsons*, I realized how utterly absurd the whole process had become. We were tiny pawns on a chessboard, moved around by Arafat, Sharon, and our own administration. Two days later Israeli forces launched Operation Defensive Shield, which involved major incursions into the West Bank and reoccupation and closure of most key cities and towns. Within three weeks 300 Palestinians and 32 IDF soldiers were dead.

I was a very slow learner. It took me a while to see that we were already in a new phase of the Israeli-Palestinian problem that would be long and transformative but would not lend itself easily to the ministrations of diplomacy.

I finally began to get the picture a week later when Zinni, Gamal Helal, and I went to Ramallah to induce Arafat to reestablish security contacts with the Israelis and with our side in anticipation of a possible Powell trip. No American diplomat had seen Arafat since Israel had bombed parts of his headquarters compound, where he now lay, as he described it, "under siege."

Security was incredibly tight, and as our three armored SUVs entered the destroyed gates of the large compound, it looked like a set from a Mel Gibson *Mad Max* movie. Overturned and burnt cars littered the walled courtyard; the bridge linking two buildings had been demolished. We halted about twenty-five yards from the front entryway, which was now barricaded and darkened. Young, heavily armed Palestinians, none of whom I recognized, peered nervously from the entranceway. The Israelis had occupied the building to our right, and their people were clearly visible.

Both sides knew that we were coming, but caught as we were in a potential crossfire, we were more than a little on edge. In a bit of masterful diplomacy Tony and I persuaded Gamal to get out of the car and announce our presence in Arabic. The men at the door motioned us forward, and we entered single file. Even by Palestinian standards, the scene was chaotic. European and

American members of the International Solidarity Movement and other peace organizations flanked either side of the narrow hallways. They had come to show support for Arafat, handing out literature and petitions protesting Israel's siege. The building reeked of foul air, body odor, and too few working toilets.

We entered Arafat's darkened conference room, the only light cast by a faint and eerie illumination from partially blocked windows. Zinni describes Arafat's men as looking like "drowned rats" around the table, and I can understand why. They'd been in that awful place for days. But Arafat was another story. It took me about ten seconds to understand that he was in his element, automatic weapon on the table, sitting defiantly at its head in his wrinkled Che Guevara outfit. Yasser Arafat might be "under siege," but in his own mind, as he told us, he was "undefeated." By turns he was both gracious and angry, eagerly describing the indignities that he and his people had suffered.

I had heard all of this before, and I guess that was really the point. Arafat didn't care much about the future, the past, his people, or the broader significance of what was happening around him. He was caught in a moment, and that moment was about him—his dignity, his place in history, and his willingness to struggle and if necessary to die in Palestine for Palestine. It was the struggle that now defined him, not its outcome. As I left the Muqataa, I wondered if that was where he had always been.

As the Israeli-Palestinian conflict intensified, pressure mounted on the Bush administration to do something. On April 4 the president delivered a tough statement urging Palestinians to stop terror and calling on Israelis to halt their incursions and stop settlements. But the administration seriously considered only two options at the time: send Powell or have the president give a speech. Powell recalls that nobody was "crazy" about the idea of sending him. Cheney was against it; Rumsfeld didn't want any U.S. effort at all until "there was a new Arafat and maybe new leadership on the other side." But the president was coming under tremendous pressure from the Arabs and Europeans to act. Having made the decision to send the secretary to the region,

Powell recalls the president saying, "I'm really troubled on this one. I need you to go. I know it's going to be bad, and I know it's probably going to hurt you. It's going to burn up, but you've got a lot to burn." The gist, Powell said to me, was that his standing in the country and the region was such that he "could take the hits." Powell told me he knew Bush had made the right decision, although he had real doubts about what could be done. "Away we go, ten long terrible days," he recalled.

The problem was that Powell, like Zinni, had no real authority, even had there been a chance to broker a cease-fire. His mandate, he recalls, was "to go solve it, but don't do anything." Even before Powell departed, critics expressed doubts about whether he should even meet with Arafat. "Are you crazy? I cannot come here and satisfy the president's political needs unless I see the Arab side of this," Powell replied. Once he launched, the second-guessing and hand-wringing started almost immediately. Armitage, who was Powell's eyes and ears in Washington, told me that he had Cheney yelling at him, "Is he negotiating? What's he doing?" En route to the region Powell stopped in Madrid, where he met with what was to become the Quartet (the United States, European Union, Russia, and United Nations). Believing the president might give him some leeway to stretch things a bit, the secretary bandied about several ideas, including a regional peace conference. This would only make the skeptics in Washington, including Condi and the president, more nervous.

On reflection, Powell recalls that the trip was the "right thing to do." But without presidential support, the visit could not possibly succeed. Even then the secretary would have had to launch a significant initiative involving negotiations on a security-political trade-off. And no one was ready for that. Powell met with Sharon and with Arafat twice, telling the latter that unless he controlled terror, "This would be the last time I'll see you."

Ironically, Sharon and Arafat proved to be the least of Powell's problems. In order to "escape" with some credibility, Powell tried to craft a tough and honest departure statement that placed responsibility for a resolution of the crisis on both Israelis and

Palestinians and included a regional conference. The NSC and the Office of the Vice President gutted the statement. That morning, Powell, who had been up most of the night, pulled me aside and put his hand on my shoulder, and jabbed his fist into my stomach, saying "Aaron, they got me." A senior Administration official told me he heard Powell say, "They're fucking telling me which way to take a piss and for how long." Some in Washington even wanted to know why Powell needed to say anything at all upon leaving the Middle East. That the administration's Arab-Israeli diplomacy had come down to arguing over language in a departure statement was all you needed to know. The trip ended much of Powell's effort and most of his influence on this issue. It was now time for a new approach much more in line with the Bush administration's broader, more ambitious and transformative regional goals.

Talking the Talk: Speech and Road Map, June 2002–2005

Colin Powell had returned from what Zinni called his ten-day "root canal" trip frustrated and still without a strategy for moving forward. He had been diddled by Arafat ("What more can I do with this guy?") and jerked around by the White House ("Nobody gave me any guidance other than don't do that"). After a year of working an issue with which he had become identified, the situation was still a mess. Bush showed no interest in a regional conference. And anyway, how would such a gathering address the situation on the ground? Sharon's tough measures had raised his poll numbers in Israel, but by mid-May suicide terror was up as well. Reveling in his role as prisoner of the Muqataa, Arafat wasn't about to budge on security without a political incentive.

If Bush thought the Arab-Israeli issue was only "Colin's baby," he was about to learn otherwise. Having finally enticed Crown Prince Abdullah to visit, the president and the Saudi leader met at Bush's ranch in Crawford. Bush got an earful about bad Israelis and suffering Palestinians. According to Rihab Masood,

Bandar's top aide, Abdullah was worried that Bush really didn't understand how bad the situation was for Palestinians. So at two A.M. he had his staff go to Kinko's to download photos of Palestinian casualties sent to the crown prince's party from the editor of a Saudi newspaper. The meeting ended on a positive note, but not before Abdullah threatened to leave unless the administration promised to act on the Israeli-Palestinian crisis. What Bush agreed to isn't clear—probably, at a minimum, a pledge to prevent the Israelis from expelling or killing Arafat. As planning for Iraq intensified, the president was more receptive to doing something in order to keep his allies in line. But what?

By June the president was "under pressure to have another Louisville moment," as Powell described the situation, referring to his own Middle East speech in Kentucky. Everyone, it seemed, wanted action on the Middle East according to Powell: "What do you believe after eight months on the war on terror, [about] what Sharon's been doing in the Muqataa, and the Saudis are continuing to go crazy, and the Jordanians are saying what is it you believe in. What is the American position?" That the administration had decided long ago to accord Arab-Israeli diplomacy a low priority didn't mean they could escape it entirely. Somehow the internal consensus ("We really don't care about this") had to be reconciled with the external pressures ("Others do"). And as the Iraq issue loomed larger in the administration's calculations, the president needed to find a way to satisfy his allies, reframe the issue, and park it somewhere so that it would not complicate the Iraq strategy.

If a serious diplomatic initiative wouldn't work, then, in a pattern of Bush administration behavior that had already become clear, words would have to do. As George Shultz had once made clear, when all else fails, the pressure mounts to give a speech.

Given the administration's mindset, there was a certain logic behind a speech. It reflected the "just leave me alone" attitude that had come to embody much of the president's reaction to this issue. Tony Blair, the Europeans, the UN, and the Arab allies had been hammering the president from day one on the Arab-Israeli peace process. If a way could be found to craft a speech that people would like but at the same time shift the onus of responsibility onto others, primarily the Palestinians, to act, then the administration might have a compelling argument to make to counter the incessant calls for Washington's engagement. In this sense, calling for a Palestinian state but challenging the Palestinians to create a new leadership to run it seemed like the perfect approach.

The president's June 24 speech was much more than a convenient set of talking points. It offers a window into the administration's policy mindset. The speech reflected the tensions between a State Department that was wedded to traditional diplomacy and still hoped for serious engagement with Israelis and Palestinians and a U.S. vision on permanent status, and a White House focused on transformative diplomacy, especially regime change and democratization. As with any new administration, it often takes time for its real policy on any issue to evolve. The speech was in fact a crystallization of that policy and was an effort to question traditional assumptions and reorient American policy in a different direction.

Powell's Louisville speech was a State Department effort with input from the White House, but the president's June 24 address was a White House show with a determined but largely unsuccessful effort by State to shape it. Bill Burns recalls that the White House speechwriters got hold of the speech draft early. But it was less the actual drafting and more the concepts that made the speech a real turning point. Driven largely by Condi Rice, conceptualizing the speech was really an effort to examine and rethink assumptions that had guided American policy, particularly since the early 1990s. Secretary Rice made clear to me in our interview that with Arafat in the Muqataa, Sharon in the West Bank, and suicide terror all around, if the "Arafat-Oslo land for peace framework isn't viable, then what is?" U.S. policy was suffering from the "absence of a framework" to guide it. According to other participants, Condi took the lead in asking fundamental questions, "big think" questions that were usually asked on other aspects of America's Middle East policy by Rumsfeld. Neither Rumsfeld, Rice, nor Cheney was enthusiastic about the speech; in fact there would be enormous hand-wringing about giving it almost right up to its delivery. But a speech was preferable to an initiative, which could divert attention and energy and might even fail. And besides, a speech was necessary to articulate what America stood for when it came to the Arab-Israeli issue.

An account of the bureaucratic ticktock over the speech will have to await the memoirs of those principally involved. But some issues are worth brief discussion now. Unlike most speeches or statements on the Arab-Israeli issue during the past twenty years, this one really was a departure in American policy; it was not some throwaway statement that the administration intended to walk away from.

The address was really two speeches in one. The first half described the process for realizing the vision of two states living side by side in peace and security. To achieve this vision, Palestinians needed to reform, to create credible institutions, to establish financial transparency, and above all to replace old leaders with new. The combination of *Karine A,* the Park Hotel attack, and Powell's trip had convinced the administration, even Powell, that Arafat had to go. That didn't mean support for expelling or killing him, but it did mean, in the words of a senior administration official, that the president believed "Arafat was done." If you go back and read the speech, Condi Rice recalls, "it's the beginning of a kernel of a notion of the democratic Palestinian state." Tony Zinni mused, "I think the president fell in love with the idea that if you could fairy-dust democracy, you could have the beginnings of the solutions of your problems, including Arab-Israel."

The second half of the speech set forth the president's vision of a Palestinian state living side by side in peace and security with Israel. If the Palestinians reformed, then a Palestinian state would be possible. He clearly laid down the marker: "Peace requires a new and different Palestinian leadership, so that a Palestinian state can be born." His thought captured the essence of Ben Franklin's immortal comment tossed off at the end of the Constitutional Convention in Philadelphia, "a republic if you can keep it." The president told the Palestinian people: here's a

Palestinian state, if you can earn it by becoming democratic. The State Department pushed for more expansive language on statehood and Jerusalem, believing that a more specific political horizon was required, but they were lucky to hold the line on statehood. As it was, the speech referred to the idea of creating a provisional Palestinian state within three years, whose final borders would have to be deferred.

Powell describes the fight over the speech as "a bear." Doug Feith remembers that his involvement in helping to formulate the speech began when the number of drafts had climbed into the twenties. There were fights about the timetable (number of years to statehood); how specific to be about permanent status issues (language on Jerusalem and refugees, which was finally very general); and even whether it was a good idea to give the speech at all. The president delivered his remarks on a Monday. That weekend the White House was still struggling with whether it was "a smart thing for the president to do," Powell recalls. "Condi was having a devil of a time" and also wondered whether it was the right thing to do. Cheney and Rumsfeld were "totally against it," although the defense secretary signed on late Sunday night. Cheney never really did, arguing on the morning of the speech that it wasn't necessary. The main source of all the hand-wringing was a strong view that the Palestinians didn't deserve the speech and that "we were giving them everything they're asking for"; as Powell recalls, the anti-speech crowd argued that the Palestinians "didn't deserve [it] because of their terrorist background and behavior."

One guy who had no doubt the president had done the right thing was Ariel Sharon. In fact, the Israelis seem to have had significant input in shaping the speech, even providing some of the language. Natan Sharansky, the Soviet dissident, former Israeli cabinet minister, and proponent of democratization as the key to peace, appears to have had influence through Vice President Cheney. At the same time the government of Israel had been analyzing the need for Palestinian reform. Efraim Halevy, the Mossad chief, recalls that Sharon received a "detailed blueprint" on the subject with some of the ideas passed to the Americans, including the need for a Palestinian CEO, consolidation of the security services, and an independent finance minister. Halevy believed Bush's speech was a "spectacular achievement" for Sharon. Dov Weisglass, who would join the prime minister's team as a key advisor in May 2002, agreed completely. He wouldn't quantify Israel's input into the speech for me, but he recalled "there was an exchange of texts, ideas, and information." For the president to "see eye to eye with us" on major principles of our policy, Weisglass recalled, was a "critical accomplishment."

No sooner had the president delivered his speech than the drumbeat began about what he would do next, specifically how to implement his vision. For the administration, European and Arab involvement in the peace process was a headache for which no diplomatic aspirin had been invented. Hadn't the president delivered a major address? What more did they want? Apparently, the answer was action. Two conflicting tendencies pulled the president and his advisors. With the focus now on Iraq, no one wanted any initiative that might drain time, energy, or political capital away from that enterprise. For some, the road to Jerusalem ran through Baghdad, so no Arab-Israeli initiative made sense until the Iraq file could be closed. On the other hand, the nagging challenge of building coalitions for containment or war required the cooperation of others in the region and in Europe. That meant checking the Arab-Israeli peace-process box. At no point did anyone, with the exception of several lonely souls at the State Department, believe that advancing the Arab-Israeli issue might actually help in the president's war on terror and his goals in Iraq.

A few of us at the State Department, largely talking to ourselves, began fashioning postspeech to-do lists for steps Israelis and Palestinians might take to create a real environment for negotiations. This was the beginning of the logic behind the road map. But the real push came from the Arabs, this time from another Abdullah, king of Jordan. Marwan Muasher, Jordan's energetic foreign minister, had raised the idea of an action plan with American officials, and in July 2002, together with the Egyptian and Saudi foreign ministers, he had come to see the president, who seemed positive about some follow-up. In early August the king himself met with Bush to reach agreement on some type of action. The president immediately rejected the king's idea. "I gave them a vision," Muasher recalls the president saying. "What do the Palestinians want from me now?" When the Jordanians pushed back, clarifying that all they were looking for was a concrete way to translate the Bush vision into reality, the president became more receptive. And with that the road map exercise was born. And it would remain just that—an exercise.

I had a hand in shaping the earliest version of what was essentially a three-phase timeline to end violence, create confidence through various Israeli and Palestinian unilateral and bilateral actions, and launch negotiations. But few people I know, and I'd put myself at the top of the list, really believed the road map had much of a chance to get the car out of the parking lot, let alone onto the highway.

The White House was never really committed to it. Powell recalls with classic understatement that it was never a "popular exercise." There was real concern that it committed the United States to "long negotiations," and that it brought "these other people [the Quartet] into the game." Powell recalls that "nobody in the administration ever said road map or Quartet except me," until the Aqaba summit in June 2003. At the same time the road map, like the June 24 speech, became a convenient administration talking point and guidepost, pointing toward what the parties needed to do.

The administration's lack of commitment ensured that the road map, to use Madeleine Albright's phrase, would never be taken out of the glove box. The document wasn't flawed, but the notion that it was self-implementing, or that Sharon and Arafat could do it by themselves without significant American help, was. To have any chance of success, the Bush administration would have to put a full-time empowered envoy on the project and work on the issue, developing detailed timelines, benchmarks, and performance standards. The work would have been messy and tough, since the envoy would have had to put a very heavy arm on both sides, especially the Israelis.

Finally, the Israelis and Palestinians never really owned the document, not seeing a first draft until the fall of 2002. Not surprisingly they had many objections. Dov Weisglass recalls "raising hell" when he saw the first draft. Once the Israelis objected, that meant we'd create a discrete channel with them to work through all their concerns, a process that still resulted in formal Israeli reservations in double digits. The Palestinians by and large went along with the road map, although unhappily and without serious intent to discharge their responsibilities for dismantling terrorist infrastructure and ending violence. In the end, the only real problem with the road map was that neither the Americans, the Israelis, nor the Palestinians were serious about implementing it. It remained unofficial until April 2003, when Tony Blair persuaded President Bush that it would help both of them with Iraq. Doug Feith put the entire enterprise in perspective: the president saw the road map as "just a halftime show" between his own June 2002 speech and "whatever serious diplomacy was going to be after the Iraq action."

Unfortunately, no serious American diplomacy followed the president's speech or the road map for the remainder of the president's first term. In the wake of what appeared to be at the time a successful outcome in Iraq, and bowing to expectations from the Europeans and Arabs, the president did meet with Mahmoud Abbas, the new Palestinian prime minister, and Sharon in Aqaba in June. There Bush demonstrated that he could be tough with Sharon. "I've taken a lot of shit for calling you a man of peace," one participant recalls him saying. "We've got to find a way to move ahead." But there would be no replay of post–Desert Storm, when the president's father and his secretary of state launched a serious diplomatic effort on the Arab-Israeli issue to exploit the opportunity of successfully pushing Saddam Hussein out of Kuwait.

Clearly, circumstances in 2003 made things more difficult for the son than they had been for the father. But the administration chose not to pursue a small opening created that summer by an Egyptian-brokered Hamas cease-fire and Abu Mazen's appointment as prime minister. Instead of empowering the secretary or another high-level envoy, they turned to a veteran Foreign Service officer with little Middle East experience. John Wolf, who claims he was selected precisely for that reason, describes his initial meeting with the president in the Oval Office, which told you just about everything you needed to know about the administration's commitment. The Palestinians, the president began, had to stop violence and start building institutions. "Look here," he said, "this office is bigger than anybody who's ever sat here. That's what the Palestinians need." "But sir," Wolf responded, "this office takes its stature from the Constitution." "That's right," Bush replied, turning to his national security advisor. "Condi, whatever happened to that Constitution we were working on?"

Without any real direction from Washington, hope for progress was slim. The president charged Wolf with "monitoring" implementation. Since neither side moved ahead on implementation, he had nothing to monitor. By the fall, the cease-fire had collapsed and Abu Mazen had resigned, principally because Arafat wouldn't empower him. And besides, by December 2003 Ariel Sharon had transformed the stage yet again by floating a new idea—unilateral Israeli withdrawal from Gaza.

Annapolis and Beyond: Better Late Than Never, 2005–2008

I have to admit I was surprised by the call. The voice on my answering machine was inviting me to a meeting with the secretary of state. I knew that Condi Rice had convened informal meetings of experts and "exes" from time to time to talk about the Middle East, but I'd never been invited. It was now early November 2007. The secretary was on her latest trip to the Middle East, perhaps only weeks away from a peace conference with Israelis and Palestinians scheduled to be held after Thanksgiving in Annapolis, Maryland. I'd been pretty critical of the administration's Arab-Israeli diplomacy over the past several years. If they were reaching out to me, I thought, how desperate were they?

And more than that. Was this newfound interest in Israeli-Palestinian diplomacy really serious, or just a last-minute bid for legacy on the part of a president and a secretary of state who hadn't done much consequential diplomacy?

Nothing in the first two years of its second term had suggested that the Bush administration was prepared to get serious about this issue. Increasingly bogged down in the war in Iraq, the administration continued to demonstrate a lack of interest and capacity to deal effectively with the opportunities and crises that beset the Arab-Israeli arena. Never persuaded that this issue was a top priority or worth real political investment, it could not even follow up seriously on its own initiatives. The road map quietly expired. The president's two-state vision became a talking point, and not a very compelling one at that. As problems in Iraq mounted, the administration's credibility both at home and in the region declined. The road to Jerusalem was still strewn with huge obstacles, but one thing was increasingly evident: it didn't run through Baghdad. Iraq would continue to suck up every ounce of political capital and energy in Washington. With Arafat still in power, the administration had little inclination to spend what it didn't have on the Arab-Israeli issue or to further the agenda of a Palestinian leader it believed to be a terrorist.

Powell left the administration in January 2005. Looking back on his four years, he told me that during the first year he wanted to test whether or not there was an opportunity to move ahead on the Arab-Israeli issue and to get Bush engaged. By the second year he'd come to realize that he could not work with Arafat. And at any rate "the president wasn't prepared to invest political capital in this." On balance, Powell concluded, "I'm not sure that it was possible to succeed. I'm not sure the Palestinian side was mature and ready enough and could have given us what we would have needed to force Sharon."

Still, at least two opportunities presented themselves that were worth testing. In November 2004 Arafat died; in January 2005 Abu Mazen was elected president in fair and free elections. For the last several years the Bush administration had been looking to marginalize Arafat and create a new leadership with responsible moderates. Now both opportunities had arrived, but instead of working hard to empower Abu Mazen and push a political process, the administration allowed the situation to drift.

Serious diplomacy—the road map—would have to have been tough, involving pressing Abu Mazen and Sharon. We never even tried. The new Palestinian leader was viewed as a good man but weak and ineffectual. "We should have stepped in with both feet," a senior official recalled. Instead we remained on the sidelines, fearful of pushing Sharon and enamored of a unilateral withdrawal option from Gaza that would take us off the hook. Already weak and dysfunctional, Fatah would grow even weaker. Hamas would fill the vacuum. Within a year, in elections ironically pushed by the Bush administration as part of its democratization agenda, Hamas would attain a majority in the Palestinian Legislative Council.

The second missed chance was to build on Sharon's Gaza disengagement strategy and see how it could be used to strengthen Abu Mazen (and not, as it turned out, Hamas). Again, we didn't try that hard. A senior administration official intimately involved in policy matters concedes that it was a "blown opportunity," but doubts that the president would have pressed Sharon at a time when he was undertaking such a bold and costly course at home. And besides, Abu Mazen was weak and unable to manage Fatah, let alone Hamas.

Knowing what I know about the frustrating nature of Palestinian negotiating behavior and Israel's own requirements, I'm persuaded that had we pressed Sharon to negotiate Gaza, the Israelis would still be there today. By the end of 2004 the administration had taken about the only steps it could have: helping Sharon get out and setting an important precedent in the withdrawal of Israeli military forces, and settlers, and dismantling settlements. In April 2004 the president had already agreed to an exchange of letters with the prime minister on permanent status issues that reaffirmed the obvious and reconfirmed what Bill Clinton had already validated in his December 2000 parameters: there would be no significant return of

Palestinian refugees to Israel proper and the June 4, 1967, borders would need to be modified to take account of Israeli settlement blocs, but only through negotiations. Although the Gaza withdrawal went better than many had anticipated, the outcome did not. Fatah couldn't control the streets and lost politically to Hamas and other groups that found new latitude to maneuver and launch rocket attacks against Israel.

The new secretary of state, Condoleezza Rice, entered office with several advantages over Powell in regard to Arab-Israeli diplomacy. She had a close relationship with her president, closer perhaps than any secretary since James Baker had with the president's father; a reelected Bush faced a second term free from political constraints and had for his use a huge reserve of political currency with Israel built up over the past four years. Finally, the president's willful disengagement had created an environment in which expectations for progress had dipped so low that just about any initiative that succeeded would have been welcomed by the Arabs and the international community.

Still, by 2005 America's hand had become weaker in many ways and the Arab-Israeli arena had become much more complicated. In January 2006 Ariel Sharon suffered a stroke that removed him permanently from political life. His successor, Ehud Olmert, was smart, centrist, and pragmatic but lacked the moral or historic legitimacy to sell big decisions. Worse still, Olmert's stock fell precipitously in July as he stumbled into a war with Hezbollah in Lebanon, then failed to win decisively or manage the home front. The image of northern Israel shut down for over a month contributed to the image of a weak prime minister and a weaker Israel. Having wrongly concluded that Israel could defeat Hezbollah and its Iranian sponsor, the administration was weakened as well by identification with an Israeli operation that claimed a thousand Lebanese civilian lives and destroyed vast amounts of Lebanon's infrastructure without dealing Hezbollah a mortal blow.

The situation on the Palestinian front was no better. In February 2006 Hamas, in elections pushed for by the Bush administration, gained a majority in the Palestinian Legislative

Council. Despite efforts by Israel, the United States, and the European Union to boycott Hamas until it accepted Israel's right to exist, the Islamists held their own, and even seemed to grow in stature, as Mahmoud Abbas grew weaker. In March 2007 Abbas and Hamas Prime Minister Ismail Haniya formed a unity government under Saudi auspices, and Hamas became a new and permanent reality in Palestinian governance and a factor in any effort to launch Israeli-Palestinian negotiations.

Matters soon got worse. "Unity" masked several worrisome trends: elements within Fatah who had never accepted Hamas's political victory looked for chances to strike out on the streets; Hamas, increasingly bowing to the wishes of its military wing, sought an opportunity to deal Fatah a resounding defeat in Gaza before it became too strong; and proliferation of too many armed men with grievances guaranteed that Gaza would be at a constant boil. Severe factional fighting erupted in June 2007. Within a week Hamas had defeated Fatah in Gaza, occupied its military positions, and laid claim to governance of the Palestinians.

The Bush administration now saw a complex and unstable situation get worse. Having backed Mahmoud Abbas and led the boycott against Hamas, the administration moved to throw its political weight fully behind the Palestinian president. With Hamas in control of Gaza, the president moved to help him consolidate his stock in the West Bank and encouraged the Israeli prime minister, and his newly appointed defense minister Ehud Barak, now head of the Labor Party, to support him by easing restrictions on Palestinian movement and releasing tax and customs revenues.

The administration's strategy of pursuing the West Bank first, however, was a highly problematic one, which was highly dependent on Israel. Mahmoud Abbas barely controlled Fatah, let alone the West Bank. The assumption that you could use carrots there and sticks against Hamas in Gaza without undermining Mahmoud Abbas's credibility and avoiding more polarization among Palestinians was at best highly questionable. In the end, any Israeli-Palestinian agreement on peace would have to be based on a coherent and united Palestinian house; otherwise, without the guarantee that its Palestinian partner could keep the peace, no Israeli government would dare risk making the concessions that needed to be made, particularly withdrawal from the West Bank. Nor could Abbas afford to be perceived for very long as presiding over a growing separation between Gaza and the West Bank or aiding one at the expense of the other.

The June 2007 crisis did, as crises often do, generate a good deal of peace-process motion; the question was whether it would lead to real movement and in the right direction. Late in the month Olmert, Abbas, Jordan's King Abdullah, and Egypt's President Mubarak met in Sharm el-Sheikh. And in a curious development former British prime minister Tony Blair emerged as the Quartet's Middle East envoy, dealing principally with economic and government/institutional support for the Palestinian Authority. On July 16, President Bush announced that he would convene an international meeting attended by Israelis, Palestinians, and their Arab neighbors, whose mandate was vague, but included support for negotiations leading to a Palestinian state. It was no coincidence that the president had noted that Secretary Rice would chair the meeting. Last time around, in 2002, Bush had referred to Powell's interest in doing something on the peace process as "Colin's baby"; now it was Condi's issue. Even at this late hour, it wasn't at all clear how committed the president was.

No, this train was being driven by a secretary of state who saw an opportunity framed by the good (Olmert and Abbas), the bad (Hamas and Iran), and the ugly (a set of huge challenges that needed to be overcome if any Israeli-Palestinian agreement was to emerge). Ironically, having criticized Powell for trying to focus on the political issues of permanent status, she was doing precisely that. And having departed from the idea of a peace process, both the secretary and the president seemed to have bought into the idea in a big way.

That November day in the meeting with the secretary, I saw a self-assured Condi Rice convinced that she understood the Arab-Israeli issue and, in the run-up to the Annapolis meeting, believing that she was on the verge of accomplishing something quite important. When I interviewed her in 2006 during the Israeli-Hezbollah war, Secretary Rice seemed less confident; but she'd still made clear that a serious negotiating process was possible. Now she appeared even more persuaded that she had been right: diplomacy was not about making deals; it was rooted in the political changes that made those deals possible.

Was her confidence justified? With only several months of Arab-Israeli diplomacy under her belt, the secretary had not yet been seriously tested. There was no doubt that regional changes were required to lay the groundwork for a serious breakthrough, but so was a strong American hand if those changes were to be exploited. Diplomacy was very much about making deals. Despite her self-confidence that day, it was still not clear to me whether the president and the secretary had sufficient will and skill to take on the challenge of brokering an Israeli-Palestinian deal on the core issues.

Still, for the first time in seven years, the Bush administration—the secretary of state really—seemed to be interested in testing whether Israelis, Palestinians, and Arabs were ready to make key decisions.

The Annapolis meeting held on November 27 had come out somewhere between what the pessimists and the optimists had predicted. In government, we used to say, there were three possible outcomes to just about everything: breakthrough, breakdown, and muddle through. Annapolis had come out somewhere well north of muddle through. It was not the result that the secretary had initially hoped to achieve—Israeli-Palestinian agreement on a document that would lay out agreed parameters on Jerusalem, borders, and refugees to guide the negotiations.

But with over forty countries participating, including senior officials from Syria and Saudi Arabia—the first time since the March 1996 summit of the peacemakers that Israelis and Arabs sat together in a high-level forum—it did signal that the peace process was once again open for business. This was no mean achievement against the doom and gloom of the previous seven years. Israelis and Palestinians agreed on the goal of seeking a peace treaty by the end of 2008; Abbas and Olmert agreed to meet biweekly and to form a steering committee to oversee negotiations which would be formally launched in mid-December. The United States also committed itself to helping to implement the much talked about but never realized road map, and a former NATO commander was appointed to deal with the security issues.

It remained to be seen, however, whether the administration's efforts could move from an event into the kind of consequential success that could produce an Israeli-Palestinian peace treaty and alter the grim situation on the ground. The challenges facing Abbas and Olmert were huge. But nowhere were the doubts greater than when it came to America's role. President Bush announced plans to visit Israel in January 2008, having never visited as President. As important a step as this was, it couldn't allay the uncertainties about his commitment to diplomacy. Had President Bush remained on the sidelines too long, now with too little leverage to affect the situation? Was the administration really committed to the kind of tough and sustained diplomacy that would be required to help Israelis and Palestinians implement the road map, let alone solve the issues of Jerusalem, refugees, and borders in their negotiations?

Both good questions to be sure, but with few good answers. In December 2007, as I write these words, the president's past behavior still seemed to argue against the more forceful and sustained American role that would be required. Was the past going to be prologue? Unfortunately, it seemed that when it came to Arab-Israeli peacemaking, the son's instincts were never as good as the father's. On this issue, and perhaps on a few others, the apple seemed to have fallen far from the tree.

Chapter Ten

One More Last Chance: Is Arab-Israeli Peace Possible, and What Can America Do About It?

Some nights after we had ended our negotiations for the day, I sat with my good friend and colleague Gamal Helal on the balcony of our Jerusalem hotel overlooking the Old City. Tired and stressed, we talked about the day's events and about history. At times we laughed ourselves silly thinking about how those two battle-hardened warriors Salah al-Din the Muslim and Richard I the Lionheart, a Christian, men of God, passion, and history, had fought over the fate of this city and now must have been rolling in their graves laughing at our efforts to craft a peaceful solution for Jerusalem, a city over which so much blood had been spilled.

What would they have made, we wondered, of American optimism, our pragmatism, and our split-the-difference approach to life? Not much, we suspected. I think back on our attempts at the July 2000 Camp David summit to persuade Israelis and Palestinians to cede or dilute sovereignty over the Haram al-Sharif/Temple Mount, and I can only shake my head. Jerusalem, history told us repeatedly, wasn't for sharing. It was to be possessed in the name of God, or at least in the name of the tribe. Were we listening? Who did we Americans think we were, trying to divide up overlapping sacred space like it was a piece of salami? Did we really believe we could use clever lawyerlike formulations to overcome the weight of a thousand years of a conflict driven by religious triumphalism and existential fears? After all, we weren't just fighting the present; we were at war with history. As William Faulkner wrote in *Requiem for a Nun*, "The past is never dead. It's not even past."

Looking back now over the past forty years of American diplomacy, particularly the twenty or so in which I was personally involved, I'm a lot more uncertain about the two questions I've posed in this final chapter title. My answers are still: "Yes, peace is possible, and America can do quite a lot about it." But my earlier exuberance and optimism are now mixed with a large dose of humility and uncertainty. Failure will do that to you. After all, the successes of the three bad boys in American diplomacy required dramatic regional changes and heroic Arab and Israeli leadership. Whether or not we choose to accept this reality, conflicts driven by history, memory, identity, and existential fear of obliteration are never resolved quickly, easily, or sometimes even at all. They certainly cannot be ended by distant great powers, no matter how well intentioned.

So where does this leave us? The pursuit of Arab-Israeli peace is excruciatingly difficult, painful, and time-consuming, but it is not impossible. It is even worth something important to America. The obstacles that block progress toward the end of the conflict aren't supernatural or metaphysical, not beyond the realm of imagining. In 1967 no one would have thought that thirty years on, Israel, Egypt, and Jordan would have signed full treaties of peace. Similar agreements between Israel, Syria, and Lebanon are possible. And a solution to the much more complex challenge of Israel and the Palestinians is still one based on two states. A point may come when that solution is no longer possible, but we are not there yet. And even though pursuing a two-state solution has become much more complex, I believe it is no less desirable than it was when I left government service five years ago.

In any case, the primary hurdle blocking peace is not what has transpired on the ground these many years, nor the absence of clever diplomatic solutions. Such solutions abounded in the discussions at Camp David, the Clinton parameters of December 2000, the ideas put forth during the Israeli-Palestinian Taba talks of January 2001, and the 2002 Geneva initiative developed by unofficial Israeli and Palestinian negotiators. What stands in the way of a solution is the absence of political will and leadership on both sides to understand what's necessary to meet the other side's needs and to take the political decisions to move forward. Clearly this challenge does not allow for softheaded Pollyannaish views about the inevitability of peace or assertions that we are "this close" to a solution. I've done more than my fair share of damage in thinking and acting this way. But neither is there much profit in granting an easy victory to cynicism and despair. Even if America did not have critically important interests in this region, there is a compelling argument to be made for our continued involvement. Unlike many other nations or organizations, what we do or don't do counts. Others may have the luxury or right to sit on the sidelines. We don't. America doesn't have the right or authority to abandon commitments we've made or to mortgage the future to unending violence and confrontation by giving up on the present or living as if we were some kind of helpless prisoner of the past.

Why Should We Care?

Why should America, thousands of miles distant from a conflict that has dragged on for generations, care at all, or at least care enough to invest serious effort, to help Arabs and Israelis resolve it?

Since the beginning of serious American involvement in Arab-Israeli diplomacy forty years ago, the "why should we care" has changed significantly. Many of the world's great religions have a home, and therefore, a stake, in the much too promised land. Critical American constituencies of 5.3 million Jews, 3.5 million Arabs, all 5 million non-Arab Muslims, and 40 million to 80 million evangelical Christians have an enormous investment in Israel and the broader region for reasons of faith, identity, religion, and family.

On the political level, however, interest in Arab-Israeli affairs had traditionally been driven, until the 1990s, by the triad of cold war, oil, and American support for Israel. During the cold war the continuation of a hot war between Israel and the Arabs had always been seen as hurting American interests by enhancing Soviet influence, jeopardizing access to oil, and alienating the Arab world, particularly as America and Israel grew closer together. This triangular set of forces came together most notably during and after the October 1973 war, but actually American influence increased rather than declined at the expense of the Soviet Union, largely as a result of Kissinger's skillful diplomacy.

Today two of the original three causative forces are gone: the Russian threat has receded, and oil shocks are much more likely to result from events in Iran or Iraq, or from market forces, than from immediate crises over Palestine. What remains is the knotty problem of how America balances its commitment to Israel with its commitments to its Arab friends in the face of an ongoing Arab-Israeli conflict. The damage to our national prestige and credibility inflicted by our invasion and conduct of the war in Iraq may have caused many Americans to forget that our uncritical identification with some of Israel's policies or our inattention to the Arab-Israeli issue has the power to erode our influence and interests even more in a critically important part of the world.

Over the years the position of the Arab-Israeli issue has shifted in the overall scheme of American foreign policy priorities as those priorities have waxed and waned. Although the Arab and Muslim world continues to attach the highest importance to the fate of Palestinians, that's not the case here, particularly since the beginning of the first George W. Bush administration in 2001. Since 9/11 a definite Arab-Israeli fatigue factor has clearly set in.

In years past the so-called experts, myself included, argued wrongly that paying continued attention to American-led diplomacy, with the goal of resolving the Arab-Israeli issue, could be the silver bullet that would protect our interests. What's clear now is that as the first decade of the twenty-first century draws to a close, no magic elixir, no protective amulet, and no high-tech solution exists to safeguard America's interests in the Arab and Muslim world. With too little democracy, too many gaps between the haves and have-nots, and between the cans and cannots (those who can participate in choosing their governors and those who can't), and too many extremists dedicated to stirring up anger and rage at the United States, this is one screwed-up region of the world. It is likely to remain so, a threat to American interests and security for many years to come.

Still, I believe the American pendulum has swung much too far away from giving proper value to Arab-Israeli diplomacy. We need a course correction. I'm absolutely convinced that managing or even solving the Arab-Israeli conflict will not protect America from oil shocks, terror, or radical regimes with nuclear weapons. But I believe with equal conviction that the Arab-Israeli issue is now more vital to our national interests, and to our security, than at any time since the late 1940s. The sooner we internalize this reality, the more effective will be our approach to the ongoing regional crisis we are now facing.

During the 1990s, with the fall of the Soviet Union, the academic experts, pundits, and intelligence analysts sat around trying to figure out what would replace the cold war as the organizing paradigm for American foreign policy in the twenty-first century. They got the answer in September 2001. The 9/11 attacks demonstrated with a terrifying clarity that the security of the continental United States was now attached to the affairs of the Arab and Muslim East, including the disposition of the much too promised land; and that in this relationship we are more vulnerable to danger than at any other point in our history. Once again, as in the 1940s with the Germans and Japanese, and from the 1940s to the 1990s with the Soviet and Chinese Communists, what people thousands of miles away from our shores care about, think about, and rail against now matters a great deal to us. This is reality—however illogical, biased, and warped some of those thoughts may seem to us. We should take no comfort from the fact that we have not been attacked again. Given our military profile and commitments in the Middle East, we are in an investment trap from which there is no escape. And given the combination of weak regimes, determined anti-American extremists, and the proliferating of weapons of mass destruction, we will likely be targeted again. Indeed, we can no longer think about 9/11 as if it were only a single, horrible day. We must adjust our time horizon to think about what happened on that day as a generational challenge. There's little doubt that that's the way our enemies think about it.

The sources of their anger at the United States and the regimes we support run deep and broad, perhaps justifying, from their distorted perspective, a thousand-year war against the Western infidels and local apostates. The response to September 11 in Afghanistan and Iraq took America deep into the heart of the Arab and Muslim world, embroiling us in the passions, hatreds, and humiliations with which much of this region now seethes. Fixing the Palestinian issue will not generate the love and respect of a region boiling over with anger at our support for authoritarian regimes, the occupation of Iraq, or the multitude of other transgressions real or imagined of which America is accused. Great powers can never be loved: at best they can hope for respect.

The veteran Yankees manager Casey Stengel once said that the key to good management is keeping the nine guys who hate your guts away from the nine guys who haven't made up their minds. Surely a serious effort to manage and resolve the Arab-Israeli conflict—an issue that still resonates with tremendous emotional and political power in a dysfunctional region—might help a great many people there and elsewhere to make up their minds about America and to associate the United States with the kind of effective diplomacy that enhances its credibility.

The serious effort I've suggested will count for naught among the disturbingly large number of Arabs and Muslims who see their confrontation with the West as a clash of values and civilization. These are enemies who, in President Bush's words, hate the United States because we love freedom. Many more oppose us because of our policies, not for our values or beliefs. A vast majority of Arabs and Muslims see their differences with America as a more traditional struggle of interests, a struggle that might be positively influenced by mutual give-and-take, reciprocity, and a more effective American approach toward an issue of such importance. We cannot expect to sway Muslim opinion by wrapping the box of American policies with a pretty bow while the contents remain unchanged. Serious public diplomacy begins with an appeal to what people perceive cognitively rather than an effort to capture their emotions. In other words, it's not hearts and minds but minds first, then hearts. This means being much more active and balanced in our approach to Arab-Israeli peacemaking.

I can already hear the groans of protest from the usual quarters that such logic is naïve, flawed, and even dangerous, a not-so-thinly veiled appeasement of the Arabs, a sacrifice of Israel, and an argument to bog America down in a problem that is really not that critical. This line of reasoning is nonsense and not even worthy of bad cable news punditry. Being smart and credible on the Arab-Israeli issue strengthens American interests and our position in a post-9/11 world and in a region in which military power and counterterrorism are necessary but not sufficient instruments to advance our goals. Without being too presumptuous, I believe a more effective approach on our part would advance the goals of Israelis and Arabs as well.

The organizing principle of every nation's foreign policy must be the protection of the homeland. We have an obligation and responsibility to our own citizens to do everything within our power to support our friends, marginalize our enemies, and enhance our credibility and influence. We will be in the Middle East for generations. The Arab-Israeli issue will continue to rattle around out there, providing opportunities for our enemies to exploit. We can't do everything or be everywhere, but on this issue uniquely, our national and moral interests combine with a demonstrated capacity, when we engage wisely, to make a bad situation better. To ignore or address ineffectively an issue that fuels so much rage and anger against us is irresponsible in the extreme.

Now the question arises: what, if anything, can we do about it? We've seen over the past four decades that America can play a critical role in helping Arabs and Israelis reach agreements, although the options, successes, and failures more often than not are shaped by regional events and by leaders willing to take grave and dramatic risks.

In 2008 these decisions are breathtakingly risky, painful, and complicated. We have used up all the "easy ones" in negotiations leading to separate peace treaties between Israel, Egypt, and Jordan. The hard ones now involve Israel, Syria, and the Palestinians. I have suggested above that during the course of the negotiations during the late 1990s, solutions to these problems are clearer now than ever before. But the leadership, political will, and environment to make the decisions and to implement them may not be. Five specific factors contribute to the enormous challenges facing Arabs and Israelis alike. We need to be honest about their impact if we are to be serious in working toward a comprehensive Arab-Israeli settlement.

It's a Bad, Bad Neighborhood The Middle East has always been a dangerous place, but since 9/11 threats against would-be peacemakers and mediators have intensified substantially. The American adventure in Iraq, once seen as a key demonstration of policies that would produce stability, democratization, and moderation, have instead given us chaos, civil war, and intensified anti-American Sunni and Shia extremism. Al-Qaeda, once on the run, has proved remarkably resilient, hiding out along the Pakistan-Afghan border, creating a new beachhead in Iraq, and even trying to penetrate Gaza. Meanwhile Iran continues to bankroll both Hezbollah and Hamas and pursue its nuclear quest. It's hard to imagine a worse environment in which to encourage risk-taking by peace-seeking Arabs or Israelis. No matter how hard we try, we can't separate the peace process from the regional environments that inevitably will distract American attention and give the top priority to Iraq and Iran.

Where Have All the Leaders Gone? The age of heroism in Arab-Israeli diplomacy is over, at least for now. The Begins, Sadats, King Husseins, and Rabins, even the Arafats and Sharons, who had the legitimacy and authority to take big risks, are gone.

Arab and Israeli leaders no longer seem to make history, but are pushed and pulled around by it in contrary directions. They have little room to maneuver and operate and have almost no margin for error in the face of historic decisions. On the Palestinian side, a dysfunctional and divided political house will continue to pose huge problems for gaining a consensus on the endgame, let alone implementing a solution. In Israel, domestic politics will continue to impose huge constraints on forging an effective strategy on peacemaking. Consider this: since 1948, Israel has had thirty-one governments; the average term was 1.86 years. Only two governments served out their lawful term of at least four years. The current reality doesn't rule out the emergence of courageous leaders, but Arabs and Israelis will need a lot of help from each other and from a third party.

Small Spoilers with Big Impact This leadership vacuum offers a splendid opportunity for small, nonstate actors to wreak havoc. In Gaza and the West Bank, Hamas has emerged as a permanent fixture in Palestinian governance, shaped by and shaping an extremist agenda and developing rockets with a range and precision that have a serious capacity to threaten Israel. In Lebanon, Hezbollah plays a key role in influencing government decisions and has refurbished the rocket and missile stock it expended in its 2006 summer war with Israel. Backed by Iran and Syria, these nonstate actors have already demonstrated a capacity as serious spoilers. They have also emerged as serious political players respected on the streets, in Arab capitals, and throughout the region. Destroying them was never really an option. Ignoring them may not be either.

The Gaps, Oh the Gaps Anyone who believes that Israelis and Palestinians came "this close" to an agreement at any recent negotiation, including Camp David and Taba, has spent too much time with the peace-process tooth fairy. All three issues that drive the Israeli-Palestinian conflict (borders, Jerusalem, refugees) and a fourth (security) represent a universe of unfinished business in terms of both substance and implementation. The past seven years of violence and terror; the al-Qaeda and Hamas focus on Jerusalem; not to mention the Palestinian refugee problem, which presents a challenge to Israel's core identity as a Jewish state—all have made far more difficult implementing the solutions we had contemplated during the Clinton years.

The Missing Will In the end, resolving the conflict is not a matter of cobbling together clever diplomatic solutions packaged in ambiguity, however creative. It is a matter of summoning up the necessary political will and courage—and not on the cheap. If both Israelis and Palestinians can do only a partial deal (and are prepared to accept this for now), fine. They will not have renounced all claims and the conflict will probably continue. Should they try to resolve it conclusively, it will likely involve an endgame pretty close to what each side is demanding, and any would-be mediator must know this as well: peace and security will need to be real and guaranteed; territorial withdrawal will need to be pretty close to total and security arrangements for Israel rock solid, even with creative arrangements to make it palatable. Otherwise, in the cruel, dangerous, and existential world of Middle East politics, neither side can defend, let alone sell and sustain, an agreement at home. Our big mistake during the Clinton years was to try to get the Arabs to accept less than 100 percent. What we should have said to Arafat and Assad is, "Fine, you want your hundred percent; here's what Israel needs. Now get serious. America will work with both of you and at some point offer a bridge to broker a deal."

The Long Journey Toward Arab-Israeli Peace: Rules of the Road

If America's stakes in Arab-Israeli peace are so high, yet prospects for quick and easy progress so low, what do we do? Taking all of America's successes and failures into account, key rules of the road must loom large in any future strategy. Some affect America's attitudes (its software); others pertain to its policies (its hardware). This to-do list cannot guarantee success, but taken together these rules offer a way to raise the odds of success in an enterprise too often marked by failure. Even if America can't deliver on its promise to help Arabs and Israelis actually achieve peace, hewing to these rules will enhance American credibility, help us avoid failure, and position the United States to at least manage the consequences should the conflict prove unresolvable.

Make the Issue a Top and Ongoing Priority... Making Arab-Israeli peacemaking a top priority will not guarantee success, but if a president does not do so, forget even getting in the game. Pursuing Arab-Israeli peace cannot be weekend work. The regional and domestic obstacles to progress are so massive and difficult that unless the president makes clear that it's important and puts some teeth into a policy, there's absolutely no possibility of success. The president doesn't have to be the peace-process desk officer; with rare exceptions, it's better not to become involved at such a level. But the president must fully empower a secretary of state or special envoy, and engage personally at times, to make it unmistakably clear to the bureaucracy, to domestic political constituencies, and to Arabs and Israelis alike that the United States takes the issue seriously because the chief executive does so. If an administration pays lip service to the conflict, or gives less than its all, the media and its opponents will identify this weakness soon enough, and the president's policy will be attacked mercilessly by forces at home and abroad.

What's more, America's engagement cannot be episodic. In the past, our involvement in the issue has arisen in response to a crisis, usually a war, or to an unexpected opportunity, such as that provided by Sadat's trip to Jerusalem. We must set a more proactive and sustained course. If dramatic openings for agreement do not emerge, the president can at least prepare the ground or prevent the situation from sliding backward.

The United States fought Communism for over four decades in a cold war, which turned hot twice in bloody Asian confrontations. Nine presidents kept the cold war at the top of America's foreign policy priorities. Since 2001 we have been engaged in a struggle to which many names have been given—the Global

War on Terror, the Long War, the War Against Islamo-Fascism—take your pick. The successor to George W. Bush knows that, whatever it is called, this new war must be kept at the top of America's foreign policy priorities. And the new president must understand and act on the fact that the Arab-Israeli conflict is, and always will be, a critical battlefield in that new war. As the effort to protect the American homeland against terror will continue to be a top priority in general for an unknown number of presidents to come, so the Arab-Israeli issue must remain a specific priority of our nation's leaders into the future.

...But Remember: It's a Long Movie The Arab-Israeli conflict evolved in phases over time. Given its complexities, it's likely to be resolved in phases over time. This is not intended as a green light to waste time or avoid tough choices. It's a reflection of the risky decisions, tough political infighting, large gaps, and deep fears that exist between and among Arabs and Israelis. Without abandoning the goal of a comprehensive peace, American policymakers must keep in mind a realistic sense and measure of time, lest they try to accomplish too much, on the one hand, or not attempt enough, on the other.

There's much America can do to support, even stimulate or cajole, Arab and Israeli decision-making. But when final status issues are up for discussion, we can neither accelerate their internal political clocks nor quickly overcome the structural problems they confront.

One example should suffice: the two-front issue of the Clinton years. Was it possible to arrive at two agreements, even in principle, simultaneously or even close in time sequentially, between Israel, Syria, and the Palestinians given the emotional, religious, and security questions involved? Could Israel make commitments to withdraw from the entire Golan Heights and nearly all of the West Bank, share sovereignty over Jerusalem and its holy sites, address the refugee question, and dismantle settlements and remove thousands of settlers, some of whom are prepared to resist with violence, all at the same time? Can Syria and the Palestinians do what is required of them on normalization and security quickly?

Recall again that it took five years to move from Sadat's historic visit to Jerusalem in November 1977 to Israel's withdrawal from Sinai in April 1982. And that was a peacemaking process made in heaven, with a cast of strong Arab and Israeli leaders and issues that paled in comparison with the complexities of Jerusalem and refugees. If there ever was a place to apply a rational cold war analogy, it is here: we will need patience, the crafting of strategy that persists from one administration to the next, and a determination to avoid the easy lapse into frustration and anger if we can't produce quick results. There's no such thing as the quick fix in Arab-Israeli peacemaking. There is simply long and longer.

And Keep It Bipartisan We must look at the Arab-Israeli issue as a problem above partisan politics. It's not about Democrats or Republicans, it's just us Americans here. Support for Israel is already bipartisan, in truth, so deeply entrenched it is nonpartisan. The president must speak openly and honestly to Congress, and particularly to the organized American Jewish and American-Arab communities, about the relationship between America's national interest in Arab-Israeli peacemaking and security. When presidents cast American involvement in the light of a broad conception of our national interest, they create more space and support at home to carry the effort forward. We must do so again.

Specifically, our approach should be decoupled from the U.S.-Israeli relationship that predated the Arab-Israeli peace process and exists for a variety of independent reasons. I am absolutely convinced that there is no contradiction between America's special ties with the Israelis and our capacity to act as an effective mediator, being both tough and empathetic with Arabs and Israelis alike. As a consequence of pressure from the Jewish community and Congress, we've convinced ourselves otherwise. We need to change our own software so we can put to rest the canard that pursuing a balanced and effective approach to Arab-Israeli peacemaking requires appeasing Arabs or sacrificing Israelis. The president must stress this point early and often.

Negotiations Can Work but Only in the Right Environment Negotiations aren't much different from good friendships or business propositions: they work when both sides get what they need. Negotiations succeed when they're based on a balance of interest, not on a skewed imbalance or asymmetry. The Egyptian-Israeli and Jordanian-Israeli peace treaties have lasted for years because of this elemental fact. The Oslo process failed because it was based on a highly skewed asymmetry of interests and ongoing day-to-day relationships between the occupier and occupied, which undermined on the ground what Israelis and Palestinians were trying to achieve at the negotiating table.

Israelis wielded the *power of the strong*, the ability to unilaterally impose and sustain facts on the ground through their preponderant military, technical, and economic advantages. Those facts fed Palestinian humiliation and rage and only made it harder to reach a final agreement. Some Israeli responses derived from legitimate security concerns about terror and violence. But too many of them were a result of political calculation and ideological fixation, especially by the settlement enterprise, which demanded settlement expansion, land confiscation, bypass roads, and a different set of legal rules to govern 2.5 million Palestinians and 250,000 Israeli Jews residing in the West Bank.

Palestinians wielded the *power of the weak*, the capacity to use whatever tool they could to level the playing field against the Israelis. For some within Arafat's Fatah (the al Aqsa Brigades) and those Islamist groups (Hamas and Islamic Jihad), that meant suicide terror against the Israeli military and civilians both in the occupied territories and in Israel proper. Arafat used terror and lost control over the Palestinian Authority's monopoly over the forces of violence within Palestinian society. This ensured not only continued conflict with Israel but a loss of legitimacy and respect for Arafat in the international community, particularly in America.

The conflict between the power of the strong and the power of the weak guaranteed the demise of Oslo, especially in the face of our refusal to hold either side accountable for its actions. One of the most important lessons to emerge from the Oslo years is that ignoring bad behavior on either side dooms any chance of serious and successful negotiations. We need to understand and act on this reality. That means imposing costs—political, moral, and financial—on each side to dissuade them from their unilateral actions; and at the same time working with them on the ground to monitor behavior, solve problems, and defuse crises. We have demonstrated that we can be tough with the Palestinians on terror and violence, even while we help Abu Mazen build up his security forces. We need to be tough with Israel, privately and publicly, on settlement activity. The fact is that settlements are totally incompatible with creating confidence, let alone with generating an atmosphere for serious negotiation. Israel must freeze these activities. And we must impose costs if they won't.

The United States and Israel: Special but Not Exclusive When I speak publicly about Arab-Israeli diplomacy, I always ask my audience why, despite our current diminished credibility, America's phone is still ringing with pleas from the Arabs, the UN, and the Europeans to be more involved in Arab-Israeli diplomacy. Nobody in the audience ever seems to know or at least volunteer the answer, but it's so obvious to me. The fact is that we are indispensable to a resolution of the issue precisely because of our close ties to Israel. Everyone and his mother has good relations with the Arabs. America is the only power that has both sides covered. That's why over the past forty years we've been involved in every successful Arab-Israeli negotiation, with the exception of the 1993 Oslo Declaration of Principles, and unfortunately in many of the failures as well. It is our capacity to gain Israel's confidence and trust, which allows us to cajole and pressure, that makes us a compelling and attractive mediator.

When we employ this special relationship wisely and effectively, we succeed, even though the process is sometimes awkward, tense, and painful. Kissinger, Carter, and Baker will tell you all about it. At the same time, when we permit our special relationship to affect our thinking prejudicially in favor of Israel, or when we take Israel's side reflexively, we can't succeed because then we are acting as an advocate for one side over the other. For many reasons, the Israelis do deserve special consideration. They're one country but are at least 50 percent of the Arab-Israeli problem, and they're living—despite their military power, much of which is not usable anyway—in a dangerous neighborhood. When they negotiate, the Israelis almost always find themselves in the position of trading the concrete and tangible (land) for commodities that are much less tangible (the promise of peace).

Forget for a minute that America, apart from Arab-Israeli diplomacy, has a stake in Israel's well-being and security as a fellow democracy and in the Jewish people as historical victims of centuries of anti-Semitism, culminating in the worst genocide in history. Our sensitivity to these key elements of Israel's national existence brings us that much closer to the Jewish state and ironically equips us to be even more effective in mediation.

But our success depends on the perception and reality that we can also be fair and effective. Too often American political leaders and diplomats have forgotten that "fair and effective" means refusing to give Israel carte blanche to influence, let alone impose, its views on America's tactics and strategies. It's important to ensure that Israel is not surprised by America's stance on critical issues, with special emphasis on security. It may even be necessary to allow some coordination when negotiations touch directly on security-related matters. But we cannot consent to giving Israel a veto over our negotiating positions, when the practical effect is to force us to ignore Arab interests or even our own.

The simple fact is that when we succeed in Arab-Israeli diplomacy, we coordinate generously, but we don't surrender our tactical independence or our capacity to judge what is required to reach a deal. When we don't succeed, it's partly because we measure requirements for an accord by Israeli rather than our own judgment, based on independent evaluation of the needs on each side.

Now that the "easy" agreements are behind us and the really tough ones remain before us, it is even more critical than ever to maintain Israel's confidence. Since the United States has never, and in my view could never, force either Israel or the Arabs to accept a final status deal that fundamentally threatened their core interests, I've never been certain what all the unhappy shouting has been about, particularly from Israel's American supporters. What I do know, after watching too many examples of American weakness and indecision in the face of Israeli and Arab nos, is that we need to protect our credibility. If Arabs, and particularly Israelis, want American help, then they need to be respectful of our interests, and we need to say no, or sometimes hell no, if we judge an idea, approach, or summit meeting to be unworkable or too risky. If we won't show resolve, independence, and toughness, we've got no business being in the peacemaking business.

Offer Love, but Make It Tough Love Here is one special albeit unsolicited piece of advice, to future presidents, contemplating getting involved in Arab-Israeli diplomacy. If you're not prepared to reassure the locals while cracking heads as needed (and both will be needed), don't bother. If you can't take a lot of heat from the Arabs as well as from the Israelis and the organized pro-Israeli community, find another conflict to help mediate or broker. And frankly, if you're not prepared to stand up for your own country's interests on an issue now more critical to our security than ever before, to lead rather than to assuage domestic lobbies, well, maybe you shouldn't be president. Sounds preachy, harsh, and unfair. Right? But those qualities are what we happen to need right now. Presidents, secretaries of state, and special envoys need to summon up and sustain tough love on this issue. They must be able to reassure yet pressure, threaten or at times walk away yet engage, and impose costs and offer incentives when necessary. Above all, they have to be real tough sons-of-bitches to succeed, but also be smart and sensitive, and just humble enough never to lose sight of the fact that in the end this is a life-and-death struggle for Arabs and Israelis, who live in one of the world's roughest neighborhoods. For us it will never be that.

The Good, the Bad, the Ugly
and America's Promise

As I look out on the long road toward Arab-Israeli peace stretching from Annapolis, it strikes me very much as a story driven by the good, the bad, and the ugly. The good is easy enough to discern: a pragmatic and well-intentioned Palestinian president in Ramallah who has given up the gun; a centrist Israeli prime minister looking for his moment in history; and a Bush administration recognizing, however belatedly, an opportunity to further its legacy and American interests. Combined with a new focus on the core issues of the conflict as well as the situation on the ground, it's possible the stage could be set for serious business. After all, in the latter part of 2007, Ehud Olmert and Mahmoud Abbas have had more hours of serious discussion on Jerusalem, borders, and refugees than any Israeli prime minister and Palestinian president—ever.

The bad is also quickly identifiable. The renewed effort to create a negotiating process of the brave is also motivated by the afraid. The rise of two nonstate actors (Hamas and Hezbollah) and the influence of their state patrons (Syria and Iran) have moved Israel, the Arab centrists, and the United States to action. These spoilers demonstrate yet again that small need not be inconsequential or weak. And they have scared would-be peacemakers into trying to preserve not only the idea of negotiations but the two-state solution as well. Today's troublemakers all have the potential to tack toward the pragmatic—indeed, in Syria's case (itself a graduate of Annapolis) even the desire to join the peacemakers; but outside the tent they also have the power to disrupt, even to destroy.

But it's the ugly that worries me most and that has the real power to lay land mines long the road from Annapolis. And the ugly—call it the mountains that now need to be climbed—rises not from external factors, but from the very nature of the Palestinians and Israelis themselves, and from the core issues that divide them. A divided Palestinian house in which no single authority controls the guns, the territory, the people, nor commands a single vision of the future, would be bad enough. But it's married to an Israeli political system which is itself divided, fractious, and unsure of what it's willing or able to pay to meet Palestinian needs and to end the conflict.

Politicians rather than statesmen or visionaries abound, lacking the historic or moral legitimacy to lead their peoples into the real promised land of a meaningful peace. The risks are enormous. Small distances, fatal proximity, terror, violence, and religious extremism and triumphalism provide almost no margin for error and little political space for trial and error. The idea of a Palestinian state with provisional borders, essentially creating a state in phases, with substantial Israeli withdrawal from the West Bank and a commitment to negotiate and resolve borders, Jerusalem, and refugees later, has a certain appeal and may raise its head again. But it also bears a certain resemblance to the broken promises and shattered trust of the incremental Oslo process. That such an idea made it into the Bush road map demonstrates that as early as 2003 solving the whole shebang was never seriously considered. Add to that the pull of a separate Israeli-Syrian negotiation over the future of the Golan Heights, and the impossibilities and improbabilities of any sort of quick comprehensive settlement mount.

Sadly, Annapolis has put America in the middle of this mess with much less leverage than it had in its previously successful peacemaking efforts. Unlike with Kissinger, no 1973 war or Arab oil embargo impels America toward forceful diplomacy. Unlike with Carter, no Arab Sadat provides the catalyst for high-level summitry. And unlike with the president's father, who used America's first victory over Saddam Hussein in 1991 to create a genuine breakthrough at Madrid, the son's second Iraq campaign has left America much weakened in a region that respects power, strength, and above all success.

Still, in taking responsibility for Annapolis, the Bush administration is now invested but also burdened with a problem it can't abandon or resolve. The all-or-nothing grand bargain was never an option; but neither is the disengagement which the administration pursued between 2005 and 2007, even after Arafat and Sharon were gone. Now America must find a role for itself appropriate to the new and difficult circumstances it partly helped to create.

In doing so, we must avoid overreaching and thus failing. We must also not make the situation worse. Here again the diplomatic equivalent of the Hippocratic oath applies: above all do no harm. The odds of a Palestinian state by the end of 2008 are long, as are the chances of an Israeli-Palestinian peace treaty. Still, there is a goal out there worth pursuing. Two, really: a framework articulated in which the principles for resolving Jerusalem, borders, and refugees are agreed, and, in parallel, an effort on the ground that ends violence and settlement activity, frees up the movement of people and goods, and generates some normalcy and real economic life. By 2009, there would be no Palestinian state, but America, Israel, the Palestinians, and the Arabs would have saved the negotiating process and the only rational solution to the conflict—a two-state solution.

Accomplishing this will be excruciatingly painful and difficult. It will require a great deal from Israel and the Palestinians, as well as a strong and deft American hand. Watching the movie *Titanic*, not a great confidence builder when discussing the Arab-Israeli issue, it occured to me that sometimes a negotiating process is like an iceberg: one-third is above the waterline, but the real mass is below.

The public and formal process launched by Annapolis is important in order to demonstrate that the peace process is open for business. The formal negotiations, the steering committees, the monitoring of the road map, and the donor effort are critically important to give the process public visibility and credibility. And the United States, together with its quartet partners and the Arab states, must drive this process.

At the same time, the post-Annapolis structure is too heavy, noisy, and public to deal with the core issues and produce a breakthrough. Even as Olmert and Abbas meet regularly and openly, there needs to be a quiet negotiation between their trusted representatives to work out a framework agreement on the core issues. If, or most likely when, the gaps emerge and an impasse occurs, America may need to be the broker. But first Israelis and Palestinians need to own their process, even if the United States must eventually put out its ideas or invest in a bridging document. Nothing will replace the trust and confidence generated by Israelis and Palestinians solving their own problems and defusing crises, even with the help of the United States. Oslo's demise lay partly in the fact that Israelis and Palestinians were left to their own devices, when it was clear that they and the process were in over their heads.

A piece of paper, however, is not enough. The reality on the ground for Israelis and Palestinians must change as well. Clearly the Annapolis process hopes to avoid this by attending to Israeli and Palestinian road-map obligations. But one huge obstacle stands in the way: Hamas and a divided Palestinian polity with two separate populations, armed forces, political leaders, and national visions. It is a great irony indeed that fifteen years after Oslo laid to rest the issue of who should represent the Palestinians— the PLO—that issue is open once again.

The Hamas problem to which there is no clear, quick, or easy solution boils down to this: without a unified Palestinian leadership that controls all the Palestinians, guns, and loyalties, no Israeli-Palestinian peace process will be possible. Whether it's the District of Columbia, Egypt, or Sweden, a central government must maintain as complete a monopoly on the forces of violence in its society as possible; otherwise your own citizens, let alone your neighbors, won't respect you. Even if an Israeli prime minister might be enticed to sign an agreement on paper, none could implement it without ironclad assurances and the reality that there is one authority and one gun on the other side. Some kind of reconciliation between Fatah and elements of Hamas is inevitable; the only questions are when and how it will occur. The problem of course is made worse by an external Hamas leadership in Damascus which has a major influence over Hamas in Gaza but which may have another agenda, more easily manipulated by its Iranian and Syrian patrons.

The current logic of Abbas, Israel, and America seems to be based on the idea that if you build a solid house, in this case an

Israeli-Palestinian agreement on the big issues, the neighborhood, so to speak, will improve. Palestinians will see that Abbas's way, not Hamas's will bring them statehood and economic prosperity. Hamas in Gaza would then have to choose between accepting a state or being marginalized or worse. Abbas would then be able to negotiate a unity deal from a position of strength, or, failing that, call for a public referendum or election to go over Hamas's head directly to the Palestinian public. There is also talk of a major Israeli operation against Gaza designed to deal with Qassam rockets but also to cripple Hamas and make it possible for Abbas and Fatah to regain control.

The "build it and they will come idea" might work if the Israeli-Palestinian agreement is rock solid and if the environment in which it is negotiated remains stable and positive. But herein lies the rub. Hamas has a capacity to disrupt matters with violence. Israel would also have to refrain from unilateral acts on the ground that would embarrass Abbas. The continued Israeli and international blockade of Gaza, as much as it undermines Hamas in Palestinian eyes, undermines Israel more and doesn't help the Palestinian Authority in Ramallah. That the West Bank gets fed while Gaza starves is not a compelling talking point without a real sense that Abbas can deliver soon on a Palestinian state.

There is another approach that turns the current logic on its head. It assumes that if the neighborhood doesn't improve, then you can't build a solid Israeli-Palestinian agreement. Trying to negotiate an Israeli-Palestinian deal on the big issues while rockets fly from Gaza, not to mention attacks from the West Bank, won't work. One bold approach—a Hamas-Israel deal that trades a real cease-fire (no Qassams, no attacks on civilians or military, and a prisoner exchange) for allowing Gaza to develop economically—would address this. But Israel at least for now would never agree to it. The current situation leaves Israel and the negotiation process with the worst of both worlds: Israel continues to bear responsibility for Gaza even though Israel is no longer there; Israel is blamed for hurting Palestinians; and Israel can't stop the Qassam rockets and attacks which can ruin the process.

Whatever option is chosen, one thing is clear: Hamas will need to be integrated in some way. We pushed for Palestinian elections in January 2006. Hamas won fairly, and we and the Israelis, helped by the Islamist movement's refusal to lay down its guns, didn't accept the outcome. Until that situation is changed, either by negotiating a cease-fire, including Hamas in real power sharing (if it accepts recognition of Israel and lays down its guns), or by forcing it from power through new Palestinian elections based on the promise and reality of statehood, implementing a meaningful Israeli-Palestinian peace will be impossible no matter how hard we try. Clearly an Israeli-Hamas deal is beyond America's capacity to shape. It's unlikely that we will change our approach to Hamas; and frankly, if Hamas is to be brought into the tent, it has to be an Israeli call. But we don't help our own case by not engaging Hamas's patrons, Syria and Iran, on the Arab-Israeli issue and other matters.

The Arab state dimension set into motion at Annapolis, particularly Saudi and Syrian participation, is also a critical ingredient in peacemaking. Whether it's empowering Abbas to contest new elections, negotiating new unity arrangements within the Palestinian house, or pressing Hamas toward pragmatism, the involvement of the Arab world, including Syria, will be critical. The United States has a more important agenda with Iran on nuclear issues, but Tehran's relationship with Hamas makes an integrated American approach, based on sticks *and* carrots, and coordinated with others in the international community, all that more imperative.

Working with the Arab world is crucial for other reasons. The core of the Arab-Israeli conflict may be the Palestinian issue, but greater involvement of the Arab states with Israel is one way to shape it in a positive direction. The conflict has always been a "twofer": one conflict between Israel and the Palestinians, and the other between Israel and the Arab states. Jordan and Syria, linked to Israel by common borders, will experience a far different relationship than, for example, Tunisia, located on another continent. Still, regional linkages are critical political inducements to Israel and to the Palestinians politically and economically as they make difficult choices in negotiations. Over time, relationships between Israel and the Arab states can begin to address any number of regional problems, from terror and proliferation of weapons of mass destruction to health and environmental concerns.

As part of any effort to resolve an Israeli-Palestinian negotiating process, the United States should coordinate a road map with key Arab states that focuses on what concrete steps Arab states would take toward Israel, and what support they are ready to lend to Palestinians as they build their institutions and economic life. The United States should also engage Syria on issues that divide the two, particularly probing prospects for resumption of Israeli-Syrian negotiations. But we need to understand the potential trap of pursuing two final-status negotiations in parallel and the stress that will put not only on the Arab side to meet Israeli needs but on the Israeli political system to accommodate Arab need and the resources of the mediator. More than likely, America and Israel will need to choose one track; otherwise, as was the case during the Clinton administration, we may find ourselves with no progress on either.

There will come a point in the next year or so when the Bush administration or its successor will have to make a decision about whether the Annapolis process is succeeding and how to calibrate an American role if it is or isn't. Above all, the United States must keep a credible negotiating process alive and not pass on to its successor a crisis atmosphere that will make it hard for a new president with a host of priorities to engage. We have seen the disastrous consequences of that movie before. This may mean outlining American ideas publicly on what elements should guide negotiations, not to force a summit, but to reaffirm the feasibility and desirability of a two-state solution; or it could mean doing crisis-management diplomacy to keep negotiations up and running and pushing both Israelis and Palestinians to implement their road-map obligations; or it could mean supporting the idea of a Palestinian state on the West Bank with provisional borders if Israelis and Palestinians agree, with the other issues (Jerusalem, refugees, and final borders) to be agreed later. Above all, we cannot risk disengaging again as we've done for much of the past six years. The stakes are too high.

As I write these words at the end of December 2007, there is hope once again for Arab-Israeli negotiations. We need to keep our expectations realistic because it will take enormous will and skill to play the mediator role. The Bush administration, having inherited the worst hand in Arab-Israeli peacemaking, has a chance to leave to its successor not only a transformed situation on the ground but a serious negotiating process that might even produce an agreement. And achieving those two objectives is well worth the effort. America has a chance now to help Arabs and Israelis climb out of the hole they've largely dug at times for themselves with considerable help from us.

We have always known that America's promise to Arabs and Israelis was really a conditional one. Even our most determined and exuberant moments in peacemaking were premised on the Arab and Israeli capacity to make decisions, constrained by all of their limitations. We also learned to condition our promise further by the undeniable fact that no matter how much of a stake we have in the outcome, it will never be as great at those who live in the neighborhood have. I remain compelled to this day by the simple fact that whenever news of a dramatic breakthrough in Arab-Israeli peacemaking arrives, we Americans are the last to know about it.

That tells you something about America's promise and role. What it tells me is that although we remain vital to peacemaking, we can't drive the train as much as I once believed. But it is very much in our interest and theirs that our promise to Arabs and Israelis remain valid; we should reaffirm it without cynicism, commit to it without illusion, and pursue it based on our national and moral interests. We must do so without deluding ourselves that somehow we alone can deliver on it or that we can simply abandon it if we run into heavy weather. Instead, we must pursue fulfillment of that promise with wisdom, resolve, sensitivity, and toughness. And together with courageous and determined Arabs and Israelis, and a lot of luck, who knows, we just might one day redeem it.

Notes

Introduction

1. Niall Ferguson, *Empire: The Rise and Demise of the British World Order and the Lessons for Global Power* (New York: Basic Books, 2002), 303.

Part I: America's Promise Challenged

1. Quoted in Thomas L. Friedman, *From Beirut to Jerusalem* (New York: Doubleday, 1988), 209.

Chapter 2: Gulliver's Troubles

1. Quoted in Thomas A. Bailey, *A Diplomatic History of the American People*, 10th ed. (Englewood, N.J.: Prentice-Hall, 1980), 4.
2. Quoted in Andrew Kohut and Bruce Stokes, *America Against the World* (New York: Times Books, 2006), 64.
3. Quoted in Hanan Ashrawi, *This Side of Peace* (New York: Simon and Schuster, 1995), 28.
4. Moshe Arens, *Broken Covenant* (New York: Simon and Schuster, 1995), 240.
5. Henry Kissinger, *Years of Upheaval* (Boston: Little, Brown, 1982), 1074; Matti Golan, *The Secret Conversations of Henry Kissinger* (New York: Bantam Books, 1976), 194.
6. Milan Kundera, "Die Weltliteratur," *New Yorker*, January 8, 2007, 28.
7. Amos Elon, *The Israelis: Founders and Sons* (London: Weidenfeld and Nicolson, 1971), 324.
8. Quoted in Amos Elon, *A Blood-Dimmed Tide* (New York: Columbia University Press, 1997), 96.
9. Paul Johnson, *A History of the Jews* (New York: Harper, 1987), 23.
10. Ashrawi, *This Side of Peace*, 29.
11. Abu Iyad, *My Home, My Land* (New York: Times Books, 1981), 214.
12. Eytan Bentsur, *Making Peace* (New York: Praeger, 2000), 37.
13. Arens, *Broken Covenant*, 54, 60.

Chapter 3: Israel's Lawyers

1. "Israel's Lawyer," *Washington Post*, May 23, 2005, A19.
2. Quoted in Shlomo Avineri, *The Making of Modern Zionism* (New York: Basic Books, 1981), 212.
3. Michael W. Suleiman, "A History of Arab-American Political Participation," *American Arabs and Political Participation*, ed. Philippa Strum (Woodrow Wilson International Center for Scholars, 2006), 12.
4. Kevin Phillips, *American Theocracy* (New York: Viking, 2006), 119.

Chapter 4: Henry Kissinger

1. "Class Notes," *Washington Post*, May 19, 2006, A19.
2. Richard Nixon, *The Memoirs of Richard Nixon* (New York: Grosset and Dunlap, 1978), 477.
3. Henry A. Kissinger, National Security Council Meeting, Friday, April 25, 1969, Item KT00019, Kissinger Transcripts, Digital National Security Archive.
4. Edward Sheehan, *The Arabs, Israelis, and Kissinger* (New York: Reader's Digest Press, 1976), 18.
5. Nixon, *Memoirs*, 786–87.
6. Henry Kissinger, *White House Years* (Boston: Little, Brown, 1979), 351.
7. Abba Eban, *An Autobiography* (New York: Random House, 1977), 498.
8. Henry Kissinger, *Crisis* (New York: Simon and Schuster, 1982), 14.
9. *Ma'ariv*, November 14, 2006, 2.
10. Richard B. Parker, *The October War* (Gainesville: University Press of Florida, 2001), 341.
11. Kissinger, *Crisis*, 139.
12. Walter Isaacson, *Kissinger* (New York: Simon and Schuster, 1996), 13.
13. Henry A. Kissinger, [Discussion with Yitzhak Rabin of Talks with Arab Leaders], October 12, 1974, Item KT01364, Kissinger Transcripts, Digital National Security Archive.
14. Shimon Peres, *Battling for Peace* (New York: Random House, 1995), 141.
15. Nixon, *Memoirs*, 787.
16. Moshe Dayan, *The Story of My Life* (New York: William Morrow, 1976), 443.
17. Henry Kissinger, *Years of Upheaval* (Boston: Little, Brown, 1982), 621.
18. Henry A. Kissinger, Secretary's Staff Meeting, November 19, 1973, Item KT00913, Kissinger Transcripts, Digital National Security Archive.
19. Kissinger, *Years of Upheaval*, 643.
20. Ariel Sharon, *Warrior* (New York: Simon and Schuster, 1989), 347.
21. Kissinger, *Years of Upheaval*, 609, 550–51.
22. Henry Kissinger, *Years of Renewal* (New York: Simon and Schuster, 1982), 420.

23. Gerald R. Ford, *A Time to Heal* (New York: Harper and Row, 1979), 246–47.

24. Charles McC. Mathias Jr., "Ethnic Groups and Foreign Policy," *Foreign Affairs* 59, no. 5 (Summer 1981), 993.

25. Henry A. Kissinger, Secretary Kissinger's Meeting with Jewish Leaders on Middle East Crisis, December 27, 1973, Item KT00974, Kissinger Transcripts, Digital National Security Archive.

26. Henry A. Kissinger, Meeting with President Sadat and Foreign Minister Fahmi, May 30, 1974, Item KT01211, Kissinger Transcripts, Digital National Security Archive.

27. Kenneth Stein, *Heroic Diplomacy* (London: Routledge, 1999), 23.

28. Henry A. Kissinger, [Meeting with Saudi Foreign Minister Saqqaf], August 29, 1974, Item KT01314, Kissinger Transcripts, Digital National Security Archive.

29. Henry A. Kissinger, [Discussion with Prince Hassan of U.N. Debates on Palestine Liberation Organization], December 9, 1975, Item KT01844, Kissinger Transcripts, Digital National Security Archive.

30. Ibid.

31. Dayan, *My Life*, 475; Yitzhak Rabin, *The Rabin Memoirs* (Berkeley and Los Angeles: University of California Press, 1979), 254.

32. Henry A. Kissinger, Cabinet Meeting, Briefing on Middle East, March 8, 1974, Item KT01059, Kissinger Transcripts, Digital National Security Archive; Kissinger, *Years of Upheaval*, 936.

33. Kissinger, *Years of Upheaval*, 781.

Chapter 5: Jimmy Carter

1. Zbigniew Brzezinski, *Power and Principle* (New York: Farrar, Straus and Giroux, 1983), 91.

2. Jimmy Carter, *Keeping Faith* (New York: Bantam Books, 1982), 282.

3. Anwar Sadat, *In Search of Identity* (New York: Harper and Row, 1974), 302; Carter, *Keeping Faith*, 284.

4. William B. Quandt, *Camp David* (Washington, D.C.: Brookings Institution, 1986), 83.

5. Jody Powell, *The Other Side of the Story* (New York: William Morrow, 1984), 57.

6. Carter, *Keeping Faith*, 294–95; Brzezinski, *Power and Principle*, 108–10; Cyrus Vance, *Hard Choices* (New York: Simon and Schuster, 1983), 192–93; Stein, see 958, fn.27 *Heroic Diplomacy*, p. 218.

7. Sadat, *Identity*, 305.

8. Carter, *Keeping Faith*, 318.

9. "Camp David 25th Anniversary Forum," September 17, 2003, sponsored jointly by the Carter Center and the Woodrow Wilson International Center for Scholars, 8.

10. Carter, *Keeping Faith*, 392–93; Brzezinski, *Power and Principle*, 272. See also
     Campusj.com 2007/01/30/Carter—reveals—camp—david—history—
     uga.
11. Quandt, *Camp David*, 240.
12. Gershon Gorenberg, *The Accidental Empire* (New York: Times Books, 2006),
     358.
13. Brzezinski, *Power and Principle*, 276–78; Carter, *Keeping Faith*, 412.
14. Carter, *Keeping Faith*, 416; Vance, *Hard Choices*, 245.
15. Moshe Dayan, *Breakthrough* (New York: Alfred A. Knopf, 1981), 272–76.
16. Carter, *Keeping Faith*, 426.
17. Memorandum from Hamilton Jordan to President Carter, June 1977, Jimmy
     Carter Library. See also memorandum "Jewish Identity, Zionism and
     Israel," November 13, 1978. Collection JC–1005 office of chief of staff,
     Files, 1977–1980 Jimmy Carter Library.
18. Ezer Weizman, *The Battle for Peace* (New York: Bantam Books, 1981), 382.

Chapter 6: James Baker

1. Daniel Seligman, "The World's Leading Pragmatist," *Fortune*, May 8, 1989, 165.
2. James A. Baker III, *Work Hard, Study...And Keep Out of Politics!* (New York:
    G. P. Putnam's Sons, 2006), 304.
3. Hanan Ashrawi, *This Side of Peace* (New York: Simon and Schuster, 1995), 87.
4. James A. Baker III, *The Politics of Diplomacy* (New York: G. P. Putnam's Sons,
    1995), 456.
5. Michael Kramer, "Playing for the Edge," *Time*, February 13, 1989, 27–33.
6. Baker, *Politics of Diplomacy*, 129.
7. Yitzhak Shamir, *Summing Up* (Boston: Little, Brown, 1994), 199.
8. Baker, *Politics of Diplomacy*, 130.
9. George H. W. Bush, "Address Before the 45th Session of the United Nations
    General Assembly in New York, October 1, 1990," *Public Papers of the
    President*, Administration of George Bush, 1990, 2:1331.
10. Baker, *Politics of Diplomacy*, 458.
11. Ibid., 457.
12. Ibid., 423–24.
13. Ibid., 507, 508.

Chapter 7: Caterer, Cash Man, and Crisis Manager: 1993–99

1. Bill Clinton, *My Life* (New York: Alfred A. Knopf, 2004), 679.
2. Uri Savir, *The Process* (New York: Vintage Books, 1999), 100.
3. Sidney Blumenthal, "The Handshake," *New Yorker*, no. 32 (October 4, 1993),
    74–6.

4. Dennis Ross, *The Missing Peace* (New York: Farrar, Straus, and Giroux, 2004), 447.
5. Clinton, *My Life*, 815.

Chapter 8: Mr. Nice Guy

1. Yitzhak Rabin, *The Rabin Memoirs* (1979), 378.
2. Madeleine Albright, *Madam Secretary* (New York: Hyperion, 2003), 602.
3. Clinton, *My Life*, 867.
4. Gilead Sher, *The Israeli-Palestinian Negotiations, 1999–2001* (London: Routledge, 2006), 4.
5. Ibid., 24.
6. Albright, *Madam Secretary*, 615.
7. Sher, *Israeli-Palestinian Negotiations*, 61.

Chapter 9: The Disengager

1. Paul O'Neill, *The Price of Loyalty* (New York: Simon and Schuster, 2004), 71.

List of Interviews

Former Presidents

Gerald Ford (April 24, 2006)
Jimmy Carter (February 16, 2006)
George H.W. Bush (July 13, 2006)

Vice Presidents

Walter Mondale (May 26, 2006)

Secretaries of State

Henry Kissinger (March 8, 2006)
Alexander Haig (May 15, 2006)
George Shultz (April 26, 2006)
James Baker (June 9, 2006)
Lawrence Eagleburger (May 16, 2006)
Warren Christopher (April 4, 2006)
Madeleine Albright (June 27, 2006)
Colin Powell (April 25, 2006)
Condoleezza Rice (August 2, 2006)

National Security Advisors

Zbigniew Brzezinski (March 2, 2006)
Brent Scowcroft (March 16, 2006)
Anthony Lake (March 13, 2006)
Samuel (Sandy) Berger (June 30, 2006)

Other American Officials

Edward Abington (April 21, 2006)
Elliott Abrams (June 30, 2006)
Richard Armitage (April 11, 2006)
William Burns (May 28, 2006)
Lynn Dent (June 6, 2006)
Edward Djerejian (June 9, 2006)
Tom Donilon (August 18, 2006)
Maria Echaveste (June 5, 2006)
Stuart Eisenstadt (March 20, 2006)
Douglas Feith (August 18; 24, 2006)
Leon Furth (April 10, 2006)
Richard Haass (June 13, 2006)
Gamal Helal (March 10, 2007)
John Herbst (June 5, 2006)
Pat Kennedy (May 25, 2006)
Daniel Kurtzer (May 12; 24, 2006)
Samuel Lewis (May 8, 2006)
Joe Lockhart (May 11, 2006)
Robert Malley (June 25, 2006)
Mike McCurry (May 24, 2006)
Stan Moscowitz (May 26, 2006)
Alfred Moses (June 1, 2006)
Robert Oakley (June 27, 2006)
Robert Pelletreau (June 7, 2006)
Thomas Pickering (June 12, 2006)
John Podesta (May 3, 2006)
Larry Pope (July 15, 2006)
Jody Powell (March 31, 2006)
William Quandt (April 27, 2006)
Bruce Riedel (May 24, 2006)
Peter Rodman (April 6, 2006)
Dennis Ross (April 17; May 11, 2006)
Richard Roth (June 5, 2006)
Mara Rudman (March 23, 2006)

David Satterfield (June 6; 12, 2006)
Harold Saunders (March 2, 2006)
Jonathan Schwartz (June 25, 2006)
Wendy Sherman (May 30, 2006)
Mark Siegel (April 7, 2006)
Robert Strauss (February 1, 2007)
John Sununu Sr. (April 5, 2005)
George Tenet (May 8, 2006)
Margaret Tutwiler (May 2, 2006)
Toni Verstandig (June 7, 2006)
Ned Walker (June 1, 2006)
Lawrence Wilkerson (March 21, 2006)
John Wolf (May 31, 2006)
Anthony Zinni (May 30, 2006)

Congress

SENATORS

Rudy Boschwitz (August 8, 2006)
Chuck Hagel (November 13, 2006)
Daniel Inouye (July 15, 2006)
Robert Kasten (April 21, 2006)
Carl Levin (May 26, 2006)
George Mitchell (June 1, 2006)
John Sununu Jr. (June 15, 2006)

REPRESENTATIVES

Howard Berman (April 7, 2006)
Rahm Emanuel (May 25, 2006)
Paul Findley (June 1, 2006)
Mark Kirk (June 28, 2006)
Tom Lantos (June 28, 2006)
Mel Levine (April 4, 2006)
John Lewis (July 19, 2006)
Nita Lowy (April 25, 2006)

James Moran (July 10, 2006)

Mary Rose Oakar (May 2, 2006)

Mike Pence (August 1, 2006)

Nick Rayhall (April 6, 2006)

Ileana Ros-Lehtinen (August 17, 2006)

Steve Solarz (May 17, 2006)

Henry Waxman (March 27; April 27, 2006)

Additional Interviews
Domestic

Morrie Amitay (March 21; May 2, 2006)

Ziad Asali (May 19, 2006)

Bob Asher (May 25, 2006)

Graeme Bannerman (April 18, 2006)

Doug Bloomfield (April 8, 2006)

Jim Bond (April 18, 2006)

Shoshana Cardin (May 30, 2006)

Zev Chafets (May 26, 2006)

Tom Dine (April 3; May 2, 2006)

E. J. Dionne (August 2, 2006)

Yechiel Eckstein (May 25, 2006)

Sarah Ehrman (May 19, 2006)

Randa Fahmy-Hudome (April 11, 2006)

Jerry Falwell (June 29, 2006)

Ira Forman (June 6, 2006)

Abe Foxman (April 23, 2006)

Monte Friedkin (May 25, 2006)

J. J. Goldberg (June 12, 2006)

Steve Grossman (May 16, 2006)

John Hagee (August 2, 2006)

Ed Hinson (June 30, 2006)

Malcolm Hoenlein (May 23, 2006)

Jess Hordes (April 27, 2006)

Hussein Ibish (May 31, 2006)

Bernard Kalb (July 24, 2007)

Marvin Kalb (June 5, 2006)
Andrew Kohut (April 18, 2006)
Pete Lakeland (May 11, 2006)
Richard Land (May 2, 2006)
Luis Lugo (May 11, 2006)
Norman Ornstein (March 24, 2006)
Ralph Reed (August 21, 2006)
Pat Robertson (June 7, 2006)
Aaron Rosenbaum (November 3, 2006)
M. J. Rosenberg (May 3, 2006)
George Salem (May 18, 2006)
Ed Sanders (April 4, 2006)
David Saperstein (March 23, 2006)
Patrick Seale (April 27, 2006)
Mel Sembler (April 26, 2006)
Neil Sher (May 15, 2006)
Harvey Sicherman (February 2, 2006)
Steve Spiegel (June 22, 2006)
Richard Straus (October 21, 2006)
Tim Weber (June 12, 2006)
Duke Westover (June 29, 2006)
Ken Wollack (May 3, 2006)
James Zogby (April 7, 2006)

International

Yasser Abd Rabbo (May 12, 2006)
Osama al-Baz (November 2, 2006)
Hanan Ashrawi (May 3, 2006)
Ami Ayalon (June 4, 2006)
Yossi Beilin (July 25, 2006)
Yossi Ben-Aharon (May 29, 2006)
Shlomo Ben-Ami (May 10, 2006)
Giora Eiland (April 25, 2006)
Avi Gil (April 27, 2006)
Amos Gilad (June 20, 2006)

Eitan Haber (June 5, 2006)
Efraim Halevy (June 10, 2006)
Menachem Klein (July 15, 2006)
Terje Larsen (May 23, 2006)
Ahmed Maher (May 12, 2006)
Rihab Masood (June 6, 2006)
Dan Meridor (July 20, 2006)
Yitzhak Molkho (June 10, 2006)
Marwan Muasher (May 11, 2006)
Nimrod Novik (July 22, 2006)
Shimon Peres (November 18, 2006)
Itamar Rabinovich (May 8; 20, 2006)
Muhammad Rashid (April 21, 2002)
Dani Seideman (July 13, 2006)
Amnon Shahak (April 26, 2006)
Gilead Sher (June 27, 2006)
Khalil Shikaki (April 24, 2006)
Zalman Shoval (May 11, 2006)
Ephraim Sneh (May 27, 2006)
Dov Weisglass (June 4, 2004)
Moshe Ya'alon (May 16, 2006)

Acknowledgments

Writing can be excruciatingly painful. A good many of my professional colleagues made it much less so for me. Lee Hamilton and Michael Van Dusen gave me the space, time, and support at the Woodrow Wilson International Center for Scholars without which I could never have completed the book. Haleh Esfanidari, a courageous woman and remarkable scholar, made me feel welcome at the Center and supported me from the start.

Numerous friends and colleagues gave me advice and counsel, some of which I solicited, some of which I did not. But there were a handful who took a special interest in the book and gave me their time and support. I want to especially acknowledge Nahum Barnea, Gamal Helal, Dan Kurtzer, Samuel Lewis, Gerald Linderman, Rob Malley, David Makovsky, Bill Quandt, Bruce Riedel, Richard Straus, Margaret Warner, and Charlie Wolfson. I would also like to thank all those who agreed to be interviewed for their time, insights, and candor. A special thanks goes to the State Department's Mark Ramee, who facilitated the clearance process.

Alan Clive, whom I've known since the good old days in Ann Arbor when we were both aspiring history PhDs, deserves more credit than I could ever give him. Despite his struggle with cancer and his own blindness, Alan read, edited, and improved this book through his wisdom and brilliant touch. I am truly lucky to have him as a friend. I also want to thank John Flicker, my editor at Bantam Dell, who taught me much about how to structure and tell a good story, and my agent Deborah Grosvenor who supported this book from the very start.

Finally, to all those researchers without whose support I could not have finished this book, thanks for putting up with me. Pride of place belongs to Ryan Sturgill, who transcribed almost all of the interviews and gave me great advice on substance throughout. This book was written longhand on yellow legal note pads, nineteenth-century-style. Ryan, together with Jeffrey Farrington, converted my barely legible handwritten scrawl into typed text, always too polite to ask why I had never learned to type. I also want to thank Elizabeth Detwiler, Moran Kedar, Elliot Leffler, Julia Shatz, Liat Shetret, and Ryan Taugher for their invaluable assistance.

Above all, I want to thank my wife, Lindsay, who's been part of my life now for fifty years. From Cleveland, to Ann Abor, to Washington, through Jerusalem and the Middle East, and finally to Maine, her love, support, and sacrifice have been unwavering. My life would be empty without her.

Index

About the Author

AARON DAVID MILLER has been a public policy scholar at the Woodrow Wilson International Center for Scholars since 2006. For the last two decades he has served as an advisor to six secretaries of state, where he helped formulate U.S. policy on the Middle East and the Arab-Israeli peace process. He lives in Chevy Chase, Maryland.